Riverside
Volume Two

**From Turkey Farm to Race Track to Shopping Mall
In Thirty Hot, Cold and Dusty Years**

Bob Schilling said:

"The track had been owned by a playboy, some car dealers, an oil man, a schemer and dreamer and finally, a real estate developer. We knew how it would turn out".

**Compiled By Dave Wolin
With an Introduction by Dan Mensinger**

Copyright 2023

**Printed in the U.S.A.
Racing History Project
Box 5578
Bakersfield CA 93388
www.racinghistoryproject.com**

Table of Contents

In Case You Missed Volume One

A Brief Note About How To Use This Book

In order to not have a 1000 page book, we split this into two volumes and cropped many the newspaper and magazine articles. You can read the full text of the articles and clippings shown in this book plus many others on the attached DVD. All the photos and videos are on the DVD also. Note the DVD is formatted to use in your computer, not a DVD player.

Note: If your book did not come with a DVD, please contact us. It's free with print book purchase, $12.95 for Kindle users. Order it at www.racinghistoryproject.com/amazon.htm.

About the Compiler: Long time racer, performance and racing industry marketer and promoter Dave Wolin has a unique background which assisted in writing these books. As he says, "like Forrest Gump, I was fortunate to be in a lot of the right places at the right time." Today he operates the non profit Racing History Project (www.racinghistoryproject.com), writes a few books and magazine articles, does some racing and driver coaching and builds a new hot rod every couple of years. He says; *"Thanks to my wife, Jane, for tolerating all the time I've put into this and the invaluable help from all those who have written about Riverside, taken photos, raced and worked on cars of the era."*

Not duplicating all the info contained in volume one but just remember this: To quote Mark Twain, "Persons attempting to find a motive in this narrative will be prosecuted; persons attempting to find a moral in it will be banished; persons attempting to find a plot in it will be shot."

As stated in volume one, while we are relating some of Riverside history, this is by no means more than an incomplete account. For historical purposes we recommend the existing well written books such as Pete Lyon's Riverside International Raceway and Dick Wallen's Palace of Speed.

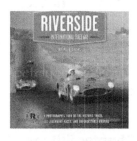 

Photo credits: Dave Friedman, David Bryant, Scott Baker, Bob D'Olivo, Eric Rickman, Pete Lyons, David Wallen, Tim Gaylean, Don Hodgdon, Scott Baker, Gary Hartman, David Allio, Bob Tronolone, Dean Lester, Tom Farrington, John Ryals, Gil Cadena, Dan Mensinger, Bruce Ward, Steve Light, Neal Bledsoe, Dante Puccetti, Frank Mormillo, Kurt Oblinger, Joe Hayashibara and all the hundreds of unattributed photos sent from my friends on Facebook..

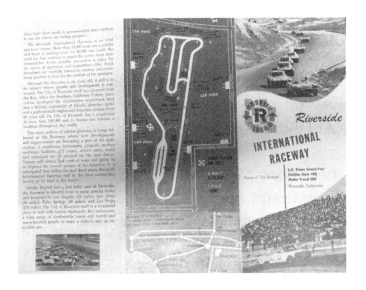

Introduction - By Dan Mensinger

I guess I was an early adopter of Riverside and it stuck with me forever. From my first visit to the track at the age of 3 ½ (Dad took me to the drag races) to my cub scout pack getting a tour of the garages before the 1963 Motor Trend 500 (Mom organized that), I was a dyed in the wool fan, as were my parents.

In the mid '60's our local Chamber of Commerce started a group of volunteers that became known as the Riverside Raceway Booster's Club, a group of racing fans and supporters who helped at the track. I jumped on that, eager to be involved and painted trash cans, swept and cleaned the main straight suites, manned the information booths on race day, helped with traffic control or whatever else might be needed. The bonus of working at a race was that we had a pair of rooms in the Goodyear Tower to watch the races from. Also, before each race, the Boosters would help promote the upcoming races by handing out posters around the SoCal area. The club hosted interviews with drivers at our meetings before races with some interesting stories shared. Come the mid '80's and the Chamber of Commerce decided to end the Booster's Club, so we became regular race fans once again. They were good times for sure. Riverside was a big part of my life and when it closed, I felt like I had lost something important.

Chapter One - Stock Car Racing

There were 47 NASCAR stock car races, and an almost equal number of supporting races held at Riverside, far more than any other pro racing series. From 1970 to 1981, the opening race of the season was held at Riverside.

First there was the December, 1957 J.C. Agajanian promoted USAC race. Bobby Unser was the pole qualifier and Jerry Unser won this last race of the USAC season as Sam Hanks, finishing third, announced his retirement.

Unser Wins Stock Car Driving Title

RIVERSIDE (UP) —Jerry Unser Jr., 23-year-old speedster from Long Beach, won the 1957 National Stock Car Driving Championship Sunday in a 250-lap USAC

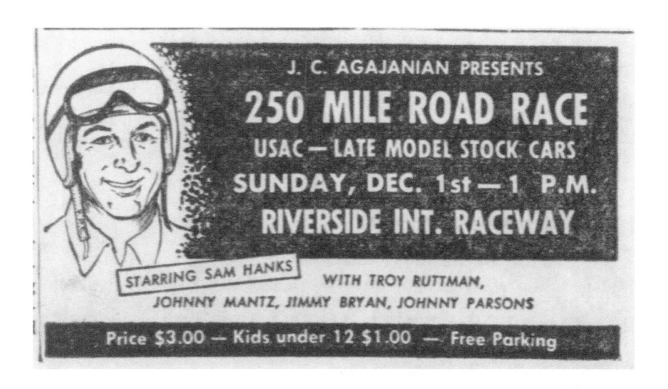

1925 Indy Winner Pete dePaolo presents the pole qualifier award to Bobby Unser

The Hot Rod Magazine Team

8

KING OF THE 500—Veteran big car and stock machine racer Sam Hanks (right), chats with promoter J. C. Agajanian during recent stop in San Bernardino to promote USAC sponsored Stock Races Dec. 1 over the Riverside International Motor Raceway road course.

Once Over Lightly

By DAVE LEWIS
Sports Editor

Moving up fast to take his place along with the Ruttmans, Bettenhausens, Bryans, Hanks, Parsons, Garretts, etc., in the auto racing world is a young fellow by the name of Jerry Unser.

Sunday he'll attempt to officially nail down the 1957 U. S. Auto Club's stock car racing championship in the 250-mile classic at Riverside's International Raceway which J. C. Agajanian calls "my biggest promotion to date."

The event not only is being regarded by racing people as the greatest stock car race of all-time, but it will be highlighted by one of the most dramatic duels for the national driving championship yet staged when Unser tries to stave off the challenge of the veteran Ralph Moody from Florida.

Unser goes into the final race of the year leading Moody by 300 points ... but the latter is working on a hot streak that threatens to take it all. The race will be worth 500 points to the winner, 400 for second, 310 for third, 300 for fourth and so on down to 12th place.

If Moody wins, Jerry will have to finish fifth or better to stay ahead of him in the stand-

THE GOOD-LOOKING, MILD-MANNERED Unser, who came to Long Beach a year ago and who moved into his new Lakewood home at 6709 Turner Grove last winter with his wife and a brand new baby boy, virtually had the driving championship salted away halfway through the season after a tremendous streak during which he won four important events, including the Pike's Peak stock car class for the second straight record-breaking year.

But Moody, a veteran NASCAR pilot making his first start in the "bigtime" on the U.S. Auto Club circuit this year, "came out of nowhere" this fall to score four straight wins and close in to a point where he can capture the title Sunday if Unser falters.

During Moody's hot streak, Jerry himself had a bit of bad luck. He had to drop out of one race and finished third and sixth in two others.

It looked as if he had the situation well under control again in the last race at Birmingham, Ala., when he held a comfortable lead going into the final laps ... but blew a tire.

Driving masterfully, Jerry kept going on the flat and succeeded in salvaging second place, but in the meantime Moody came charging down the stretch to post his fourth straight triumph.

Troy Ruttman, Sam Hanks and Jimmy Bryan are considered the biggest threats to Unser and Moody in Sunday's race. But Jerry is quick to say ... "don't forget about my brother Bobby." Bobby, of course, is quite a car jockey himself, having won the championship class in the '56 Pike's Peak competition.

The two 1957 Fords that Jerry and Bobby drive have been the two fastest cars in the practice runs at Riverside the

Riverside Raceway oval March 6th. George Durade (#4) dives to the inside to make a pass in turn 3 during a CAR super modified race. (Bob Holbert collection)

Agajanian also promoted the three race 1958 Memorial Day weekend event; 500 mile races for sprint cars, midgets and stock cars. The sprint and midget portion was covered in volume one. Of interest here was the Monday NASCAR event; where Bill France Sr. flew in and demanded payment, in cash, for the promised prize money. Once that was sorted, pole sitter Parnelli Jones (who also competed in the sprint car and midget 500 milers) led the first 147 laps, then blew his engine and crashed, turning the win over to Eddie Gray. Another first, NASCAR also had a class for imports. The race ran six hours and seventeen minutes.

Ken Clapp: *"This race marked my first job as a crew chief. At nineteen, I had been helping on a variety of racecars, somehow got a NASCAR mechanics license and was offered this opportunity by Bob Keefe, a pretty successful driver. Keefe had a 1956 Ford, an ex Pete de Paolo factory car. Keefe unfortunately had some bad habits; drinking, fighting and chasing women, He got into a fight in Whittier and was locked up, just before the race. My buddy and I had towed the car down from Northern California and we were the crew and I was crew chief. Now we didn't know what to do. We ended up staying in a two dollar flophouse in Riverside and I had to qualify the car, never having driven a racecar anywhere, much less at Riverside. So, I put on Keefe's helmet, stuck a cigarette in my mouth, hoped no one would recognize me as not Keefe and turned in a lap good enough to get us 41st on the grid. We got Keefe out of jail on Sunday morning, showed him a map of the track and Parnelli Jones gave him a few tips. He actually drove a good race; our pit stops went well and we ended up in fifth and made $925."* Compiler's Note: Ken Clapp went on to be a significant figure in west coast stock car racing, a NASCAR vice president and now heads he West Coast Stock Car Hall of Fame. Look for his new book by Bones Bourcier; From the West to Daytona.

Record Field Seen For 3-Day Run At Riverside

The big three 500-mile auto races on May 30, May 31, and June 1 at Riverside International Raceway will see a record number of race cars, midgets, and stock cars to qualify this weekend with more than a hundred speed pilots expected to jam the starting line.

To date 57 cars have qualified, with Colby Scroggin racking up the hottest time — a top speed of more than 155 miles per hour and the fast 2½-mile lap time of 97 miles per hour.

Time trials will be held Saturday and Sunday beginning at 1:00 p.m. Sunday's qualifying will feature a 2½-hour live telecast at the track over KTTV with Bill Welch, veteran announcer, handling the mike. The fastest man on the speedway will be presented a gold cup, with ceremonies to be seen on the air. It is expected that the 100-mile-an-hour mark will be hit during the telecast.

Another feature of the Sunday program will be radar timing of the races by the Riverside Police Radar Unit, the same equipment which checks motorists on the highways.

A highlight of the time trials

Riverside Motor Speedway Features Three Auto Races

Riverside, Calif. — European and American late model stock cars will battle in the climax of three 500-mile auto races to be held here May 30 weekend on the new 2½-mile paved track at Riverside Motor Raceway.

The NASCAR sanctioned Grand International Stock Car Race will feature 1956-57-58 models on Sunday, June 1, preceded by a racecar 500-miler on Memorial Day (May 30) and a midget 500-miler classic on Saturday (May 31).

Bill France, NASCAR president, approved the $25,000 Grand International this week, according to Charles A. Curryer, racing director for Crown—America, a California racing group presenting the three 500's.

LIL LEAGUER

BASEBALL TODAY

"Ye gads! We're not reaching for the moon ... We just want it to get us over the fence!"

Galard (AI) Slonaker, Crown-America president brought out that the International 500 is unique because "it will be the first time that American and foreign sedans have ever competed on United States' soil."

A large portion of the purse will go to "makes of cars" winners, with the balance of money alloted to overall competition," Slonaker said. Makes of cars have been grouped as follows:

Group A—Bentley, Cadillac Eldorado, Continental, Imperial, Facel Vega, and Mercedes-Benz 300.

Group B— Chrysler, Cadillac, Daimler, Lincoln.

Group C—Buick, DeSoto, Packard, Jaguar, Mercedes-Benz 220.

Group D—Dodge, Lancia, Edsel, Pontiac, Mercury, Studebaker, Oldsmobile.

Group E—Alfa Romeo, Alvis, Ford, Chevrolet, Plymouth, Rambler, BMW, Borgward, Bristol, Citroen, Goliath, Mercedes-Benz 180, Riley, Rover, Sunbeam, Volvo.

Group F—Austin, DKW Fiat, Zephyr, Hillman, Humber, Lloyd, MG, Morris, Opel, Panhard, Renault, Saab, Simca, Singer, Triumph, Standard Malcs, Taunus, Vauxhall, Volkswagen, Wolseley, Skoda.

Races will start all three days promptly at 11 a.m. Time trials are scheduled for three weekends prior to May 30. Inquiries should be sent to Big Three 500-Mile Auto Races; Riverside Motor Raceway, Riverside, California.

Read about Indy Cars and Midgets in Volume One

Eddie Gray passing Bill Jones in the Citroen

13

In May, 1961, a NASCAR sanctioned Pacific Coast Series race (later Winston West), held in conjunction with an SCCA event, was won by Lloyd Dane in a Ford. The 39 lap, 100 mile race paid $825 to the winner. Second was Don Noel with third going to Dick Smith. Newspapers reported a disappointing crowd of 3500.

Frank Secrist: *"I wrecked my record setting Studebaker at the modified race at*  *Daytona in February. Fortunately my girlfriend's father stepped up with a stockcar for me. Blew it up in practice; never made the race I got to race there again in '67, went ten laps and broke an a arm "* Compiler's Note - Secrist is a legend in California; winning in stock cars, sprint cars and midgets. He set a record at the Daytona modified race in 1961, beating Fireball Roberts and Cale Yarborough.

—Al Powers

WINNING Citroen ID-19 takes a tight turn In the first California NASCAR-sanctioned race to include European cars. A pair of Citroen ID-19s with air-oil suspension and front-wheel drive won "First in Class" honors at the 500-mile Riverside event, June 1.

Citroens Class Winner in "500"

Les Richter recognized the need for money making high attendance stock car races and in 1962, negotiated the deal that would bring NASCAR to Riverside twice a year, continuing through the last race in 1988.

Winners over the years included Bobby Allison - 6 times, Dan Gurney - 5 times. Richard Petty - 5 times, Darrrell Waltrip 5 times, Parnelli Jones, David Pearson 3 times, Tim Richmond 3 times, Terry Labonte, Ricky Rudd and Rusty Wallace twice.

LLOYD DANE WINS 100-MILE NASCAR RACE AT RIVERSIDE

BY BILL DREDGE
Times Staff Representative

RIVERSIDE — Stock car veteran Lloyd Dane won the 100-mile NASCAR road race Sunday at Riverside Raceway.

The Buena Park driver went the route without a stop. He averaged 81.60 m.p.h. and collected a purse of $800.

It took 13 laps of hub-to-hub driving before Dane's new Chevrolet finally took over from Eddie Gray of Gar-

Gray lost his '61 Ford in a spin and never got back into contention.

Second spot went to Don Noel of Arleta in another '61 Ford. He made one stop for fuel and dashed back without losing the position.

Crowd of 3,500

Third place was taken by Dick Smith, Lakewood, in a '60 Ford; Jim Cook of Norwalk was fourth in a '60 Dodge; fifth place went to Bob Perry, Hawthorne, in a '59 Ford. Nineteen cars fin-

pointing 3,500 for the benefit event sponsored by the Riverside Press - Enterprise. Sports car portion of the event sanctioned by NASCAR, was also disappointing. Only two sports machines turned up running and drivers Billy Krause of Long Beach and Pete Woods of La Habra staged two short exhibition races.

Gray set a track record during the morning qualifying trials, turning the circuit in 1:48.80. The old record

Pauley, Levy Buy Into Riverside Raceway

EDWIN PAULEY

ROY LEWIS

FRED LEVY

Edwin Pauley, wealthy independent oil producer and Democratic party chieftain, and Fred Levy, Jr., have purchased a substantial interest in Riverside Int'l Raceway and have become stockholders and directors, it was announced by Roy G. Lewis, Riverside president.

No figure was announced, but it is believed they have invested "at least $1 million."

This bids fair to make Riverside one of the biggest and outstanding road racing courses in the world.

Both Pauley and Levy are part owners of the LA Rams pro football team with Dan Reeves, Bob Hope and Hal Seley.

Pauley was associated years ago with Paul Schissler, Riverside general manager, in ownership of the old Hollywood Bears pro football team that played at Gilmore Stadium.

The USAC stock car In March 1962 race featured two 37 lap heats, the first won by Troy Ruttman in a Ford, the second, shortened to 27 laps by rain, was won by Paul Goldsmith.

Top Stock Car Race Set at Riverside

RIVERSIDE—One of the finest fields of drivers to ever take part in a stock car race on the west coast is shaping up for next Sunday (March 18) afternoon's 200-mile USAC National Championship late model stock car race at Riverside Raceway.

Already in the fold for a crack at the $10,000 purse are such "500" veterans as winner A. J. Foyt, Bill Cheesbourg and Paul Goldsmith, 1961 national stock car champion, as well as such standouts as Dan Gurney, runner-up for the 1961 world's sports car championship, and Norm Nelson, 1960 national stock car champion.

Reported ready to enter the race for 1960-61-62 cars over the paved 2.59 mile road course is a quartet of "500" veterans

The January 1963 Riverside 500 offered a number of firsts; the first appearance of 1963 model stockcars; the first event where drivers from USAC, NASCAR and SCCA all raced together and the first time a purse of $66,000 had been offered in a west coast auto race. Dan Gurney qualified on the pole and won in a Holman Moody Ford in front of a crowd of 52,500, collecting $13,600, followed by A.J Foyt and Troy Ruttman.

Ron Hornaday

Wendell Scott

Gurney wins at Riverside

RIVERSIDE, Calif. (UPI)—Dan Gurney — ex - motorcycle racer, Grand Prix sports car driver, and

Parnelli and Gurney

A.J Foyt and Troy Ruttman

GOING OVER: The 1962 Pontiac driven by Danny Weinberg of Downey, Calif., is going backward (upper left) and heading up an embankment after its wheels locked during the running of Sunday's $66,245 stock car race at Riverside (Calif.) International Raceway. The car is turned broadside at upper right and rolling over back on to the track in lower left. It landed back on its wheels (lower right) and Weinberg remained in his seat, only slightly hurt, but the car was out of the 500-mile race (AP Wirephoto).

19

Les Richter Looks Forward to Big Season at Riverside Raceway

By Bob Thomas

"We've got a lot of things going for us this time."

That's the way the new year looks to Les Richter, the popular ex-football star who is so wrapped up in his efforts to make Riverside Raceway into a successful, money-making auto racing plant that he didn't want to be considered for the head coaching job of his alma mater, California.

The old year didn't fade out quite so brightly for the So-Cal All-American and one-time Ram All-Pro. Things definitely weren't going for him when the Riverside general manager promoted a 400-mile stock race last month.

Caught in Middle

Richter was caught in the crossfire of a battle between America's two major professional auto racing bodies—USAC and NASCAR. The United States Auto Club boycotted the event and held out such gate-appeal stars as

Les Richter

Parnelli Jones, A. J. Foyt and Rodger Ward, all Indianapolis champions, and Dan Gurney.

The race was an artistic success with the NASCAR hotshots on hand but not the financial whopper that it might have been.

The story for 1964, in contrast, looms bright. The war clouds have dissipated. As a result, Richter is attacking his upcoming 500-mile stock car race (Jan. 19) with enthusiasm.

All Top Drivers

"We should have all the top drivers for this one," he said, referring to the stars of NASCAR, USAC and the Sports Car Club of America (SCCA).

This, of course, means Jones, Ward, Foyt, Freddie Lorenzen, Joe Weatherly, Gurney, Richard Petty, Times Grand Prix winner Dave MacDonald, Ned Jarrett, et al.

"We've got 20 of the top West Coast drivers already signed," Richter says.

Incidentally, virtually all of the leading late-model drivers on the Pacific will close out the year with a 50-lap NASCAR race at Ascot Park Sunday afternoon.

That ol' pro, Eddie Gray of Gardena, is the pre-race favorite, driving a 1963 Mercury over the Ascot half-mile oval, isn't surprising.

Gray, a silver-thatched veteran who won a 500-miler at Riverside (1958), has some proven long-timers to battle, such as Marv Porter (Pontiac), who is a two-time NASCAR national short-

track champ; Lloyd Dane of Buena Park (1963 Ford), Clem Proctor of Paramount (1963 Pontiac), Jim Cook of Norwalk (1963 Ford), and Jim Blomgren of Paramount (Pontiac).

The stockers will share the Sunday card with a program of super stocks from the California Jalopy Association.

RIVERSIDE — Richter says the Raceway will launch its most ambitious year in history

with the Motor Trend [...] next month. Not yet an[...] in fact, is an interd[...] championship event to [...] Nov. 12-15. It will [...] champions of the 17 [...] visions in the country. [...] tion, the California Sp[...] Club will hold a regio[...] at Riverside on Feb. [...] divisional in June. Th[...] States Road Racing Ch[...] ships, which embrace [...] in the country, will b[...] at Riverside April 25[...]

In May, 1963, a crowd of 11,295 watched Roger Penske, in a Ray Nichels Pontiac, win the Riverside 250, a 93 lap, 251 mile NASCAR Pacific Coast series event, Penske led 22 laps and collected $3500. Second went to Darel Dierenger in a Bill Stroppe prepared Mercury and third was Joe Weatherly in another Ray Nichels Pontiac

DIERINGER STREAKS 1:40.52 TO WIN RIVERSIDE 250 POLE

RIVERSIDE—Darel Dieringer, 37-year-old Charlotte, N.C. charger, won the pole position for next Sunday's "Riverside 250" late model stock car race by streaking around the Riverside Raceway oval in 1:40.52 in qualifying runs Sunday.

a hassle over driver affiliations that the Carolinan was on deck at Riverside at all. The Stroppe Mercury had been assigned to U.S. stock car champion Joe Weatherly.

But after Weatherly won the Darlington "200" Satur-

So Weatherly was force to vacate the ride, leaving open for Dieringer, wl finished seventh behir Weatherly at Darlington.

Weatherly now will mo to either a 1963 or 19 Pontiac for the "Rivers:

Roger Penske wins $16,800 in Riverside 250

RIVERSIDE (UPI) — Roger Penske, who started a series of sports car race triumphs here last Fall, perked up the ears of

Penske Wins At Riverside

RIVERSIDE, Calif. (UPI) — Roger Penske, who started a series of sports car race triumphs here last fall, perked up the ears of the stock car racing fraternity Sunday by winning the $16,800 Riverside "250."

It was only the second late model stock car race for the confident 26-year-old driver from

Roger Penske and Marilyn Fox

Penske Roars From Last To Win Riverside 250

By BRUCE GRANT
(Sun-Telegram Sports Writer)

RIVERSIDE—Roger Penske, in a dramatic drive from dead last, made it two in a row at Riverside International Raceway yesterday by winning the 250-mile stock car road race.

The 26-year-old aluminum salesman from Gladwyne, Pa., victor in the Times Grand Prix on this same course last October, out-dueled pole position winner Darel Dieringer on the final 29 laps to seize first prize money of $2,500.

field of 27 cars had gone by before Roger got back into the race.

Methodically, Penske used tremendous skill to pass car after car until he reached third place on the 10th lap. In the meantime, Dieringer was setting a torrid pace at the front of the pack.

Weatherly forged into the No. 2 position on the 40th lap, with Marvin Porter, in a 1963 Ford, third and Penske a rapidly closing fourth.

Dieringer was running well

Sixteen cars finished the rigorous test. There were several spinouts, but no serious damage was inflicted upon the cars and no drivers were injured. Driver Bruce Worrell collapsed from heat and fatigue during a pit stop, but was listed as "okay" by his crew chief.

Penske heaped praise upon the Ray Nichels pit crew, headed by Ralph Knopf. "The car ran beautifully — you really gotta hand

YOU CAN WIN A PAIR OF TICKETS TO SEE THE "RIVERSIDE 250"

You may be one of five local residents selected today to receive a pair of tickets to see the exciting late-model stock cars in action at the Riverside Raceway next Sunday. All makes of 1960-61-62-63 cars—including Chevrolet, Ford, Plymouth, Dodge, Mercury, Pontiac, Oldsmobile, etc. —will compete in the "Riverside 250" for a purse of more than $16,800. Many of the nation's top drivers will be in action over the 2.7 mile high speed course in the 95-lap chase for the prize money. It's mile-a-minute action, so turn now to the classified pages of this section to learn how you may be one of the five local residents who will win a pair of tickets.

DEAD END—Don Noel spins into fence on No. 6 turn on Riverside course Sunday during Riverside '250' race. Noel walked away from the wreck. Race was won by Times Grand Prix winner, Roger Penske.

A crowd of 32,500 attended the November 1963 Golden State 400; won by Darel Dieringer in a Stroppe prepared Mercury. He led a total of 35 laps and made $7875. Second place Dave Macdonald led 92 laps and finished second after having transmission issues, A number of well known California racers, best known for their performance in sportscars, included Ken Miles in 11th, Pete Brock in 16th, Skip Hudson in 26th and Bob Bondurant in 29th. USAC banned it's drivers from competing, leaving Parnelli Jones, A.J. Foyt and Rodger Ward as spectators.

RIVERSIDE STOCK CAR RACE HIT BY USAC, NASCAR 'WAR'

By Bob Thomas

Riverside International Raceway has become a battleground for a "war" between the country's two major auto racing bodies—USAC and NASCAR.

And the loser of the first battle appears to be the FIA stock car race at Indianapolis in April.

Also, Riverside's tie-up with NASCAR for a 500-mile race last January can be listed as painful for USAC. Binford himself commented that USAC always considered Southern California as "USAC territory."

champion Joe Weatherly, Fireball Roberts, Junior Johnson, Dick Petty . . . fellas like that. It's a shame, though, to deprive the fans of drivers like Jones, Ward and Foyt."

Fireball Sizzles in

Champ Weatherly Enters Riverside Auto Race

RIVERSIDE — Defending will be on hand for the event.

Dieringer Wins Golden State 400 In A Mercury

RIVERSIDE, Calif. (AP) — Darel Dieringer won the race and Joe Weatherly won his sec- | Marvin Panch, of I Beach, Fla., finished thi 1963 Ford and Glen (F Roberts of Daytona Bea

Joe Ruttman: "*My first NASCAR race was in 1963 at Riverside. I was 18, used my brother Troy's year old stockcar, a 1962 Mercury. My parents let me use their passenger car to towbar the race car to Riverside from Detroit. Took all the spare pieces and put them inside that car. Proceeded to California, met Bill Stroppe who was kind enough to let me and my crew member stay in one of his shops until racetime. In those days, there were volunteers used to pit the cars during this race. After successfully starting 30th and finishing the race in 10th place, I started back home to Detroit and we were involved in a road accident in Tucumcari, New Mexico. The other car was at fault but had no insurance. My parent's insurance covered their own personal vehicle which I was riding in but not the racecar that we were towing. It totaled both my parents and Troys racecar. That slowed down my NASCAR racing career for a period of time with no racecar, towcar and funds to finance. It also left a scar on my forehead which I fondly point to and refer to as Riverside*" Compiler's Note: Joe went on to run 255 races and have 60 top ten finishes and 19 top fives in NASCAR Cup racing and 172 races and 13 wins in NASCAR truck racing. He was also 1980 USAC Stock Car champ.,

Marilyn Fox flags off the field for practice

Ken Miles poses with his "bent" Ford after rolling it in practice. The car (Lorenzen's alternate mount) was put into shape in time for the race.

'63 NASCAR Golden State 400

Dave Macdonald leads the field in the Woods Brothers Ford

Pete Brock and Bob Bondurant. They would finish 11th and 29th respectively

Pace Lap

The January 1964 Motor Trend 500, 185 laps on the 2.7 mile course, was won by Dan Gurney in the Woods Brothers Ford, followed by Marvin Panch and Fireball Roberts. The race was marred by the death of Joe Weatherly,

Weatherly Killed; Gurney Wins Race

RIVERSIDE, Calif. (AP)— Defending champion Dan Gurney made it two in a row Sunday by breezing to an easy victory in the 500-mile stock car road race at Riverside International Raceway.

Joe Weatherly of Norfolk, Va. was killed midway through the event when his 1964 Mercury skidded and struck a retaining

View the 1964 Motor Trend 500 on the attached DVD

Bob Petersen, Linda Evans and Dan Gurney

Pace Lap

Dan Gurney and the Woods Brothers Pit Stop

**Fireball Roberts with Skip Hudson and Dave MacDonald
following through turn six**

The January 1965 Motor Trend 500 was won for a third time by Dan Gurney who collected $13,625 and a Pontiac GTO convertible in front of a crowd of 61,474. Junior Johnson started from the pole and finished second with Marvin Panch third. Chrysler teams were missing as NASCAR had banned their Hemi powerplants. An odd incident marred the race; a spectator was killed and three others injured when the forklift he and friends were using as a viewing platform rolled over.

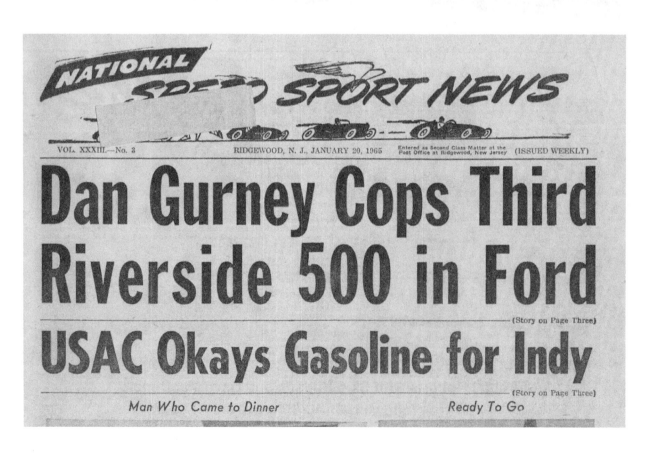

NATIONAL SPORT NEWS

VOL. XXXIII.—No. 3   RIDGEWOOD, N. J., JANUARY 20, 1965   Entered as Second Class Matter at the Post Office at Ridgewood, New Jersey   (ISSUED WEEKLY)

Dan Gurney Cops Third
Riverside 500 in Ford

(Story on Page Three)

USAC Okays Gasoline for Indy

(Story on Page Three)

Man Who Came to Dinner   *Ready To Go*

Pace Lap

Larry Frank had a camera car

Jerry Grant

1964 Motor Trend 500 Parade

**A.J. Foyt – Battling with Gurney, he crashed on lap 169,
resulting in serious injuries**

Also in 1965, California Auto Racing Inc. (CAR), who produced racing around southern California (605, Ascot etc) also scheduled some Friday night stock car racing on Riverside's half mile oval. Don Noel dominated the series which featured fields of as many as fifty modified stock cars.

Stock cars to race at Riverside

Stocks will race Friday night on Riverside International Raceway's ½-mile oval for the first time.

The Raceway, which helped to change the flavor of NASCAR's Grand National circuit when they introduced modified racing to the sport, will offer its high-

At Riverside
Stock Car Races Set

RIVERSIDE — Super modified stock cars will be the next type of racing equipment to test the high banked paved oval at Riverside International Race-

The January 1966 Motor Trend 500 was again won by Dan Gurney with David Pearson in second and Paul Goldsmith in third. A crowd of 73,331 saw Gurney collect $20,080 for the win.

Gurney victor fourth time in Riverside 500

kuk, Iowa, in a 1966 Ford also was fifth, and Jim Hurtubise North Tonwanda, N.Y., in 1965 Plymouth, was sixth.

Turner bumped Pearson whe they were jockeying for positio on lap No. 146 and his car be gan spewing gasoline. He sper an expensive 55 seconds in th

Dan Gurney with Curtis Turner following

Billy Foster

Curtis Turner

In January 1967, a new event added as a prelude to the NASCAR Motor Trend 500, the 100 mile Permatex 100 Late Model Sportsman race.. Oren Prosser won in 1957 Ford followed by Frank Deiny and Russ Bullen. 80 cars entered with 44 starting after qualifications and mechanical issues ruled out some of the slower cars. Jerry Titus qualified on the pole but had engine problems and DNF'd.

Oren Prosser Wins Preliminary Race To Rich Riverside Classic

RIVERSIDE, Calif. (UPI) — Oren Prosser of Reseda, Calif., drove a 1957 Ford to victory in the Permatex 100 National stock car race Saturday in a prelude to today's rich $85,000 Motor Trend 500 at Riverside International Raceway.

Prosser averaged 78.077 miles per hour in covering the 38 laps. The race was slowed by two accidents, but there were no injuries.

Frank Deiny of Los Angeles finished second in a '58 Ford, while Dave James of Los Ange-9 on the 2.7 - mile course and demolished the car. Brown escaped injury.

Brown's mishap means that first alternate driver Don Noel of Arleta, Calif., will start in the race in his '67 Ford.

The pole position in the rich event belongs to Dick Hutcherson of Keokuk, Iowa, who qualified Thursday in 106.-660 mph.

But many observers were sticking with Dan Gurney and his 1967 Mercury Cyclone.

Driver Billy Foster, 29, was the wreckage said they determined that the drums had failed at a speed of between 134 and 140 miles an hour as Foster came down the back straightaway.

The brake drums on Foster's car were not stock equipment but were special drums modified for racing events as permitted under stock car racing regulations.

Five more cars qualified for the race following the accident and raceway officials ruled that Foster's ninth place among the

Permatex Winner Oren Prosser

Jerry Johnson, who finished back in 23rd said: *"The first time on a road course; my only experience before that was on the local short tracks, Ascot and Orange Show. We had no idea what to do for road racing; we put a stiffer springs in the left front; that seemed to work o. k. Started seventh' early in the race we developed a leak in the oil cooler and got black flagged. My crew bypassed the cooler and we went back out, Ended up down eight laps but we finished."*

Jerry Titus

Oren Prosser

Tenth place finisher George Beall said: *"I'd been to a couple of road course events at Willow Springs; a fast track but nothing like that long straight and turn nine at Riverside – and the esses - we figured it out eventually. Late as usual getting our '55 Olds car ready. Neglected a fan shroud, ran fine in practice and qualified eleventh but overheated during the race; had to back off but still managed tenth"*

Some of this happened – and some didn't...............

Riverside Pit Improvements Combine Beauty With Safety

By DAVE DANIEL

Riverside International Raceway, in the midst of a nine million dollar improvement program, is nearing the end of one phase, $200,-000 worth, this week.

A permanent garage area and a redesigned safety barrier along the front straightaway will be finished by the time the Trans-American Sedan races roll around on Sept. 18. The safety barrier is already completed and the garages are rapidly nearing completion.

According to Les Richter, former Ram football great

and now president of the Raceway, the latest construction, besides providing permanent garage facilities, adds a touch of beauty to the area, located near the pits in the paddock area.

Two permanent garages, each 60 by 140 feet, contain seven 20-foot work bays, each accomodating two race cars, In addition to the work area, a drivers' lounge and meeting area, containing showers, lockers and gymnasium - type facilities will occupy the rear portion of one of the buildings, while the front of each building will house per-

manent office space and storage areas.

Future projects for Riverside include permanent and covered grandstands, an 18-hole golf course, restaurant, motel, additional permanent rest rooms, snack bars and landscaped rest areas and an automotive museum making Richter one of the most forward-looking executives anywhere. He has already seen to numerous improvements for the course itself and has also developed most of the successful racing events themselves.

The usual Sunday stock

The 1967 Motor Trend 500 Grand National race was won by Parnelli Jones in a Stroppe Ford, paying $18,720. Paul Goldsmith second and Norm Nelson third. Rained out after 50 laps, it continued a week later day with only 12 finishers. Sadly, promising driver Billy Foster was killed in a practice accident.

Riverside 500 Grand National:
It Rained on Their Parade

RIVERSIDE, Calif., Jan. 22 — The only thing that didn't surprise the 61,000 fans here for the Riverside 500 NASCAR Grand National was the rain that halted the race at 50 laps.

It had been storming all over California for days and only this outlying desert community was tem-porarily immune.

Officials who finally called the event when mere rain became a deluge announced it would restart under the yellow Jan. 29 and pick up from lap 50.

Until the rains came on lap 40, the race had been a wild affair with USAC stars A. J. Foyt and Parnelli Jones battling for the lead most of the way.

Four-time winner and favorite Dan Gurney led only two racing laps but was always within striking distance.

Jones and Foyt were in '67 Fair-lanes. Gurney led the two-car Mer-

(Continued on page 10)

COMPETITION PRESS &
AUTOWEEK

Vol. 17, No. 6   Entered as second class mail at
Lafayette, California   February 11, 1967

Winner Parnelli Jones in a Stroppe Ford

NONE MORE FORLORN THAN ANDRETTI . . .   . . . AT FUNERAL FOR BILLY FOSTER

'I've Lost Best Friend I Ever Had'

By DOUG PEDEN

If you don't think Billy Foster was a special kind of man you should talk to Mario Andretti, the two-time U.S. national car-racing champion from Nazareth, Pa.

From the time they met as rookie drivers at the famed Indianapolis 500-mile race in 1965, Mario and Billy were buddies. It was a rare, almost-instant type of friendship that seemed to grow in depth as the months went by — until last Friday.

That was the day Foster, taking a practice spin in preparation for a stock-car race at Riverside, Calif., was helplessly trapped by brake failure as his machine hurtled toward a turn at better than 140 miles per hour. The car crashed into a retaining wall and Foster, the Victoria driver with a touch of greatness, was dead.

That was the day Andretti's former fun-filled world of screaming rubber and roaring engines suddenly became sad and lonely.

Mario was in Victoria Tuesday, joining dozens of other famous men of the automobile circuits in paying final tribute at Foster's funeral. Friends and admirers of Foster, probably more than 100, from Boston, Akron, Peoria, Indianapolis and other places, arrived in the city to say farewell.

All were sad. But none seemed more forlorn or more helpless than Andretti, the slender little man who becomes such a fearless giant behind a wheel that he has won the national title in both his years on the big-time sprint car circuit.

"Words are hard to find." said Andretti, "but I'll tell you one thing. I've lost the best friend I ever had, in racing and away from the track.

"What makes it the hardest is that Billy was loved so much by everyone. If he hadn't been that way this would have been easier.

"He was a great driver and a wonderful man. More than that; he was a special kind of a man, a very easy man to get to know. Everybody seemed to like him instantly.

"I don't make friends easily, but Billy and I were buddies right from the start. He had a special way about him and he's the only really close friend I ever had.

"We talked about this several times," added Andretti, "but we were confident it wouldn't happen to us.

"Now it has happened and I doubt if things will ever be the same."

Jim Meyer: *"There must have been fifty cars there, and the big names got all the inside garages, so we were out in the gravel. Pitted next to us were some guys from Alabama with a Ford, driven by Jack Hardin. Well, here we were at the big time, but no one on our crew had ever done a pit stop before, There were a bunch of us; a few more than we has passes for, and there were only the two of them. So e made a deal; if they would train and coach us, we'd crew both cars. They did, and we did, and we made some pretty respectable stops and both cars finished.. This was January and it rained;; there was a week's rain delay, Bo was sick on the second Sunday so Cliff Garner finished for us. Jack tangled with someone and we had to do some body and chassis repairs, but our crew pulled it off. Bo finished 11th and Jack finished 12th"*

43

Jerry Grant was impressive at Riverside in the first round of the two-weekend Grand National. A third Plymouth, a '67, is due to be acquired by the Friedkin stable.   (Cam Warren photo)

Miss Motor Trend 500

Jim Meyer: *"My first NASCAR race was the 1967 Motor Trend 500. I had been helping Bo Reeder with his 1964 Ford for a while. My dad, Bill Meyer, was a metallurgist and I got interested in the team. He helped upgrade some suspension, steering and drive train components for Bo. They forged and machined a couple of different sway bars, made and heat treated axles and some other bits, had everything magnetic inspected, and shot peened. When we got to pick up our credentials, NASCAR tech chief Bill Gazaway says and I quote; "We don't allow no hippies in the NASCAR garage. Y'all need to go get your hair cut. So I went off to nearby Sunnymead and got a haircut.*

The NASCAR tech crew, all southerners, made it difficult for a west coast guy to get through tech. As they came by and checked out your car, they'd make a list of five or six things that you needed to fix or change. A lot of our west coast cars had aluminum aircraft surplus bucket seats; they were a no-no, and we all had to find something else. Other stuff was just to screw around with you, like they made us cut out one of our door braces and move it up or down one half inch. The guys were furious, but so they put me in charge of smiling and saying "Yes Sir" and "No Sir", so we just did what they asked, and, as I said earlier, we were one of the first west coast cars to get out on the track. One of the funniest (to me, not to the other team) things that I remember was when Joe Gazaway, Bill's brother and a tech guy, presented his list of things to the west coast car pitted on the other side of us. This was an old time west coast, tough as nails guy and he was furious. He told the tech crew exactly what he thought of their five or six silly changes. He ranted, raved and turned purple. And when he was all done, Joe calmly reached into his back pocket, pulled out another bigger list list, handed it to the driver and said, "and when you finish with those first items, here are some more things that we'd like you to fix before Y'all bring yore car to tech. Now "y'all have a nice day now, y'hear!", and just walked away.

"NASCAR owned the garage area – no one got in without credentials, On Friday, I was standing by the gate waiting for one of our crew to show up so I could get him his pass and I'd just been chatting with the NASCAR guy who was manning the gate. Bob Hope and some pretty lady came driving up in a golf cart. The guard stops them, and says "Sorry, you can't come in here without a garage pass" Bob Hope tells him who he is. The guard repeats, "Sorry, you can't come in here without a garage pass". Bob Hope gets a bit agitated, and proceeds to tell the guard that not only is he Bob Hope, but that he owns some stock or something in the raceway. The guard is not overly impressed, so he calmly repeats, for the third time, "Sorry, you can't come in here without a garage pass". Then he adds, "Sir, let me tell you something. If our Lord, Jesus Christ, Himself came up to this gate and He didn't have His garage pass on, I wouldn't let Him in." And Sir, let me tell you one more thing. If our Lord, Jesus Christ, Himself come up to this gate and He had on fifty passes, and he was with a woman. I still wouldn't let him in!"

Richard Petty

A.J. Foyt

Richter Keeps Riverside Raceway Humming

RIVERSIDE—In 1963, the year after he became general manager of Riverside International Raceway, Les Richter was offered the job of head football coach at a major university.

He won't say which one (because he doesn't want to identify the man eventually picked for the job as a second choice), but he does say it was a very appealing offer. He would have had tenure, a professorship, the whole issue.

"My wife, Marilyn, and I talked about it for three days," Les told us Tuesday. "Finally, at 3 o'clock one morning, I woke her up and told her I'd made up my mind. I was going to stay on at Riverside.

"She'd been hoping I'd say that. It meant I would be home more.

"The story, of course, is that I'm almost never home. It's pretty much a seven-day-a-week job.

"From right now until Jan. 23, the track will be busy every day except Christmas, either with racing or testing. Last week, Warner Brothers shot some scenes for 'The FBI' series here. Toyota ran some tests the same day. Ford has a car out on the track right now and Wednesday — weather permitting — they'll start practice runs for our big race Sunday, the Rex Mays 300.

"Next year, we will have 56 days of competition. And we're working for the day when the track will be busy 340 days out of the 365, with racing or testing.

"In 1963, the president of Autolite asked me, 'Just where is Riverside located?' Today, Autolite knows just where Riverside is located."

When Richter went to work full time at Riverside five years ago, after nine seasons with the Rams, he sensed there was something in the air here. It was dust. "Outside of asphalt and a fence, that's about all there was," he said.

"Our only major event was The Times Grand Prix. We had to develop a master plan and we had to get more activity. Since then, we have put up a maintenance building, a garage area that we think is the finest in all of auto racing (it has a lounge and a sauna bath for drivers, among other things), permanent concession stands and improved viewing for spectators.

"Eventually, we'll have a motel, a restaurant, a golf course and an auto museum. We're hopeful that by the first part of next year the hotel and restaurant will be in the planning stage. The golf course is a little further away. The museum we could build any time, but it isn't programmed yet.

"We are now planning permanent grandstands. We'll probably start with

Les Richter

about 10,000 seats and build up to who knows! Indianapolis has 172,000 permanent seats and we are in as great an area of auto enthusiasm as there is in the world.

Many Events

Besides The Times Grand Prix, the raceway now offers such annual events as the Motor Trend 500 for stock cars, the Hot Rod magazine championship drag races and, starting this year, the Rex Mays 300 for Indianapolis-type cars.

Before he went to Riverside, Richter was a casual racing fan. "I was born and raised in Fresno," he said, "and racing was very big there in the late 30s. Our family used to go out on Sunday and watch the midgets.

"I followed racing later on, but I wasn't a buff by any means. In my last years with the Rams, I was building toward a career in real estate. When I went into pro ball, I made a vow that I'd try to make enough in the off season to live on and whatever I made in football I would invest.

"I went in on a deal with Frank Gifford and Bob at Bakersfield High when I was captain at Fresno High. Bob and I went to Cal and Frank went to SC, and the friendships sort of crossed over. We started a company called CALSC— for Cal and SC. We kept making investments. In fact, we're still doing it.

"We have half ownership of a cattle feed lot in Bakersfield and we own several apartment houses in Bakersfield. We also have some land in Kern County and interests in office buildings and stores. And some trust deeds.

"The company doesn't have a president, but Bob is the spokesman. He is president of the California Real Estate Assn. Quite an achievement for a man his age.

The January 1968 Permatex 100 late model sportsman race was won by Jerry Titus in front of a crowd of 11,800, not bad for a Saturday supporting race. George Follmer finished second and J.R. Skinner third. Titus collected $4000 for the win.

Jerry Titus

The Permatex Field

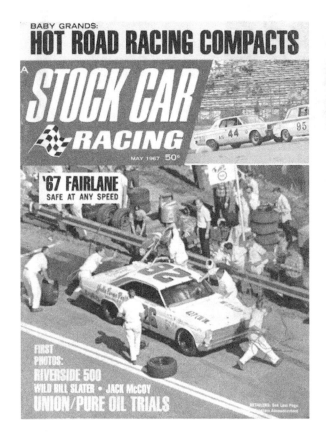

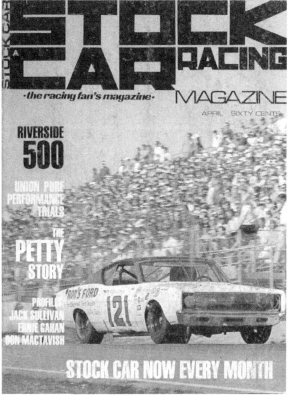

Jerry Titus

"... but who is to say that he had not seen more, done more, and learned more ... than many people do in a lifetime? ... It would be a waste of life to do nothing with one's ability, for I feel that life is measured in achievement, not in years alone."

Bruce McLaren, 1964

The over 80,000 people attending the 1968 Motor Trend 500 Grand National race saw Dan Gurney win $21,250 in a Woods Brothers Ford, with David Pearson second and Parnelli Jones third. For the first time, NASCAR mandated a window net; a reaction to Joe Weatherly's 1964 accident.

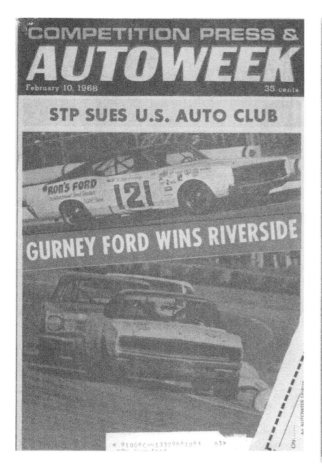

Gurney proves perennial king of 500

Escondido's Grant has engine explode

RIVERSIDE, Calif. (UPI)— There's no truth to a report that Dan Gurney has bought Riverside International Raceway. It just seems that way.

The veteran Corona del Mar, Calif., driver Sunday scored his fifth win in the sixth annual Motor Trend 500 stock car race over the raceway's 2.7-mile road circuit course.

Gurney's NASCAR victory came in a record time of four hours, 57 minutes and 38 seconds — an average of 100.999 miles per hour. The old mark was five hours, five minutes and 39 seconds set by Gurney in 1966.

The winner, who was the top qualifier at 110.971 m.p.h., drove a 1968 Ford and earned $21,250.

Escondido's Jerry Grant, driving a '67 Plymouth, worked his way from 11th to 6th position

returned to the track. At last report he was fine.

Gurney finished 36 seconds in front of David Pearson of Spartanburg, S.C., and 46 seconds ahead of last year's winner, Parnelli Jones of Torrance, Calif. Pearson and Jones also piloted 1968 Fords.

Pearson's runner-up finish was worth $9,550 of the $90,000 purse.

The lead changed hands 13 times in the race with Gurney and Jones sharing first place from the 8th lap on. Gurney went ahead to stay for good on the 160th lap of the 185-lap, 500-mile event.

Bobby Allison of Hueytown, Ala., and Cale Yarborough of Timmonsville, S.C., both in 1968

* * * * * * *

Fords, collected fourth and fifth places, respectively.

Al Unser of Albuquerque, N.M., was sixth in a 1967 Charger and Bobby Isaac of Catawba, S.C., piloting another 1967 Charger, finished seventh.

Rounding out the top 10 finishers, in order, were Dave James, Los Angeles, 1967 Plymouth; Scotty Cain, Fresno, Calif., 1968 Ford, and Richard Petty, Randleman, N.C., 1967 Plymouth.

Petty, last year's NASCAR champion, was forced to retire after hitting a retaining wall on the 165th lap. He was not injured.

Two other nonfinishers were A. J. Foyt of Houston, Tex., the 1967 Indianapolis 500-mile race winner, and Mario Andretti of Nazareth, Pa.

Foyt's 1968 Ford blew its engine on the first lap while Andretti left the race on the

Roger McCluskY

Mario Andretti

NOW HEAR THIS — As Les Richter, president of Riverside International Raceway (right), bends the ear of A. J. Foyt during a lull in a practice session. Roy Hord stands in on the conversation Richter and Hord work very closely coordinating functions at the track.

Richter and Foyt

QUIET MAN — Hord surveys the vast 550-acre raceway from the 75-foot Goodyear tower. Hord mans the center of the communications center during a race from the tower. With the ear phones he is in constant contact with all points at the raceway and can keep in touch with what is happening where.

Roy Hord

Anonymous: *"I was two years old, going to my first race at Riverside. Apparently I was fascinated by the race, kept quiet and watched !! The folks said "we found a way to keep him quiet." After the race my dad took me into the garage area to meet his favorite drivers, Freddy Lorenzen and Richard Petty. Petty offered to let me sit in his car as he and my dad were talking. Then Richard fired up the car with me in it, scared me and I had an accident; wet my pants. Richard said, "it's OK, we're going to clean the car when we get home". I've been a race fan ever since"*

Gurney won after this pit stop to change a flat tire

The 1969 Permatex 200 Late Model Sportsman race drew 19,200 fans on a foggy, drizzly day and was won by Herschel McGriff followed by Ron Grable and Clem Proctor. The race was cut short at 62 laps due to rain.

McGriff Wins Race In Drizzle

By RYAN REES
Sun-Telegram Auto Racing Editor

RIVERSIDE Hershel Mc-Griff survived oil in the cockpit, a crash into a wall and a possible blowout yesterday to win the rain - curtailed Permatex 200.

TIGHT TURN—Ray Johnstone (00) of San Bernardino, steers his 1957 Chevy through Turn 8 yesterday while leading the field in the Permatex 200 stock car race. He crashed on the 50th lap and finished 13 in the final tally. Hershel McGriff won the race which was shortened by the heavy drizzle that turned the course into a slippery ice rink.

10-Year Agreement Confirmed

Riverside Gets NASCAR

RIVERSIDE — A major new road race was added to the racing fare of Western America today with the signing of a new 10-year contract by Riverside International Raceway and the National Assn. for Stock Car Automobile Racing (NASCAR).

The contract provides for a 400-mile Grand National late model stock car road race annually beginning June 14, 1970. It also affirms the long-standing date in January for the Motor Trend-Riverside 500, one of the nation's $100,000 stock events.

The new race will revive the Golden State 400, a NASCAR Grand National race held in

November of 1963 that was won by Darel Dieringer. When signing William G. France, President of NCASCAR commented, "NASCAR is very proud to be expanding its Grand National program in California by adding a second race at Riverside.

"After studying the current improvement plans at Riverside and considering the market potential for racing in the nation's most populous state, I feel this new race will help to meet the demand for big time motor racing."

The signing of the long-term contract by France and Les Richter, President of Riverside International Raceway, coincides

with the closing of a multi-million dollar transaction that makes Michigan International Speedway, Inc. a controlling stockholder in the Riverside operation and signaled the start of a $3-million construction program at the Raceway.

The agreement between Michigan International Speedway and Riverside was approved by the Boards of Directors of both companies and the first two phases of a long-term improvement financing program has been completed, according to Lawrence H. LoPatin, President of Michigan International Speedway, Inc.

Michigan acquires 625,000

shares of stock in Riverside International Raceway for $1,250,000 and lends the Raceway an additional $950,000 secured by a first trust deed to the 600-acre property. This provides Riverside with $2.2 million with which to begin construction of new facilities for spectators and competitors.

According to Richter, in previously reported plans for Riverside's improvement program, the road course will be redesigned to include a wide sweeping turn that replaces part of its 1.1-mile straight-a-way, and permanent grandstand seating for more than 20,000 spectators will be erected.

Rain was expected and the 1969 Motor Trend 500 Grand National race was postponed twice due to rain. Cars were held under armed guard in the garages until two weeks later when it was finally won by Richard Petty followed by A.J. Foyt and Parnelli Jones. Petty got $21,750 for the win.

Parade to Honor Racers

RIVERSIDE — A special Riverside 500 parade will be held in downtown Riverside this morning in connection with the Motor Trend/Riverside 500 race tomorrow.

The parade will begin at Magnolia Avenue at 11 a.m. It will move down Magnolia to Merrill Avenue and then turn back on Riverside Avenue.

Numerous television and

movie personalities are expected to be in the parade.

The Riverside Jaycees sponsor the event and hope for 110 units including 17 of the top marching bands in Southern California.

More than 30,000 attended last year's parade.

The Permatex 200 for NASCAR Sportsman stock cars will begin at Riverside Raceway at 1 p.m.

RAIN AGAIN KO'S 500; RESET SATURDA

BY SHAV GLICK
Times Staff Writer

RIVERSIDE — For the second straight week the 7th annual Motor Trend 500, scheduled to be run today at Riverside International Raceway, has been postponed.

The 500-mile race for stock cars has been rescheduled for next Saturday at 11 a.m., it was announced Saturday by Les Richter, raceway president.

Cars Impounded Again

"If the rains had stopped, the track itself would have been fine, but everywhere else around the track is one big lake," said Richter. "By scheduling it for next Saturday we hope we will be able to dry out by then."

Pit crews returned to the garages Saturday morning and worked on their cars, hopeful of running today. However, when the second postponement was announced, the cars were impounded again and the garages locked until next Friday. Practice is scheduled for 2 to 4 p.m. Friday.

There is a possibility some of the 44 cars may pull out of the race because of the added expense of another week's delay. At least 15 of the cars are either owned or driven by NASCAR members who live in the Southeast part of the country. This is NASCAR's lone Grand National race on the West Coast, but not its first experience with rain this season.

The Motor Trend is race No. 3 on the 1969 Grand National circuit and all had been postponed by the rain. The Georgia 500 at Macon and the Alabama 200 at Montgomery were both delayed one week. Both were won by Plymouths driven by Richard Petty and Bobby Allison, respectively, which may be some kind of omen.

This is the first time Motor Trend 500 has twice delayed. Two years ago it was interrupted rain after 115 miles, restarted and completed week later with Parnelli Jones winning.

Petty 'On Track' With 500 Win

RIVERSIDE, Calif. (AP) —"I just managed to stay on the track most of the time," said Richard Petty after his blistering 186-lap victory at the Riverside International Raceway.

By so doing, he won the Motor Trend 500 for stock cars, good for $21,750. He averaged 105.51 miles an hour.

"In the past races here I always managed to spend more time off the track than on it and you just can't do when he missed shifts and finally retired to the pits on the 68th lap.

The race, delayed from last month because of heavy rainstorms, was run in clear, dry weather. Not once did the yellow caution light blink — another first for the 500.

Amon's Ferrari Wins

BRISBANE, Australia (AP) —Chris Amon of New Zealand took the lead at the start in an Italian Ferrari yesterday

Mario Andretti

NASCAR held two Grand National races at Riverside in 1970, the January Motor Trend 500, won by A.J. Foyt and the June Falstaff 400, won by Richard Petty. The January Permatex 200 Late Model Sportsman race, with a crowd of 12,750 on a Saturday, was won by polesitter Clem Proctor in a Thunderbird followed by Sonny Easley and Bud Hickey. There was an interesting tire issue; as the NASCAR Goodyears didn't fit the late model wheels; they ran on Firestones. 80 cars entered, 44 qualified to start. In the following day's Motor Trend 500, 43,200 saw A.J Foyt win $19,190 in a Ford Torino. Roger McCluskey in a Plymouth Superbird was second with Lee Roy Yarborough in third.

January 1970 Permatex Winner Clem Proctor – 1963 Thunderbird

Foyt Overcomes Early Trouble, Wins 500

RIVERSIDE, Calif. (AP) — Veteran A. J. Foyt of Houston, Tex., captured a crash-marred Riverside-Motor Trend 500-mile stock car race Sunday by about three seconds in his 1970 Ford Torino.

Two drivers were hospitalized, one in critical condition, during the test over a road race course which saw the yellow

In third place came Lee Roy Yarbrough of Columbia, S.C., who also drove a Torino. He finished eight seconds behind McCluskey.

Foyt, already a millionaire, collected $19,100 for his triumph. McCluskey's second place was worth $8,600 with third valued at $5,300 to Yarbrough.

"When I was 18 seconds in front of McCluskey I drove cautiously and just didn't want to make mistakes."

Foyt recalled that in this race five years ago he flipped his car and suffered a broken back.

Many of the yellow flag periods were caused when cars blew engines and

Accident Mars A. J. Foyt's Riverside Victory

RIVERSIDE, Calif. — A. J. Foyt won the 500-mile Riverside Motor Trend stock car ... going into turn No. 9 of Riverside International Raceway. "If you're going only 100 ... going around it on the outside. Instead he slammed head-on into the wall. The 45-year-old father of ... Earlier another driver, Buddy Young of Fairfax, Va., escaped serious injury even though his car rolled about 15 ... Equipment wouldn't take this much beating in 200,000 miles of highway driving." ... Houston, three-times winner of the Indianapolis 500, and Roger McCluskey of Tucson, ... seconds by being careful. I didn't want trouble on the final couple of laps." ... used on six occasions, the speed was far below the record 105.516 by Richard Petty

Jim Cook recovered from this crash but was confined to a wheelchair. Thirteen years later, he was beaten to death with one of his trophies by an intruder who broke into his home.

In June 1970, Ron Hornaday Sr. won the California 100 Late Model Sportsman race, followed by Brad Weber and Vallie Engelaf.

Proctor's Problems Clears Path for Hornaday

Ron Hornaday Cops 100-Miler At Riverside

RIVERSIDE (AP) — Ron Hornaday of Chatsworth, Los Angeles County, came from 13th place Saturday to win the California 100 sportsman stock car race at Riverside International Raceway, a companion to today's Riverside 400.

Driving a 1964 Ford Mus-

George Beall: *"I always ran in the top ten, 'cept for the occasions where the motor blew up (or in the summer race, when the car overheated). But the best story was, on my way to the track early on a Sunday morning, I got stopped for speeding. I told the cop I had been going 150 mph at the track and it was hard to readjust. He let me go with a warning"*

Richard Petty won the June 1970 Falstaff 400 Grand National race in a Plymouth Superbird, followed by Bobby Allison in Dodge and James Hylton in a Ford. Petty received $18,840 for the win in front of a small crowd, 18,500.

Richard Petty Whips Around Turn Six Searching for Victory . . .
. . . and He Found It Yesterday at Riverside International Raceway in the Falstaff 400

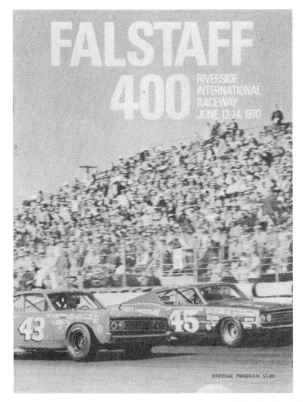

Petty Captures Falstaff 400

By RYAN REES
Sun-Telegram Auto Racing Editor

RIVERSIDE — Perhaps no one informed Ford Motor Company of the Falstaff 400 stock car race. Perhaps FoMoCo didn't care.

With only three otther factory-sponsored cars to challenge him, Richard Petty spread-eagled the 40-car field in his Plymouth SuperBird enroute to a one-lap victory in the first annual Falstaff 400 held at Riverside International Raceway.

Ford had won every previous major stock car or Trans-Am event at Riverside before yesterday.

The Randleman, N. C. stock car great captured the Riverside 500 in 1969 while driving a Ford Torino. But yesterday he was back in the familiar "Petty blue" Plymouth.

Petty led all but one lap of the four-

Runner-up Bobby Allison led for one lap while Petty was in the pits.

Allison, who captured the pole position with an average speed of 111.621 miles per hour, held on for second.

In the unofficial tally, James Hylton, in a factory-backed Ford, was third 10 laps back while Johnny Soares of Hayward was fourth in a SuperBird. However, Hylton was running very slow the final 20 laps of the race when the left front suspension broke and Soares made up several laps on the crippled Ford.

Dick Guldstand was fifth with Jack McCoy in a badly battered Dodge Charger sixth. Neil Castles claimed seventh, Bob McDonald eighth, Mel Larson ninth and Bob England tenth. Larson drove the car originally intended for Cale Yarborough. However, Yarborough wasn't satisfied with the 1969 Ford and decided not to enter.

Watch the 1970 Falstaff 400 on the attached DVD

The 1971 January Motor Trend 500 Grand National race, the first race run as "Winston Cup", was won by Ray Elder, followed by Bobby Allison and Benny Parsons. Elder picked up $18,715 for the win in front of 33,300 people on a sunny but cold day, In January 1971, Ray Elder won the Motor Trend 500, collecting $18,715 followed by Bobby Allison and Benny Parsons in front of 33,300 people on a cold, blustery day. The June Golden State 400 was won by Bobby Allison, followed by Ray Elder and Cecil Gordon. Allison took home $14,395 for the win in front of 18,700 fans who braved 105 degree weather. Allison used two way radios, a first in a NASCAR race.

Ray Elder Takes Motor Trend 500

Southern Superstars In Independent Debut

Bobby Allison, '70 Dodge, prepares to lap the '69 Chevelle of Friday Hassler during the Motor Trend/Riverside 500 Jan. 10. Allison took second after a duel of pits stops with eventual winner Ray Elder. (Edwin Ingalls photo)

By Mike Knepper
Managing Editor

RIVERSIDE, Calif., Jan. 10 – Ray Elder, star of short track events in NASCAR's Western Grand National division, held off the best the South had to offer to win the Motor Trend/Riverside 500-mile Grand National stock car race at Riverside International Raceway here today before 33,500 enthusiastic fans.

Elder's 1970 Dodge, which he owns, prepares and independently enters, performed flawlessly throughout the race. Riverside's nine turns, however, proved too much for the machines of pre-race favorites Richard Petty, '70 Plymouth, and David Pearson, '70 Ford.

BOBBY ALLISON SECOND

Still around at the finish were Bobby Allison, who drove his '70 Dodge to second place; Benny Parsons, '69 Ford, third; Bobby Isaac/David Pearson, '70 Dodge, fourth, (Pearson took over for Isaac late in the race); and James Hylton, '70 Ford, fifth.

The event was the first for the Grand National drivers after Ford's complete pullout from racing and Chrysler's cutback. Only Petty and Buddy Baker, who didn't make this race, are still enjoying factory sponsorship.

The rest of the traditional factory drivers, now finding
(Continued on page 20)

Kershaw's Permatex

RIVERSIDE, Calif., Jan. 9 – Today's Permatex 200 for NASCAR early model stock cars should have been Clem Proctor's race, but when the dust cleared, Proctor's 1963 Thunderbird was dead on the course and Gary Kershaw, driving a 1965 Chevelle out of Victoria, B.C. in his second road race, was the winner.

Following Kershaw was Johnny Anderson in a 1964 Chevelle. Then, a lap in arrears, were Romie Alderman, '64 Buick; Sonny
(Continued on page 22)

COMPETITION PRESS & AUTOWEEK

LATE NEWS

● Following the death of Ignazio Giunti in Buenos Aires, the Italian Automobile Sports Commission has requested that Ferrari withdraw its entry for the Jan. 24 non-championship Formula 1 Argentine Grand Prix. Mario Andretti, Clay Regazzoni and Jacky Ickx were scheduled to drive for Ferrari in the race.
● Ferrari and Matra factory teams have not been entered in the Jan. 30 24 Hours of Daytona. Ferrari will be represented in the race with nine private entries, six of them the 512S model.

WINNER—The victory in the Riverside 500 brought cheer to three members of the Elder family: Ray (center) who drove, brother Richard (left) and dad, Fred, who handled most of the pit duties.

Ray Elder Captures Riverside 500 Miler

By Art Glattke

McClatchy Newspapers Service

RIVERSIDE, Calif. — Coming on late, Ray Elder of Caruthers won the ninth Riverside 500 for NASCAR late-model stock cars.

Elder outdrove 38 other driv-

This will be a big boost to West Coast racing."

He was commenting, too, about the factory help which prior to this event had been given in abundance to southern drivers — the hotbed of stock

and Bobby Isaac if it was just a flat out race," he said. Petty, in the only factory-sponsored car in the race, had won the pole position. Petty, in a 1970 Plymouth, led for a while but Elder blew him off, literally, after

Motor Trend 500 Parade

NATIONAL SPEED SPORT NEWS

25¢

VOL. XXXIX—No. 2   RIDGEWOOD, N. J., JANUARY 13, 1971   Entered as Second Class Matter at the Post Office at Ridgewood, New Jersey   (ISSUED WEEKLY)

Wins in a Dodge:

West Coast Ace Elder Bags Motor Trend 500

Dan Gurney (1931 – 2018)

It's pretty difficult to describe Dan Gurney in just one page: a winner in Formula One, Trans Am, Indy Cars, Can Am and Stock Cars; a noted innovator and successful car builder and a really nice guy. Winning at Riverside five times in stock cars, he became a fan favorite.

Les Richter convinced him to come out of retirement after 10 year hiatus in 1980; Dan qualified seventh and ran as high as second before the gearbox broke. Compilers Note: Les Richter allegedly insisted that Dan attend the Bob Bondurant Driving Scholl prior to the race. Bondurant said; *"He didn't need the school – He was always faster than me and still is"*

Grinning."Wood remembers one instance in which a clowning Gurney pulled all the lining from his helmet, and then put on the helmet to the amusement of those around him."

Dan receiving the Peter Bryant Award

Dan and Bobby- Legends of Riverside

Watch the Dan Gurney Video on the attached DVD

14,500 spectators, the largest crowd to ever watch a Saturday Permatex 200 saw Gary Kershaw of Vancouver win the January 1971 Late Model Stock Car event in a Chevelle, followed by Johnnie Anderson and Richard White.

(Continued on page 23)

Eventual winner Gary Kershaw, '65 Chevy, leads the '67 Chevy of Jack Jeffery and the '61 Ford of Ray Elder during Permatex action.   (Edwin Ingalls photo)

Truck Driver Wins Permatex 200

By RYAN REES
Sun-Telegram Auto Racing Editor

RIVERSIDE — Former winners Clem Proctor and Ron Hornaday both lost chances at victory yesterday and a truck driver from Victoria, Canada, took home all the marbles in the Permatex 200 at Riverside International Raceway.

Proctor, who won the

"My pit crew was a little excited I guess," he answered.

For Kershaw, 33, it was his biggest victory and first ever on a road course. He has been racing in the Northwest the past two years in Sportsman races. "I won about six races last year," he said.

Kershaw qualified fourth on

lead when Proctor pitted but spun going through turn two and landed near the wall. By the time he had gotten out of the ice plant and back on the track, Proctor was well out in front.

On the 62nd lap, Proctor again pulled into the pits and the crew put in more gas. Still holding the lead, Proctor

Baldwin of Highland. He spun at least five times, once bringing out the yellow flag when he rammed into the dirt embankment near turn five. He had spun earlier going through the esses and then spun coming out of turn nine. He managed to keep going on the latter spins. He also had his troubles getting

13	13	George Soink, Riverside, 64 Pontiac	73
14	19	Larry Funkhouser, Riverside, 63 Chevy	73
15	15	Joe Ruggles, Granada Hills, 66 Ford	73
16	88	Jack Jeffrey, Seattle, 67 Chevelle	72
17	01	Jim Whitt, El Cajon, 67 Chevelle	71
18	22n	Roy Bleckert, Riverside, 64 Pontiac	71
19	33n	Jerry Green, Las Vegas, 64 Pontiac	70
20	35	Pat Mintey, San Valley, 66 Chevelle	70
		Bill Foster, Santa	

Gary Kershaw

The June 1971 California 100 Late Model Stock Car race was won by Clem Proctor, followed by Gene Riniker and Billy Foster.

Going Around on the Outside in Turn 6
... California 100 winner Clem Proctor (33) passes a slower car to stay in front

Clem Proctor Coasts to Cal 100 Win

By RYAN REES
San-Telegram Auto Racing Editor

RIVERSIDE — Clem Proctor stopped for 22 seconds to add a couple of gallons of gas and then went back out and won the California 100 yesterday at Riverside International Raceway.

The California 100 for sportsman racers was the companion feature to the Winston-Golden State 400 which begins at 1 p.m. today.

Proctor, who has taken the pole after the last four sportsman races at Riverside, would have liked a little longer stop than he took. Under the conditions, he couldn't very well afford to take any longer.

"I was hit hard by 'Montezuma's Revenge' last night and was almost looking around for another driver this morning.

"However, a pint of Pepto Bismo took care of things and I feel good now," Proctor said in the winner's circle.

Proctor tooled his 1963 T-Bird around the twisting road course with a no stream of trouble. The only time he had the lead was after the only yellow flag of the race and when he stopped briefly for gas.

Does Anybody Have a Road Map?
... several drivers in yesterday's California 100 at Riverside Raceway find the going confusing in the race

74

SEE THE BIG ONE SUNDAY!!!
MOTOR TREND'S
9th Annual
RIVERSIDE 500
RIVERSIDE INTERNATONAL RACEWAY
11:00 AM

THE RACE THAT WON THE WEST

TALK ABOUT TRADITION! The Motor Trend 500 has it all. Take NASCAR's 4,000 pound, 600 horsepower stockers with the country's top drivers — men like Richard Petty, Bobby Allison, James Hylton, David Pearson and Bobby Isaac — and put them all on Riverside's famous 2.62 mile, twisting eight-turn road course for the most exciting 500 miler in the West. It's the only 500-mile race of the year in which these rugged stock car pilots have to turn right as well as left, go uphill

and down, shifting more than a thousand times as they go from 180 miles an hour down Riverside's long back straightaway to less than 60 around the hairpin turn 8. Infield parking is welcome. Come in, move around and see it all. Come early and join the thousands who camp overnight on the 400 acre infield and pick your spots. See the race that won the West—the Motor Trend Riverside 500.

5th Annual
PERMATEX 200

On Saturday, it's the fifth annual Permatex 200 for late model (1960-67) sedans with the West Coast's finest behind the wheels. Same course, same excitement as the Motor Trend 500, except this one is decided 300 miles sooner. Clem Proctor, Ron Hornaday, Cliff Garner, Hershel McGriff—just a few of the West Coast boys who'll be doing their stuff in the Permatex 200. Saturday, 3 p.m.

DAN GURNEY DAY

If you've ever been a Dan Gurney fan, this is your chance to come out and say thanks. The Motor Trend Riverside 500, which Dan has won five times, is being dedicated to his sort. Sunday and sponsors, fans and friends will participate in a special pre-race appreciation day ceremony. Best—Dan Gurney banner displayed during the ceremonies wins the owner a pair of season passes to Riverside and a ride in the pace car with Dan.

ONE TICKET WILL DO IT ALL
Buy any Sunday ticket in advance and see all previous days' activities—Thursday and Friday Motor Trend 500 qualifying and Saturday's Permatex 200—FREE.

Motor Trend 500 Prices:

General Admission . . . . . $ 6	Esses Grandstands $10
Grandstand A (Start/Finish) . . . $10	Grandstand B (Turn 6) . $10, $12, $15

Grandstand Prices include General Admission. General admission free to children under 12. At all Wallichs Music City Stores, Ticketron (213) 878-2211, Master Charge or Riverside International Raceway (714) 653-1161.

ALLISON PACES FIELD

Bobby Allison shows why he won the Winston Golden State 400 at Riverside Sunday in his 1970 Dodge (12). Ray Elder finished second with Cecil Gordon placing third. (Photo by Gil Frazee)

Allison leads Petty and Elder

NATIONAL SPEED SPORT NEWS

25c

VOL. XXXIX—No. 2   RIDGEWOOD, N. J., JANUARY 13, 1971   Entered as Second Class Matter at the Post Office at Ridgewood, New Jersey   (ISSUED WEEKLY)

Wins in a Dodge:

West Coast Ace Elder Bags Motor Trend 500

(Story on Page Three)

STRATEGY TALK—STP crew chief Vincent Granatelli confers with New Zealander Chris Amon prior to the opening race of the 1971 Tasman Cup series at Levin, New Zealand. The STP Racing Team is making an all-out effort in the Tasman.

HONORING THE CHAMPS—United Racing Club sprint car champion Gino Swarthout, second from left, and champion car owner Jimmy Shaw were honored Saturday night at the club's 23rd annual awards banquet at Wieland's Steak House in Mountainside, N. J. Taking part in the ceremonies were, from the left, Ty Berger of NATIONAL SPEED SPORT NEWS, newspaper editor Jack Schwartz and Art Maxim representing the STP Corporation.   (Dusty Fraser photo)

LANCASTER CHAMPS — The Lancaster, N.Y., Speedway recently concluded their season with a gala awards banquet. The four track champions with their trophies are l. to r. Merv Treichler, modified-sportsman; Bruce Bolitsky, three-quarter midgets; Fred Rounds, mini stocks; and Pete Snyder, late models. Rounds has been confined to the wheel chair for ten years following a street accident, and operates his Datsun mini stocker with hand controls. (Merrill Stearns photo)

TASMAN ACTION—New Zealander Chris Amon in the STP March, leads Australia's Niel Allen in a McLaren during the opening round of the 1971 Tasman Cup series at Levin, New Zealand, January 2. Amon finished third despite having shifter problems.

Juliette
Miss Winston Western 500

Coming to Riverside International Raceway as Miss Winston Western 500 is a homecoming for Juliette Ashdown. Although she was born in Panama City, Florida, the auburn-haired beauty considers herself a native of California. And Riverside was her "hometown" during her father's tour of duty at March Air Force Base.

You'll see Miss Winston Western 500 throughout the race activities, and she'll be on hand in the Victory Circle to greet the winner of the 1972 Winton Western 500.

Juliette was born in Panama City, while her father was stationed at Merced, California, and as soon as she was old enough to travel, she and her mother returned to Merced. The family left as her father received other Air Force assignments, but returned to Merced where Juliette graduated from high school.

After high school, Juliette began her college study at InterAmerican University in San Francisco, where she earned money for her college expenses working as a model. An offer for a "great" modeling job caused Juliette to move to San Higerman, Puerto Rico where she continued her studies for a couple of years. Later, she transferred to Florida State University.

When she had completed the courses for a degree in education, Juliette found that she had not attended any one college long enough to meet the residency requirements for a degree. Undaunted, she applied for teacher certification which was granted, and then she attended graduate school at Florida State University.

Her two years of study and work in Puerto Rico indirectly led Juliette to what she considers her most unusual job. She had moved to Las Vegas and was looking for modeling jobs. "I needed a regular job, but still needed to be free during the day to accept modeling assignments. I learned that the Sheriff's Department needed a Spanish interpreter. I applied for the job and became the youngest member of the County Vice Squad." (That's right—Vice Squad.) "I took calls and served as interpreter for Spanish-speaking people coming in contact with the Vice Squad. It was interesting, but as I got more and more modeling jobs, I left the Sheriff's Department."

Now, the green-eyed Miss Winston Western 500 lives in Atlanta where her talents as a model require her full attention.

For hobbies, Juliette says she changes from time to time. "While I lived in California, snow skiing was my favorite pasttime." Later, tennis moved into the spotlight, and she was on the Florida State University tennis team.

What's her number one hobby now? "Why, stock car racing, of course," replies Miss Winston Western 500.

J.D. McDuffie – Dick Guldstrand behind him

Mark Donohue, at the wheel of American Motors' latest racing endeavor, talks with Roger Penske, boss of the project, at Daytona International Speedway. The 366 cubic inch-engined Matador has equaled Penske Racing's hopes for a competitive Grand National car. Today's race is the first outing for the car under competition conditions.

Read Jean Calvin's stock car article on the attached DVD

Rotary Engine Mazda RX-2 Selected Official Pace Car At Riverside International Raceway

By Wally Wyss, Associate Editor, *Motor Trend*

It's a race day at Riverside International Raceway and the announcer's voice is drowned out by the incredible RHUMPA-RHUMPA-RHUMPA as 40 squat beasts growl and prowl on bulging rubber paws ready to do battle. The crowd buzzes expectantly, hoping to see the first of the pack as they take the pace lap, restrained as if on a giant leash.

But, wait, what's that in the lead? It looks like a small import coupe. An economy car? What's that doing as a pace car? Why, it won't be able to get out of its own way.

Unless, of course, it's a Mazda.

You see, back at MOTOR TREND, we had occasion to test one of those innocuous looking little Mazdas. It didn't have a humped hood, or strobe stripes, or a leather-steering wheel or jumbo white-lettered tires. But we still ended up calling it "the muscle car of tomorrow."

Not just because the Mazda RX-2 comes with lots of trick stuff like a four-speed stick, a four-barrel carb, a tach, and even an oil cooler. But because it comes with a *rotary* engine—the ultimate in trick engines.

What's so different about the Mazda rotary engine? For one thing, its simplicity. In fact, the rotary engine is *so* simple, one wonders why it wasn't thought of *before* the reciprocating piston engine. Basically, the rotary engine consists of a combustion chamber shaped like a fat peanut (or a Mae West life jacket) inside of which a triangle-shaped rotor rotates. Since the rotor is mounted on an eccentric crank, it not only revolves but roves around the entire inside of the chamber, continually varying the volume between each side of the rotor and the chamber wall.

This rotor manages to perform all of the necessary operations for an internal combustion engine—intake, compres-sion, power and exhaust. A valve train, pistons and connecting rods are unnec-essary. There is less power loss because there's no up-and-down motion to be converted into rotary motion. The Maz-da rotary is far smoother than the high winding "singy" engines in most im-ports. You might even fool somebody into thinking you've got a mini V-12 under the hood.

The lack of a valve train has one other great advantage, as any racer whose car has ever "swallowed a valve" can tell you. Without valves, there are no valves to swallow or float. That means that going past redline on the tachometer does not mean irrevocable disaster. (Exceeding the redline on a Mazda is definitely *not* recommended, just as with any other car, but at least you won't float a valve.) Besides, with the Mazda redline of 7,000 rpm, at which time you're doing roughly 120

Read about the Mazda pace car on the attached DVD

2nd ANNUAL GOLDEN STATE 400

JUNE 20, 1971 1:00 P.M.

Riverside International Raceway

ENJOY THRILL PACKED RACING

See top names in NASCAR stock racing... Including: Richard Petty, Bobby Isaac, David Pearson, Bobby Allison and other top names, roaring down the long back straight at speeds up to 160 MPH; racing over Riverside's 8-turn road course for a purse of $65,000.

The Golden State 400, one of two major stock car road races in the world, is sanctioned by the National Association for Stock Car Automobile Racing (NASCAR). Riverside is the only road course where Grand National events are scheduled.

SATURDAY'S EVENTS — JUNE 19th
CALIFORNIA 100 —
Sportsman 1961-67 stock cars
Final Qualifying for GOLDEN STATE 400

25% DISCOUNT TICKETS

Regular Price	Sears Price	You Save
$12	$9	$3
$10	$7 50	$2 50
$8	$6	$2
$6	$4 50	$1 50

Available ONLY at
SEARS TICKETRON

Shop Sunday 12 Noon to 5 p.m.
Monday thru Friday 9:30 a.m. to 9 p.m.
Saturdays 9:30 a.m. to 6:00 p.m.

Satisfaction Guaranteed
or Your Money Back
Free Parking Available

Allison races to Golden State win

RIVERSIDE (UPI) — Before Sunday's $80,000 Winston Golden State 400, Nascar veteran Bobby Allison cracked:

"When you're hot, you're hot."

The 33-year-old Hueytown, Ala., driver continued to sizzle in the year's 24th Grand National race, posting his fourth consecutive victory for a first prize of $14,395.

Allison averaged 93.622 miles per hour in his 1970 Dodge in 100-degree weather, leading 136 of the 153 laps in the Winston Golden State event.

The pole sitter with a 107.351 miles per hour qualifying speed, he finished the race in four hours, 17 minutes and five seconds.

"I didn't run as hard as I had to," Allison admitted. "I kept reminding myself during the race that I have to save the car. I knew I could outrun (Richard) Petty. It was just a question of how fast I would have to run."

Petty, the defending champion from Randleman, N.C., and the No. 2 qualifier, wasn't around at the end.

Petty's '71 Plymouth blew an engine on the 114th lap while running four laps behind the leader. The car hit the wall on turn nine. Petty was unhurt.

Ray Caruthers, the racing farmer from Caruthers, Calif., was second on the same lap in a '71 Dodge for $7,695.

Six laps back in third place was Cecil Gordon of Arden, N.C., in a '69 Mercury followed, in order, by James Hylton of Inman, S.C., in a '70 Ford and Jerry Oliver of Concord, Calif., in a '71 Olds.

The temperature hit 105 degrees during the race and only 10 cars in the field of 40 were running over Riverside's 2.62-mile, eight-turn road course at the end.

Allison used a two-way radio to talk to his pit crew during the race.

"The radio really helped me," the driver said. "At one time my pit crew warned me about a crash ahead of me. If I hadn't known about the crash coming up, I might have run into it."

The NASCAR Grand National circuit continues at Houston, Tex., Wednesday night with a 150-miler.

Bobby Allison

Bobby Allison had 43 starts at Riverside led 1003 laps and won six times (1971, 1973, 1975, 1979 and twice in 1981). He said *"My first win here was in the June race in '71 and it was a pretty big thrill for me just to finish. The hardest thing we had to learn was not to over-rev the engines. We'd miss a shift and tear up the transmission and we'd never finish. When I conquered that, and drove a whole race without tearing anything up, I won the race."*.

Bobby Allison: *"I'd been racing at Riverside since 1965 or so; always liked road courses, especially ones with long straights like Riverside had. I had the good fortune to have a local road racing expert give me a few tips – I learned to not over rev and miss shifts. My first win here in '71, was really a thrill, driving for Holman – Moody, battling with Ray Elder, as was my win in '75, leading 175 laps, a tough fight with David Pearson, driving for Roger Penske in the AMC Matador. And being able to run the last race, in 1988, was also a thrill, just because it was the last race at one of my favorite tracks. Didn't do to well as I recall"* Compiler's Note: Bobby had 6 wins at Riverside, a number of top tens and is in the NASCAR Hall of Fame.

Allison in the Mario Rossi Daytona

Watch the Bobby Allison video on the attached DVD

Winning races never gets old for Allison

By KATIE CASTATOR
Sun Sports Writer

RIVERSIDE — That's no baby on board the Miller American Buick.

Sitting in the driver's seat is a lean, rangy, middle-aged man as weathered and enduring as an ancient redwood. However, Bobby Allison, Hueytown's most famous citizen, has given new meaning to the philosophy "young at heart."

On May 4, the 48-year-old racing legend won the Winston 500 at Talladega, Ala., to become the oldest driver to win a NASCAR Winston Cup race.

Allison was "pleased" but couldn't help putting the win in perspective.

He said: "Look at Hershel McGriff (who at 58 years old is still one of the top drivers on the Winston West Tour). You know, he obviously has a little bit on me. He won the Mexican road race when I was in the fourth grade of school. That's not because I was a slow learner, either."

Allison may not be quite as old as McGriff, but it's still a little wondrous that he's currently third in the season points standings with eight top-10 finishes in 11 starts. And he's looking forward to winning his second Winston Cup championship. He cinched the 1983 points race with a ninth-place finish in the season-ending race at Riverside International Raceway.

Allison is back at Riverside this week, starting 11th in today's $250,000 Budweiser 400.

This is his 36th Winston Cup race on the course; his first was in 1965. He remains the statistical leader in the 41 events conducted at the 2.62 mile, eight-turn course with six victories, and 16 top-five finishes. He's also won $292,010 here.

Allison is proving this year he hasn't lost an rpm since he was 17 and strapped into his first race car. In the years that followed, Allison collected 82 Winston Cup career victories.

Amazingly, those years haven't dimmed his enthusiasm or competitive fires. That's because the easygoing leader of racing's Alabama Gang has never approached racing as a job.

"I'm going to run about 75 races this year, and would probably run more," Allison said. "What

Bobby Allison, 48, is oldest-ever NASCAR winner.

think ought to have priority over my golf game, which is short-track racing. I've even missed a fishin' trip or two for a race."

Even a broken back couldn't keep Allison out of his stock car. In 1974, he crashed in Saturday's race of a doubleheader weekend at Riverside. He was taken to the hospital and X-rayed.

"Then they stuck me back in a space in the emergency room and must have forgotten about me," Allison said. "About two hours later when some of my friends from Alabama came in to check on me, I had them get my clothes and we left. I figured they wouldn't miss me."

The group then went out to dinner and headed back to the motel. Allison was getting ready for bed when the phone rang. It was the doctor. He asked Allison to come back to the hospital because X-rays had shown a fracture in his back. Allison declined but promised to be careful.

"I got up the next morning and I hurt, but I was determined to race anyhow," Allison said. "I got in the car and took off. I got a good lead and ran the cleanest race I ever ran out there. I never got off the pavement because the bumps really made the pain so much worse."

Allison won the race, but it took a long time for him to get over the pain.

Racing became painful again for Allison in 1985. Somehow the DiGard team was out of sync. For the first year since 1971, Allison went winless in the Winston Cup series, and finished out of the top 10 in points for the first time in 10 years.

This year, he has new owners — Bill and Mickey Stavola. The marriage appears to be a good

Straightaway

RIR Tough On Stocks

By JIMMY JOHNSON
Sun-Telegram Sports Writer

RIVERSIDE — Stock cars racing on a road course is indeed a unique happening.

It only happens on one track in the country — Riverside International Raceway.

The massive 4,000-pound stock car was built with the high-banked oval in mind. The twisting and turning of a road course is often too demanding for both automobile and driver.

In the words of the jovial giant Buddy Baker, "I can't stay on a road course. The last time I raced at Riverside was a humiliating experience.

"The first time I went through turn six and stayed on the asphalt," he recalled, the fans gave me a standing ovation. I don't need that kind of humiliation."

Although Buddy Baker flatly refuses to drive at Riverside, there are many stock cars drivers who do drive there and do it well all considered.

In fact, the combination of road course and heavy stock cars makes for an exciting race.

The ice plant at Riverside sees a lot of traffic during the Golden State 400, but there's nothing like fast gals, fast cars and spin-outs to attract a crowd.

Outlook Good for Golden State

The third annual Golden State 400 will be run at Riverside on June 18, and the outlook is optimistic, track officials say.

However, they still recall last year's disaster when the race was almost canceled.

Trouble for the 1971 Golden State started at the close of the 1970 season when Ford Motor Co. pulled out of stock car racing, leaving seven top line drivers adrift.

David Pearson, Lee Roy Yarbrough, Cale Yarborough and Donnie Allison were left without factory contracts.

Also, Dan Gurney, A. J. Foyt and Parnelli Jones, who could race Ford stock cars in fully sanctioned FIA races, were also without factory sponsorship.

If Ford dropping out wasn't enough, Chrysler Corp. cut way down. This left Bobby Isaac, Bobby Allison, Roger McCluskey, Don White and Charlie Gotzbach without factory support.

Plymouth kept only Petty Enterprises, two cars during the 1971 season and everyone knows what Richard Petty did that year. He won 22 races, the NASCAR Grand National Championship and more than $300,000 in purse money.

Money Short on Grand National

Then at the end of the short season, Chrysler dropped Petty and Buddy Baker, eliminating all factory money in Grand National racing.

Long before then there was a lack of money on the Grand National circuit. So when it came time to run the Golden State 400 (1971 version) many name East Coast drivers couldn't afford to haul their cars all the way across country.

With Ford out of racing and Chrysler Corp. cutting way down, only three name drivers — Petty, Bobby Allison and Bobby Isaac — made the trip.

By the start of 1972 there wasn't a single factory tie-up in Grand National racing. That meant no free parts, no free chassis, no homologated parts (specially tooled parts for a particular car) or no easy rides.

Until then, certain names were magic in stock car racing. Factory money had assured this, but with a that money gone it was a whole new ball of wax so to speak.

Probably the only man cheering at that point was the farsighted Bill France, former president of NASCAR. France said "Bravo," because he knew it would benefit the game by making it more competitive.

And when Ray Elder won the 1971 Winston Western 500 it was the first time an independent driver had won a Grand National race in years.

Meanwhile, General Motors had refused to officially get into the racing game. This wasn't good for the fans, because in stock car racing, the fans likes to identify with the car as well as the driver.

Chevrolet Fans Were Slighted

In other words, there were a lot of Chevy fans who were being slighted, and when Bobby Allison won the Atlanta 500 this year, the Chevy fans went into orbit.

For good cause, too. It was the first time a Chevy had won a big race since Junior Johnson did in 1963.

Now there are five competitive brands of cars to root for. If you drive a Dodge you can yell for Isaac; if you drive a Chevy it's Allison; Plymouth it's Petty; or Mercury it's Pearson.

These four drivers will run in the Golden State this year. One thing NASCAR did to make 1972 better for everyone was to come up with a pre-season commitment from these four drivers.

So the Golden State is almost a carbon copy of the January race. The only exceptions are Foyt and Mark Donohue.

The American Motors car will run in the 400, but there's a very strong possibility Donohue will not be at the wheel. He might if he can get permission from USAC, but vibrations from USAC are strong . . . a strong permission denied.

However, Jackie Oliver, a well-known Formula 1 driver, will race for the first time at Riverside, and he'll be driving a red hot stocker on his kind of track.

Les Richter, president of RIR, feels good about this year's race. "It takes two or three years to make a race a success," he says. All considered, this should be the year.

NASCAR Changes Point System

Another thing Richter has going for the Golden State is the change in the point system. NASCAR has eliminated all short-track races from the point system, leaving only 32 Grand National races this year.

Just about everyone concerned believed the old system was unfair and that the new setup will make it possible for a lot more drivers to compete for championship points.

Money for championship points is dished out in three legs. Petty has already won the first leg, edging out Jamie Hylton in the point race.

This is the start of the second leg, so all the drivers will be gunning for the point money as well as the purse in the Golden State.

Riverside has reason to be optimistic.

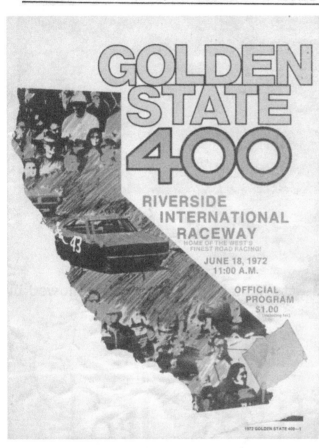

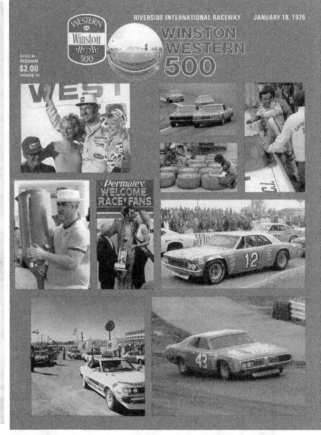

The 1972 Permatex 200 was won by Herschel McGriff, followed by Clem Proctor and Eddie Bradshaw.

Hershel McGriff Captures Permatex for Second Time

By RYAN REES

RIVERSIDE — Men with very humble backgrounds are beginning to dominate the winner's circle at Riverside International Raceway.

Last January, Ray Elder, a man from Bridal Veil, Ore., won the Permatex 200 before a record crowd of 18,600.

It was McGriff's second Permatex victory, having won the event in 1969. He is the only two-time winner.

an hour for the 200-mile chase in his 1966 Chevrolet.

It was the same car he drove to victory in 1969. "I've just changed a little sheet metal here and there the past three years," McGriff said.

don't think I ever left the pavement.

"When I saw Clem (Proctor) pit for fuel near the end I knew I had the race won," McGriff said.

Proctor, who has won the

The Inside Line Is the Fastest . . .
. . . as Permatex 200 winner Hershel McGriff proves

Sun-Telegram photo by Ron Takaca

Sonny Easley won the June California 100 Late Model Sportsman race followed by Eddie Bradshaw and Gene Riniker.

Easley Battles To Riverside Victory

By Art Glattke
McClatchy Newspapers
Motor Racing Writer

RIVERSIDE — Sonny Eas-

seconds in front of Oildale's Eddie Bradshaw, but not before outlasting Clem Proctor of Paramount and Les Los-ser of Modesto

The January 1972 Winston Western 500, formerly the Motor Trend 500, started two hours late and was shortened due to fog to 149 laps or 390 miles It was won by Richard Petty as 47,200 fans braved the fog and chilly weather. The win paid $11,870 to Petty who was followed by Bobby Allison and Bobby Isaac.

Staff Photos by Larry Littlefield

'Petty Power' provides Winston win

Richard Petty, who had 140 NASCAR Grand National victories going into the 1972 season opener at Riverside Raceway Sunday, made it 141 with a victory in the Winston Western 500. Petty (car 43) passed Jim Danielson (car 61) going into turn No. 6 and later gave the old victory sign in the winner's circle. Petty, who topped Bobby Allison, was driving for the first time for STP.

Ray Elder passing or being passed by Herschel McGriff

Richard Petty wins Riverside stock race

RIVERSIDE, Calif. (UPI) — Andy Granatelli, whose name is almost synonymous with Indianapolis, may be ready to change his image.

The fat man who sells STP on television got into stock car racing in a big way last week when he bought Richard Petty's operation for a reported $1 million.

Petty, the 1971 Nascar Grand National Champion from Randleman, N.C., showed Granatelli Sunday that he made a good investment, winning the $103,000 Winston Western 500 in his 1972 Plymouth.

"I love stock car racing," said the man who likes to refer to himself as Mr. 500. "I love Richard Petty, too, but I'm not going to kiss him."

Granatelli bussed Mario Andretti in that famous Italian hugging scene after they teamed to win the 1969 Indy 500 USAC race.

A winner of 21 races and $333,148 on the Grand National

series this year got under way two hours late because of heavy fog and was cut short because of impending darkness.

The Martini & Rossi driver of the year in 1971 led 39 of the 149 laps, completing his day's work in three hours, 45 minutes and 11 seconds.

The veteran from North Carolina, whose victory was worth $11,870, took the lead for good on the 110th lap.

Allison, who had the faste qualifying time but started 16 because he couldn't get his c onto the track when the po was up for grabs Thursda was in front 100 laps.

But he lost his chance to w when he dropped a valve ar had to complete the race seven cylinders

"I still was going pret good," Allison said. "But knew there was no way I cou catch Petty."

Three make trip

Bulldog track team takes 11th in NAIA

University of Redlands made the most of a small track and field traveling squad over the weekend. The Bulldogs finished in a tie for 11th place in the Seventh Annual NAIA Indoor Track and Field championships

third in the finals.

Winner of the event was Do Hampton of Simon Fraser wit a a 2:15.0 time.

The third member of th local thinclad squad in Kansa City was quartermiler Ji

Ray Elder won $12,375 at the June 1972 Golden State 400 Grand National race. Second was Benny Parsons and third was Donnie Allison in a one off drive in the Penske Matador.

Benny Parsons

Golden State 400 Entry Record Set

By JIMMY JOHNSON
Sun-Telegram Sports Writer

RIVERSIDE — Entries for the third annual Golden State 400 have already climbed to a record high.

More than 70 of NASCAR's top drivers on the Grand National circuit have entered the race which will be run over a 2.62-mile road course at the

500 and Daytona 500 in will be driven by Pearson. Since the Spartanburg, S.C., driver took over the Woods car he has won the Darlington 400 and the Talladega 500.

Pearson claims one win at Riverside. He drove a Cougar to victory in the Mission Bell Trans-Am race back in 1966.

r Elder Beats NASCAR's Best In Golden State 400

RIVERSIDE, Calif. (AP) — Ray Elder may have learned patience as a farmer, but he's applying it as a race driver.

The 29-year-old cotton and alfalfa grower from Caruthers, Calif., didn't have the fastest car in Sunday's $75,000 Golden State 400 at Riverside International Raceway. But at the finish, it was Elder who took the checkered flag with a lap to spare.

"After the first few laps I knew I couldn't run with the leaders, so I just picked my own pace and stuck with it," he said.

For 95 of the 153 laps the

Ray Elder

Elder, who had started seventh, took over and nursed his lead over the final 43 laps, babying his

the race. The mishap delayed him four laps.

"It was my mistake. I could have won the race if I hadn't done that," said Allison, who was subbing for Indianapolis 500 winner Mark Donohue in a Matador. Donohue was refused U.S. Auto Club permission to drive in the National Association for Stock Car Auto Racing-sanctioned event.

Elder won the Western 500 here last year, becoming the first non-factory team driver to win a major NASCAR 500-mile event, and decided to take a crack at the Eastern cir-

Ray Elder Wins Riverside Race

RIVERSIDE, Calif. (AP) — Ray Elder may have learned patience as a farmer, but he's applying it as a race driver.

The 29-year-old cotton and alfalfa grower from Caruthers, Calif., didn't have the fastest car in Sunday's $75,000 Golden State 400 at Riverside International Raceway. But at the finish, it was Elder who took the checkered flag with a lap to spare.

"After the first few laps I knew I couldn't run with the leaders, so I just picked my own pace and stuck with it," he said.

For 95 of the 153 laps the strategy looked only good enough for a third-place check, as Richard Petty, the Randleman, N.C., driver who has won over a million dollars and was the fastest qualifier for this event, opened up a wide lead on the twisting eight-turn road course, with Bobby Isaac second.

But on the 96th lap Petty moved out to lap the third-place driver, Elder, and his crankshaft broke, forcing him out of the race

Isaac took over and led for 14 laps. On the 110th lap, the Catawba, N.C., veteran left the race with transmission failure.

Elder, who had started seventh, took over and nursed his lead over the final 43 laps, babying his 1971 Dodge to compensate for a brake problem. At the finish, several drivers were gaining on him, including runner-up Benny Parsons and third-place Donnie Allison. But the lead was never in real danger.

"The car ran perfect and when the time was right there I was," said Elder, who collected $11,625. His average of 98.747 miles per hour was well off the track record.

Donnie Allison, whose brother Bobby was the defending champion but finished sixth this time, spun out on the 115th lap and said he felt it cost him the race. The mishap delayed him four laps.

"It was my mistake. I could have won the race if I hadn't done that," said Allison, who was subbing for Indianapolis 500 winner Mark Donohue in a Matador. Donohue was refused U.S. Auto Club permission to drive in the National Association for Stock Car Auto Racing-sanctioned event.

Elder won the Western 500 here last year, becoming the first non-factory team driver to win a major NASCAR 500-mile event, and decided to take a crack at the Eastern circuit.

Unable to break through Southern drivers' domination of racing on their own ground, he returned home to win the Grand National West division of NASCAR for the third time.

This time, the co-proprietor of a 240-acre family farm in Fresno County said, he's sticking close to home.

"I'm going to concentrate on the West Coast races and try to win a fourth championship," he said. "I've got a race Friday night in Medford, Ore., Saturday night in Longview, Wash., and Sunday in Portland."

Ray Elder (1942 - 2011)

Calling his team "The Racing Farmer's", Elder ran his operation out a barn on the family cotton and alfalfa farm in Caruthers, CA, near Fresno. Not just any barn, Ray had a dyno, built his own motors and bought cars from Petty. He was the first non factory driver to win a NASCAR 500 mile even and a six time winner of the NASCAR West Series.

Racing Farmer Wins Golden State 400
California Luck Holds Up for Elder

By Associated Press

Ray Elder is finally getting his message across to the National Association for Stock Car Auto Racing's top stars from Dixie. "There is still some gold in California but it belongs to me."

Second place went to Benny Parson in a Mercury, third to Donnie Allison in an American Motors Matador, fourth to James Hylton in a Ford and fifth to Carl Joiner in a Chevelle.

Another Californian, George

doubleheader at Watkins Glen, N.Y. He was paid $4,000.

The 35-year-old Follmer, selected for the All-America driver team in 1971, now has won three of the four Trans-Am races and appears headed for his first national title.

Graham McRae was the overall winner in a Leda machine powered by a domestic stock block engine. McRae won the second of two heats and placed fourth in the first for take-home pay of $25,000.

Second place over-all went

de Adamich of Italy and third to another Italian, Nanni Galli.

Sonny Easley of Van Nuys, Calif., won a 100-mile race for NASCAR older model sportsman cars at Riverside Saturday — his first triumph four years.

Elder, who won the

Vanguard Photography

'RACING FARMER'
Elder, a Central Valley farmer, upset
Bobby Allison to win the Riverside 500 in 1971.

NASCAR'S RAY ELDER SAYS:

"You've really got to bear down to out-drive NASCAR's finest. That's why I use nothing but the best...Pennzoil."

Ray Elder knows what he's talking about. With his victory in the 1971 Motor Trend 500, he became the first Western Division driver to win a major NASCAR race. Ray's in a class by himself...like Pennzoil.

PENNZOIL COMPANY • OIL CITY, PENNSYLVANIA

MOTOR TREND / AUGUST 1971 $6

SPONSOR: **OLYMPIA BREWING COMPANY**   *OLYMPIA DODGE*   DRIVER: RAY ELDER
WINNER: Winston Western 500
Golden State 400

Permatex®

Riverside
PERMATEX® "200"

West Coast Late Model Sportsman Championship Race
Riverside International Raceway
Riverside, California
January 22, 1972

PERMATEX COMPANY, INC.
"OUR NAME IS OUR BOND"
P. O. Box 1350, Permatex Building
West Palm Beach, Florida 33402

Permatex® RIVERSIDE
LAP SPEED CHART
2.6 MILE COURSE

Lap Time	M.P.H.	Lap Time	M.P.H.	Lap Time	M.P.H.
1:18.0	120.000	1:24.0	111.428	1:30.0	104.000
1:18.1	119.847	1:24.1	111.296	1:30.1	103.885
1:18.2	119.693	1:24.2	111.163	1:30.2	103.769
1:18.3	119.540	1:24.3	111.032	1:30.3	103.655
1:18.4	119.387	1:24.4	110.900	1:30.4	103.539
1:18.5	119.236	1:24.5	110.769	1:30.5	103.426
1:18.6	119.083	1:24.6	110.638	1:30.6	103.311
1:18.7	118.933	1:24.7	110.508	1:30.7	103.198
1:18.8	118.781	1:24.8	110.377	1:30.8	103.083
1:18.9	118.632	1:24.9	110.248	1:30.9	102.970
1:19.0	118.481	1:25.0	110.117	1:31.0	102.857
1:19.1	118.331	1:25.1	109.989	1:31.1	102.744
1:19.2	118.182	1:25.2	109.859	1:31.2	102.631
1:19.3	118.033	1:25.3	109.731	1:31.3	102.519
1:19.4	117.884	1:25.4	109.601	1:31.4	102.407
1:19.5	117.736	1:25.5	109.218	1:31.5	102.295
1:19.6	117.587	1:25.6	109.345	1:31.6	102.183
1:19.7	117.441	1:25.7	109.474	1:31.7	102.072
1:19.8	117.293	1:25.8	109.090	1:31.8	101.960
1:19.9	117.147	1:25.9	108.964	1:31.9	101.850
1:20.0	117.000	1:26.0	108.837	1:32.0	101.739
1:20.1	116.854	1:26.1	108.711	1:32.1	101.629
1:20.2	116.708	1:26.2	108.584	1:32.2	101.518
1:20.3	116.563	1:26.3	108.459	1:32.3	101.409
1:20.4	116.417	1:26.4	108.333	1:32.4	101.298
1:20.5	116.273	1:26.5	108.208	1:32.5	101.189
1:20.6	116.129	1:26.6	108.083	1:32.6	101.079
1:20.7	115.985	1:26.7	107.958	1:32.7	100.971
1:20.8	115.841	1:26.8	107.834	1:32.8	100.862
1:20.9	115.699	1:26.9	107.710	1:32.9	100.754
1:21.0	115.555	1:27.0	107.586	1:33.0	100.645
1:21.1	115.413	1:27.1	107.463	1:33.1	100.537
1:21.2	115.270	1:27.2	107.339	1:33.2	100.429
1:21.3	115.129	1:27.3	107.216	1:33.3	100.322
1:21.4	114.987	1:27.4	107.093	1:33.4	100.214
1:21.5	114.847	1:27.5	106.972	1:33.5	100.107
1:21.6	114.705	1:27.6	106.849	1:33.6	100.000
1:21.7	114.566	1:27.7	106.728	1:33.7	99.894
1:21.8	114.425	1:27.8	106.605	1:33.8	99.786
1:21.9	114.286	1:27.9	106.485	1:33.9	99.681
1:22.0	114.146	1:28.0	106.363	1:34.0	99.574
1:22.1	114.008	1:28.1	106.243	1:34.1	99.469
1:22.2	113.868	1:28.2	106.122	1:34.2	99.363
1:22.3	113.730	1:28.3	106.003	1:34.3	99.258
1:22.4	113.592	1:28.4	105.882	1:34.4	99.152
1:22.5	113.456	1:28.5	105.763	1:34.5	99.048
1:22.6	113.317	1:28.6	105.643	1:34.6	98.942
1:22.7	113.180	1:28.7	105.525	1:34.7	98.839
1:22.8	113.043	1:28.8	105.405	1:34.8	98.734
1:22.9	112.907	1:28.9	105.287	1:34.9	98.630
1:23.0	112.771	1:29.0	105.168	1:35.0	98.526
1:23.1	112.636	1:29.1	105.051	1:35.1	98.423
1:23.2	112.500	1:29.2	104.932	1:35.2	98.319
1:23.3	112.365	1:29.3	104.815	1:35.3	98.216
1:23.4	112.230	1:29.4	104.697	1:35.4	98.113
1:23.5	112.096	1:29.5	104.581	1:35.5	98.011
1:23.6	111.961	1:29.6	104.464	1:35.6	97.907
1:23.7	111.828	1:29.7	104.348	1:35.7	97.806
1:23.8	111.694	1:29.8	104.231	1:35.8	97.703
1:23.9	111.522	1:29.9	104.116	1:35.9	97.602

The January 1973 Permatex 200 Late Model Sportsman race, held in front of a record crowd of 18,650 on a clear crisp winter day, was won by Jack Jeffrey, followed by Harry Jefferson and Bob Forster.

Washington Drivers Run 1-2 in Permatex

Exclusive to The Times from a Staff Writer

RIVERSIDE—A mantle of low-lying snow which seemed to surround Riverside International Raceway on three sides helped make a pair of Washington neighbors, Jack Jeffrey and Harry Jefferson, feel at home Saturday.

Jeffrey, a part-time car builder and full-time mechanic from Yakima, and Jefferson, a logger from Naches, finished 1-2 in the 7th annual Permatex 200, companion race to today's $100,000 Winston Western 500.

A record Permatex crowd of 18,650 watched in clear, crisp weather.

It was an easy win for

California favorites in the race for late model stock cars of 1961-1969 vintage suffered a variety of woes, generally succumbing to broken engines and clutch problems. Pole sitter Sonny Easley of Van Nuys lasted only 27 laps and Jimmy Insolo, Mission Hills, who had the fastest qualifying time, went only 14.

PERMATEX 200 (77 laps)—1. Jack Jeffery (Yakima, Wash.), '69 Dodge, 77 laps ($4,500); 2. Harry Jefferson (Naches, Wash.), '68 Ford Torino, 76 ($2,700); 3. Bob Forster (Montclair), '66 Chevelle, 76, ($1,600); 4. Dan Clark (Riverside), '63 Ford, 76 ($800); 5. Bob Johnson (Neosho, Mo.), '69 Ford, 76 ($750); 6. Jim Bettini (Eagle Rock), '65 Chevelle, 75 ($600); 7. Gene Riniker (Riverside), '64 Oldsmobile, 75 ($550); 8. Richard White (Escondido), '63 Ford, 75 ($350); 9. Bill Scott (San Bernardino), '66 Chevelle, 74 ($225); 10. George Beall (Glendale), '65 Chevelle, 74 ($200). Winner's speed: 97.107 m.p.h.

Jeffery captures Permatex

Jack Jeffrey

Riverside 200
Jeffery Permatex Winner

RIVERSIDE (AP) — Jack Jeffery, Yakima, Wash., ran away from the other starters late in the race and easily won the Permatex 200 late model sportsmen's race Saturday at Riverside International Raceway.

Jeffery completed the 77 laps around the 2.62-mile road course in 2 hours, 4 minutes and 39 seconds for an average speed of 97.129 miles an hour. He drove a 1969 Dodge Charger.

At the finish he held an advantage of just over a lap on Harry Jefferson of Naches, Wash., the second-place finisher in a 1969 Ford.

Third place went to Bob Forster of Montclair, in a Chevelle. Dan Clark, Riverside, came in fourth in a 1963 Ford, while fifth place went to Bob Johnson of Neosho, Mo., in a 1969 Ford.

Jeffery won $4,500 from the $30,000 purse. Jefferson took $2,700.

Others finishing in the top 10, and at least two laps back, were Jim Bettina of Eagle Rock, Gene Riniker, Riverside; Richard White, Escondido, Bill Scott, San Bernardino, and George Beall, Glendale.

Ron Hornady of Sepulveda, and Jefferson were the only other leaders during the race period. Hornady was sidelined later by a broken engine, while pole sitter Sonny Easley of Van Nuys, also went out with mechanical problems.

Clem Proctor, a strong driver in late model sportsman competition on the West Coast for years, made a strong showing early in the race. He started 31st in the field of 40 and had moved into third place by lap 24 when his engine broke.

The June 1973 California 100 Late Model Sportsman race was won by Herschel McGriff, followed by Ron Hornaday and Roy Bleckert. For the first time, the race ran on Sunday, before the NASCAR Grand National race.

McGriff wins California 100 with ease

By RYAN REES
Sun-Telegram Sports Writer

RIVERSIDE — Hershel McGriff, a Bridal Veil, Ore., lumberman, made the rest of the field in the California 100 look like it was driving lumber trucks as he raced to an easy victory at Riverside International Raceway, yesterday.

For McGriff, it was his third victory in a sportsman car over the tricky Riverside road course. He won similar races in January of 1969 and 1972.

"I could have gone a little harder had I been pressed and needed to," said the

Hornaday Second in Riverside Auto Race

By United Press International

RIVERSIDE — San Fernando Valley drivers made their "marks" yesterday in the annual California 100 NASCAR late model stock car race at Riverside International Raceway here.

Ron Hornaday of Simi Valley 1964-'65 Pacific Coast NASCAR champion and former early model champ at Saugus Speedway, finished second to winner Herschel McGriff of Bridlevale, Ore.

McGriff, driving a 1969 Chevelle, averaged 91.962 miles an hour in chalking up the victory.

Hornaday, service manager at Galpin Ford in Sepulveda, picked up $1025 for his second place finish, while McGriff took home $1875.

Hornaday drove a 1963 Ford Thunderbird.

Oren Prosser of Agoura, successful in recent years at Saugus, drove a 1968 Chevelle, and was involved in a pileup with a car driven by Bob Switzer of Van Nuys.

Prosser plowed into Switzer during a dust cloud created on the 20th lap when the Van Nuys driver's car went into a spin.

Switzer was uninjured, but Prosser injured his knee and had to be taken to Riverside Community Hospital, where his condition was listed as good.

The race was run as a preliminary to today's $90,000 Tuborg 400, and featured 40 cars, 23 of which finished.

Top five finishers:

1 Herschel McGriff, Bridlevale, Ore. 1969 Chevelle, $1875. 2. Ron Hornaday, Simi, '63 Thunderbird, $1025; 3. Ron Bleckert, Sunnymead, '64 Pontiac, $750. 4. Ivan Baldwin, Highland, '65 Chevelle, $500. 5. Jim Anderson, Las Vegas, Nev., '66 Chevelle, $300.

102

51,000 people braved the heavy overcast and fifty degree weather to see Mark Donohue win the January 1973 Winston Western 500 in a Penske AMC Matador. Second was Bobby Allison with Ray Elder third. Donohue won $15,170.

West Coast Drivers Top Second-Round Qualifying For Winston Western 500

RIVERSIDE, Calif. (AP) — A trio of West Coast drivers paced second round qualifying Friday as 15 more starters were added for Sunday's $100,-000 Winston Western 500 stock car race.

Gerald Thompson, a 25-year-old from Caluson, Mich., who plans to race in California this year, won the 16th spot in the 40-car lineup by driving a Pon-

Inslo of Missin Hills Calif., recorded 104.823 in a Chevrolet.

Other top qualifiers were Elmo Langley of Charlotte, N.C., 104.648 m.p.h. in a Ford; Jack McCoy of Modesto, Calif., 104.590 in a Dodge, and Harry Jefferson of Naches, Wash., 104.267 in a Ford.

Sonny Easley of Van Nuys, Calif., will start from the pole position for the Permatex race.

Donohue Wins Western 500

By BLOYS BRITT
AP Auto Racing Writer

RIVERSIDE, Calif. (AP) — Mark Donohue, a member of Philadelphia's social set, has officially joined the exclusive club that belongs to the "good old boys" of Southern stock car racing.

He acquired his membership Sunday when he drove a boxlike American Motors Matador to an easy victory in the $100,000 Winston-Western 500 at Riverside International Raceway.

The race opened a 31-event schedule for the National Association for Stock Car Auto Racing and it drew 51,000 persons into the sprawling road course grounds.

Donohue, 35, who lives in the Philadelphia suburb of Newtown Square, Pa., didn't become involved in NASCAR doings until last year, when he made his debut in Roger Penske's untried Matador in the traditional Riverside opener.

He came to that race with good credentials. He had won the old U.S. Road Racing title twice and had captured TransAm championships in 1968 and 1970.

His Matador wasn't reliable or strong enough to cause the stock car boys even mild concern last year, but the moon-faced Pennsylvanian was hot as a pistol elsewhere. He won the Indianapolis 500, among other racing plums, and came back to Riverside with even better credentials.

He displayed them almost immediately, qualifying the red, white and blue machine fourth fastest among 40 starters—just slightly behind frontrow sitters David Pearson in a Mercury and Bobby Allison in a Chevrolet. Next to Donohue in the second row was Hershel McGriff, third fastest qualifier, in a Dodge.

But when the race got under way, it became evident that the combination of Donohue's road course ability and the Matador's handling qualities would become a major factor over the 500-mile distance.

He raced strongly with early leaders Pearson, Allison and Richard Petty, stock car racing's all-time champion.

When Pearson was forced out by mechanical woes, to be followed a short time later by Petty's Dodge, Donohue had things pretty much his own way.

Allison was his only major competition over the final 300 miles around the eight-turn, 2.62-mile circuit. Allison, top money winner in stock cars last year with $284,735, drove the final miles with a sick engine and was almost two laps behind at the finish.

Third place went to Ray Elder, Caruthers, Calif., in a Dodge, fourth to Bobby Unser of Albuquerque in a Ford and fifth to Jimmy Insolo, Mission Hills, Calif., in a Chevrolet.

Donohue was paid $11,770 for first place. His average speed was 104.056 miles per hour.

What's a Matador?
Winner of the NASCAR Winston 500 at Riverside!

Mark Donohue, driving a specially modified 366 cubic inch American Motors Matador, raced to an impressive victory in the $100,000 Winston Western 500 at Riverside International Raceway.

The AMC Matador and Donohue beat a field composed of veteran NASCAR cars and drivers. Matador's domination was so complete that it led 139 of the 191 laps, and finished almost five miles ahead of last year's top NASCAR money winner. The Matador's great stability, cornering and high-speed dependability sped it to victory.

The Matador *you* can buy wins another contest. It has more head room, hip room, rear seat leg room and trunk room than any other intermediate. And it's backed by the exclusive American Motors Buyer Protection Plan.

Test drive the Matador. Even if your name isn't Mark Donohue, you'll find it a winner.

AMC ◢◤ Matador
We back them better because we build them better.

A crowd of 43,700 watched Bobby Allison win the June 1973 Tuborg 400, followed by Richard Petty and Benny Parsons. Allison's win paid $12,750. George Follmer, in a Penske Matador, was the pole qualifier

Follmer tops qualifiers for Riverside Tuborg 400

RIVERSIDE, Calif. (UPI) — Veteran George Follmer, who considers Riverside International Raceway his home course, grabbed the pole for Sunday's $80,000 Tuborg 400 with a clocking of 109.555 miles an hour Friday in the first day of qualifying.

Follmer, Huntington Harbor, Calif., qualified on Riverside's 2.62 mile, eight-turn course with a 1974 Matador that had to be cleaned out just before his runs.

The Roger Penske-owned car caught fire in a garage during practice runs Thursday when Follmer's crew squirted gasoline into its carburetor and the fuel ignited. It was not damaged.

Bobby Allison, Hueytown, Ala., joined Follmer in the first row with a 109.304 mph clocking in his '74 Chevelle.

The Tuborg 400 is the 14th race on the Grand National Winston Cup circuit.

Fifteen nascar drivers qualified Friday. The 20 other starting positions will be determined in runs Saturday.

RIVERSIDE, Calif. (UPI) — The drivers who qualified Friday for Sunday's $80,000 Tuborg 400 at Riverside International Raceway:
First row
1. George Follmer, Huntington Harbor, Calif., '74 Matador, 109.555 mph.
2. Bobby Allison, Hueytown, Ala., '74 Chevelle, 109.304 mph.
Second row
3. Cale Yarborough, Timmonsville, S. C., '74 Chevy, 108.528.
4. Richard Petty, Randleman, N. C., '74 Dodge, 107.596.
Third row
5. Benny Parsons, Ellerbe, N. C., '74 Chevy, 106.971.
6. Jimmy Insolo, Mission Hills, Calif., '72 Chevy, 106.203.
Fourth row
7. Cecil Gordon, Horse Shoe, N. C., '72 Monte Carlo, 105.959.
8. Dave Marcis, Skyland, N. C., '73 Dodge, 105.736.
Fifth row
9. Carl Adams, Harrisburg, N. C., '72 Ford Torino, 104.727.
10. Chuck Brown, Portland, Ore., '72 Dodge, 104.636.
Sixth row
11. Sonny Easley, Van Nuys, Calif., '73 Ford, 104.322
12. Glen Francis, Bakersfield, Calif., 104.015.
Seventh row
13. Tony Bettenhausen, Charlotte, N. C., '72 Monte Carlo, 103.866.
14. James Hylton, Inman, S. C., '74 Chevy, 103.575.
Eighth row
15. Dick Bown, Portland, Ore., '72 Dodge, 103.525.

Allison beats Petty in RIR's Tuborg 400

RIVERSIDE (UPI)— Bobby Allison's victory Sunday in the Tuborg 400 at Riverside International Raceway—a repeat of his win two years ago—couldn't have come at a better time.

"We have had less than a delightful year so far," said the 35-year-old Hueytown, Ala., race driver, who collected a Father's Day present of $14,000 and his first win of the season on the NASCAR Grand National stock car circuit.

Averaging 100.215 miles per hour in his 1973 Chevelle, Allison led in 84 of the 153 laps in the race, staving off a last minute assault by Richard Petty, the only other driver on the final lap.

"We've been playing a catch up game all year," said Allison, who this year began building his own cars and managing his own team.

"In fact, we were the last car on the grid this morning," he said.

Both Petty and Cale Yarborough, of Timmonsville, S.C., challenged Allison through the first two thirds of the $90,000 race. Yarborough, who led for 15 laps, dropped out with a blown engine while leading on the 114th lap, when Allison finally took over for good.

Petty, the defending NASCAR Grand National driving champion from Randleman, N.C., driving a '73 Dodge, finished second, one minute and 13 seconds behind Allison, and collected $8,075.

Finishing third, one lap back, was Banney Parsons, Ellerbe, N.C., a former Detroit cab driver, in a '73 Chevy, and a lap

BOBBY ALLISON

.... Tuborg 400 winner

(UPI Telephoto)

time, and spun off the track, losing 10 seconds to Petty who was then leading.

Petty had taken the initial lead from his pole position, had led for 54 laps, but lost it for the last time on the 81st lap as he was pulling away from the

track. He was not hurt.

Herschel McGriff, averaging 91.962 miles per hour in his 1969 Chevelle, won the California NASCAR late model sportsman stock car road race at Riverside International Raceway Saturday, a preliminary to the

COMPETITION PRESS &
AUTOWEEK®

JULY 7, 1973

50 CENTS

The Le Mans Experience
VW's New Thing
L&M Glen

NASCAR War Wagons
Move West!

Compiler's Note: David Pearson was quoted as saying. *"It was three years before I realized the esses were paved"*

.

Pace Lap

The January 1974 Permatex 200 Late Model Sportsman race, back to running on Saturday, was won, after a two hour fog delay, by Herschel McGriff who led every lap. Bobby Allison was second and Harry Jefferson third. The crowd was a record 19,200

McGriff wins Permatex

The June 1974 California 100 Late Model Sportsman race, back to a Sunday race preceding the Tuborg 400, was also won by Herschel McGriff, his fifth win at Riverside, with Ivan Baldwin second and Pat Mintey third.

Prelude to $80,000 Tuborg 400
McGriff heads California 100 field

By ALLEN WOLFE
Staff Writer

RIVERSIDE—Although Les Richter isn't about to hang up the "For Sale" sign at Riverside International Raceway, if he ever entertained the idea a logical customer would be Herschel McGriff.

Plain fact of the matter is, ol' Hersh loves the 140-acre racing plant and particularly its most dominant feature, the 2.62-mile, 8-turn road course.

It was six years ago last January that McGriff ended a self-imposed 14-year retirement from auto racing at age 40 by competing in—and winning—the Permatex 200 for NASCAR Sportsman stock cars. It was a $20,000 prelude to the $100,000 Motor Trend 500, since renamed the Winston Western 500.

Now it's 1974—and McGriff is six years older —and that much better.

The millionaire lumber mill owner from Bridal Veil, Ore., remains one of

MOTOR SPORTS

the dominant factors in Grand National West and Pacific Northwest Sportsman-division racing and he will once again be favored among a field of

enters the California 100 as defending champion.

Normally, practice and qualifying for the California 100 is scheduled over a two-day Saturday-Sunday format, but due to the energy crisis it is being consolidated into one eight-hour session.

Sunday, an entry field of between 60 and 70 cars and drivers begin practice at 9 a.m., followed by two-lap time trials against the clock at 1 p.m. to determine a 40-car starting grid for the 11 a.m. race on June 9.

Also bidding for the pole position with McGriff is Paramount tavern owner Clem Proctor, winner of four Permatex-type Sportsman races at Riverside and Ontario over the last six years. He drives a '69 Ford Torino.

Other entries have been received from Ron Hornaday of Simi Valley and Roy Bleckert of Sunnymead, the 2-3 finishers behind McGriff last year.

along with Sam Beler of Lakewood, Richard White of Escondido, Ivan Baldwin of Highland and the Esau brothers (Ron and Larry) from San Diego.

HERSHEL McGRIFF
Going strong at 46

ease the line at 1 p.m. Saturday for a two-hour enduro. Action begins both days at 8 a.m. One of the entrants is John McGowan, who along with his tank-riding dog Kookie, was featured in Bruce Brown's documentary movie, "On Any Sunday." Indian Dunes Park is located on Highway 126, two miles west of the Golden State Freeway.

Two of the entrants for the Tuborg 400—formerly known as the Falstaff and Golden State 400—are NASCAR regulars Richard Petty, Bobby and Donnie Allison, Cale Yarborough, Benny Parsons and James Hylton.

SPRINT CARS—Two-time SCCA national sports car champion John Morton...

Follmer ready for Tuborg 400

George Follmer of Arcadia, a newcomer to the NASCAR Grand National stock car circuit, said Thursday he will drive Roger Penske's American Motors Matador in the $80,000 Tuborg 400 June 9.

Follmer, 40, and car owner Bud Moore parted company last week before the World 600 at Charlotte, N.C. Moore replaced Follmer with Buddy Baker.

The Tuborg 400 will be held over the Riverside

Charlotte, he called me and asked me if I'd be interested in driving at Riverside.

"I began driving for Roger in 1967. I finished third in his Camaro (Chevrolet) in a Trans-Am race at Mid-Ohio."

Follmer, who ranks 10th in NASCAR's Winston Cup Grand National point race this year with his best finish a fourth place at Atlanta, said he left Moore "with no hard feelings."

"There was no reason

Intruder Insolo chases big boys at Riverside

By ALLEN WOLFE
Staff Writer

RIVERSIDE — When the rain-delayed Winston Western 500 picks up today where it left off last Sunday, the "boys up front" will be names synonymous with winning NASCAR Grand National races.

Bobby Allison ... Richard Petty ... David Pearson ... Herschel McGriff ... Jim Insolo ... Benny Parsons ... Cale Yarborough.

Jim Insolo?
Where did he come from?
When the ribbon of 27 cars

led away in single file to the Porsche for the first of two yellow caution warmup laps, Insolo and his blue '71 Chevrolet Monte Carlo No. 36 will occupy the fifth position on the grid.

A 26-year-old machinist who works swing shift at a Van Nuys hydraulics plant during the week and a man with only limited road racing experience, Insolo...

Insolo's car is strictly a "backyard special." He, along with friends Roger Pasquette and Bill Martin Jr., paid $600 for the frame and main chassis shell from an insurance salvage yard. Then in-

McGriff grabs Cal 100 victory

RIVERSIDE — Hershel McGriff cut through the 40-car California 100 field about as easily as one of the buzz saws in his lumber mill.

McGriff, a 46-year-old millionaire lumberman from Bridal Veil, Ore., captured his third straight Sportsman event at Riverside International Raceway yesterday.

McGriff had a comfortable 40-second margin over Ivan Baldwin of Highland

Johnstone fell to sixth, and Harold Harcrow of Bloomington took seventh place.

McGriff won $2,000 for the victory with Baldwin collecting $800 for second place.

It was no surprise to the rest of the competitors that McGriff won. He captured this event last June and also won the 200-mile race last January. He has also won the 200-mile race two other times.

44,500 people saw 63 laps of the January 1974 Winston Western 500; then rain postponed the race until the next Saturday. 32,000 saw Cale Yarborough win, collecting $15,000. Second was Richard Petty with pole sitter David Pearson in third.

Yarborough Holds Off Petty To Win Rain-Delayed Winston 500

RIVERSIDE (AP)—Cale Yarborough held off a charging Richard Petty in a final stretch battle Saturday and won the hotly-contested, rain-delayed Winston Western 500-mile stock car race.

Petty, down by as much as 20 seconds with only 15 circuits of the 2.62-mile Riverside Raceway road course left, cut the margin to less than five seconds at the finish. He drove a dodge.

It was the first major stock-car race of the season, and the victory gave the Chevrolet-driving Yarborough an early lead in a drive he will make to win the Grand National Championship of the National Association for Stock Car Auto Racing.

David Pearson, who will retire his Mercury to a museum in two weeks, finished a distant third after having been in a close battle for the lead much of the way.

Fourth place went to Benny Parsons, the 1973 Grand National titleholder, and fifth to Bobby Allison, both in Chevrolets.

The first 164 miles of the $103,000 event were run last Sunday before being halted by rain. After 3½ half laps under a yellow light slowdown, Saturday's final 335 miles got under way under bleak, overcast conditions.

But the second phase of race drew a hardy crowd of 32,500—down about 11,000 from a week ago.

Jack McCoy of Modesto, driving a 1972 Dodge, placed 21st, completing 123 laps. He had held the lead from the 12th through 15th laps last weekend prior to the rain-delay.

The West Coast stock car champ was running 11th after a pit stop when the race was red-flagged.

Yarborough completed the 500 miles in an elapsed time of 4 hours 58 minutes 20.05 seconds. His average speed was 100.643 miles an hour and his share of the purse was about $15,000.

Yarborough, Petty and Pearson were the only drivers in the same lap at the finish. Allison, who had started the day in front of the 26 survivors from last Sunday, was in contention until his gear box went sour in the final 100 miles. He and Parsons were a full circuit back at the end.

Donnie Allison finished sixth in a Chevrolet, trailed by Garry Bettenhausen in a Matador, Richie Panch in a Chevrolet, Cecil Gordon in a Chevrolet and Herschel McGriff in a Dodge.

"I played a 'Cool Luke' hand there at the finish," the short stocky Yarborough said. "I knew Petty was gaining a little bit on me every lap, but my crew people told me on the radio not to lose my cool.

"It's sort of like having an ace in the hole and one up, and letting the other plays out-draw you," added Yarborough, who is a Republican county supervisor in Florence County, S.C.

The NASCAR entourage now heads for Daytona Beach, Fla. to begin preparations for the circuit's richest event, the $200,000 Daytona 500 Feb. 17.

Collombin Breaks Killy's Ski Mark

KITZBUEHEL, Austria (AP) — Switzerland's Raymond Collombin won his fourth straight World Cup downhill ski race Saturday, smashing the seven-year-old course record held by Jean-Claude Killy and taking an 18-point lead in the over-all World Cup standings.

With a clocking of 2 minutes, 3.29 seconds over the 3,516-meter course, with a vertical drop of 890 meters, Collombin destroyed Killy's standard of 2:11.92 set in 1972.

ships at St. Moritz, Switzerland.

Collombin described the triumph as his most difficult of the season. "I took every risk and almost tumbled a couple of times," he said, "but that is what you have to do to win—go all out."

Behind Anzi and Besson came another Italian, Herbert Plank, at 2:04.36. Klammer, at 2:04.81, edged Switzerland's Walter Vesti for fifth place. Vesti was clocked in 2:04.91.

Rounding out the top 10 fin-

ing it out

Herschel McGriff leading Richard Petty through Turn Six

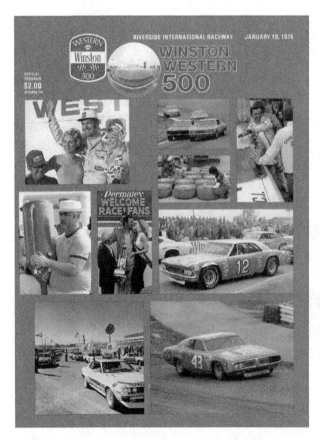
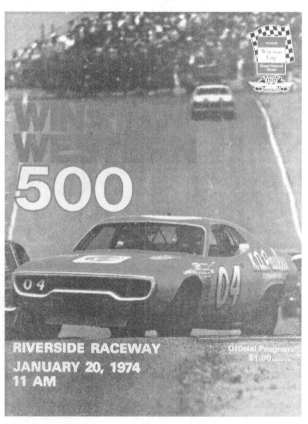

The June 1974 Tuborg 400 Grand National race was won by Cale Yarborough in 92 degree heat in front of 41,000 fans. Second was Bobby Allison followed by 1973 NASCAR Champ Benny Parsons. Yarborough collected $14,125 for the win.

Yarborough Claims Riverside Victory

RIVERSIDE, Calif. (AP) — Cale Yarborough, gutting it out to the end with a rapidly emptying gas tank, scored his second straight Riverside National Association of Stock Car Auto Racing victory Sunday.

Yarborough finished the 360-mile, 138-lap race 2.7 seconds ahead of Bobby Allison, who apparently lost the race when he elected to stop for fuel near the end. The top four cars in the race were Chevrolets.

Allison, of Hueytown, Ala., had a nine-second lead and was pulling away, but pulled into the pits on the 130th lap. After the pit stop, Allison returned to the race nine seconds behind Yarborough.

The last eight laps brought the 41,000 fans to their feet as

In the two races, Yarborough has led 215 of the 329 laps, including 91 Sunday.

Pole-sitter George Follmer of Huntington Beach, Calif., dropped out of the race after leading the first lap and appearing to make a runaway out of the event, when he broke a timing chain in the engine of his Matador. Car owner Roger Penske reported that Follmer apparently missed a shift and overrevved.

The race then became the two-car battle between Allison and Yarborough to the end, with Richard Petty's Dodge challenging them at mid-race until his engine blew on the 50th lap.

Third place, two laps behind, went to Benny Parsons, the

Yarborough came close to collapsing in the winner's circle, and Allison was treated in his garage.

"I ran out of water in the container in my car about halfway through the race," Yarborough said. "Then I started to dehydrate.

"I could keep cool by sticking my hand out the window down the straightaways and getting some air on me, but when I came to a stop with all those people around in the winner's circle, I thought I was going to pass out."

Allison's crew chief, Dick Hamner, said he believes Allison's final pit stop, the one that probably cost him the race, may have been unnecessary.

"We had been coming in ev-

Cecil Gordon - Fourth Place

115

Sun-Telegram photo by Sam Spina

Bobby Allison (12) leads Cale Yarborough (11)
. . . Yarborough went on to win Tuborg 400 with empty gas tank

Elder boycotting RIR's Tuborg 400

Remember the short-lived television series "Car 54, Where are you?"? Race fans may be asking the same question Sunday of Car 96.

West Coast race fans know that Car 96 belongs to Ray Elder. However, Elder will not be in Sunday's Tuborg 400 at Riverside Raceway.

He is boycotting the race in a one-man protest against NASCAR rules that provide guaranteed money to Eastern

political. They keep changing the rules to suit the guys with the most money. Every time they make a change, it seems to end up helping Richard Petty. If they change them to hurt him, he yells and they end up changing them back.

"His 366 (cubic inch engine) couldn't run with the Chevy 366s. But his 340 will out-run the Chevy 350s," Baldwin said.

Baldwin, who is leading the

Follmer, Allison Claim Front Spots At Riverside

RIVERSIDE, Calif. (AP) — George Follmer pushed his 1974 Matador 109.555 miles an hour Friday and withstood Bobby Allison's late challenge for the pole position in Sunday's National Association of Stock Car Auto Racing Grand National 400-mile race at Riverside International Raceway.

Allison will start alongside Follmer in the first row. Allison's 109.304 in a 1974 Chevelle came late in the qualifying session in which the first 15 spots in the 35-car field were settled.

Cale Yarborough in a '74 crew replaced burned wiring from a fire Thursday afternoon. After brief practice runs, the crew was trying to restart the engine in the garage when gasoline being squirted into the carburetor ignited. The spectacular, 30-second fire caused only minor damage.

First Row
1. George Follmer '74 Matador 109.555
2. Bobby Allison '74 Chevelle, 109.304

Second Row
3. Cale Yarborough '74 Chevrolet, 108.538 4. Richard Petty, '74 Dodge, 107.596

Third Row
5. Benny Parsons '72 Monte Carlo, 106.971 6. Jimmy Insolo, '72 Chevrolet, 106.203

Fourth Row
7. Cecil Gordon '72 Monte Carlo,

George Follmer To Drive For Penske In Tuborg 400

LOS ANGELES (UPI) — George Follmer of Arcadia, Calif., a newcomer to the NASCAR Grand National stock car circuit, said Thursday he will drive Roger Penske's American Motors Matador in the $80,000 Tuborg 400 June 9.

Follmer, 40, and car owner Bud Moore parted company last week before the World 600 at Charlotte, N.C. Moore Camaro (Chevrolet) in a Trans-Am race at Mid-Ohio."

Follmer, who ranks 10th in NASCAR's Winston Cup Grand National point race this year with his best finish a fourth place at Atlanta, said he left Moore "with no hard feelings."

Snappe

In January 1975, the Permatex 200 Late Model Sportsman race was won by pole qualifier Jimmy Insolo in front of a record Saturday crowd of 21,500. Second was Hershel McGriff followed by Harry Jefferson. Unfortunately, Bill Spencer, 605 Speedway track champ, was killed in a crash at turn six, most likely due to brake failure.

Enters Permatex 200 at Riverside
Rodger Ward returns to racing

By ALLEN WOLFE
Staff Writer

You can take the man out of racing, but you can't take racing out of the man.

A little play on words, but it applies. Particularly in the case of Rodger Ward.

One of the greatest drivers America has ever produced, Ward retired from the sport nine years ago in a manner many drivers wish they could—pulling into his pit stall during the 1966 Indianapolis 500 and dramatically

having fun on a Saturday afternoon," explains Ward. "At the same time, if I didn't think I could win the race, I wouldn't be in it.

"The real reason I'm coming back is the fact I miss the competition and excitement. I don't care if you're racing at Indy or a go-kart, you get the same kind of charge out of it. I felt stock cars were the way to go—they're relatively safe and the competition is close."

Ward has three sons, two of whom are older

an expected turnout of 45,000.

OFF ROAD RACING—Defending champion Bobby Ferro of Sherman Oaks leads the list of entries for the fourth California 400 Saturday in the desert surrounding Barstow. Ferro will drive a new Sandmaster Funco single-seat buggy in the $30,000 event. The 8:30 a.m. race starts adjacent to the Lenwood exit on Interstate 15, near Barstow. Other off road heavyweights entered are Roger Mears, Johnny Johnson, Walker Evans, Malcolm Smith and Don Roundtree. Mickey Thompson reports a record early draw of 262 competitors for starting positions in the SCORE Parker 400 to be held Feb. 1 near Parker, Ariz.

MOTOCROSS RACING—The

July, drew more than 70,000 spectators.

STOCK CAR RACING—Figures rivals Ed Ferro and June Tanasi head the lineup of Sunday's Ascot Park triple header program that also includes men's and women's division stocks and destruction derby. Racing begins at 1.

FORMULA ONE—The 1975 Formula One Grand Prix season begins Sunday with the Grand Prix of Argentina in Buenos Aires. A field of 22 cars will compete on the municipal track in the 53-lap, 196.5-mile event, the first of 15 world driver's championship events this year. Mario Andretti debuts behind the wheel of a Parnelli, built in Torrance by Vel's Parnelli Jones Racing, is the first all-U.S. car to campaign on the Formula One circuit. Another American car, the

Spencer dies after Permatex 200 crash

By ALLEN WOLFE
Staff Writer

Jimmy Insolo of Mission Hills scored a nose-to-tail victory over Hershel McGriff in the Permatex 200 Saturday at Riverside International Raceway, a race marred by the death of stock car driver Bill Spencer.

According to observers at the scene, Spencer lost control of his 1966 Chevrolet when his brakes failed to function, hurtling head-on into the turn 6 crash-

when removed from his crippled car, which suffered minimal body damage.

Spencer was given a tracheotomy by ambulance attendants enroute to Riverside Community Hospital, where he died minutes after arrival. Cause of death was listed as multiple chest and neck injuries, resulting in cardiac arrest.

Spencer is the third stock car driver to die at Riverside since the track

ing practice for Formula 5,000 sports car event.

The accident proved a critical factor in the outcome of the $25,000 race prelim to today's $114,000 Winston Western 500.

With rescue crews on the course, the yellow caution flag was displayed for six laps, enabling leaders Jimmy Insolo and NASCAR veteran Bobby Allison to pit for fuel and prepare for the sprint to the finish.

By ALLEN WOLFE
Staff Writer

RIVERSIDE—The Permatex 200 today at Riverside International Raceway is being called a "co-feature" to the Winston Western 500 Sunday.

But the $25,000 event for 1961-72 model Sportsman stock cars could be the best race of the weekend.

It's not hard to see why. For example:

—The field is loaded with talent, the best in the event's eight-year history.

—Veteran West Grand National driver Jimmy Insolo of Mission Hills captured the pole position last week, setting a track record of 109.589 mph in his '72 Chevrolet Monte Carlo.

—He will be flanked on the front row by George Follmer, a three-time starter in the Indianapolis 500 and Can-Am sports car champion two years

Ore., will be attempting to win this race for the fourth time. All told, McGriff has won seven Permatex events since coming out of retirement in 1969.

—The race signals the return of one of auto racing's greatest drivers, Rodger Ward. The 54-year-old two-time Indianapolis 500 winner, a tire dealer in Rosemead the last few years, qualified a '69 Ford Torino in 40th place in the 45-car lineup despite having gear box problems during time trials last Sunday.

Unlike the bigger Winston Western 500 for Grand National stock cars, where pit stops play a crucial role, the Permatex is a 200-mile sprint to the checkered flag with drivers only expected to make two stops for fuel. "In this type of race, the idea is to get the lead and

ROW TWO—Bobby Allison (Hueytown, Ala.) '66 Chevelle, 108.787; Ivan Baldwin (Highland) '66 Chevelle, 107.800.

ROW THREE—Bill Spencer (Pomona) '66 Chevrolet, 107.443; Harry Jefferson (Naches, Wash.) '68 Ford, 107.231.

ROW FOUR—Bill Osborne (Rialto) '69 Ford, 106.916; Hershel McGriff (Bridal Veil, Ore.) '69 Chevelle, 106.862.

ROW FIVE—Larry Esau (El Cajon) '69 Chevelle, 105.464; Ray Johnstone (San Bernardino) '64 Chevelle, 105.298.

ROW SIX—Hugh Pearson (Bakersfield) '66 Chevelle, 105.234; Ron Esau (San Diego) '66 Chevelle, 104.766.

ROW SEVEN—Sam Beler (Lakewood) '61 Ford, 104.738; Norm Palmer (Torrance) '70 Plymouth, 104.716.

ROW EIGHT—L.D. Ottinger (Newport, Tenn.) '69 Chevelle, 104.280; Glen Steurer (Granada Hills) '64 Chevelle, 104.006.

ROW NINE—Ross Surgenor (Victoria, B.C.) '68 Ford, 103.833; Max Dudley (Sumner, Wash.) '65 Chevelle, 103.500.

ROW 10—Sam Stanley (Castaic) '71 Ford, 103.425; Pat Mintey (Arleta) '67 Chevelle, 103.129.

ROW 11—Joe Chamberlain (Tigard, Ore.) '72 Chevrolet, 103.123; Don Noel (Northridge) '71 Ford, 103.024.

ROW 12—John Weibel (Yucaipa) '64 Chevelle, 102.678; Rick Becker (Highland) '69 Chevelle, 102.633.

ROW 13—Duke Dunn (Escondido) '69 Ford, 102.567; Sonny Easley (Northridge) '68 Chevelle, 102.409.

ROW 14—Mike Walsh (Reno) '70 Chevelle, 102.341; Tony Heckart (Yakima, Wash.) '71 Ford, 102.223.

ROW 15—Alan Brown (San Bernardino) '66 Chevelle, 102.206; John Borneman (El Cajon) '62 T-Bird, 101.737.

ROW 16—Vick Irvin (Los Angeles) '66 Chevelle, 101.626; Roy Bleckert (Sunnymead) '70 Chevelle, 101.465.

ROW 17—Bob Ruppert Jr (Las Vegas) '67 Chevelle, 101.352; Joe Naccitelli (Sepulveda) '63 Ford, 101.146.

Rodger Ward

119

Jim Short: *"Very few of the things I remember about NASCAR at Riverside International Raceway have anything to do with the races. I remember: Benny Parsons sitting at my desk at The Press Enterprise newspaper in January, 1974, explaining what it meant to be the reigning Winston Cup champion; flying to San Diego with Bobby Allison for a local television appearance; sitting on the pit wall getting to know Ricky Rudd as he honed his road racing skills; chauffeuring Davey Allison from Ontario Airport to RIR after an SOS from raceway management; Breakfast interviews with Rusty Wallace and Darrell Waltrip; working dinner interviews with Richard Petty, Dale Earnhardt, Dave Marcis and others; an unexpected but most enjoyable evening with Neil Bonnett; and a banquet in the mid 1980s where one of Riverside's veteran politicians asked me "why do we need the raceway anyway? What do we get from it?" and I knew there would be no reprieve for a unique road course that was known around the world.*

I was there for most of the races in the '70s and '80s, but I can't remember if I was there for what I consider perhaps the most significant event in NASCAR history – the initial public appearance of newlyweds NASCAR and Winston and the first race in the Winston Cup series on January 10, 1971. The race was won by Ray Elder, the racing farmer from Caruthers, California, and that's always seemed fitting to me since in those formative years NASCAR relied on West Coast racers to fill in for the teams that wanted nothing to do with what one of my Southern friends mistakenly called "a test track in the desert until someone said 'why don't we have a race there."

The sport was entering puberty then and everything seemed easy. The atmosphere was relaxed, the drivers approachable and cooperative, the few PR people around would go out of their way to help and each race had its own story. Then slowly Winston's money and marketing begat change and NASCAR spread its arms and invited the nation to come and adore it. From a distance. NASCAR got more controlling, the atmosphere became stressful, the drivers less accessible as demands on them grew and the PR people were displaced by marketing types whose favorite word was no. Finally, long after Riverside, the championship was decided without winning a race, Winston walked away new sponsors like Nextel came aboard real racing became "The Chase" and stages and I quit paying any attention"
Compiler's Note: Jim Short was the Riverside Press Enterprise Motor Sports Editor for many years.

The June 1975 California 100 Late Model Sportsman race ran at 11AM prior to the Tuborg 400, The winner was Herschel McGriff followed by Vince Giaformaggio, Ed Ash and Eddie Bradshaw.

ESAU WINS POLE IN CALIFORNIA 100

Ron Esau of San Diego, in a 1966 Chevelle, was a surprise winner of the pole for next Sunday's California 100 late model sportsman car race at Riverside International Raceway with a qualifying speed Sunday or 106.292 m.p.h.

Defending champion Hershel McGriff, of Bridal Veil, Ore., who also won in 1973, elected not to attempt to qualify Sunday and will shoot for one of five berths at the back of the field in a special qualifying session Saturday. Also attempting to make the 40-car field Saturday will be 1972 winner Sonny Easley and two-time Indianapolis 500 winner Rodger Ward, both of whom had engine problems Sunday.

1. Ron Esau (San Diego), '66 Chevelle, 106.292 m.p.h.; 2. Ray Johnstone (San Bernardino), 64 Chevy, 105.6777; 3. Eddie Bradshaw (Bakersfield), 68 Chevelle, 104.080; 4. Ivan Baldwin (Highland), 66 Chevelle, 103.835; 5. Richard White (Escondido), 67 Chevy, 103.736; 6. Joe Muccitelli (Sepulveda), 63 Ford, 103.656; 7. Norm Palmer (Torrance), 70 Plymouth, 103.566; 8. Dan Clark (Riverside), 69 Torino, 103.452; 9. Pat Mintey (Arleta), 67 Chevelle, 102.949; 10. Sam Stanley (San Fernando), 71 Ford, 102.496.

11. Vince Giamformaggio (Van

23. Mark Stall (Chula Vista), 69 Ford, 99.035; 24. Harry Hageman (Lakeside), 72 Chevelle, 98.956; 25. Dale Perry (Riverside), 70 Road Runner, 98.890; 26. Bob Earnshaw (Bakersfield), 65 Chevelle, 98.536; 27. Larry Esau (San Diego), 66 Chevelle, 98.300; 28. Rick Titus (Van Nuys), 68 Torino, 98.141; 29. Richard Escalante (La Puente), 66 Chevelle, 97.599; 30. Tom Montes (Los Angeles), 68 Chevelle, 97.323; 31. Arnie Krueger (Pasadena), 72 Chevy, 96.960. 32. Roy Cline (San Bernardino), 71 Chevelle, 96.837; 33. Ed Ash (Azusa), 66 Chevelle, 96.140; 34. Brownie Brown (Las Vegas), 66

Rick Titus: *"I'd never driven a NASCAR stocker before. Much bigger than the Formula Ford I got my SCCA license in. To make matters just a bit more challenging it was a 427 inch Ford in a sea of Chevys. I was fitted to the seat, borrowed from a Sprite and contoured by fender covers. The stock steering wheel had about seven rolls of electrical tape wrapped around it and we were off to the races. Good news was at least I knew Riverside pretty well, bad news was I didn't know NASCAR flags well. Turns out in NASCAR the white flag means "last lap", in SCCA the white flag means "slow vehicle or emergency vehicle on track".*

I learned this the hard way during qualifying when on lap two of my two lap qualifying they throw the white flag and I promptly slowed down — BAD CALL — that put us 28th on the grid. That discouraged my car owner enough that he figured I was not going to much more than wear out his tires so he installed what turned out to be a faulty "rev limiter" in the car which would only turn the engine 4800 rpm. However my road racing background came somewhat to my rescue against largely circle track guys and I was able to drive to ninth place having turned my second quickest time in the race. Learned a lot, mostly learned every sanctioning body's flags and whenever the track in blocked by dust and dirt, don't lift, as Skeeter McKitterick pointed out to me afterward, you're just as dead at 100 mph as you would be at 110 mph. It was my first professional racing paycheck, liked that."

Bradshaw fourth in California 100

RIVERSIDE — Hershel McGriff's come-from-the-back victory in Sunday's California 100 at Riverside International Raceway was reminiscent of a short-track event, where the fast cars start in the rear.

McGriff, of Bridal Veil, Ore., had the third quickest qualifying time but was forced to start 36th because he wasn't present on the first day of time trials. That small inconvenience didn't bother the 47-year-old McGriff, whose 1967 Chevelle was third by the 10th lap and in front to stay with 35 miles to go. His average speed was 91.029 miles per hour.

It was the lumberman's third consecutive victory in the 100-miler and his sixth NASCAR Late Model Sportsman win at Riverside's 2.66 mile road course. He earned $1,550 from a purse of $5,250.

The second and third place cars also came from deep in the pack as the top qualifiers all ran into problems. Vince Giaformaggio of Van Nuys, starting 11th, was second, 8½ seconds behind McGriff, while 33rd starter Ed Ash of Azusa was third. They also drove Chevelles.

Bakersfield's Eddie Bradshaw started third and led briefly early in the event but saw all hopes for victory vanish near the end when he stalled the engine of his 1968 Chevelle during a caution light pitstop for a tire. Bradshaw roared back from out of the top 10 to finish fourth, a second behind Ash.

Ivan Baldwin of Modesto, who took the lead on the first lap and battled with McGriff most of the way, fell out with a blown engine while in first place.—Owen Kearns Jr.

Other finishers: 22. Marlen Collins (Bakersfield), 1972 Dodge, running, 7 laps down; 31. Bob Earnshaw (Bakersfield), 1965 Chevelle, 15, broken linkage; 37. Roger Mears (Bakersfield), 1966 Chevelle, 8, broken water pump.

The January 1975 Winston Western 500 Grand National race was won by pole qualifier Bobby Allison in Roger Penske's AMC Matador, followed by David Pearson in the Woods Brothers Mercury and Cecil Gordon in his own privateer Chevrolet, seven laps back. 55,000 fans saw Allison win $14,735.

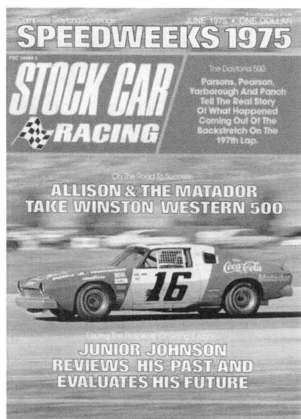

Allison captures pole

RIVERSIDE — Is Bobby Allison's slump finally coming to an end?

It certainly appears that way, judging from his performances during the last few months.

Ever since the 37-year-old Hueytown, Ala., native joined the Roger Penske Enterprises team for the Firecracker 400 at Daytona last July 4, nothing but nice things have happened to him.

He won the final NAS-CAR Grand National of

His speed was only a stopwatch tick off the Riverside track record of 110.856 mph.

Allison, however, was in no danger of breaking the outright track record of 113.310 mph, set by Parnelli Jones in the days before carburetor restrictor plates became mandatory to reduce speeds.

Twenty-five cars qualified in Friday's first round with another 10 to be added in today's second round between 9 a.m. and noon, just prior to the start of the Permatex 200 for Sportsman division cars at 1 p.m.

—ALLEN WOLFE

WINSTON 500 QUALIFIERS

ROW ONE—Bobby Allison (Huey-town, Ala.) '75 AMC Matador, 110.382 mph. David Pearson (Spartanburg, S.C.) '73 Purolator Mercury, 110.026.

ROW TWO—Richard Petty (Randleman, N.C.) '74 STP Dodge, 109.176;

Allison triumphant in stock car series

Associated Press

RIVERSIDE, Calif. — Bobby Allison, driving the only American Motors Matador in the race, turned the Western 500 into a one-man show Sunday, easily outdistancing David Pearson to capture the $114,000 opener of the 1975 stock car series.

Saturday's Permatex 200, run in conjunction with the Western 500, was marred by the death of Bill Spencer.

Allison captured the finale of the 1974 series at nearby Ontario, a victory tainted by

Boise approved

charges of cheating. This time he declared the legality of his car and took command.

At the conclusion, Allison and Pearson were the only drivers on the same lap. Cecil Gordon of Horse Shoe, NC, finished third, a full lap behind and others were seven or more laps back of them.

Richard Petty, the 1974 series champion, hit a wall early and lost seven laps although c o n t i n u i n g in his Dodge with much of its right front side torn off and portions of the body reinforced with tape.

He had spun after trying to pass Allison on the inside.

Lin Kuchler, executive vice president of the National Association of Stock Car Auto Racing, said an examination of the car showed no major mechanical failure, either in the brake system or in the transmission.

Midget record in high jump

TORONTO (CP) — Julie White, 14, of Toronto jumped five feet, 10½ inches Saturday to set a new midget women's world age-class record for high jumping.

The three-year veteran of high jump broke the previous

Allison leads Pearson and Petty

PENSKE PREPARED 1975 AMC 🏁 *Coca-Cola* MATADOR

WINNER OF THE L.A. TIMES 500 • WINSTON WESTERN 500 • DAYTONA 125 • REBEL 500

Driver — BOBBY ALLISON

It was hard to be a non smoker with all the free cigarettes

Bill Phillips: *"I was covering the races for the Anaheim Bulletin and got invited to a test session at Riverside with the Penske Matador. Most of the day I just watched the crew changing springs, shocks and swaybars. Bobby Allison said, "We're done, wanna go for a hot lap or two?" No fool, I jumped at the chance and climbed in through the passenger window of the Matador. No seat, I just hung onto the bars of the rollcage and braced my feet against some round canister on the floor. He proceeded to take two laps at a bit less than racing speeds, but just a bit. Barreling through the esses and turn six, 170 down the back straight, turn nine at what seemed to be an incredible speed for a turn while I held onto a rollbar tube or too, getting bruised and battered along the way. But what a ride. After the breathtaking ride, my rear end was cooked (the floor was hot) and I asked what that canister was. Bobby said it was the brake booster; good thing I didn't break it or we'd have been dead !!!"*

Allison Makes It One Matador Show

RIVERSIDE, Calif. (AP) — Bobby Allison, driving the only American Motors Matador in the race, turned the Western 500 into a one-man show Sunday, easily outdistancing David Pearson to capture the $114,000 opener of the 1975 stock car series.

Allison also captured the finale of the 1974 series at nearby Ontario, a victory tainted by charges of cheating. This time he declared the legality of his car and took command.

At the conclusion, Allison and Pearson were the only drivers on the same lap. Cecil Gordon of Horse Shoe, N.C., finished third, a full lap behind and others were seven or more laps back of them.

Richard Petty, the 1974 series champion, hit a wall early and lost seven laps although continuing in his Dodge with much of its right front side torn off and portions of the body reinforced with tape.

He had spun after trying to pass Allison on the inside.

Allison trailed only on 18 laps of the 191 in the 500.42-mile race over the eight-turn Riverside International Raceway road course.

Petty, Pearson, Sonny Easley and Ray Elder had only brief tours heading the pack of 35 starters.

Last November, Allison's Matador was found to have illegal valve lifters and he was fined $9,100 of his $15,125 purse.

"I'll guarantee there are no roller tappets in there now," he said in reference to the illegal equipment of last fall.

Allison won a base purse of $11,035 for this 1975 inaugural as he averaged 98.627 miles per hour.

Pearson, of Spartanburg, S.C., earned $8,135 as he finished 23 seconds behind, even though aided by yellow flags following late race accidents which allowed him to close distances previously established by Allison.

After the first three were Dave Marcis, Skyland, N.C.; Elmo Langley, Charlotte, N.C.; James Hylton, Grambling, S.C.; Petty; Gary Mathews, Fresno, Calif., and Ed Negre, Concord, Calif.

Allison, who qualified his Matador at a speed of 110.382 m.p.h., grabbed the lead from the pole position and held it for 12 laps until Petty overtook him.

Then Pearson, in a Mercury, overhauled Petty, who dropped back into second. Trouble for Petty came on the 33rd lap as he attempted to go inside to pass Allison on the final turn of the 2.62-mile course, hit the dirt and spun up into the wall.

Although he managed to drive his car to the pits for repairs, Petty had lost seven laps. After the yellow flags following that crash, Californians Easley of Van Nuys and Elder of Caruthers had one lap apiece at the front before giving way to Allison again.

A pit stop put Allison behind Pearson for one lap, but the Alabama driver took over on the 65th again and his duel with Pearson turned the race into a two-car battle.

When Chuck Wahl of Burbank, Calif., and Bill Osborne of Pomona, Calif., had engine trouble late in the race, the caution flag allowed Pearson to take over briefly as Allison pitted for gas.

But by the 163rd lap, Bobby had surged well ahead.

Allison, 37, had won stock car races during June at Riverside in 1971 and 1973 but never had won this Western 500 in January.

He had finished second three times in the past four years.

Cale Yarborough, the winner at Riverside last year, did not enter this time. Allison had finished fifth in 1974 behind Yarborough, Petty, Pearson and Benny Parsons.

A blown piston on the 74th lap put Parsons out of this 1975 race on a sunny Sunday when 53,000 watched the competition, the largest crowd here in five years.

Allison Gets The Flag

RIVERSIDE — Bobby Allison, driving the only American Motors Matador in the race, flashes past the finish line and takes the checkered flag here Sunday afternoon as he wins the Winston Western 500 stock car race. Allison's triumph came in the season-opener for NASCAR's 1975 grand national stock car series, a 30-event tour. (AP Wirephoto).

The June 1975 Tuborg 400 Grand National race ran in typical 80 degree California weather and was won by Richard Petty, collecting $14,885. This was his fourth Riverside and 171st Grand National win. Bobby Allison was second followed by Benny Parsons and Ray Elder. West coast driver Jimmy Insolo led for few laps but lost a motor and retired.

Petty hails crew after Tuborg win

RIVERSIDE, Calif. (AP) — Richard Petty said his boys had a thing or two they wanted to prove to Bobby Allison and his crew, and they did just that.

"Maybe they was wantin' to win a race," Petty drawled after some sure-handed work by his pit crew helped him beat Allison and win the NASCAR 400-mile Grand National stock car road race at Riverside International Raceway Sunday.

Petty started his brightly-hured 1974 Dodge in the front row next to Allison's 1975 Matador that had grabbed the pole with a record speed of 110.753 miles an hour on the nine-turn, 2.62-mile road course.

But during the race Petty spent nearly a half-minute less in the pits, including a crucial series late in the race, and beat Allison by more than nine seconds for his seventh NASCAR victory of the season.

"The big difference was the pit stops," said Petty, who leads the Grand National circuit point standings seeking an unprecedented sixth NASCAR

RICHARD PETTY
Wins at Riverside

maybe that's why they wanted to win this race. Ever since Bobby won the Western 500 here in January they've been arguin', getting ready.

"My crew has been arguin' with his crew because they feel that's where we can beat him

al West driver from Mission Hills, Calif. driving a 1974 Chevrolet, set the pace in the early going. Petty let his suspension settle in and hounded the front-runners.

Insolo took the lead on the 29th lap of the 153-lap race when Allison pitted but lost it to the red, white and blue Matador 16 laps later.

After Insolo went out with engine trouble Petty started working on Allison.

Petty and Allison swapped the lead on pit stops the rest of the way except once when Allison slipped by on the sweeping ninth turn which comes at the end of a long straightaway.

In the deciding series of stops Petty managed to get in and take on two tires along with fuel in 15 seconds while Allison needed 22. Allison ducked in and out on a five second stop later but the earlier pit work had already paid off for Petty, who won $14,885 from the $80,-000 purse.

Petty has had some pit problems with the crew. "I guess we've had for a year or two."

PETTY WINS IN PITS ... AND ON THE TRACK

Crew's Quick Work Instrumental in Close Victory Over Allison in 400-Mile Stock Car Race at Riverside

BY SHAV GLICK
Times Staff Writer

RIVERSIDE—If ever it could be said a major automobile race was won in the pits, it was Sunday's Tuborg 400 in which Richard Petty defeated Bobby Allison in a tense contest that kept the 46,000 spectators on their feet much of the time.

After 400 miles around the nine turns of Riverside International Raceway's 2.62-mile road course at a record 101.029 m.p.h., Petty's margin at the checkered flag was 9.4 seconds. Each of stock car racing's superstars made six pit stops but Petty's crew—headed by cousin Dale Inman—got his Dodge in and out 26.6 seconds quicker than Allison's Matador, handled by Roger Penske's crew.

"Bobby and I seemed to be running pretty even all day," said Petty, who collected $14,885 for the 3-hour 38-minute 4-second drive in 80-degree weather. "It was my crew that did a little better job today . . . Last spring we lost the race here because the pilot lost his head once down there in Turn 9, and (Allison's) crew has been givin' it to my boys pretty good since then. I think Dale had his boys ready for a big effort today."

Petty and Allison were running nose-to-tail in the 500-miler here last January when Petty hit the wall in Turn 9 and lost a couple of laps.

Twice Allison came into the pits while leading, but Petty came in

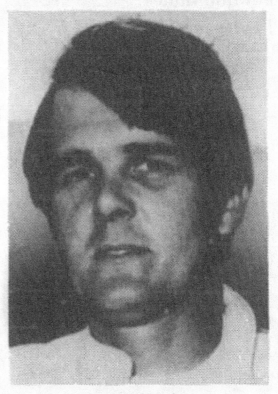

Jimmy Insolo

the front—and he was still hot-footing it with them when his engine gave way and the car quit on the 56th lap.

From then to the finish it was a two-car race, and the lead changed six more times between Petty, five-

Allison, Follmer, Insolo try new 'shoes'

Disc brakes: Key in Tuborg 400?

By ALLEN WOLFE
Staff Writer

RIVERSIDE—The driver who wins the Tuborg 400 today at Riverside International Raceway may not necessarily be the one who goes the fastest. It could be the one who stops fastest.

NASCAR Grand National stock car drivers readily admit that Riverside's 2.62-mile, 9-turn road course presents a whole new set of problems from those they normally encounter on the high-speed banked ovals of the South.

"Brakes are about as important as horsepower in a stock car race at Riverside," says former Can-Am champion George

GEORGE FOLLMER
Likes his chances

Lakewood shines in Legion opener

Stan Williams fired a two-hitter, striking out 10, and knocked in the only run he needed as Lakewood opened its American Legion season with a 4-0 conquest of Alamitos Bay at Wilson High.

Williams followed catcher

slugging a first-inning grand slam to left-center and Mike Maloney launching a three-run shot to right in the eighth. Charles Gwynn went seven innings to pick up the win.

Shea used a five-run

Follmer. "These cars weigh in the neighborhood of 3,800 pounds, so that puts quite a burden on the brakes when you go from 170 mph down to 80 in turn nine. If you can depend on the brakes for four hundred miles, you can make up a helluva lot of ground."

It is Follmer's contention that he and only two other drivers—Bobby Allison and Jimmy Insolo—are properly equipped to cope with the stresses and strains facing them in the four-hour endurance test, which begins at 12:30 p.m. before an expected crowd of 35,000.

Follmer's '75 Chevrolet, Allison's '75 Matador and Insolo's '75 Chevrolet are the only ones shod with disc brakes on all four wheels. The remainder of the field will be using traditional drum brakes.

"There's no question disc brakes perform better than drum brakes," says Follmer, a resident of Huntington Harbour. "They dissipate heat better and if you don't abuse them, they'll perform forever."

The superiority of disc brakes was graphically

illustrated during the first round of time trials Friday when Allison, Follmer and Insolo qualified 1-5-6 for today's $90,-000 event, the 14th of 30 stops on this year's Winston Cup Grand National trail.

Disc brakes aren't new to the NASCAR ranks. Two years ago, Mark Donohue drove a Roger Penske-prepared AMC Matador to victory in the Winston Western 500 at Riverside, then Allison repeated by winning the same race last January in the car he drove to the pole position for today's race.

Follmer, 40, and Insolo, 32, will be using disc brakes recently fabricated and developed by Hurst Airheart in San Fernando Valley. Follmer spent two days testing the new "shoes" at Riverside two weeks ago and the preliminary engineering reports are glowing.

"You begin to lose drum brakes after about 10 laps at Riverside," says Follmer. "But in the tests, we lost nothing. I think they'll be as strong at the end of the race as they are at the start."

Follmer believes he will have the strongest advantage in turns six and eight, the slowest turns on the course. "The deeper a car can go into the turn before braking, the quicker a driver can get the car through it," explains Follmer.

Despite their obvious benefits, disc brakes haven't become the rage in NASCAR racing simply because they aren't needed. Twenty-eight out of 30 races each year are run on ovals, where braking is of minimal concern and only comes into play when cars enter the pits for service.

Disc brakes are also three times as expensive as drum brakes, so the difference in price weighed against their "marginal" benefits doesn't warrant their use.

"We can't tear down and completely re-work

our brake systems just for two races a year," says one NASCAR veteran. "But I have to admit, those guys with the disc brakes have an edge on us."

Not to be discounted—even if he has drum brakes—is NASCAR's all-time kingpin, Richard Petty.

The 37-year-old driver from Randleman, N.C., enters the race merely $82,612 shy of becoming stock car racing's first $2 million career winner. He has won 170 races spanning 17 years, including three at Riverside—the Winston Western 500 in 1969 and '72 and this race in 1970 when it was known as the Falstaff 400.

The Tuborg 400 will be preceded at 11 a.m. by the California 100, a $7,000 preliminary race for NASCAR Sportsman stock cars.

IT ONLY TAKES ONE — George Follmer's stock car hits the wall in Turn 4 Sunday during 400-mile race in Riverside. It put Follmer out for the day. Notice the windshield: it's on its way out, too.

Times photo by Joe Kennedy

130

Bill Phillips: *"Petty had blown up three or four engines in practice. I was standing at*  *the garage entrance when Petty stopped to talk to his crew chief Dale Inman. Chris Economaki came running up, microphone in hand, asked Richard, "How is it running ?" He replied, "looking good, we'll be ready for Sunday" He left and Inman looked into the car and said well?". Petty replied, "this piece of junk won't get out of its own way". Later that night, they took parts from three or four other engines and assembled a motor. Seemed to work as he won"*

The January 1976 Permatex 200 Late Model Sportsman race was a Chevelle sweep; Jim Walker won, pole sitter L.D. Ottinger was second and Gary Crossland was third.

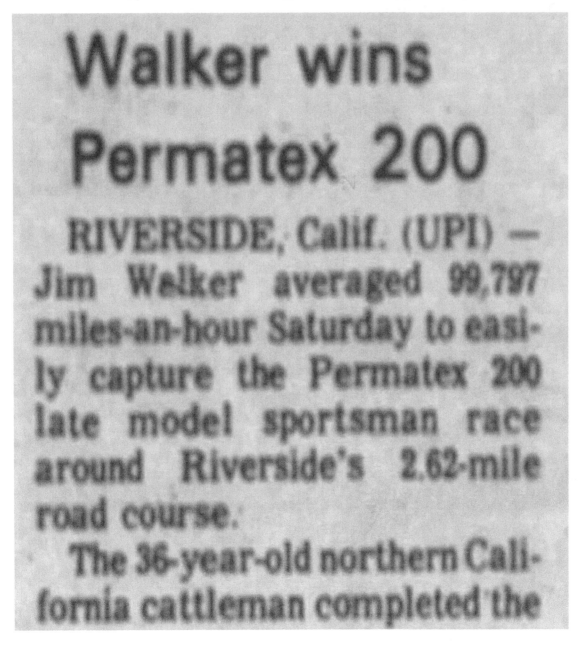

Walker wins Permatex 200

RIVERSIDE, Calif. (UPI) — Jim Walker averaged 99,797 miles-an-hour Saturday to easily capture the Permatex 200 late model sportsman race around Riverside's 2.62-mile road course.

The 36-year-old northern California cattleman completed the

Stock Car Racing at its Best !!

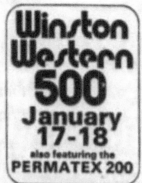

Lenny Pond

Jim Insolo

The June 1976 California 150 Late Model Sportsman race ran at 11 AM on Sunday, prior to the Winston Cup race. Ivan Baldwin won with Dan Clark second, James Sanderson third and Ron Esau fourth.

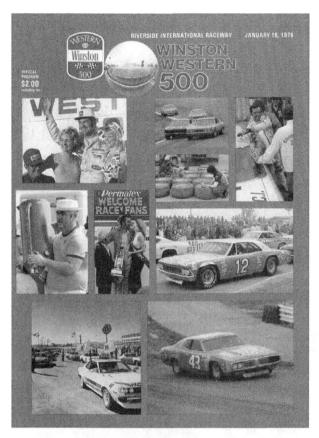
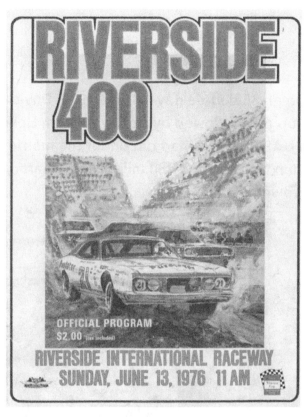

The January 1976 Winston Western 500, attended by a crowd of 54,700 on Super Bowl Sunday was won by David Pearson in a Woods Brothers Mercury, his 88th NASCAR victory, Second was Cale Yarborough in a Chevy with west coaster Jimmy Insolo and Ray Elder in third and fourth.

FLAGGED HOME—David Pearson of Spartanburg, S.C., takes the checkered flag to win the Winston Western 500 stockcar race at Riverside International Raceway yesterday. Not visible at the finish line is second place finisher Cale Yarborough.
(UPI Telephoto)

After 12 stock car losses

Pearson finds 13 lucky number, wins RIR 500

RIVERSIDE, Calif. (UPI) — David Pearson, the "Gray Fox" of the NASCAR Grand National curcuit, has finally won a stockcar race on Riverside's demanding road layout.

But the taciturn veteran from Spartanburg, S.C., didn't want to make anything of it.

"You can't think about jinxes," Pearson said. "You just keep coming back and trying again and again."

"Besides, I've won at Riverside before. That was a long time ago and it wasn't in a stockcar, but it was a win."

A loser here in a dozen previous NASCAR starts since 1963, Pearson proved 13 was his lucky number Sunday. Driving the Wood Bros. 1976 Mercury Montego, he led 85 of the 191 laps en route to a convincing 35.9-second triumph in the

four years ago, Pearson raced despite being weakened by a bout with the flu. He was virtually speechless Friday.

"I didn't know if I would make it this morning," he offered. "But I felt a whole lot better after I saw what happened to Petty and Allison.

"I felt worse after 500 miles, too. I'd rather not run 500 miles when I'm sick, though."

Pearson did capture a Trans-Am sedan race in a Cougar over Riverside's eight-turn 2.62-mile road course in 1967. He was runner-up to Allison here in the 1975 Western race after sitting on the pole the two previous years.

"I don't mind the road course," he emphasized. "In fact I enjoy it. It's a nice change of pace. You just have to set your car up so you can turn left and right."

race at Riverside International Race
1. David Pearson, Spartanburg, '76 Mercury, 191 laps, $15,245; 2. Cale Yarborough, Timmonsville, S.C., '75 Chevy, 191, $9,820; 3. Jimmy Insolo, Mission Hills, Calif., '74 Chevy, $8,220; 4. Ray Elder, Caruthers, C '74 Dodge, 190, $6,545; 5. Benny Parsons, Ellerbe, N.C., '75 Chevy, 189, $4,045; 6. Lennie Pond, Petersburg, Va., '75 Chevy, 183, $2,695; 7. Richard Childress, Winston Salem, N.C., '76 Chevy, 183, $2,695; 8. Dave Marcis, Skyland, N.C., '74 Dodge, 182, $2,496; 9. James Hylton, Grand N.C., '75 Chevy, 180, $2,345; 10. Schmitt, Redding, Calif., '75 Chevy $2,145.

11. Frank Warren, Harrisburg, N.C., Dodge, 177, $1,995; 12. D.K. Ull Harrisburg, N.C., '75 Chevy, 174, $1 13. Larry Esau, San Diego, '75 Chevy, 154, $1,645; 15. Bobby All Hueytown, Ala., '75 Matador, 149, $1 16. Chuck Bown, Portland, Ore. Dodge, 141, $1,445; 17. Gary Matt Marina del Rey, Calif., '74 Dodge, $1,395; 18. Eddie Bradshaw, Bakers Calif., '72 Chevy, 135, $1,345; 19. McDuffie, Sanford, N.C., '75 Chevy, $1,295; 20. Carl Joiner, Portland, Ore, Chevy, 180, $1,240.

COMPLETE

On an 85 degree day in June 1976, David Pearson won the Riverside 400 Winston Cup race followed by Bobby Allison, Benny Parsons and Ray Elder. For the first time a NASCAR race had run under the metric system (400 kilometers) and was shorter than the previous 400 mile races. Pearson picked up $15,150 for the win in front of a crowd of 29,300.

Daily Press photo by John Lucero

Car No. 89, owned by Bill Riley of Hesperia stopped in the pits during the recent running of the Riverside 400. Riley, who already has a "For Sale" sign painted on the Grand National auto, is contemplating selling the car next fall but would much prefer to find a sponsor to help finance the costly "hobby." Riley's car finished 18th in this year's Riverside 400 and will be running at Ontario Speedway in November.

Pearson is enjoying his greatest start

By DON BRADLEY
PB Staff Writer

RIVERSIDE — Luck rode with David Pearson Sunday.

That is not to say that the "Silver Fox" was lucky to win the "short ...

Pearson maintained he "ran hard" all day.

"This short a race, you naturally jes gonna have to run hard," he grinned. "You can't lay back. But I got more blisters today than when I was runnin' 500 miles.

finished fifth. Darrell Waltrip started 10th and finished sixth. Yarborough started sixth and finished seventh.

Jimmy Insolo started fifth and finished eighth. Richard Petty started seventh and finished ninth.

134

Everything is metric for Riverside 400

RIVERSIDE, Calif. (AP) — Riverside International Raceway opens to practice Thursday for the $124,925 Riverside 400 NASCAR Grand National stock car race, but there will be major differences as this year goes metric.

For one, the eight-turn track will be measured at 4.22 kilometers, and speeds on the back straightaway will hit 265 — that's kilometers roughly equivalent to 165 miles an hour.

Buddy Baker, at 6 feet 5 and 230 pounds the largest driver on the circuit, will be listed at 19.5 decimeters and 104 kilograms.

The reason for this is that Riverside will make history this weekend as the first site of a metric distance race in American stock car history.

The distance for Sunday's 14th event on the 30-race Winston Cup circuit is officially 400 kilometers, shortened from 400 miles, and the reason has little to do with the fact that the U. S. will soon, by perhaps as early as 1980, adopt the metric system.

Promoter Les Richter thinks 400 kilometers (just under 249 miles) will make a better race for the spectators to watch.

Drivers, many of whom believe the shorter race will cut down on their expenses and eliminate a lot of the boredom of endurance-type driving, agree with Richter.

"It's the best thing since axle grease," Cale Yarborough said.

"Anything to shorten that race," said Daytona 500 and Charlotte World 600 winner David Pearson, "will make it better."

The drivers aren't enthusiastic about 400 miles on the eight-turn Riverside road course, where average speeds approximate 100 miles an hour during a long afternoon.

But why does Richter believe a shorter race will give the fans more for their money?

"In the longer races," he said, "the drivers have to wait each other out and save their equipment in the middle of the race. In effect, they just drive around and around, waiting for something to happen to their opponents.

"In a shorter race, there is no middle part, only a sprint at the start for position and a sprint at the end for the checkered flag."

As Richard Petty puts it: "We'll have to run this one a lot different than we've been doing. We used to let them other cats go out and burn themselves out, but now we've got to pass that cat out in front right away, because we might not get another

npic bid

a sure-fire pro prospect despite being hidden by Centenary's NCAA probation thoughout his career there. He averaged 18 rebounds a game last year which would have led the nation had he been listed in NCAA statistics. The probation,

INLAND

EMPIRE

JUNE 1976 $1.00

The Prestige Publication for the Greater Riverside and San Bernardino Areas **MAGAZINE**

SHAPE UP FOR SUMMER • LIVING WITH ART

Read This Article on the Attached DVD

• RIVERSIDE INTERNATIONAL RACEWAY •

The January 1977 Permatex 300 Late Model Sportsman race was won by Ivan Baldwin with James Sanderson second and Ron Esau third.

In June 1977 Glen Steurer won the Black Gold 150 Late Model Sportsman race, followed by Roy Smith and Jim Walker, all driving Novas.

60,000 attended the January 1977 Winston Western 500 Winston Cup race in perfect weather. The race was won by David Pearson who earned $15,400 for his efforts. Second was pole sitter Cale Yarborough with Richard Petty third and Dave Marcis fourth. The race was changed from 500 miles to 500 kilometers, primarily to keep spectators happy.

Pearson wins opener as Yarborough spins

RIVERSIDE (UPI) — As Cale Yarborough saw it, he was a victim of racing fate.

In the new season's NASCAR Grand National opener Sunday, Yarborough lost to an old rival, David Pearson, when he should have won.

"I had 18 seconds on him when I spun out," explained the defending NASCAR king from Timmonsville, S.C. "I was just at the wrong place at the wrong time."

Yarborough, who wound up nine seconds behind Pearson, lost his lead — and the race — on turn eight of Riverside's ardulous 2.62-mile road course 15 laps from the end of the Winston Western 500.

"There was sand and dirt all over the turn this particular time," he said. "I saw it, but I couldn't do anything about it. I hit it and spun."

"As far as dirt on the racetrack," declared Pearson. "That's the worst I ever saw it here."

"There's no doubt about that," echoed Yarborough, ruefully shaking his head.

Pearson, winner of 10 of 22 Grand National events last year, posted his fourth straight California stock car victory. He won the two Riverside NASCAR races in 1976 and the Ontario 500-miler last November.

On a beautiful Southern California winter day when the temperature hit 76 and an estimated 60,000 fans turned out, Yarborough led from the second lap until the 104th in the 119-lap race.

Riverside International Raceway president Les Richter this year cut the race from 500 miles to 500 kilometers, approximately 310 miles, because he felt five hours of driving around the tight road course was too hard on cars and drivers.

"I knew if I could push him I could try to get him to run a little harder," Pearson said of Yarborough. "But that ain't what done it. He just got into that corner a little wide.

"I kept talking to my crew during the race on my car radio and asking them where Cale was and how many seconds he was ahead. But I was driving as hard as I could without tearing my car up."

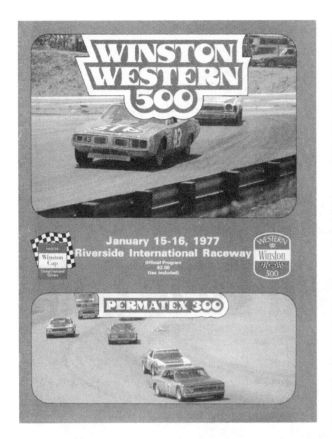

Winners and losers

Cale Yarborough (left) and David Pearson pace the field at the beginning of Sunday's Winston Western 500. At the end of 500 kilometers, Pearson crossed the finish line ahead of Yarborough and the rest of the field. In between, some drivers like Greg Francis (below) had a little trouble and weren't around for the checkered flag.

David Pearson gets trophy and kisses after winning the Western 500 at Riverside, Calif., Sunday. Salley Fuller, the Raceway Queen, is at left. Susan Brinkley of Greensboro, N.C., is the Winston Girl. — AP Wirephoto.

NATIONAL
Speed Sport NEWS

VOL. XLV No. 3   RIDGEWOOD, N.J. JANUARY 19, 1977

Biggest Riverside Crowd Watches David Edge Cale

(Story on Page Three)

THE ESSES — The portion of California's Riverside Raceway leading to turn six is called the "esses." Here Cale Yarborough leads out of the esses in Sunday's NASCAR Grand National season opener during the early laps of the Winston Western 500. Darrell Waltrip (88) is trying to duck under David Pearson as Dave Marcis, Jimmy Insolo, Richard Petty and Buddy Baker trail. The race drew the track's biggest January crowd. (Bruce Wylie photo).

60,000 saw pole sitter Richard Petty win the June 1977 NAPA 400. Second was David Pearson with Cale Yarborough third. This was Petty's 184th career win and paid $18,255.

Top racing field prepared for prestigious NAPA 400

Yarborough seeks third straight win on Riverside track

King Richard wins pole for Riverside 400 race

Petty Quiet After Win In Winston Cup National

RIVERSIDE (UPI) — Richard Petty didn't have too much to say after he won his second Winston Cup Grand National race in a row and the 18th of his career.

It apparently was enough that he won.

"Darrell (Waltrip) ran real good at the start," said Petty, who averaged 105.022 miles an hour, "Then he started having trouble. That's about it, I guess."

The win in the NAPA Riverside 400 at Riverside International Raceway Sunday was Petty's fourth victory this year and earned him $19,600, a record for the 20-year-old race track.

Petty, of Level Cross, N.C., came in 9.5 seconds ahead of

ers on the corners "really helped."

"They made the track stay cleaner. Even last spring you couldn't get around No.6 and 8 up there and it was just as neat as a pin.

"I think it helped everybody because the way it was we couldn't hang our wheels off the corners because of the dirt. It makes cars handle better, run a little quicker and also keeps the track clean."

There was one yellow caution period lasting six laps after Don Puskarich, Garden Grove, Calif., blew an engine.

It was Petty's fifth win at the Riverside track and boosted his career victory on the NASCAR Winston Cup circuit to 184. He

now trails Yarborough, who has 2,346 points in the championship race, by only 93 points. Waltrip has 2,080 points.

Two weeks ago Petty won a record NASCAR payoff of $62,300 in the World 600 at Charlotte, N.C.

In an earlier event, Glen Steurer, 22, Granada Hills, Calif., averaged 99.956 miles an hour to win his first major stock car race in the California 150 for NASCAR late model sports cars.

Steurer took command in the 22nd lap of the 36-lap race to edge out Roy Smitt of Victoria B.C. by 11.6 seconds, to claim the $3,400 purse.

Polesitter Ivan Baldwin of Modesto, Calif., Vince Gianformaggio of Whittier, Calif., and

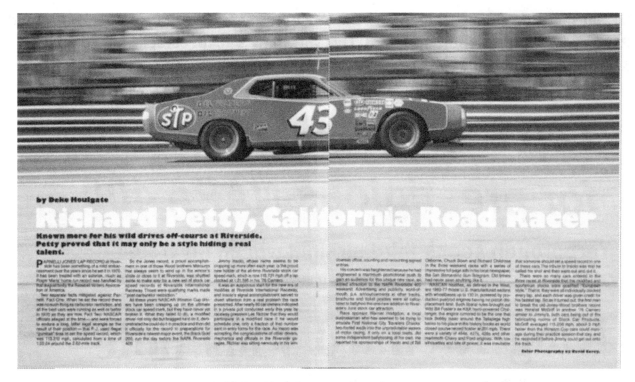

by Deke Houlgate

Richard Petty, California Road Racer

Known more for his wild drives off-course at Riverside, Petty proved that it may only be a style hiding a real talent.

PARNELLI JONES' LAP RECORD at Riverside has been something of a mild embarrassment over the years since he set it in 1970. It had been treated with an estimate, much as Roger Mears' home run record was handled by that august body the Baseball Writers Association of America.

Two separate facts mitigated against Parnelli. Fact One: When he set the record there was no such thing as carburetor restriction, and all the best cars were running as well or better in 1970 as they are now. Fact Two: NASCAR officials alleged at the time — and were forced to endure a long, bitter legal wrangle as the result of their position — that P.J. used illegal "gunboat" tires to set the speed record, which was 115.310 mph, calculated from a time of 1:33.24 around the 2.62-mile track.

So the Jones record, a proud accomplishment in one of those Roush brothers Mercurys that always seem to wind up in the winner's circle or close to it at Riverside, was shuffled aside to make way for a new set of stock car speed records. Which is now 115.721 mph off a lap clocked at 1:21.395 in his '76 Camaro.

It was an auspicious start for the new era of modifies at Riverside International Raceway, and Insolo's signal accomplishment served to divert attention from a real problem the race presented. After nearly 80 car owners indicated in a private poll conducted early this year the raceday pressures Les Richter then they would participate in a modified race if he would schedule one, only a fraction of that number sent in entry forms for the race. As major sponsor. Warner Hodgdon, a local businessman who has seemed to be trying to outsnobman who has seemed to be trying to buy himself into a position in the history books as quickly as possible, bankrolled all the congratulations of other drivers, mechanics and officials in the Riverside garages. Richter was sitting nervously in his win-

overseas office, counting and re-counting signed entries.

His concern was heightened because he had engineered a maximum promotional push, to gain an audience for this unique new race, as added attraction to the NAPA Riverside 400 weekend. Advertising and publicity, word-of-mouth, p.a. announcements and other tracks, brochures and ticket prizes were all calculated to ballyhoo the one-new addition to Riverside's June stock car attraction.

Osborne, Chuck Bown and Richard Childress in the three weekend races with a series of impressive full-page ads in the local newspaper, the San Bernardino Sun-Telegram. Old timers had never seen anything like it.

NASCAR Modifies, as defined in the West, are 1960-77 model U.S. manufactured sedans with wheelbases up to 130 in. powered by production pushrod engines having no pistol displacement limit. Such liberal rules brought out Wild Bill Fosler's ex-K&K hemi-powered Chargers, the engine rumored to be the one that took Bobby Isaac around the Talladega high banks to his place in the history books as world closed pushrod record holder at 201 mph. There were a variety of 454s, 427s, 426s and other mammoth Chevy and Ford engines. With low silhouettes and lots of power, it was inevitable

that someone should set a speed record in one of these cars. The tribute to Insolo was that he called his shot and then went out and did it.

There were so many cars entered in the three races at Riverside that the modified and sportsman checks were qualified "European style." That is, they were all individually clocked every lap, and each driver was given credit for his fastest lap. As it turned out, the first man to break the old Jones-Wood brothers record was Hershel McGriff in another '76 Camaro similar to Jimmy's, both cars being out of the fabricating rooms of Stock Car Products. McGriff averaged 115.206 mph, about 5 mph faster than the Winston Cup cars could manage during their practice session that day, and he recorded it before Jimmy could get out onto the track.

Salar Photography by David Carey.

Deke Houlgate wrote the article for the September 1977 issue of Stock Car . Read the entire article on the attached DVD

Rocky Moran: *"We thought we'd try stock car racing; what an awakening. I would drive a precise line through the esses, clipping the apexes perfectly. Did well and qualified third. Raceday, the NASCAR guys just straightened then out, blew through the dirt and most of them passed me before turn six – I ended up 23rd"*

Darrell Waltrip led the first 20 laps

The January 1978 Stock Car Products 300 Grand American (formerly Late Model Sportsman) race was won by polesitter Jimmy Insolo, followed by Joe Ruttman and Gary Johnson. Tragically, veteran driver Sonny Easely and a spectator were killed in a practice crash.

Zach Topeleski signals driver Tim Fleenor of San Bernardino, who finished ninth.

Note; The sign said "haul ass" and NASCAR made them change it

Stock Car Products 300 drivers go through the esses during the pace lap Saturday.

Tim Fleenor: *"This was the first race for the new Grand American cars, mixing the old Sportsman cars built to different rules. NASCAR decided to pay extra money to the old style cars who could qualify. It had rained heavily all week before the event. This was Kyle Petty's first Grand National race; he had issues in the first practice so they stopped practice and Richard drove him around on a station wagon. While we waited, I sat next to Sonny Easely and we made small talk. This was a big deal for me because this my second race and he was a west coast hero. Then the session starts; the track is dry but there is a lot of mud and standing puddles. On the third lap as I go under the Champion Bridge I can see smoke and flying mud at the dog leg where Sonny Easely had just crashed. A terrible incident, bothered me for days as I just talked with him. 105 cars attempted to qualify: I qualified 26th out of 40 with my 1974 Nova. By lap ten I was tenth, stopped for right side tires and fuel under a yellow and finished seventh, second of the sportsman cars."*

Ruttman donates winnings to fund for Easley family

RIVERSIDE (AP) — Joe Ruttman, who finished second in Saturday's Stock Car Products 300 NASCAR modified-sportsman stock car race at Riverside International Raceway, donated his winnings to the Sonny Easley Fund.

The 39-year-old Easley, of Van Nuys, was killed last Sunday during practice runs for Saturday's race.

Ruttman, of Upland, and formerly a resident of Livonia, Mich., turned

A trust fund for the four children of driver Sonny Easley, who was killed last week in a freak racing accident at Riverside, has been established by Steve Smith of Santa Ana. Smith hopes to raise $20,000 toward their college education. Joe Ruttman of Ontario, who finished second in last week's Stock Car Products 300, and his sponsor, Haddick's Towing Service of the City of Industry, donated their purse of $4,200 to the fund. Checks may be made payable to Steve Smith, Trustee, and mailed to Easley Trust Fund, c/o Steve Smith, P.O. Box 11631, Santa Ana, 92711.

Freak Accident Claims Two Lives

RIVERSIDE (AP) — A freak accident has claimed the lives of veteran stock car race driver Sonny Easley and racing mechanic Douglas B. Gruntz.

The pair died Sunday at Riverside International Raceway after Easley's 1968 Camaro, which he was driving in practice to prepare for next Saturday's Stock Car Products 300 NASCAR modified sportsman race here, slid out of control at high speed into a group of parked pit vehicles.

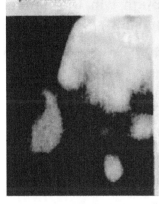

Officials said Gruntz, 37, of La Crescenta, was pinned between a truck and a van struck by the race car. Gruntz was a member of a pit crew working for driver Tiny Keith of Van Nuys.

The car impacted sideways into a trailer attached to a pickup truck, pushing the truck into the van, officials said. Gruntz was trapped between the two vehicles and Easley, 39, of Van Nuys, was fatally injured when he was struck by the twisted metal of the three vehicles.

The accident occurred on an escape road leading away from the high speed back straightaway. All the cars on the 2.62-mile road course were driving at reduced speeds due to a yellow caution flag, according to Ken Piper, West Coast supervisor for NASCAR.

Piper said observers reported that Easley's car dropped a wheel off the pave-

ment into the muddy corner of a dog leg bend in the road, and then slid out of control sideways, across the track and down the road.

The accident brought activity to a stop on the track just before qualifications were scheduled to begin, forcing postponement of time trials until Tuesday.

Paramedics at the track worked over the two victims for more than an hour at the track and the hospital but failed to revive either one.

Easley's biggest victory came in 1973 when he won the first stock car race ever held on the road course at Laguna Seca and he was also noted for losing a hairline decision to driver George Follmer in a 250-mile stock car race at Ontario Motor Speedway in 1972.

Easley's record on the Winston West Grand National circuit was eight wins, 40 finishes in the top five and

63 in the top 10 out of 98 races since 1972.

He had been entered in next Sunday's Winston Western 500 as well as the Stock Car Products 300.

He is survived by his wife, Sonja, and four children.

Easley, one of the most highly regarded race drivers on the Pacific Coast, finished second in points to six-time champion Ray Elder of Caruthers, Calif., in 1975, winning two races. But Easley had been less active the last two seasons.

Easley had turned in the fifth fastest lap time in practice shortly before the fatal accident.

Right behind Steurer on the clocks were Bobby Allison of Hueytown, Ala., in a 1978 Concorde at 107.807 mph; Jim Walker of Ferndale, Calif., in a 1974 Camaro at 107.375 mph and Hugh Pearson of Bakersfield in a 1977 Camaro at 106.285 mph.

In June 1978, on a very hot day, Herschel McGriff won the Warner Hodgdon 200 Grand American race, his seventh win in that category. Second was Jimmy Insolo followed by Ron Esau and Tim Williamson. Twenty laps were run under yellow due to a number of incidents.

Local racers need money to beat the heat

By JIM MATTHEWS
Sun-Telegram Sports Writer

RIVERSIDE — For the past three days the heat has nearly equaled the qualifying speeds drivers have clocked at Riverside International Raceway in preparation for today's Warner W Hodgdon 200 NASCAR race.

The excess of heat presents a major problem for drivers and their cars in the race, but the lack of something else presents just as big a problem.

Most entrants in the companion feature to the NAPA 400 are "local boys," as opposed to "good ol' boys," and their money just doesn't compare. Combine that with the excessive heat that is expected to burn out 30 per cent of the competitors and you have two major reasons why many local racers decided to stay out of the Hodgdon event.

"It's a big waste of time, they don't pay anything — you can't even pay for tires unless you finish third or better," said Fontana driver Bill Osborne this week.

Osborne was one of the many local

drivers expected to enter the race, but who didn't because the purse was too small. When tires cost you $100 a pop, and you don't have a semi truck to haul you and your crew all over the country, and you don't have a sponsor who'll feed you $2,000 a race, and the heat makes you run so hot you could blown an expensive racing engine, and ...

'You gotta darn near win it to pay for everything'

Osborne was echoing the sentiments of dozens of local drivers in and out of the Hodgdon 200 race. They can make more money, at least cover costs, by running at some of the smaller races in Southern and Central California. Bakersfield pays $1,000 for a first place finish in its much shorter Saturday night event, while the Hodgdon race is paying a total of $18,000. First draws $3,600 but places much

below fourth in this race won't cover the cost of tires.

"If we didn't have someone give us eight tires," said Berdoo driver Tim Fleenor Saturday. "We couldn't have afforded this, although we probably would have come anyway."

"You gotta darn near win it to pay for everything," said Fleenor as his crew put a new transmission in his '74 Nova. Fleenor is racing the Nova because there are bonus bucks for the better finishers in the large wheelbase cars ($500, $200 and $100 for the three top finishers in cars with a 112-inch wheelbase or better).

None of these drivers kid themselves into believing they'll win this event, they're self-sponsored and don't have the money to maintain a super car. They agree that it's going to be a dual between sponsored Jimmy Insolo and Herschel McGriff for the first spot with the rest of the field scrambling for places below that.

"I feel like we can run in the top six or seven," said Alan Brown of San

Bernardino. To win... He smiled and shrugged his shoulders.

"The heat's the real killer. That'll take em," said Brown, pleased that his car was running cool and counting on that factor to give him a place or two in the final standings.

Ralph Davidson, one of Brown's mechanics, said he didn't expect more than about 15 of the 35 cars in the field to finish the race because of the heat.

Of the three area drivers in the Hodgdon 200, Bill Rozhon of Rialto posted the best qualification time Friday and sits on the 4th row in the 8th position. Fleenor and Brown qualified for the 14th and 16th spots respectively. All three look to be fair prospects for good finishes — if they can beat the heat.

"It's gonna be a race of attrition. I'm sure," said Fleenor. "A lot of cars will be falling apart because of the heat."

"And a lot more cars won't be in the heat because there's not enough money to stoke their fire."

Staff photo by Greg Schneider

Al Brown of San Bernardino.

McGriff captures Hodgdon 200; Insolo second

RIVERSIDE — You'd think a 50-year old man would be content to stay home on Sundays watching TV and playing with his grandchildren.

Not Hershel McGriff.

Instead, he chose to race around Riverside International Raceway's 2.62 mile course with about 30 younger men and showed them a thing or two by winning the Warner Hodgdon 200 NASCAR race.

And the enthusiasm he showed after the victory could have rivaled that of a 15-year-old.

"It was really neat driving in this race," beamed McGriff. "I'm really sorry Jimmy (Insolo) broke down because we could have had a good race."

Insolo led for 23 laps of the 48-lap, 200-kilometer event, but had trouble with a wobbly back tire on his '76 Camero. He was forced to pit five times, all during the race's three yellow flags. To compound the problem, his car slipped off a jack while the left-rear wheel was off, bending the axle.

Insolo was 13th after the second yellow was lifted but managed to weave through the field to move into third place before the final caution period.

By lap 39, Insolo had pulled to within a second of McGriff's '78 Camaro, but McGriff steadily moved away, winning by a 19-second margin. Ron Esau finished third.

San Bernardino drivers Alan Brown and Tim Fleenor had a spirited battle with Riverside's Dan Clark for the 9th, 10th and 11th spots. Brown took ninth in his '74 Pontiac after passing Fleenor near the mid-way point. Near the finish Clark also passed Fleenor to end up 10th in his '78 Mustang. Fleenor was 11th in his '74 Nova.

Rialto's Bill Rozhon, who was sitting 6th on the starting grid, finished 14th.

Twenty of the 48 laps in the race were run under yellow flags. The first was called when Jerry Jones engine blew going into turn nine. He coasted up on the turn and clipped the car driven by Donald Lowrey of Riverside hard enough to knock it out of the race and cover the track with oil. Two cars spun on the slick but remained in the race.

The second yellow occured when Bill Clarkson of Orange scattered his engine at the start-finish line, showering the track with oil and slowing the race for 10 laps while the mess was cleaned up. The same thing happened to Bob Brown of Bakersfield going into turn 8 on the 31st lap, forcing four more laps under the yellow.

"I reported a flat to the pit crew coming out of turn eight," said McGriff about his car dancing through the oil. "But it was OK down the back straightaway, so I told 'em to cancel the flat."

But that was about the only thing McGriff had to cancel Sunday as he collected the $6,050 first prize. But like the kid craving more chocolate cake after its all gone, McGriff seemed to want more.

"The yellows kind of take the real race out of it," he said. "Jimmy's car is a little faster, but I figured with strategy and our pit crew we could do alright. I wanted to race."

— By JIM MATTHEWS

70,000 fans, the largest crowd since 1968, saw Cale Yarborough win the January 1978 Winston Western 500 Winston Cup race in an Oldsmobile, This was Oldsmobile's first NASCAR race win since 1959. Benny Parsons was second and pole sitter David Pearson was third.

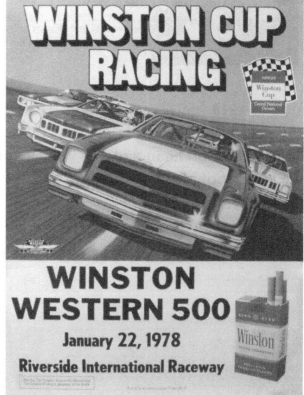

David Pearson (21) follows the leader, Cale Yarborough, through a turn during Winston Western 500 Sunday

Staff photo by Tom Kasser

Yarborough gets even at Riverside

By RYAN REBELLO-REES
Sun-Telegram Sports Writer

RIVERSIDE — Cale Yarborough was tasting the sweet fruits of victory — and revenge — Sunday after capturing the Winston Western 500 at Riverside International Raceway.

A year ago, Yarborough had a sour taste in his mouth after David Pearson passed him late in the race to take the victory.

"Last year I had the race won with 15 laps to go until somebody put sand on the track and Pearson got by me and won the race. All year long I felt like I gave that race away. Today, we got it back," Yarborough said in Victory Circle.

The stocky blond driver had a slim, one-second lead over Benny Parsons and Pearson when he took the checkered flag.

Parsons and Pearson were tail to nose as they futilely chased Yarborough the final eight laps of the race before an estimated 70,000 cheering fans spread around the sprawling road course. It was the largest crowd at Riverside since 1968.

The final eight-lap chase was set up when a yellow flag was brought out after Richard Petty got stuck in the mud on Turn 6 when the differential on his 1974 Dodge locked up.

It was an inglorious end for Petty, the winningest driver in NASCAR history. But it created one of the greatest finishes ever in Riverside racing.

With the yellow out for Petty, the leaders dashed into the pits for fuel and new tires. Yarborough, the first

It's been almost 20 years since an Oldsmobile won a stock car race — but it won't take twenty more. C-3.

one in, was the first one out in his 1977 Oldsmobile.

Parsons exited right on his bumper in his 1978 Chevrolet.

Pearson, who normally benefits in these situations by the crack workmanship of the Woods Brothers crew, took an abnormally long time in getting new rubber on the right side of his 1977 Mercury and trailed Yarborough and Parsons by several car lengths when he finally got out of the pits.

There was less than a car length between the three front runners when the racing resumed However, in the final two laps, Yarborough

edged away slightly while Pearson moved right onto Parsons' bumper.

On the last lap, Pearson went off the track and into the dirt to get around Parsons as they entered Turn 8, halfway to the finish line. But Parsons drafted Pearson down the back straight and passed him before they entered the last turn.

That final effort by Parsons earned the former Detroit taxi driver almost $2,000 extra.

Yarborough won $16,550 for the victory while Parsons collected $11,125 for second. Pearson received $9,350 for third place.

Yarborough's win represents the first time an Oldsmobile has won a NASCAR event since 1959 when Lee Petty, Richard's father, won at the Charlotte, N.C. fairgrounds.

Neil Bonnett finished fourth, the

only other driver on the same lap with the winners. One lap down was Dave Marcis in fifth and Herschel McGriff sixth. McGriff, a racing grandfather from Bridal Veil, Ore., started the race 29th out the 35 starters.

Seventh went to Jimmy Insolo, winner of Saturday's Stock Car Products 300. Insolo had challenged for the lead early in the race but fell back after 80 laps when he began having troubles with fourth gear.

Road racing specialist Al Holbert was eighth, Roy Smith ninth and D.K. Ulrich 10th.

Rick McCray of Riverside, the only local entry in the field, finished 12th, six laps behind the winners.

Yarborough averaged 102.269 miles per hour for the three-hour

(Continued on C-2, column 1)

Cal Yarborough / Benny Parsons

Petty Pit Stop

CALE'S CONQUEST — Grand National racing champion Cale Yarborough waved following the finish of Sunday's Winston Western 500 event at Riverside International Raceway. Yarborough outlasted Benny Parsons and David Pearson to post the victory in a tight finish. —AP Laserphoto

Pearson seeks 100th win in Western 500

Lineup, D9

By Mike Morrow, staff writer

RIVERSIDE — David Pearson will start from the pole today in the $147,470 Western 500 stock car race, an event he's won two straight years, in the 1978 NASCAR grand national opener.

The 43-year-old Pearson was the leading qualifier in his Wood Bros. 1976 Mercury in 113.204 miles per hour, the fastest lap for a grand national car at Riverside since

PEARSON IN FAMILIAR SPOT AGAIN

BY SHAV GLICK
Times Staff Writer

RIVERSIDE—David Pearson, the Old Gray Fox from South Carolina who has won the last two Winston Western 500 stock car races, put himself in a good position Fri-

Pearson won a $500 beer keg and the first leg toward the $10,000 Busch Beer Trophy, to be awarded the driver winning the most pole positions at the end of the 30-race season.

1. David Pearson (Spartanburg, colo). 108.252. 14. Gary Johnson

28,000 fans watched the June 1978 NAPA 400 Winston Cup race on an 85 degree day. The race was won by Benny Parsons who collected $22,750.. Second was Richard Petty followed by Bobby Allison. Pole qualifier David Pearson DNF'd with engine problems.

Benny Parsons in Victory Circle after winning the NAPA 400 Sunday.

Staff photo by Ron Hann

148

Parsons Battles Heat for NAPA 400 Win Over Eight-Turn Road Race Layout

By JIM COUR
UPI Sports Writer

RIVERSIDE, Calif. (UPI) — Benny Parsons took over the lead from Bobby Allison 16 laps from the finish Sunday and then went on to post his first victory at Riverside by capturing the NAPA 400 NASCAR Grand National stock car race by 29 seconds.

The 36-year-old Ellerbe, N.C., veteran finished in front of Richard Petty of Randleman, N.C., who is in the throes of the longest losing streak of his illustrious career, for his third win of 1978 and the 12th of his nine-year stock car racing career.

Clark Second in Fun Run

DALEVILLE — Jeff Clark, 13-year-old son of Mr. and Mrs. Phil Clark, Daleville, surprised a big audience and a big field Sunday when he ran second in the Anderson "Fun Run," a distance race of three miles through Anderson and its

Allison, winner of the prestigious Daytona 500 last February, was third.

Parsons, the son of a Detroit taxicab company owner who was the No. 4 qualifier, waved triumphantly to the main grandstand crowd as he crossed the finish line in his 1977 Chevrolet. He averaged 104.313 mph around the Riverside International Raceway's 2.62-mile, eight-turn road course.

Racing in 85 degree weather, Parsons led from the 79th lap on in the 95-lap race, the second NASCAR event of the year at Riverside.

He led 25 of the 95 laps and got his big break of the day when Cale Yarborough, a wire-to-wire winner in the last NASCAR race in Nashville, Tenn., had a flat tire on the 55th lap after leading 47 of the first 54 laps.

Pole-sitter David Pearson went out on the 66th lap with a broken valve while running fourth.

There were six different leaders in the NAPA race and nine lead changes. Only

For the 40-year-old Petty, it was the 28th straight race in which he has failed to win. His last victory came last July 4 in the Firecracker 400 at Daytona.

In the Warner Hodgdon 200, a preliminary event for the NASCAR race, the winner was Herschel McGriff, a 50-year-old Bridal Veil, Ore., lumberman, who won the Mexican road race in 1950.

He finished 14 seconds ahead of Jimmy Insolo.

Ongais Wins USAC Ontario Road Race

MOSPORT, Ont. (UPI) — Danny Ongais rocketed ahead of the field to win the United States Automobile Club championship series road race Sunday, avoiding the troubles that afflicted most

---

The January 1979 Warner Hodgdon 200 Grand American race was won by Tim Williamson followed by Bobby Allison and Herschel McGriff.

Tim Williamson

Vince Giaformaggio

300-miler today at Riverside

By JIM MATTHEWS
Sun Sports Writer

RIVERSIDE — Jimmy Insolo was standing by the garages watching other cars qualify for Sunday's race. Listening to him talk, it was clear that he was just as interested in today's 1 p.m. Stock Car Products 300 at Riverside International Raceway.

"These big cars are really something to drive compared to my smaller car," said Insolo, comparing the difference between the larger Grand National car he's driving in Sunday's Winston West 500 and the Grand American car he's driving in today's event.

"The big cars feel sluggish coming out of a turn, you press the excellerator and unghhhh. But the little car comes out faster — and you can go deeper into the turn before you have to brake. It's 600 pounds lighter and I use the same brakes as on the big car.

"That's why there were quicker times for today's race," said Insolo.

And Insolo should know about quick times, he set a course record last Sunday while qualifying for today's pole position — 117.585 mph. But the record he broke was his own, set last year in June while qualifying for the Warner Hodgdon 200.

Other top qualifiers for today's race are Tim Wil-

liamson, Bobby Allison, Dave Marcis, Vince Giamformaggio, and Herschel McGriff.

There will also be four local drivers entered in the 200-kilometer event. Greg Scheidecker of Highland is starting in the 31st position after clocking a 107.533 mph speed Sunday in his 1977 Camaro. A couple of spots below him will be San Bernardino's Alan Brown, with Rialto's John Haney down a couple of more notches.

Rick Becker of Highland, while not qualifying for the regular field, was admitted to the starting grid as an alternate when another driver withdrew.

The race begins at 1 p.m. today. Tickets are still available at Ticketron and the raceway. The cost is $6 for general admission and $3 to enter the paddock area.

winston western 500 schedule

Saturday
Grand National practice from 9 a.m. to noon.
The Stock Car Products 300 for Grand American cars begins at 1 p.m. General admission $6, paddock $3.

Williamson wins 300 . . .

(Continued from F-1)

straight after three laps under a yellow flag.

On the 11th lap, Williamson blew the right rear tire on the back straight and had to baby his machine through turn 9 and into the pits. He got back on the track just ahead of Insolo, so he wasn't lapped.

Oil from a blown engine two laps later brought out another yellow flag and tightened up the leaders again, allowing Williamson to start closing the gap between himself and the leaders — Dave Marcis, Insolo and Allison.

Williamson and Insolo traded the lead five times between the 26th and 64th lap, when Williamson stormed past Insolo in the esses for the final time.

Marcis, who led for four laps while Insolo and Allison were pitting under a yellow, came out of

Before that however, Williamson was making himself known all over the West. He finished second to Insolo in the Cooper World Classic open competition race, the first time he ever drove on the one-mile oval at Phoenix International Raceway.

He also won his first NASCAR Winston West race at Stockton — again beating Insolo and Allison. Then he headed north to Washington and British Columbia to drive in a seven-race International Drivers Challenge where he finished third overall.

After qualifying for the pole in another Winston West race at Sears Point, he led until mechanical problems forced him out of the race. The same thing happened in another open competition race in Stockton. After becoming the first driver to ever break the 14-second barrier on that ¼-mile, his water

In a very short time his credentials have become impressive. It's not surprising that the young driver has big plans — to be the first driver to win both the rookie of the year award and overall championship on the Winston West circuit.

And the way he's been driving, it doesn't seem all that unlikely.

The June 1979 Warner Hodgdon 200 Grand American race was won by Tim Williamson once again with Joe Ruttman second and Ron Esau third

Ruttman and Williamson

Williamson rallies past Ruttman to take Hodgdon 200

By JIM SCHULTE
Sun Sports Writer

RIVERSIDE — With just nine laps to go Sunday, Tim Williamson knew he had to shift into high gear if he wanted to catch leader Joe Ruttman of Upland.

There was only one problem. The last thing Williamson wanted to do was shift — period.

The shifter knob on his '77 Camaro had fallen off at the start of the race and the 23-year-old had quickly rubbed his right palm raw.

However, Williamson overcame the pain and, after a furious three-lap duel, also overcame Ruttman to win the Warner W. Hodgdon 200 at Riverside International Raceway.

The action actually started when a yellow flag came out on lap 32. Williamson pitted for fuel and new tires.

Ruttman came in the next lap for tires but there was a communication mix-up and he only got fresh rubber on the left side.

"It was a major boo-boo," said Ruttman. "Our communications went awry and instead of four new tires I only got the two. The tires on the right had been on the car for the entire race and were worn out.

"But that's just making excuses," continued Ruttman, who started on the pole. "Timmy was just faster at the end of the race than I was. I held out for as long as I could but . . . Timmy didn't beat us. We beat ourselves."

Williamson passed Ruttman on Turn 7 on lap 43 and then steadily increased his lead to win the 46-lap event by a comfortable 6.1-second margin. Third was

Ron Esau while San Bernardino driver Alan Brown pushed his '74 Pontiac to a fourth-place finish.

Williamson's was almost secondary in interest to the road racing debut of Kyle Petty, son of NASCAR star Richard Petty.

But an auspicious start by the 19-year-old turned into a premature ending.

Petty started the race 12th in the 34-car lineup, quickly moved into sixth and took the lead on the 16th lap during a caution period when the other leaders made pit stops.

On the restart, Williamson beat Petty, who faded to fourth, then dropped out on lap 29 with transmission troubles. He unofficially was posted 15th.

"The transmission started leaking fluid on about the 10th lap," Petty explained. "Then it started

smoking. Finally it wouldn't go in gear, and wouldn't come out of gear. It stuck in fourth, so I just coasted it down through the dirt into the pits.

"I enjoyed it as long as it lasted. In the early going, I was just trying to get acquainted with the race track and the other cars. Finally I got to feeling pretty comfortable. I'd run a good lap, then a bad lap, depending on the traffic."

Hodgdon 200 notes

Of the six S.B. County drivers in the race, the only other one still running at the end besides Ruttman and Brown was Rialto's C.H. Pound, who completed 40 laps in his '77 Camaro to finish 13th.

Rick Bacher of Highland ended up 14th, blowing his engine in Turn 5 on lap 31. Glen Cummings, also of Highland, went out with mechanical problems in the 24th lap while Steve Eschleman of Fontana finished just 11 laps after sustaining front-end damage in a crunch in Turn 4.

Williamson also drove in the NAPA 400 but only lasted until lap 32 before a carburetor fire sidelined his '76 Chevelle.

NAPA 400 CO-FEATURE
Riverside's fastest car on tap for Warner Hodgdon 200

The fastest stock car in the history of Riverside International Raceway was not driven by Cale Yarborough, Richard Petty or David Pearson — but by Jimmy Insolo.

It's not a Chevy, Olds or Ford but a

from Simi Valley, Richard White from Escondido and Jim Walker from Ferndale are a few of the added favorites.

Grand American stock cars are 1960-79 compacts, such as Cougars, Darts, Javelins, Mavericks, Camaros, Firebirds

Richard Petty's son to celebrate 19th birthday in Hodgdon race

Young Kyle will pilot '78 Pontiac Grand Am in prelim to Riverside's NAPA 400

The road to fame for Kyle Petty, son of stock car racing great Richard Petty, took an unusual and unexpected turn with announcement that the aspiring young race driver will test the 2.62-mile road course at Riverside International Raceway on Sunday.

Kyle, whose 19th birthday is this Saturday, will drive the STP-Haddick's '78 Pontiac Grand Am in the Warner W. Hodgdon 200 for NASCAR Grand American stock cars, a preliminary to the NAPA 400 in which his daddy is entered.

King Richard's only son (he has three daughters) will be driving in only his third race and first on a road course. He'll be in a car which has proven its winning potential, although it is yet to win in three previous races, driven by Dave Marcis at Riverside, Joe Ruttman at I-70 Speedway in Missouri and Larry Phillips at Mesa Marin in Bakersfield.

Kyle burst into the news last Feb. 4 when he led 51 of the 80 laps to win his maiden race, the ARCA 200 at Daytona. Soon afterward, STP Corp. announced that the teenager would begin gaining experience in NASCAR Winston Cup racing for an assault on the 1980 "rookie of the year" title by driving in five events, beginning with the World 600 at Charlotte on Memorial Day weekend.

Two crashes during a test session at Charlotte interrupted that program,

Pettys by giving Kyle some experience at Riverside, we went back to work on the Pontiac again."

The trip to Riverside won't be the first for Kyle, who has served on his father's STP Racing Team crew several times in recent years.

"I've been there, and I know the track," Kyle said. "But running on the road course at Riverside ought to teach me something. I need all the racing I can get."

A 1978 graduate from Randleman, N.C., High School, where he was a star quarterback on the football team and played guard in basketball, Kyle entertained scholarship offers from several colleges before deciding to concentrate on the sport of his father and Lee Petty, his grandfather.

Kyle is now a business administration student at Ashboro Business College in North Carolina.

Last February, just before leaving for Daytona, he was married to a Sofia, N.C., kindergarten teacher and former Winston Cup representative, Patti Huffman, 26. They now live on a 147-acre farm near the Level Cross, N.C., compound where Petty Enterprises turn out those famed red and blue racing cars.

At Riverside in the Warner W. Hodgdon 200 young Petty will drive an all-black STP-Haddick's Pontiac against such talented West Coast drivers as Jimmy Insolo, Tim Williamson, Ron

Bobby Allison: *"I'd been racing at Riverside since 1965 or so; always liked road courses, especially ones with long straights like Riverside had. I had the good fortune to have a local road racing expert give me a few tips – I learned to not over rev and miss shifts. My first win here in '71, was really a thrill, driving for Holman – Moody, battling with Ray Elder, as was my win in '75, leading 175 laps, a tough fight with David Pearson, driving for Roger Penske in the AMC Matador. And being able to run the last race, in 1988, was also a thrill, just because it was the last race at one of my favorite tracks. Didn't do to well as I recall"* Compiler's Note: Bobby had 6 wins at Riverside, a number of top tens and is in the NASCAR Hall of Fame.

Allison races to Golden State win

RIVERSIDE (UPI) — Before Sunday's $80,000 Winston Golden State 400, Nascar veteran Bobby Allison cracked:

"When you're hot, you're hot."

The 33-year-old Hueytown, Ala., driver continued to sizzle in the year's 24th Grand National race, posting his fourth consecutive victory for a first prize of $14,395.

Allison averaged 93.622 miles per hour in his 1970 Dodge in 100-degree weather, leading 136 of the 153 laps in the Winston Golden State event.

The pole sitter with a 107.351 miles per hour qualifying speed, he finished the race in four hours, 17 minutes and five seconds.

"I didn't run as hard as I had to," Allison admitted. "I kept reminding myself during the race that I have to save the car. I knew I could outrun (Richard) Petty. It was just a question of how fast I would have to run."

Petty, the defending champion from Randleman, N.C., and the No. 2 qualifier, wasn't around at the end.

Petty's '71 Plymouth blew an engine on the 114th lap while running four laps behind the leader. The car hit the wall on turn nine. Petty was unhurt.

Ray Caruthers, the racing farmer from Caruthers, Calif., was second on the same lap in a '71 Dodge for $7,695.

Six laps back in third place was Cecil Gordon of Arden, N.C., in a '69 Mercury followed, in order, by James Hylton of Inman, S.C., in a '70 Ford and

Jerry Oliver of Concord, Calif., in a '71 Olds.

The temperature hit 105 degrees during the race and only 10 cars in the field of 40 were running over Riverside's 2.62-mile, eight-turn road course at the end.

Allison used a two-way radio to talk to his pit crew during the race.

"The radio really helped me," the driver said. "At one time my pit crew warned me about a crash ahead of me. If I hadn't known about the crash coming up, I might have run into it."

The NASCAR Grand National circuit continues at Houston, Tex., Wednesday night with a 150-miler.

MICHELIN X

Ivan Baldwin

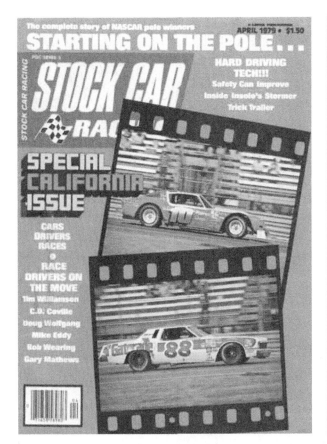
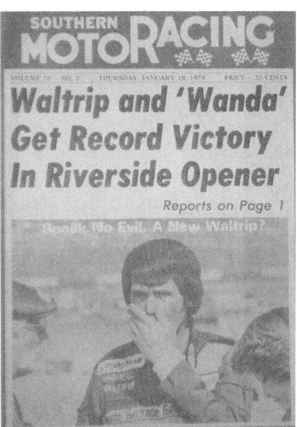

68,000 saw Darrell Waltrip win the Winston Western 500 Winston Cup race in January 1979, collecting $21,150. The threatened rain held off until six laps from the end. David Pearson was second with Cale Yarborough in third.

THEY'RE OFF—Cale Yarborough leads the field of Sunday's Winston Western 500 at the start of the race at Riverside International Raceway. Yarborough, who had won the pole position, finished third behind winner Darrell Waltrip and David Pearson.

Times photo by Mike Meadows

Waltrip records an easy Western 500 victory

By JIM MATTHEWS
Sun Sports Writer

RIVERSIDE — You may find this difficult to believe, but not only did Darrell Waltrip win the $160,000 Winston Western 500 with a record average speed at Riverside International Raceway Sunday, but the race was completed without a yellow flag.

"We've been here so many times," said Waltrip, whose best prior finish at Riverside was a sixth last June. "Last January I spent most of my time out in the mud. I've jumped every fence here. But today everything ran so well. I wish it would have been 500 miles (instead of kilometers) the way the car was running."

Waltrip (driving a Chevrolet Monte Carlo) passed David Pearson on the 105th lap of the 119-lap feature to take the lead for the final time in the rain-threatened race.

Pearson, who had been running strongly all day after qualifying for the pole position in record time, had a chance to challenge Waltrip in the final laps. But a costly 22-second pit stop for fuel and tires 11 laps from the end momentarily dropped him back into third place behind Cale Yarborough.

Pearson made one more pit stop than Waltrip or Yarborough, making the late-race stop a crucial factor. He pitted sooner than the other two drivers earlier in the race and was hoping for a yellow flag.

But the yellow never came. Pearson ended up having to pit under the green and re-entered the course behind Yarborough.

The duel wasn't for the lead anymore, but for second — between Yarborough and Pearson. Pearson won that battle in the middle of Turn 9, going above Yarborough just before both drivers took the white flag.

Pearson finished two seconds ahead of Yarborough.

"When it started raining, I was sure pleased I had that lead," said Waltrip of his winning margin of 32.08 seconds. "Those raindrops kept getting bigger and bigger and I could hear the thunder of that No. 11 car

(Yarborough). I didn't know where he was, but I could hear him.

"Cale and some of the other Chevys have dominated the course, and while we won today, the others — the Mercurys and Fords, did real well," said Waltrip of Pearson's second place finish in a Mercury. "But the Fords normally have to make an extra pit stop over the Chevrolets."

Because of the absence of any yellow caution periods, the extra stop cost Pearson a shot at winning. Pearson wasn't the only driver who didn't have things go his way Sunday.

• Bobby Allison, after running with the top four cars all day, burned a valve on the 105th lap and left the race. He had been leading from the 95th lap when he passed Pearson, and looked to be in the car that would show up in the winner's circle.

(While Allison didn't hold onto his lead, he did gain a sponsor for the grand national season. Allison announced the night before that San Bernardino businessman Warner Hodgdon would fill in where Norris Industries left off.)

• Richard Petty, recovering from stomach surgery, blew an engine after only 14 laps. His quick exit failed to end speculation on whether or not he can run a whole race without being relieved by veteran driver Hershel McGriff.

"The iron broke, I didn't," said Petty. "I'm feeling pretty good and I was going to go as far as I could."

• Yarborough, after leading the first three laps, battled an ill-handling car all day. He was bumped by Petty in Turn 9 and nearly careened into the wall on the same turn a lap later, dropping back to fifth place. He also cut a tire early and struggled with the car.

"This could be the best race I've ever driven because of all the difficulties I faced during the day," said Yarborough after his third-place finish.

"On the third lap I knew we had problems — after that it was catch up all day."

• Jimmy Insolo, last year's Winston West champion, also was with the leaders all day. He was in fourth place when he pulled into the pits with oil pump

(Continued on C-2, column 1)

Vince Giaformaggio spins in front of Cale Yarborough

The spoils of victory

AP Laserphoto

Stock car driver Darrell Waltrip of Franklin, Tenn., gets a double kiss from his wife Stevie, right, and race queen Doshia Wall after his victory in Sunday's Winston Western 500 at Riverside, Calif. Waltrip averaged 107.841 m.p.h. in his Chevrolet in winning the 500-kilometer event, the season opener for the Winston Cup Grand National circuit.

The June 1979 NAPA 400 Winston Cup race, run in 103 degree temperatures, was won by Bobby Allison. Followed by Darrell Waltrip and Richard Petty who relieved Jummy Insolo. Allison collected $22,700 for the win.

Top racing field prepared for prestigious NAPA 400

Yarborough seeks third straight win on Riverside track

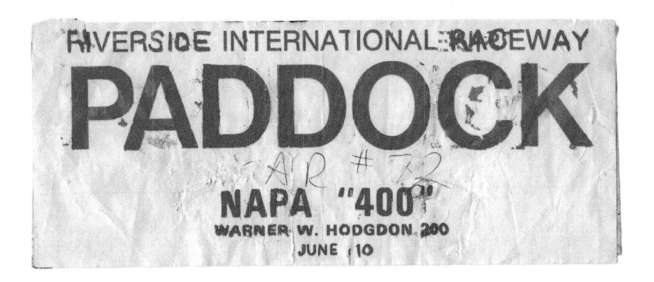

RIVERSIDE INTERNATIONAL RACEWAY
PADDOCK
CAR # 72
NAPA "400"
WARNER W. HODGDON 200
JUNE 10

Allison runs away with 400 win

By JIM SCHULTE
Sun Sports Writer

RIVERSIDE — It was the 10th running of the NAPA 400 at Riverside International Raceway Sunday and the emphasis was on running.

Neil Bonnett ran into a wall. Cale Yarborough ran into tire problems. Dale Earnhardt ran into reality. A car ran into Darrell Waltrip. Darrell Waltrip ran into a car. Everybody, but especially Richard Petty, ran into the blistering heat.

And Bobby Allison easily ran into the winners circle — with the emphasis on easily.

The Hueytown, Ala., driver finished 33 seconds ahead of Waltrip's battered machine, 35 seconds ahead of Petty's car (being driven at the end by Jimmy In-

solo), and 40 seconds ahead of a frustrated Yarborough.

Allison, who started fourth and took over the lead 125 kilometers from the finish when Yarborough and Waltrip had their problems, actually ran into some luck on the way to the win.

"We did pretty well for having no clutch linkage," said the hot, weary Allison. "I got pushed into the dirt by a car I was lapping and that broke the linkage. The crew had to push me to get me started after the last pit stop. But actually the car ran all right without it.

"In all it was a pretty uneventful race for us. It wasn't the coolest day I've ever spent, though."

An understatement of the highest order.

The temperature at the start of the 1 p.m. race was 103 degrees and

climbed to a high of 106. Added to that was a parching Santa Ana wind that swirled dust and blew debris onto the track. It was estimated that the temperature inside the cars was about 130 degrees.

The weather also forced John Borneman's retiring from the race due to heat exhaustion and was the major cause of the prevelent tire problems.

Even Allison, who ran relatively free of trouble all day, started to experience tire problems on his '79 Ford Thunderbird. Fortunately it was near the end of the race.

"I noticed this bad vibration and knew that the tires were going," said Allison, who is sponsored by San Bernardino businessman Warner Hodgdon through his National Engineering Company.

"I figured if I kept going fast

then I could pit and maybe not lose the lead. But if I backed off, then for sure I would lose it," Allison said. He made the right choice.

Yarborough didn't have any choice. He paced the race much of the way, taking over from Waltrip on the eighth of 95 laps. But on the 65th lap, the left rear tire on Yarborough's car suffered a cut from debris on the track. He made a pit stop to change the tire, and was assessed a 30-second penalty for entering the pit area from the back door.

Then a flat tire and the ensuing pit stop 14 laps from the finish robbed him of any chance of catching Allison.

Waltrip, who had been running second most of the race and fig-

(Continued on C-2, column 5)

Bobby Allison waves to crowd after winning NAPA 400.

Staff photo by Goli Fisher

Allison Takes the Heat and 400

Continued from First Page

Insolo was already out of his racing suit and into his street clothes when Ralph Salvino, an STP team official, came running up to him and said the Petty crew wanted him to drive for Richard.

"I got changed back in a real big hurry," said Insolo, a long-time West Coast champion driver who has hungered for a solid chance to drive on the NASCAR Grand National circuit. "I threw my street clothes to someone, I'm not even sure who it was."

The driver change was made in 33 seconds, and when No. 43 returned to the track it was fourth behind Allison, Waltrip and Yarborough. On lap 89, Yarborough went into the dirt at Turn 2 and Insolo passed him for third.

Sunday was a euphoric day for Warner W. Hodgdon, the San Bernardino business tycoon who sponsors both cars and races. His car won the NAPA 400, while his own races —the Warner W. Hodgdon 200 for Grand American cars— had one of the most exciting finishes in recent years at Riverside.

Tim Williamson and Joe Ruttman, turned loose nose-to-tail with 11 laps remaining after a yellow caution flag, put on a pass and re-pass show that had most of the sunburned crowd of 30,000 on its feet cheering.

Ruttman, the younger brother of the 1952 Indianapolis 500 winner, Troy Ruttman, was in front twice during the late stages, but coming to the crest of the hill at Turn 6, three laps from the end, he got his Camaro out of shape and Williamson slipped past. The 23-year-old driver from

The race started with Dale Earnhardt, the rookie pole sitter from Kannapolis, N.C., leading the 35 cars through a single-file snake dance up the esses on the first lap. Barnhardt and Insolo, who started on the front row, were soon caught by Waltrip, the pre-race favorite, who took over the lead on lap 3.

Yarborough, seeking his fourth straight Winston Cup championship, overhauled Waltrip and moved his Busch-sponsored Monte Carlo in front on the eighth lap, acting as if he were going to win his third race of 1979. Each lap he seemed to gain ground on his pursurers, relinquishing the lead for only one lap in 57 while he pitted.

On lap 65, two-thirds of the way through the race, a tire went flat on Yarborough's car. He took a shortcut back to the pits, had the tire changed, but was held in the pits for a 30-second penalty for the shortcut. It was a curious rule that dropped the Timmonsville, S.C., veteran out of the chase.

There is a 30-second penalty if a driver brings a slow car —not up to race speed—around Turn 9 and then into the pits. But there is also a 30-second penalty if a driver slips into the pits from the back road to keep from creeping through Turn 9.

Whatever the situation, the flat tire and the resultant penalty gave the lead to Allison, and for the last 30 laps he was never seriously challenged.

"Bud (Moore) told me on the radio that the tires were worn badly on the insides so I didn't back off," said Allison. "I figured if I had a problem I needed as big a lead as I could have. The last couple of laps I slowed a bit, figuring if I had a serious tire problem I could limp around and still hold my lead."

Bobby Allison

Dale Earnhardt

Neil Bonnett

Terry Labonte

Earnhardt, Insolo, Waltrip and Petty

Dave Hill won the rain delayed January 1980 Stock Car Products 300 Grand American race followed by Ray Elder and Ernie Irvan. The event was marred by the death of last year's winner and Winston West Rookie of the Year, Tim Williamson.

Hill works his way to SCP 300 victory

By JIM SCHULTE
Sun Sports Writer

RIVERSIDE — Just moments before, Dr. David Hill was telling a trackside announcer that "this is the best race of my career. In fact, this is the best day of my life."

He had every reason to be happy. He had just captured the Stock Car Products 300 Grand American race at Riverside International Raceway for his first victory ever.

Now he was standing in an empty corner of the press box, wiping away tears and taking deep breaths, trying to control his emotions.

He had just been told of the death of Tim Williamson, who was fatally injured in a crash on the 10th lap of the race. (See accompanying story)

After several minutes, Hill finally composed himself.

"This is kind of hard . . . I just found out about Timmy," Hill softly said, his voice shaky. "It's just a terrible, terrible tragedy. I just can't believe it happened. He was a real racer and was a super guy. It's making it kind of hard for me to talk right now."

But with Williamson's death still on his mind, Hill went on and talked about his victory.

"I never had a greater day in my life in racing than this. I beat a bunch of great guys. I probably had a lot of luck but it was also a bunch of super hard work by my crew and the guys that put up the dough besides

Williamson's accident). Elder roared back to lead from 18-22.

Then it was Thirkettle's turn at the front for the next seven laps. Insolo retook the lead at 31 and held it until lap 41, when Thirkettle had another go at it. However, he lost the lead back to Elder at lap 56.

Meanwhile, Insolo had fallen victim to broken front shocks and had retired at lap 48.

All through this leapfrogging by the leaders, Hill had hung back in the pack. He weathered a spin and minor collision in Turn 9 on lap 24 and, by lap 50, had worked his way into sixth.

At lap 57, Thirkettle was out of the running, stalling on the course at Turn 5 due to distributor problems.

Three laps later, Hill found himself riding Elder's bumper.

"My car was running real good," noted Hill. "It was starting to miss a little bit right at the end . . . it felt like an ignition thing. But it was plenty strong."

While Hill's 1978 Camaro was having minor difficulties, Elder was experiencing major ones with his '78 Firebird.

Elder's car suddenly seemed slow up and Hill passed him on lap 65.

"I knew he was having troubles," said Hill. "He could run real hard down the back chute but he was having a lot of problems. I think his tires were gone. Riverside's a hard place to pass, especially a driver like Ray.

Despite the relatively easy ending to the victory, Hill said the key to his win was his new pit help.

"I had the Gatorade pit guys and Darrell Waltrip's pit crew helping me out. It's just unbelievable to have a guy like 'crew chief' Buddy Parrot sitting there telling you what to do," Hill said. "You feel like he's in there driving it, he's so smart. I couldn't hear him very well but when he said 'go' I went.

"Buddy in the pits was the only reason I won. There's no doubt about it."

Hill earned $7,450 for the victory. Elder held on for second to pick up $4,900 while Ernie Irvan was third and Ron Esau fourth.

Race notes

The WINSTON WESTERN 500 is set to begin today at 11 a.m. The last 18 spots were filled Saturday in a qualifying session that went on until dark following the SCP 300. Don Whittington, who is being sponsored by San Bernardino businessman Warner Hodgdon and will be running a DiGard car, posted the top time Saturday with a 129.430 mph clocking to start 24th today. His brother Bill, driving former San Bernardino resident D.K. Ulrich's entry, will start 28th after running a 127.769. Rick McCray of Bloomington qualified 30th (127.489). A complete list of the 35 starters can be found in scoreboard, D-2.

In the SCP 300, Joe Ruttman of Upland dropped out with linkage problems after completing 16 laps. He had started 9th. Bill Rothen of Rialto completed 37 laps before retiring. Official results for Alan Brown of San Bernardino and Greg Scheidecker of Highland were unavailable by press time and will be published in Monday's sports section. They were both still running at the end of the race but did not finish in the top 10.

Dave Hill and Ray Elder; entering turn six

Williamson, 23, killed in wreck at Riverside

By JIM SCHULTE
Sun Sports Writer

RIVERSIDE — The good die young.

That's how the ancient Greeks tried to explain away the unexplainable — the death of someone in his prime, the death of someone who had the best still ahead of him.

At 23, Tim Williamson was just entering his prime . . . he was already good at what he did . . . nothing but the best was expected of him.

But he will never fulfill those promises.

Tim Williamson died Saturday from injuries suffered after his 1977 Camaro crashed during the

running of the Stock Car Products 300 at Riverside Raceway.

The accident occured on lap 10 of the rain-delayed race. Williamson, who started fourth in the 46-car field, was running third at the time and charging hard.

Entering the esses, Williamson attempted to get around Glen Steurer, but Steurer closed the gap on the Seaside resident. The nose of Williamson's machine bumped the rear of Steurer's '79 Camaro, forcing Williamson to back off.

Williamson then went off the track slightly at Turn 3. However, he was able to get back onto the pave-

ment. He was entering Turn 4 normally when he again got off the track and into the mud that bordered the course.

Williamson suddenly lost control. The car skidded off the track into the infield at Turn 5 and hit the retaining wall. The car rebounded off that wall and started to spin. It crossed the track and then, sliding backwards, slammed broadside into the wall approaching Turn 6.

"It looked like he hit the wall at full speed," said Ray Elder, who was running right behind Williamson at the time of the crash.

The impact was so violent it ripped away all the

sheet metal from the passenger side of the car and blew out all the glass. The car ended up partially on the track after bouncing off the wall.

Trackside medical personnel got Williamson out and administered mouth-to-mouth resuscitation before placing him in an ambulance and taking him to Riverside Community Hospital.

Williamson, who was unmarried, was pronounced dead on arrival. Survivors include his parents and a brother. His parents were at the track Saturday watching the race. His brother was also at Riverside.

(Continued on D-8, column 1)

The June 1980 Sharon Hodgdon 200 Grand American race was won by Ron Esau, followed by Roy Smith and Ray Elder.

ESAU FINALLY GETS A VICTORY
From a Times Staff Writer

RIVERSIDE—Ron Esau is only 25 but he has been coming to Riverside International Raceway from San Diego since he was 17 in quest of a stock car win.

He had been second several times, third and fourth but never first. Sunday he made it .

Esau drove his 1980 Camaro to victory in the Sharon Hodgdon 200, a race for Grand American cars as a preliminary to the Winston Cup Grand National race. He finished five seconds ahead of Roy Smith of Canada with veteran Ray Elder of Caruthers and Kevin Riniker of Riverside the only other cars on the same lap.

Pole-sitter Joe Ruttman, who led the early going, pulled off the course with mechanical problems while leading on the twelfth lap. Esau took over and led all but nine remaining laps of the 48-lap race.

Car driven by Paul Carrara of La Habra spins out in dirt on Turn 5 during Sharon Hodgdon 200.

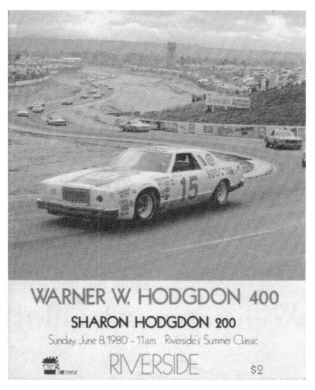

WARNER W. HODGDON 400
SHARON HODGDON 200
Sunday, June 8, 1980 - 11 am   Riverside's Summer Classic
RIVERSIDE $2

In the rain delayed January 1980 Winston Western 500 Winston Cup race the race started on January 13th and finished a week later), Pole sitter Darrell Waltrip won for the second straight time (and his third win at Riverside), followed by Dale Earnhardt and Richard Petty. 22,000 fans came back to see Waltrip collect $24,700 for the win.

Winston Western 500 postponed by rain

By MIKE KAPUSTA
Daily Press Sports Editor

RIVERSIDE — The 1980 NASCAR season got off to a less-than attractive start this weekend as Saturday's Stock Car Products 500 was marred by a fatal accident, and Sunday's Winston Western 500 was rained out, here at the Riverside International Raceway.

On lap 10 of Saturday's race, rookie sensation Tim Williamson of Seaside Calif. was attempting to pass Glen Steurer through Turn Six, but went off the track and ran into the wall, suffering fatal injuries.

Sunday's race was already shadowed by the black cloud of the accident from the day before, plus had the additional drawback of the storm front that had moved into the area overnight.

The entire infield at the racetrack was the same consistency as chocolate pudding, and the track was wet from the rainfall to add to the hazardous conditions.

It took four hours of futile attempts at drying the track

before RIR officials finally announced that the race would be postponed until Saturday — weather permitting.

At 1:15, two-and-one-half hours after the race was to begin, the drivers started around the track for warm-up laps, with the race officially starting at 1:30.

They managed to get in 24 laps before rain started to again fall at turn eight, forcing the postponement.

"It doesn't look too bad right here in Riverside," said pole sitter Darrell Waltrip from the start-finish line. "But it's starting to rain there in Redlands, near Turn Eight," he joked.

All 24 of the laps were run under the green-yellow flag, meaning that they counted toward the 119-lap total, but there was no actual racing as the laps were run under yellow-flag conditions.

At 1 p.m., Waltrip admitted that the race wouldn't be run Sunday, and commented that he wished they could have quickly made the official announcement and let the fans and drivers go home for the week.

"I just wish they could hurry and make a decision," said an anxious Waltrip. "It's just a shame to have all these fans wait all day, to go through all this trying to dry off the track, just to have it all cancelled in the long run."

Waltrip commented that he was quite impressed with the fans that did show up to the race, although it was a much smaller crowd than the event drew the year before.

"They've got a helluva crowd here for it to be raining," Waltrip said from the pits, looking up at the one-third full main grandstand. "It's great to see these fans that have stuck it out here (pointing at the stands) and there's a lot of people down yonder (referring to the Turn Six grandstand)."

Waltrip, and second position sitter Cale Yarborough took a lap in a street car to check out the track conditions, and both were leary that the race would be run Sunday.

"Hell it'll be three hours before the track would dry now, even if it doesn't rain," said Yarborough at 12:36. "We've got to get something decided before two if we're going to run this race at all."

Throughout the entire morning volunteers with their personal cars ran laps around the racecourse trying to dry the track by spreading the water thinner, and forcing evaporation by the friction.

A helicopter also flew over the course, setting down on especially wet portions, in a vain attempt to get the track race ready.

"I'd just like to get back to my motel and sit in front of the TV...maybe have a Gatorade," joked Waltrip, who is sponsored by the same beverage company, after the postponement.

The race has been re-scheduled for Saturday, Jan. 19, with an 11 a.m. starting time.

The starting grid will remain the same, although they will be starting the race on lap 25, "under the green flag," promised an RIR official.

All tickets from yesterday's race will be accepted for the Saturday run, and tickets will be on sale at the gates for those who still wish to see the opener of the 1980 NASCAR season.

Gurney Gets the Cheers; Waltrip Gets the Win

By SHAV GLICK
Times Staff Writer

RIVERSIDE—The Big Kid from Newport Beach (he'd be 49 in April) looked like he'd just been given a electric train for Christmas. The train broke down while he was having fun but the disappointment couldn't wipe the smile off Dan Gurney's face.

For 75 laps Saturday, from the cheers of the modest sized crowd, you'd have thought Gurney—out of retirement after almost 10 years—was driving the only car on the track. As the white No. 88 with the blue trim moved up from seventh to third place in the Winston Western 500 at Riverside International Raceway, the opening race of the 31-million Winston Cup series seemed more a showcase for Gurney than a battle among the world's fastest stock car drivers.

Then abruptly it ended. Gurney left the gear box gurgling as his Monte Carlo crossed the start-finish line on lap 79 and he coasted to a stop in the dirt apron off Turn 6—right

the dirt between the third and fourth turns to make the pass.

Earnhardt, 1979's NASCAR Rookie of the Year and the surprise pole sitter here for last June's NAPA 400, came back later in the race to briefly challenge Waltrip for the lead.

Earnhardt finished second, 2.91 seconds back, with Petty third, Millican fourth and Sehnack, the Winston West champion from the Banning, fifth. All were on the same lap with Waltrip when the race ended—30 seconds shy of six days. Realistically, the 500 kilometers took 3 hours 36 minutes 58 seconds for a 94.974 m.p.h. average.

Waltrip collected a track record $24,600 and the point lead in the first of the 1980 31-race season.

"This is an awful good way to start off a year," said Waltrip, who lost by a paltry 21 points out of more than 15,000 last year. "We won the pole and we won the race and that has to give the crew, the owners, the engine man and the driver a big boost for the Daytona 500. Our team

has enjoyed a whole lot since last November. I think we've profited by our experiences, the good times and the bad ones. This is a new year and there's no better way to start than by winning.

Waltrip said he had two close calls during the 500 kilometers, both coming out of high-speed Turn 9.

"The first time the No. 2 car (Dave Marcis) was heading for the pits and I came off nine pretty hard and we made a little contact. The next time it was kinda the same situation; I don't know who it was but it seemed I was running through nine a lot harder than anyone else so when they cut into the pits I was running up their back. My car was so stable I had no trouble running so hard so I had in each other on the track."

During mid-race, Yarborough seemed to have the strongest car on the track. He led for 31 laps and had only Waltrip to contend with when his car's ignition system went on the blink around lap 98.

Waltrip inherited the lead at this point and except for

one lap when he pitted and permitted Petty to take the lead, Waltrip was in command. Petty's last chance was lost when he had to pit for fuel and two tires only 12 laps from the end. This permitted Waltrip the luxury of stopping for a touch of gasoline without losing the lead.

"I thought I had plenty of room to spare when I stopped," Waltrip said, "and all of a sudden the crew just ran about the No. 3 car (Earnhardt). I hadn't noticed him; I thought all we had to beat was Petty. I found out I could pull him through nine and down the backstretch so I just stopped worrying."

Waltrip's win from the pole was only the third time it had happened in 10 winter races here. Bobby Allison did it in 1975 and Gurney in 1968.

Gurney in 1968 didn't do it but it was the former Riverside Junior College student who became America's most popular driver in the 60s and made the race a memorable affair. After such a fine showing, is Gurney going to continue his comeback?

"No, I'm not going to do it again," he said. "Not unless I change my mind again, anyway."

Any bets?

Buddy Arrington and Richard Childress

Darrell Waltrip

Dan Gurney

Waltrip, Yarborough and Petty

Darrell Waltrip also won the June 1980 Warner Hodgdon 400 Winston Cup race followed by Neil Bonnett and Benny Parsons. Waltrip collected $22,100 for the win.

Waltrip Wins, but It Was Touch and Go

Darrell Squeezes Past Bonnett on Last Turn of Last Lap for Riverside Victory

Staff photo by Tom Kasser

Darrell Waltrip leads Warner Hodgdon 400 field through Turn 8. Waltrip edged Neil Bonnett at the finish to win.

There were three Grand American races in 1981, January, June and November. The November race was the result of the closing of Ontario Motor Speedway. In January, Joe Ruttman won the Warner Hodgdon 300, followed by Jim Neal and Dave Hill. In June, the Sharon Hodgdon 200 was won by Herschel McGriff. Second was Duke Hoenshell with Don Noel in third. In November, Glen Steuer won followed by Jim Neal and Rod Hetrick.

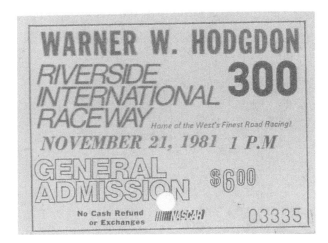

Steurer Winner in 300

From a Times Staff Writer

RIVERSIDE—Glen Steurer of Simi Valley Thwarted Hershel McGriff's bid for a record ninth win at Riverside International Raceway Saturday by winning the Warner W. Hodgdon 300.

McGriff, 53-year-old veteran from Bridal Veil, Ore., led three Times in the 72-lap race for Grand American cars but finished seventh when his Camaro quit running seven laps from the end. He had won eight times before at Riverside, a record he shares with Dan Gurney.

Steurer, 26, came out of retirement only a month ago after two years inactivity. He won the Black Gold 150 here in June 1977. His Camaro averaged 103.759 m.p.h. for the 300 kilometers and was a lap and seven seconds ahead of runnerup Jim Neal of Huntington Beach.

McGriff continues success

RIVERSIDE (AP) — Hershel McGriff's success in races at Riverside International Raceway continued Sunday as he drove a 1980 Camaro to victory in the Sharon Hodgdon 200 kilometer NASCAR race for Grand American cars.

McGriff, a veteran driver from Bridal Veil, Ore., who won the 1950 Mexican Road Race, captured his eighth event at Riverside to tie Dan Gurney for the career lead in victories at the 2.62-mile road course opened 25 years ago.

McGriff averaged 101.533 miles per hour to win the 48 lap race by 47 seconds over Duke Hoenshell of Orange, who drove an 81 Camaro.

The winner started on the pole in the preliminary to the Warner W. Hodgdon 400 kilometer race for grand national

stock cars later in the day. In the major race, McGriff's 1981 Buick went out with engine trouble after 52 laps and he finished 25th of 36 starters.

In the 200 kilometer event, McGriff led 18 of the first 19 laps, but he had to slow down for most of the 20th lap because of worn tires. After his pit stop he did not regain the lead until the 32nd lap.

Don Noel of Northridge, driving a 1978 Firebird, finished third, followed by Chuck Phillippi of Santa Fe Springs in a 1981 Camaro and Richard White of Escondido in a 1980 Camaro. The top five were the only drivers in the field of 35 to complete 48 laps.

(Hodgdon 200 RESULTS, B-4)

At 11 a.m. Sunday

Grand Am cars to duel in Sharon Hodgdon 200

At 11 a.m. this Sunday, the top stock-car drivers of the West compete in the Sharon Hodgdon 200 NASCAR Grand American race at Riverside International Raceway.

The Sharon Hodgdon 200 is a preliminary to the Warner W. Hodgdon 400 NASCAR Cup feature. In four years there have been four winners of the 200. Jimmy Insolo, Hershel McGriff, the late Tim Williamson and Joe Ruttman.

McGriff returns to rank as the favorite in the $30,000 race on Riverside's 2.62-mile, 9-turn course.

Among the other leading drivers entered are Russ Haus of Lakeside, former champ from Cajon Speedway; Ruben Garcia of San Dimas, Duke Hoenshell of Orange, Gary Meade of Riverside, "Bonnie"

Steve Beuck of Los Alamitos; Dale Perry of Riverside, Greg Scheidecker of Highland, Carl Wayne Smith of Bakersfield, Robert Switzer of Chatsworth, Richard White of Rosamead, and John Wilson of La Puente.

Grand American stock cars are 1966-1981 American-manufactured sedans in the intermediate and compact classes. They have a 108-inch wheelbase and weigh 3,100 pounds. With a 430-cubic inch maximum piston displacement for engine size and body modifications permitted, they are the fastest stock cars ever to run at Riverside.

The all-time stock car speed record at Riverside is 117.565 m.p.h. by Jimmy Insolo in a '77 Camaro in the Sharon Tran in Race 11. Cal 4

Robert Switzer (51) and Roy Smith (11) seen to avoid collision during NASCAR action at Riverside.

Don Noel

Joe Ruttman

1981 marked the first time NASCAR held three Winston Cup races at Riverside; the January Winston Western 500, the June Warner Hodgdon 400 and another Winston Western 500 in November, replacing a date previously held at Ontario.

35,000 spectators saw Bobby Allison win the January 1981 race in a Rainier Racing Monte Carlo after an hour and a half rain delay. This was the last time a race other than Daytona would kick off the season. Terry Labonte was second and Dale Earnhardt third. Pole qualifier Darrell Waltrip ended up in seventeenth.

Associated Press Laserphoto

Rain doesn't bother Allison; wins Winston Western 500

RIVERSIDE, Calif. (AP) — Bobby Allison didn't let anything bother him.

The rain was a nuisance and starting at the back of the pack because of a last-minute mechanical problem was unnerving, but the veteran stock car racer just went after the car in front of him.

Eventually, there was nobody else to pick off, and Allison had a victory in the Winston Western 500 Grand National race Sunday at Riverside International Raceway.

"It's unpleasant and uncomfortable to be in the situation of starting at the back, especially when you have a lot of car under you," explained the 43-year-old from Hueytown, Ala. "But it's not disastrous.

"I've been there before. I started 33rd at Daytona (last July) and won. It's not the ideal situation, but you just live with it."

Morning rains delayed the start of the race for 1 hour and 28 minutes. In fact, the cars ran 16 uncounted laps under a caution flag in an effort to dry out the soaked 2.62-mile course.

He was among a handful of drivers who ducked into the pits for adjustments or more fuel before the green flag dropped.

"I just had a little mechanical problem and I had to have the guys take care of it," Allison explained. "It was a situation where we made a change after practice ended and didn't have a chance to try it out until just before the race started.

"We were probably lucky we had to chance to do it the way we did. But I had to play catch-up, catch-up, catch-up early in the race."

Allison, who now has won 59 NASCAR races, made his way steadily through the stretched-out field, moving into first place on the 52nd lap.

He then battled a pair of 24-year-old youngsters, first Ricky Rudd, then Terry Labonte, for the lead most of the way.

Rudd, who never has won a NASCAR race, fell by the wayside on lap 98 when he blew an engine, bringing out the last of six caution flags in the race.

Labonte, winner of one race, took the lead during the caution period, but watched helplessly as Allison sped

Richard and Kyle swapped rides

WINSTON WESTERN 500 WEEKEND
SATURDAY AND SUNDAY, JANUARY 10 & 11 RIVERSIDE INTERNATIONAL RACEWAY

Winston Western 500: first race of the season
1981 NASCAR circuit opens with swan song for behemoth stock cars

The first race for NASCAR's new down-sized racing stock cars will also be the swan song for the behemoths of the speedways as Riverside International Raceway opens the 1981 season with the Winston Western 500 on Sunday.

In the first major technical change for race cars since the advent of carburetor plates, NASCAR will introduce the new smaller model American stock cars to competition, and many of the major teams are expected to bring their new equipment to Riverside.

The down-sizing is from 115-inch to 110-inch wheelbase cars, reflecting the change in character of the

American stock cars on the highways. However, for the final time ever in NASCAR Winston Cup competition, owners of Chevrolet Monte Carlos, Oldsmobile 442s, Ford Thunderbirds, Dodge Magnums and Mercury Cougars will be in action on the 2.62-mile, 8-turn road course.

Also new will be the NASCAR team alignments that show two-time 500 winner Darrell Waltrip switching to the Junior Johnson team, Kyle Petty now a full-time STP team campaigner on the Winston Cup trail, Ricky Rudd now driving for DiGard Gatorade, and other driver shifts affecting Cale Yarborough, Benny Parsons, Bobby Allison, David Pearson and Buddy Baker.

The Winston Western 500 purse, now in excess of $175,000, will also lure the strong contingent of NASCAR Winston West drivers, whose championship was expected to be decided in Phoenix a week after the Los Angeles Times 500 at Ontario Motor Speedway.

Four drivers who battled down to the wire, Winston West champion Roy Smith of Victoria, B.C., Canada, Bill Schmitt of Redding, Jim Robinson of Sylmar and Rick McCray of Bloomington, can be counted on to challenge the Eastern contingent on the tricky road course that has frustrated so many top NASCAR drivers for so many years.

Please Turn to Page 10, Col. 1

NASCAR champion Richard Petty (43) of Randleman, N.C., is hotly pursued, at left, by Bill Schmitt (73) of Redding, Calif., and others in the scramble for the lead. The Winston Western 500, the '81 season opener, will feature the final race of these behemoths with the first race of the new smaller cars on Sunday at Riverside International Raceway. Top contenders for the Winston Western 500 are pictured below.

| Neil Bonnett | Bobby Allison | Richard Petty | Benny Parsons | Bill Schmitt | Darrell Waltrip | Dale Earnhardt | Elliot Forbes-Robinson |

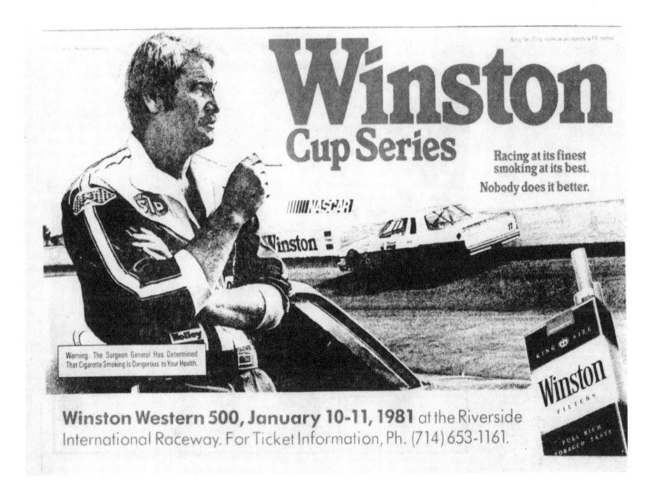

SOUTHERN MOTORACING

VOLUME 18 – NO. 2   THURSDAY, JAN. 22, 1981   PRICE 50 CENT

Allison Is Winner, Nosing Out Labonte In Riverside Opener

Report on Page 1

Neil Bonnett leads Bobby Allison into turn eight

Darrell Waltrip leads into turn six

In the June 1981 Winston Cup race, the Warner Hodgdon 400, Darrell Waltrip won $23,650, followed by Dale Earnhardt and Richard Petty,

JAYNE KAMIN / Los Angeles Times

Mechanic—NASCAR driver Kyle Petty does some close-in tuning on his Buick for Warner Hodgdon 400 at Riverside Raceway. Petty qualified 13th.

Darrell Waltrip celebrates win in Hodgdon 400

...the pole sitter didn't take lead for good until next-to-last lap

Veteran driver wins Hodgdon 400

Waltrip does it the hard way

RIVERSIDE (AP) — "Every year I have to do it the hard way," Darrell Waltrip said after he survived a flat tire with 13 laps remaining, and came from third place in the next-to-last lap to win the Warner W. Hodgdon NASCAR stock car race Sunday.

Dale Earnhardt had taken the lead away from Richard Petty with 2¾ laps remaining at Riverside International Raceway, but Waltrip passed both of them in the next lap and easily

trip said of the furious finishing laps.

"I've got a real chance now to go for the championship the last half of the season," said Waltrip, who trails points leader Bobby Allison by 232 points with 15 races remaining. Allison went out early Sunday with a blown engine.

Allison has 2,332 points, Rudd is second at 2,139 and Waltrip remained in third with 2,100 as he gained 109 points on the leader Sunday

Earnhardt, the 1980 NASCAR de-

then Petty to take the lead with 2¾ laps to go.

But Waltrip had even more car left for the closing rush. He was the race qualifying leader on Friday with a 114.419 mile per hour average, almost one second per lap faster than runner-up Earnhardt in qualifying, and Waltrip went past Petty early in the next-to-last lap and then caught and passed Earnhardt just before the final

left-hand turns of most NASCAR tracks.

Waltrip averaged 98.103 mph in a race slowed by six caution flags, and won by six-tenths of a second.

The NASCAR points leader, Bobby Allison, dropped out with a blown engine after 27 laps. Waltrip, winning his fifth race of the year compared to three for Allison, won $23,400 but more importantly gained ground in the Win-

Ricky Rudd ahead of Richard Petty and Benny Parsons

The Road to Glory

Pole-sitter Darrell Waltrip leads the field through Turn 6 at Riverside after the start of the Warner Hodgdon 400 Sunday and a little later celebrates victory in the winner's circle. With Waltrip are, from left, wife Stevie, Sharon Hodgdon and her sons, Aaron and Justin, and California Lieutenant Governor Mike Curb.

RANDY MCBRIDE / Los Angeles Times

Tim Richmond

Ricky Rudd

Most Riverside Winston West races were run as part of the Winston Cup events. There were a few exceptions; In August 1981, NASCAR held a stand alone Winston West race, the Warner Hodgdon 200 as a supporting event to the L.A, Times 500 Indy car race. Roy Smith won, followed by John Borneman Jr. and Bill Schmitt.

NASCAR Winston West is war on wheels

Traditionally, the NASCAR Winston West stock car series is wheel-to-wheel war. And 1981 is no different.

One of the more decisive battles will be fought Sunday, Aug. 30 at Riverside in the $34,025 Warner Hodgdon 200K, companion feature to the Times/California 500.

Currently, North Hollywood's Jim Robinson leads defending Winston West champion Roy Smith by 16 points, 498-482. Rookie Jim Bown, of Portland, Ore., is third with 447.

Robinson, driving the Hammer Security/Del Ray Builders Oldsmobile, increased his point lead over Smith by scoring his third win of the season Aug. 8 at Shasta Speedway in Anderson, Calif. edging Bown by six seconds.

Smith also has three 1981 wins and continues to lead in money won, with $29,150 to Robinson's $27,295. In 1980, Smith, from Victoria, B.C., became the first Canadian driver to win a national championship when he edged Bill Schmitt, of Redding, Calif., by eight points. Robinson finished third in 1980.

Bown, driving a Buick for Rose Auto Wrecking, has a substantial lead in the Reed Cams Winston West Rookie-of-the-Year race, leading Gene Thonesen of Reedley, Ca., by 10 points. (19-9).

Robinson and Smith have had mixed success on Riverside's road course in 1981. At the January Winston Western 500, Robinson finished sixth and Smith eighth. In June, Smith finished eighth in the Warner Hodgdon 400, with Robinson tenth.

Smith Nearly Stuck in Pits

He Loses Lead on Long Stop but Wins Hodgdon 200

By BILL DWYRE, *Times Sports Editor*

RIVERSIDE—To the auto racing purist, Sunday's Warner Hodgdon 200 was a little like being handed an all-expense paid trip to LeMans.

The 125.76-mile race (202 kilometers), a stock car preliminary to the Los Angeles Times/California 500 Indy car race, had the kind of finish that interests even those who buy tickets to root for wrecks.

The winner was Roy Smith, a onetime sprint-car driver from Victoria, Canada, who has made the shift to stock cars on the NASCAR Winston West circuit with a flair that showed up well on the closing laps here Sunday.

Smith led for most of the race, after taking over from pole-sitter Hershel McGriff on lap 10 of the 48-lap race. But on lap 39, during a yellow caution flag caused when Jim Robinson spun out, Smith dashed into the pits for a quick change of his left-side tires and immediately ran into problems.

The automatic wrench that turns the lug nuts tight on the wheels failed to operate and by the time a backup wrench could be located, a 15-second pit stop had turned into a 40-second disaster.

Schmitt Takes Lead

While Smith fidgeted in his driver's seat, John Borneman of Lakeside, Bill Schmitt of Redding and Garry Johnson of Modesto flashed past, leaving Smith in fourth position by the time he got back onto the track. In fact, including a couple of slower cars not on the same lap, there were six cars between Smith and leader Borneman. And he had just eight laps left in the race to catch up.

But shortly, Schmitt took the lead from Borneman

still anybody's."

Not really. Smith was just too fast and too powerful in his 1981 Buick, although his winning margin was a mere 1.28 seconds.

"I felt that, if I could keep him within two or three lengths going into the eighth turn on the last lap, I might have a shot at him," Borneman said. "But with the amount of power he had all day, once he got away from me there, all I could hope for was that he made a mistake in 9 (last turn before the start/finish line). He just had me. He had the horsepower."

Smith also had a car that was four years newer than Borneman's, a fact that made Borneman's strong second-place finish even more noteworthy.

Borneman was in the race field only through a special invitation, extended by promoters when there was a need to fill out the field. According to NASCAR rules, established in June, the Winston circuit can include only 1981 model cars.

Smith Takes Point Lead

Borneman, who owns three older cars and runs without a sponsor, was out of luck when the rule was announced and gets into races now with special dispensation only. His second-place finish Sunday was achieved in a '77 Pontiac Ventura (even older than the '79 Pontiac listed incorrectly on the program as his car).

"I've got $75,000 invested in my three cars, and I just can't afford to start over," Borneman said. "I've been invited to a race in Phoenix, but unless something happens, this race today is pretty much it for me."

172

The November 1981 Winston Cup race, another Winston Western 500, was won by Bobby Allison, his eighth win at Riverside. Second was Joe Ruttman with Terry Labonte in third. Allison earned $24,300 and Darrell Waltrip won the championship.

RIVERSIDE: Allison Wins Race but Loses Out to Waltrip

Waltrip cinches Winston Cup

Examiner news services

Like a teenager out for a Sunday drive with his dad, Darrell Waltrip kept revving up the car and Junior Johnson kept telling him to take it easy.

"I felt like I could have won," Waltrip said, "but every time I started to running pretty good, Junior would say, 'Hey, you take care of that car, boy.'"

The strategy didn't win yesterday's Winston Western 500 at Riverside for Waltrip and the Johnson Team Buick, but it did give Waltrip a bigger prize — the 1981 Winston Cup points championship.

Bobby Allison won the stock car race at Riverside International Raceway, edging Joe Ruttman by a mere .24 of a second. But Waltrip, who finished sixth, did what he had to do to beat Allison for the points title.

The points championship was the first for Waltrip, 34, who finished the 31-race series with 4,880 points to Allison's 4,827.

Allison averaged 95.288 mph for 119 laps over the 2.62-mile Riverside road course. The time for the 500-kilometer, 311.98-mile race was 3 hours, 27 minutes, 19.44 seconds, as seven caution flags slowed it up.

173

Miss Winston

Kyle and Richard

No more January races as NASCAR wanted Daytona and Speed Weeks to be the opening events – The June 1982 Budweiser 400 Winston Cup race and $21,530 in prize money was won by Tim Richmond in front of a crowd of 45,000. Terry Labonte was second followed by Geoff Bodine.

Richmond gets his luck on track, wins Bud 400

By JIM SCHULTE
Sun Sports Writer

RIVERSIDE — Tim Richmond says he has no complaints about his luck, at least off the race track.

But it has occurred to him more than once that when he most needs a bit of that elusive commodity on his side — such as when he's competing in a race — that's when fortune has been positively loathe to step in.

Sunday, though, luck finally answered Richmond's call and stepped in. Jumped in, actually. With both feet. And they landed squarely on the back of any unfortunate who happened to be in the way.

In this case it was several members of a storied field of NASCAR Grand National drivers who dared covet a victory in the Budweiser 400 at Riverside International Raceway, but ended up sidelined by mechanical problems.

Richmond, riding high on the unexpected bonanza of good fortune, simply bided his time and allowed events to be worked in mysterious ways.

When it was all over, it was Richmond taking the checkered flag by a mere 3.82 seconds and handing yet another bouquet to the growing collection belonging to

NASCAR bridesmaid Terry Labonte. Labonte ended up with his fifth second-place finish in 14 races this year against zero wins.

A surprising third was Geoff Bodine, followed by Dale Earnhardt and Neil Bonnett. The rest of the top 10 was hardly a rollcall of NASCAR greats — Roy Smith, Jody Ridley, Mark Martin, Ron Bouchard and Jim Reich. But it was that kind of a race — unusually exciting and fraught with the unusual.

The victory gave Richmond his first-ever Grand National victory, $20,000 in mad money and a noticeable high.

"Damn, I really won that doggie," Richmond muttered to himself afterwards. "How 'bout that! How 'bout that!"

Later, after he calmed down a bit, Richmond said, "I'm high on the win," but added that his immediate "thought right now is 'Lets get the next one.'"

Tough talk, but even he admitted he barely got this one.

"Yeah, we got lucky, really," he said. "I tell you, my luck is so tremendous off the track it's amazing. On the track today, it worked well. But in the past, it was not been

(Please see Richmond, C-4)

Tim Richmond lets the world know how happy he is to have wo[n] Budweiser 400 at Riverside Raceway Sunday as he climbs out of hi[s] car in victory circle.

Benny Parsons and Tim Richmond

Dave Marcis is pulled from his car after crashing into Turn 6 wall on 31st lap of Budweiser 400 at Riverside Raceway. He wasn't seriously hurt.

Randy Becker

Bill Elliott

Ricky Rudd

Neil Bonnett

Dale Earnhardt / Lake Speed

Bill Schmitt

In August 1982, another standalone Winston West race, the Warner Hodgdon 200, was held a as a support event to the Air Cal 500 Indy car event. Rick McCray won, followed by Jim Bown and Roy mith.

Winston West stock car drivers to mix in Warner Hodgdon 200

The NASCAR Winston West stock cars will return to Riverside International Raceway at 10:30 a.m. Sunday, Aug. 29 during the AirCal 500 weekend.

A starting field of the West Coast's fastest stock car drivers will compete in the Warner Hodgdon 200K doing 48 laps on Riverside's demanding 2.62-mile road course.

To date, the race for the 1982 Winston West championship has been a tight contest between rookie Jim Reich, who has driven his Baldwin Engineering Chevy to one race victory and 335 points. He is only a point ahead of Jim Brown of Portland, Ore. Brown, last season's Winston West rookie of the year, has two race victories in 1982, with two races remaining prior to the Hodgdon race at Riverside.

Third place in the standings is held by Sylmar's Jim Robinson.

Last year, Robinson lost the Winston West championship by 19 points to Roy Smith from Victoria, British Columbia. Smith, twice the series champion, is in fourth place, three points ahead of veteran Don Waterman, also of Portland, Ore.

Also racing will be Hershel McGriff. McGriff, a veteran of five decades of NASCAR racing and winner of the most races ever at Riverside, currently holds 13th place in the standings.

Another young driver to watch, Ron Eaton has entered only four races — but he won two of them. His 185 points place him 14th in the Winston West standings.

Other entries to watch in the 125.76-mile race are Bill Schmitt of Redding, a two-time Winston West champion and the leader

Please see WINSTON, page 2

McCray wins Warner Hodgdon 200

RIVERSIDE (AP) — Rick McCray, from nearby Bloomington, Calif., streaked to his second straight NASCAR Winston West stock car victory, winning Sunday's Warner Hodgdon 200 at Riverside International Raceway.

The November 1982 Winston Western 500 Winston Cup race was won by Tim Richmond, collecting $24,730. Second was Ricky Rudd followed by Darrell Waltrip in third. Waltrip's third place secured his second NASCAR championship..

Richmond wins Western 500, while Waltrip is NASCAR champ

RIVERSIDE (AP) — Tim Richmond raced to a solid victory Sunday in the Winston Western 500 Grand National stock car race, but it was Darrell Waltrip who took home the biggest laurels in the form of his second straight Winston Cup season championship.

While Richmond was running off to a big lead, Waltrip was able to nurse an ailing gearbox through more than half the race and finish third, giving him the decision in the much-ballyhooed title race with hard-luck Bobby Allison.

Allison, who lost a big point lead earlier this season because of a series of broken engines and other mechanical problems, this time was knocked off the pace by two flat tires and a spin, then finally retired for the day by a blown engine with just eight laps remaining.

That left the 44-year-old from Hueytown, Ala., without a championship in 18 years of Grand National racing. Meanwhile, the 35-year-old Waltrip, a resident of Franklin, Tenn., shut off Allison's title chances in this race for the second straight season after entering the race just 22 points ahead.

"We squared off at one point early in the race, and that's when Bobby had his tire trouble," Waltrip said. "We knew he was going to run hard and try to win, and the idea was just to lead the first lap, get that out of the way (and take the five points for leading a lap), then just stay with him.

"After he had his problems, I really didn't know where he was. I didn't really know I had it sewed up until they (his crew) told me when I came in at the end. I thought he was still out there."

Looking at the hard-earned second championship, Waltrip said: "I believe this one is actually sweeter for everybody on our team because we were in the limelight all year and had to produce. This will give everybody on the team a lot of pride and good feelings."

Richmond, 27 and in his second year of Grand National racing, was elated with his second victory of the season on Riverside International Raceway's 2.6-mile circuit, the only road course in Grand National racing.

"Winning the June race applied a lot to this one," Richmond explained. "That (first victory) told us to actually race the track and let the car determine where we run. And we were able to keep the car in the first spot most of the race without abusing it."

Waltrip, driving the Buick Regal owned by Junior Johnson and sponsored by Mountain Dew, clinched the second title of his career by 72 points. Allison's engine quit just seven laps from the end, while he was running fifth, a lap behind the leaders. He wound up 16th.

Ricky Rudd was second, 7.85-seconds behind Richmond. Neil Bonnett, who was running a strong second, fell off the pace with a flat tire just eight laps from the end, but came back to finish fourth.

Richmond, the 1980 Indianapolis 500 Rookie of the Year, drove a Jim Stacy Buick, sponsored by Stacy-Pak, to an average speed of 99.823 mph. The youngster will drive for the new team started by drag racer Raymond Beadle next season.

Terry Labonte, who finished a distant third in the season point race, was injured in a crash just 24 laps from the end of the race. It appeared the brakes in his Buick failed as he headed down the long backstretch into the sweeping ninth turn.

The car slammed hard into the metal railing and the 27-year-old driver had to be pried from the battered car.

(Winston Western RESULTS, Page C-5)

Waltrip takes second national crown

RIVERSIDE (AP) — Tim Richmond was excited about his second victory in Grand National stock car racing, but he deferred to Darrell Waltrip, the man who finished third and wrapped up a second straight Winston Cup national championship.

"I won the race, but it's Darrell's day," Richmond said after he ran off to an easy triumph in the Winston Western 500 Sunday at Riverside International Raceway.

Waltrip couldn't seem to make up his mind how to act about the second national title of his 11-year Grand National career.

"After I took the (checkered) flag, all the emotions of the day and the championship and everything hit me all at once and I cried all the way around the track," he said with a big smile breaking across his dark, handsome face.

"Then, when I got to the crew and Junior (car owner Junior Johnson), I was just so happy I didn't know what to do. And, tomorrow morning (today), when I wake up and really feel what happened, I expect I'll be so proud I won't be able to stand myself.

"We knew before the race it was just belly up to the bar and get the job done. And that's what we did."

The day began as a shootout between the 35-year-old Waltrip and Bobby Allison, 44, the challenger who came into this season-ending race just 22 points behind Waltrip and practically tasting his first Winston Cup title in 18 years of Grand National racing.

Neil Bonnett

Rick Rudd

Bill Elliott

Joe Ruttman and Tim Richmond

Bill Schmidt

Jim Insolo

The June 1983 Warner Hodgdon 200 Grand American race, the supporting event to the Budweiser 400, was won by Herschel McGriff followed by Jim Neal and Ron Esau.

—AP
Hershel McGriff, left, of Bridal Veil, Ore., empties a bottle of Cold Duck over the head of a crew member with the help of "Miss Winston" Becky Carter after winning the Warner Hodgdon 200 NASCAR race at Riverside Raceway Sunday.

In the preliminary Warner Hodgdon 200, Herschel McGriff of Bridle Vail, Ore., captured first in a 1980 Camaro at an average speed of 98.037 mph. McGriff, 55, crossed the finish line with a seven-second margin over Jim Neal of Huntington Beach, Calif.

John Borneman

Ron Esau

Hershel McGriff, Nearly 56, Wins the Hodgdon 300 at Riverside

RIVERSIDE—Hershel McGriff will be 56 years old in two weeks, but he's not slowing down. At least, not on the Riverside International Raceway.

McGriff won his 12th Riverside race Saturday in the Warner Hodgdon 300-K, beating many drivers who weren't born yet when he won the Mexican Road Race in 1950. He led 40 of the 72 laps, including the last 11

The November 1983 Warner Hodgdon 300 Grand American race, was also won by Hershel McGriff in a Camaro, followed by Vince Giaformaggio in a Trans Am and Rick Ware, also in a Camaro.

Perennial companion feature Warner Hodgdon 300 will get under way 1 p.m. Saturday at Riverside

The Warner Hodgdon 300 Grand American race, the traditional companion feature to the annual Winston Western 500 is scheduled to begin Saturday at Riverside International Raceway at 1 p.m.

And, for the 15th straight year, the day has been designated "Scout Day" with anyone involved in scouting—Cubs, Brownies, Girl Scouts, Camp Fire, Boy Scouts and any type of Explorer Scout—admitted free.

Scouting uniforms are not mandatory but encouraged for quick identification when entering. If uniforms are not worn, some form of scouting identification will be required for free admittance.

The Hodgdon 300 features 1965 to 1983 NASCAR Grand American cars. These are U.S.-made sedans in the compact and intermediate classes such as Camaros, Novas, Firebirds, Venturas and Omegas.

This year's entry list is again dominated by popular West Coast short track veterans including Glen Steurer of Simi Valley, Jim Neal of Huntington Beach, Ron Esau of Lakeside, Kevin Riniker of Riverside and Herschel McGriff of Bridal Veil, Ore. McGriff is the only driver expected to compete in both the 300 and Winston Western 500.

The 303-kilometer (187-mile) race will be run over a distance of 72 laps around Riverside's 2.6-mile road course, and the day's activity will also include final qualifying for Sunday's 500.

General admission for the Hodgdon 300 is $7 and includes open grandstand seating. Tickets may be purchased Saturday at the gated beginning at 8 a.m.

Hodgdon 300 features NASCAR Grand American cars in model years 1965 to 1983.

Another standalone Winston West race in August 1983, the Warner Hodgdon 200, was a supporting race to the L.A. Times Budweiser 500 Indy Car race. Herschel McGriff won with Scott Miller in second and Bill Schmitt in third.

McGriff posts victory in Hodgdon 200

RIVERSIDE — Hershel McGriff drove the final three laps with a flat tire, but was able to hold off Scott Miller for a three-second win in the Warner Hodgdon 200 stock car race Sunday.

The 55-year-old McGriff is the winningest driver at Riverside International Raceway, and he was able to pick up his 10th win there despite the problem.

"It was pretty frightening," he said. "But luckily it didn't go down until the final turn. I'd have driven in on the rims."

The win moved McGriff a little closer to second-place Jim Robinson in the Winston West Grand National points standings. McGriff (320) is third behind Robinson (351) and Bill Schmitt (328).

"All we have to do is win the next two and hope that Robinson slows down a little," McGriff said.

In Sunday's race, which was a preliminary to the Los Angeles Times-Budweiser 500, Robinson finished eighth after starting in the front row next to Jim Bown, who was on the pole. Bown finished fourth.

McGriff took the lead on the 32nd lap of the 48-lap race, but then lost it to Miller on lap 36 when he made a pit stop. However, McGriff got the lead right back when Miller stopped.

"Hershel was just a little too fast for us to catch today," Miller said.

Randy Becker of Highland finished fifth. The only problem he had came early when he had to stop on lap 17 for right-side tire changes and then again on lap 18 for left-side changes.

Rick McCray of Bloomington finished 14th and is now 10th in the point standings. He got off to a bad start when he had a problem with his car on the fourth lap and had to pull into the garage. He wasn't able to rejoin until the leader's seventh lap.

—STUART DURANDO

JOE KENNEDY / Los Angeles Times

Winner—Herschel McGriff celebrates his victory in Warner Hodgdon 200-kilometer race at Riverside Sunday. See Bill Dwyre's story, Page 7.

McGriff Isn't Getting Older, Just Better

By BILL DWYRE, *Times Sports Editor*

RIVERSIDE—As fellow drivers on the Winston West stock car circuit will attest to, nobody does it better than Hershel McGriff. Or, more accurately put, nobody does it better for longer.

McGriff won Sunday's Warner Hodgdon 200 (200 kilometers, 125.76 miles) at the Riverside International Raceway, a preliminary to the Times/Budweiser 500 Indy car race. And with his victory, by a three-second margin over Scott Miller of Garden Grove, McGriff continued to defy both logic and father time.

McGriff, from Bridal Veil, Ore., is 56 years old. That's not exactly an age where a rocking chair on the front

185

45,000 spectators attended the June 1983 Budweiser 400 Winston Cup race won by Ricky Rudd who collected $24,530 for the win. Second was Bill Elliott followed by Harry Gant.

Ricky Rudd Wins 400 at Riverside; Waltrip Places 7th

By RICH ROBERTS, *Times Staff Writer*

The first race car Ricky Rudd ever drove was owned by his father, who did the body work. His brother and a neighbor back in Chesapeake, Va., were the mechanics, and his sister handled publicity for the team.

With that basic backyard operation, they plunged straight into NASCAR's Winston Cup Grand National circuit in 1975. Rudd was 18 at the time and probably didn't know any better.

"It was a family affair, and we went as far as we could with it," Rudd said Sunday after collecting his first win in a wild Budweiser 400 before an estimated 45,000 spectators at Riverside International Raceway. "I started playing big league ball right off the start. It was a hard way to come up, but it's paid off now."

Please see RIVERSIDE Page 10

Darrell Waltrip (11) leads pack while Jim Brown (96), Neil Bonnett (75) spin out on first lap of Budweiser 400 at Riverside Sunday.

Bill Elliott won the November 1983 Winston Western 500 Winston Cup race collecting $26,380. The race started an hour late and had another brief rain delay, Second was Benny Parsons followed by Neil Bonnett. Allison won the championship.

Elliott wins the battle, Allison wins the war

RIVERSIDE (UPI) — There were seven cars between them, but both Bill Elliott and Bobby Allison finished as winners Sunday.

Elliott, of Dawsonville, Ga., who was winless since his 1976 debut on the NASCAR tour, became the 12th driver to win on the tour this year by capturing the Western NASCAR 500.

Allison, of Hueytown, Ala., one of nine drivers in the same lap as the winner, finished ninth in a Buick and won the tour's title by 47 points. Allison needed only a 13th-place finish to clinch the title that eluded him for 20 years.

"I knew we needed to win but the odds were all against us," Elliott said. "When there was all the attention with Allison versus (favored Darrell) Waltrip, I thought there was a chance the two cars could come together and I had to be ready."

Elliott, who has four second-place finishes this year and nine in his career, led for the last five laps of the 119-lap race, which was run under intermittent rain that forced a 63-minute delay on the 89th lap. He averaged 99.993 miles per hour in a Ford and earned $26,380 for the victory.

Allison didn't know who to thank first.

"There were people who inspired me, including Pope John Paul II and Ronald Reagan," he said. "I wanted to lead that race so bad I couldn't stand it.

"It really feels great to win after 25 years. Little things kept happening out there. First I had a flat right wheel, then a flat left wheel. I got down to 27th and I was one lap down and my crew backed me all the way."

Benny Parsons of Ellerbe, N.C., was second in a Chevrolet; Neil Bonnett of Hueytown, third in a Chevy; Dale Earnhardt of Mooresville, N.C., fourth in a Ford; and Tim Richmond of Mooresville, fifth in a Pontiac.

There were eight leaders, 13 lead changes and six yellow caution flags — four coming because of rain.

On the 113th lap, with Richmond leading and Waltrip of Franklin, Tenn., needing to win to take the tour's championship, Waltrip passed Richmond. He came out of the turn on the outside, Richmond touched Waltrip's left-side door and the two cars spun into the infield. A yellow flag had just come out and the two drivers were racing to the flag 200 yards away.

"When Waltrip and Richmond came together, I thought I had a chance," Elliott said. "When they gave me the green, I thought I'd go for it."

Waltrip, the pole-sitter and pre-race favorite, finished sixth. He led for all but one of the first 34 laps, but after the first yellow flag he was forced to come from behind the rest of the race.

After the rain delay, Richmond pitted and Parsons took the lead. A succession of leaders followed before the Waltrip-Richmond collision.

The race began an hour late due to the weather and was run in 3 hours 15 minutes 9 seconds.

Allison Edges Waltrip For Winston Cup Title

DAYTONA BEACH, Fla. (AP) — Bobby Allison topped his nearest competitor, Darrell Waltrip, by 47 points to take his first Winston Cup championship in 20 years of NASCAR Grand National racing.

Allison clinched the title Sunday with a ninth-place finish at the Winston Western 500 at Riverside International Raceway.

Allison finished the 30-race NASCAR Winston Cup season with 4,667 points and six victories. Waltrip, who placed second, completed the year with 4,620 points and six wins. Waltrip won the title the previous two years.

Third-place Bill Elliot, with 4,279 points, won the Western 500 for his first career Winston Cup victory.

Bill Elliott of Dawsonville, Ga., celebrates under umbrella Sunday's rain-soaked win in Winston Western 500 NASCAR race at Riverside International Raceway. With Elliott are his wife, Martha, right, and Margaret Claud, Miss Winston Western.

Watch the WTBS 1983 Winston Western 500 Broadcast on the attached DVD

The June 1984 Warner Hodgdon 200 Grand American race was won by Duke Hoenshell. Second was Herschel McGriff with Glen Steurer in third and Bill Cooper in fourth. Pole qualifier Ron Esau did not finish.

Duke Hoenshell

Frank Loverock

Herschel McGriff

McGriff, Hoenshell and Steurer

Hoenshell Gambles, Wins

RIVERSIDE—A gamble on not pitting for tires under a yellow caution flag paid off with a win for Duke Hoenshell Sunday in the Warner W. Hodgdon 200 at Riverside. It was the first win of Hoenshell's nine-year racing career.

Hershel McGriff, the 54-year-old favorite, had stopped for four new tires and then began to rapidly reel in Hoenshell, but another caution flag came out when Walt Snow spun and crashed three laps from the end. In the race to the finish line, Hoenshell squeezed his unsponsored Camaro across the white stripe less than a foot ahead of McGriff's Mark C. Bloome Camaro. The race ended under the caution flag, and Hoenshell, 27, of Orange, collected the $3,500 first prize.

—SHAV GLICK

Esau captures Hodgdon 200 pole position at Riverside

RIVERSIDE — Ron Esau of Lakeside lapped the 2.62-mile, eight-turn Riverside International Raceway course at 114.325 mph to nab the pole position for the Warner Hodgdon 200, a Winston West series race that precedes today's Grand National Budweiser 400.

Esau's Pontiac will share the front row with Hershel McGriff of Bridal Veil, Ore., who qualified his Camaro for the second spot at 114.258 mph. Esau and McGriff also qualified Friday for the Budweiser 400.

A win today for McGriff would represent his fourth consecutive victory at Riverside and 13th career win there.

On Friday, Terry Labonte won the pole for the Budweiser 400 with a speed of 115.921 mph. Esau's Hodgdon qualifying speed matches Labonte's 115.325 mph in 1982 when he won his first Budweiser 400 pole.

Other Hodgdon qualifiers were Steve Bare of Ontario in a Camaro (18th at 107.356 mph) and Don F. Ewing of Colton (19th at 107.278 mph).

The Hodgdon 200 gets underway at 11 a.m. today. The Budweiser 400 follows at 1 p.m.

Hershel McGriff leads the field through the esses

The November 1984 Warner Hodgdon 300 Grand American series race was won by Herschel McGriff, his thirteenth win at Riverside, with Rich Loch in second and Tom Hanson in third. Pole qualifier Jimmy insolo did not finish.

Paul Dube: *"My first race at RIR was in a formula vee with SCCA. Then I was also offered a ride in a stock car refitted to compete in the Grand American series. I had never driven a high powered stock car on anything bigger than the Mesa Marin oval in Bakersfield and was in for a real surprise. The first time I ever drove the car was during the first practice session. Our plan was simple, Get through tech, qualify and hopefully finish the race. During practice I took a while to get out of third gear as the car was so fast; finally shifted into fourth and went faster yet. By lap six I was*

running wide open and looking for more. Then I looked in the rear view mirror and couldn't see anything but the inside of the roof. The wind pressure had pushed the roof down so far I couldn't see out the back window. Luckily we found a guy with a welder to build an inside brace for the roof. I don't think I have ever been that nervous as when we came around turn nine for the start of my first ever NASCAR race. We qualified 26th and finished 10th and I went on to do a couple more Grand American races"

Hershel McGriff, 56, Still Giving the Kids Lessons at Riverside

RIVERSIDE—Hershel McGriff, the ageless lumber baron from Bridal Veil, Ore., gave the kids another racing lesson Saturday.

McGriff, 56, led the last 31 laps to finish more than a mile ahead of Rich Lach of Simi Valley to win the Warner Hodgdon 300 for Grand American cars at Riverside International Raceway.

It was the 13th win for McGriff on Riverside's 2.62-mile road course. Only two drivers finished on the same lap with the winner, who averaged 97.949 m.p.h. for the 300 kilometers (188 miles). Tom Hanson of La Habra was third.

Pole-sitter Jimmy Insolo was involved in an accident with Dale Perry in Turn 9, on lap 17, and dropped out with a bent frame.

No sooner had McGriff finished the 1-hour 52-minute race than he climbed into a Grand National Pontiac to practice for today's 500-kilometer Winston Western race.

—SHAV GLICK

The June 1984 Budweiser 400 Winston Cup race was won by pole qualifier Terry Labonte in front of a crowd of 32,000. Labonte collected $31,955 for the win. Second was Benny Parsons, substituting for Neil Bonnett, followed by Bobby Allison.

Harry Gant and Tim Richmond

Bobby Allison and Dale Earnhardt

Greg Sacks

Richard Petty

Labonte wins Budweiser 400

RIVERSIDE (AP) — Turn nine at Riverside International Raceway, where Terry Labonte once slammed into the wall in a violent crash, didn't scare him during the Budweiser 400, the young stock car driver said.

"I just shut my eyes when I went into that turn," Labonte said, laughing Sunday after he'd won the Budweiser 400 NASCAR race at Riverside.

"On the other hand, it would have been hard to shut my eyes every time, since I had to go around there 95 times," added Labonte, who suffered facial injuries and a number of fractures in the 1982 accident at Riverside.

Labonte, a 27-year-old driver who'd won just two NASCAR races previously, took the lead for good after a quick pit stop on the 73rd lap, finishing the event a comfortable 9.4 seconds in front of Benny Parsons, who was filling in for Neil Bonnett.

Bobby Allison, the leader at three different stages of the race, finished third.

Labonte, who'd won the pole position in his Chevrolet, took the lead for keeps when his pit crew got him in and out in 29 seconds, as Allison, who pitted at the same time, was in nearly five seconds longer and dropped to second.

"I think my pit crew was the difference in the race," said Labonte.

Tim Richmond made a run at Labonte later, moving up right behind the frontrunner. But Richmond's Pontiac lightly brushed Labonte's car on the 87th lap, with Richmond's car suffering minor fender damage that sent him into the pits for a tire change five laps from the finish.

When he returned to the track, he had dropped back and eventually wound up sixth.

Labonte, a native of Corpus Christi, Texas, who now lives in Archdale, N.C., averaged 102.91 mph for the 400 kilometers (248.9 miles) over Riverside's demanding 2.62-mile, 8-turn track, the only road course used on the Winston Cup circuit.

The race lasted 2 hours, 25 minutes and 48 seconds.

The victory boosted Labonte, fourth in the points standings heading into the race, into second. He now has 1,897, just 15 behind leader Darrell Waltrip, who wound up 11th in the race.

The second-place finish by Parsons, in the Chevrolet usually driven by Bonnett, actually counts in Bonnett's column in the points standings.

Parsons' Finish Halts a Brewing Controversy

By MIKE KUPPER, Times Staff Writer

RIVERSIDE—If you are one of those cynics who figure that big-time sports are more arranged than contested, what happened in Sunday's Budweiser 400-kilometer race at the Riverside Raceway might just change your mind, at least as far as stock car racing is concerned.

If this race had been arranged, there would have been absolutely no question. Benny Parsons would have won.

As it was, he only finished second.

Why, you ask, would Parsons have won?

Well, start with the name of the race, the Budweiser 400. That tells us that a certain St. Louis brewery had a fairly substantial investment in the event.

Then consider that the car Parsons drove, a Chevrolet, was one of two sponsored by that same certain St. Louis brewery. In stock car-advertising circles, it is considered extremely good form if a sponsor's race is won by the same sponsor's car. In fact, it doesn't get any better than that.

Consider further that Parsons, as a relief driver for Neil Bonnett, had to start dead last and work his way through the pack. Wouldn't an arranged race, in the best manner of underdog tales, have him going from last all the way to victory? In the sponsor's car? In the

LORI SHEPLER / Los Angeles Times

Terry Labonte starts and finishes first in Sunday's stock car race at Riverside Raceway.

Super Service Helps Labonte Win
Fast Pit Work Moves Him From Third Place Into Lead

Buddy Arrington, one of the last "Moonshiners" and also at one time a Chrysler dealer, had 20 starts at Riverside from 1977 to 1987. Always running as an independent, he put on a good show

The way it was clocked at 180 mph hauling shine in a 429 cj Torino

CARLOAD OF MOONSHINE - Henry County Deputy Sheriff Melvin Brown, left, and Pittsylvania Deputy Doug Parrish take a look at the 249 gallon of illegal whiskey in the Ford Torino Cobra 429 owned by NAS-CAR driver, Buddy Rogers Arrington of Martinsville. The vehicle and the driver were taken into custody last Saturday afternoon in Pittsylvania County by the deputies.

Rogers, who served as grand marshall of the Martinsville-Henry County Christmas Parade, was boxed in by deputy sheriffs as he proceeded in an easterly direction on the Martinsville-Danville road. Arrington, who was released on a $500 bond, told the deputies that he was "in the business" so he could buy a new race car.

At Chatham the $4,000 worth of moonshine was poured down the drain, with the exception of two of the plastic gallon cartons saved for evidence. The car, especially equipped with 11 additional springs and inflatable shocks on the rear, was capable of about 180 miles-per-hour.

The Cobra was compounded by the Sheriff's Department. When stopped Arrington said he thought he had been spotted by radar when he saw the police cars. He offered no resistance saying that he alone was in the operation and that he regretted "letting down my friends". His wife came to Chatham with $500 in cash for the bond.

26,000 fans braved rainy weather and a two hour delay to watch Geoff Bodine win the Winston Western 500 In November 1984. Tim Richmond was second and Terry Labonte third. Bodine picked up $31,900 for the win. Labonte won the championship.

Kyle Petty, Derrick Cope and Ruben Garcia

Photo for The Times by Randy Leffingwell

Terry Labonte, this year's stock car champion, leads the pack of 40 entries through the esses on the way to Turn 6 in the Western 500 race Sunday at Riverside International Raceway.

Bodine Wins the Western 500; Labonte Takes Championship

By SHAV GLICK, *Times Staff Writer*

RIVERSIDE—Late on a dark and dank Sunday afternoon in the Winston Western 500, the media voted the Goody's Headache Award to Darrell Waltrip for having a bit of bad luck. He had led most of the early laps before losing his engine on the 71st lap—adequate cause for a headache.

It was a premature decision. The $500 (and more) should have gone to Bobby Allison.

The defending Winston Cup champion appeared to be a going-away winner of the rain-delayed race at Riverside International Raceway when his right front tire went flat three laps (less than eight miles) from the end of the 500-kilometer race.

This enabled Geoff Bodine, a New Yorker making a name for himself in the Southern-dominated NASCAR stock car circuit, to cruise by in his Chevrolet and win the final event of the season by five seconds over two-time winner Tim Richmond.

Terry Labonte, by finishing third in a conservative and well-planned effort directed by crew chief Dale Inman, became the second youngest driver to win the Winston Cup championship and its end-of-season bonuses totaling more than $300,000. Labonte was 28 last Friday. Richard Petty won his first title when he was 27.

Inman was also Petty's crew chief for all seven of his Grand National championships, starting with the first in 1964. Labonte's made it eight for Inman.

Even Bodine, 33, was quick to admit that he would not have caught Allison, who was seeking his fourth Winston Western 500 win.

"Bobby would have won," said the former super modified driver from Chemung, N.Y. "He ran a very good race. I tried to pass him several times, but he held such a steady line that I never really had a chance. His car was strong all the way around the track. But a flat tire is part of racing. We've had things like that happen to us, too."

Bodine received $31,900 for winning his third race of the season—and his NASCAR career. His other wins were on short tracks at Martinsville, Va., and Nashville.

Allison, after pitting for a new tire, finished seventh and collected $16,750. Allison led 55 laps, Bodine three.

Harry Gant, who started the day with a remote chance of beating Labonte for the national championship, knew early that it was not

Please see BODINE, Page 21

BODINE

Continued from Page 1

New Yorker making a name for himself in the Southern-dominated NASCAR stock car circuit, to cruise by in his Chevrolet and win the final event of the season by five seconds over two-time winner Tim Richmond.

Terry Labonte, by finishing third in a conservative and well-planned effort directed by crew chief Dale Inman, became the second youngest driver to win the Winston Cup championship and its end-of-season bonuses totaling more than $300,000. Labonte was 28 last Friday. Richard Petty won his first title when he was 27.

Inman was also Petty's crew chief for all seven of his Grand National championships, starting with the first in 1964. Labonte's made it eight for Inman.

Even Bodine, 33, was quick to admit that he would not have caught Allison, who was seeking his fourth Winston Western 500 win.

"Bobby would have won," said the former super modified driver from Chemung, N.Y. "He ran a very good race. I tried to pass him several times, but he held such a steady line that I never really had a chance. His car was strong all the way around the track. But a flat tire is part of racing. We've had things like that happen to us, too."

Bodine received $31,900 for winning his third race of the season—and his NASCAR career. His other wins were on short tracks at Mar-

ing to Vegas."

Gant finished eighth, but even if he had won, it would have made no difference. All Labonte needed was to finish seventh. He ended the 30-race season with 4,508 points to 4,443 for Gant, who will collect $165,000 as the Winston Cup runner-up.

"We ran the kinda race we wanted to run," said Labonte, who made one brief run at the lead and then thought better of it. "One particular time late in the race I felt I could get the lead, but when I got up close to Bobby (Allison) and Bodine I knew I couldn't get by them without abusing the car, and I felt it was not the time to do that so I backed off.

"I'm sure a lot happier now than when I came out here a couple of years ago."

That was when Labonte's car hit a concrete abutment head-on going into Turn 9. Labonte spent a week in a Riverside hospital recovering from head injuries.

Labonte's only concern was the growing darkness that enveloped the track in the late laps.

"It was dark and hard to see," he said. "I was concerned there might be oil on the track and I wouldn't be able to see it."

Bodine put on a spectacular show when his car bottomed out on several dips in the road and sent sparks flying.

"We lit up the track, didn't we?" he said. "Night racing is unusual in NASCAR, but we let the fans know where we were. The race didn't end any too soon."

Bodine said the sparks came

Another time I came up on a slow car and figured it was quicker to cut across the dirt to save time. Dale Earnhardt taught me that trick last June when I saw him take a shortcut through the dirt to get by a slow car and I followed him. I remembered that today."

A slow drizzle that started just as the cars began their first pace laps caused a two-hour delay and threatened to postpone the race until next Saturday.

The first nine laps were run under yellow caution flag conditions to allow the cars to dry the track. This enabled Labonte, who started on the pole, to pick up a five-point bonus for leading at least a lap.

Once the cars got up to speed, Labonte dropped back to protect his car and Waltrip took command. He and Allison controlled the first half of the race except for brief flurries during pit stops when Benny Parsons, Hershel McGriff and Gant got to the front for a lap or two.

McGriff, 53, who won the Warner Hodgdon 300 Saturday, finished ninth, highest of all Winston West drivers.

Indy-car veteran Bobby Rahal, making his first start in a stock car, dropped out on lap 47 with a bad vibration in the Wood Brothers Thunderbird. Although Rahal was not expected to be among the leaders, the loss was significant in stock-car racing history. It was the first time since 1962 that a car prepared by the Wood Brothers went through a season without winning a race.

Motor Racing / Shav Glick

Vast Stock Car Empire of Warner Hodgdon Ends in Bankruptcy

Three years ago, Warner Hodgdon appeared on his way to becoming the most powerful figure in stock car racing.

The San Bernardino businessman owned or had a major interest in six race tracks, had NASCAR races carrying his name at Riverside International Raceway and North Carolina Motor Speedway in Rockingham, N.C., and sponsored Neil Bonnett's car in the Winston Cup championship series.

His wife, Sharon, had a race in her name at Riverside, the Sharon Hodgdon 200. It was a companion feature to the Warner Hodgdon 400.

One of Hodgdon's sons, Aaron, was vice president of the board of directors at Phoenix International Raceway, which Hodgdon owned at the time. Aaron was 14. Another son, Justin, worked as a crewman on Hodgdon's teams. Justin was 9.

When racing associates asked Hodgdon about his long-range plans, he smiled and said: "The only plans we have are to win races, improve our facilities, help

the Johnson-Hodgdon team has fielded two cars, one for Darrell Waltrip and one for Neil Bonnett, both operating out of Johnson's shop in Ronda, N.C.

"There will be no Warner Hodgdon races at Riverside this year," General Manager Walt Carter said. "Our contract with him ran out last November, and we are not renewing it. We're just hoping to get back what we're owed."

The Warner Hodgdon 500 at Rockingham, N.C., has been renamed the Carolina 500.

Hodgdon has also divested himself of control of two golf courses, Shandin Hills in San Bernardino and Quail Lake (now Quail Valley), east of Riverside.

MOTOCROSS—The Supercross season will open Saturday night at San Diego Jack Murphy Stadium and as usual the favorites are from the San Diego area—**Broc Glover, Rick Johnson, Ron Lechien** and **Scott Burnworth.** The last three winners of the opening race—**Donnie Hansen, David Bailey** and **Johnny O'Mara**—have gone on to win the Supercross championship. Those three openers were all at Anaheim Stadium, however, where the second Supercross will be held Feb. 2.

Grand American was now the All American Challenge Series. The June 1985 All American 200 was won by Duke Hoenshell in a Pontiac. Hoenshell led every lap. Second was Ron Esau, also in a Pontiac with Richard Lach third in a Chevrolet.

Orange's Hoenshell Races Out of Own Garage

Driver Started on His Own and Is Still Fending for Himself

By JOHN PENNER

When he was 16, Duke Hoenshell constructed his first race car in his garage, using parts he had collected from the auto wrecking yard where he worked. When it was finally completed, he would drive it to a local race track as often as possible, race a few laps and then drive it home.

Now 28, Hoenshell, who lives in Orange with his wife Nancy, is a professional race car driver, still designing and building cars in his garage. The last car he and his crew completed, he drove last Sunday at Riverside International Raceway, where he won his second consecutive LA 200 race for Grand American cars.

Hoenshell was born on an Air Force base in Africa, where his father was stationed, but after six months, his family moved to Santa Ana. He has been an Orange Coun-

'With somebody else's financial support, it's a whole lot easier. When you gotta take the punch in the chops (while racing) and in the wallet, it's tough. I can take it in the chops, but I don't know how much I can take in the wallet.'
—Duke Hoenshell

Hoenshell wins LA 200; Cummings sidelined early

By KATIE CASTATOR
Sun Sports Writer

RIVERSIDE — When it's June and the track is Riverside, Duke Hoenshell, like his feisty cat, always lands on his feet.

Hoenshell successfully defended his title Sunday in the LA 200 at Riverside International Raceway, leading wire-to-wire and taking the checkered flag with a 20-second margin of victory over Ron Esau of Lakeside.

His winning time was 1 hour 13 minutes 19 seconds at

Parts Chevrolet.

Hoenshell, a resident of Orange, has rotten luck racing at Riverside in November. In 1983, he missed the Hodgdon 200 after his cat bit him and he came down with cat fever.

"I've still got the cat," Hoenshell said. "But he looks more like a giraffe now."

Last year at the November race, Hoenshell left a rag in his intake manifold and ruined his engine.

Time ran short for the Hoenshell team building a new

Watch the All American 200 on the attached DVD

The November 1984 Warner Hodgdon 300 Grand American series race was won by Herschel McGriff with Rich Loch in second and Tom Hanson in third.

Paul Dube': *"My first race at RIR was in a formula vee with SCCA. I was also offered a ride in a stock car that we refitted for road racing to compete in the Grand American series. I had never driven a high powered stock car on anything bigger than the Mesa Marin oval in Bakersfield and was in for a real surprise. The first time I ever drove the car was during the first practice session. Our plan was simple, Get through tech, qualify and hopefully finish the race. During practice I took a while to get out of third gear as the car was so fast; finally shifted into fourth and went faster yet. By lap six I was running wide open and looking for more. Then I looked in the rear view mirror and couldn't see anything but the inside of the roof. The wind pressure had pushed the roof down so far I couldn't see out the back window. Luckily we found a guy with a welder to build an inside brace for the roof. I don't think I have ever been that nervous as when we came around turn nine for the start of my first ever NASCAR race. We qualified 26th and finished 10th and I went on to do a couple more Grand American races"*

In November 1985, the Pep Boys 300 All American Challenge race was won by Herschel McGriff in a Camaro, followed by Kevin Riniker in a Nova and Dick Cobb in another Camaro.

McGriff, 57, Still Running Strong

RIVERSIDE—Thirty-five years after beating his opposition in the 1950 Mexican Road Race, Hershel McGriff is still winning.

McGriff, who will be 58 next month, won the Pep Boys 300 for Grand American stock cars by 49 seconds Saturday at Riverside International Raceway. It was McGriff's 14th victory on this track.

Kevin Riniker of Riverside was second. Defending champion Duke Hoenshell of Orange led the first 35 laps before McGriff took over and stayed in front to the finish. Three laps after losing his lead, Hoenshell crashed in Turn 6.

—SHAV GLICK

Herschel McGriff and Dick Taylor

The June !985 Budweiser 400 Winston Cup race was won by Terry Labonte followed by Harry Gant and Bobby Allison, A crowd of 32,000 saw Labonte pick up $39,200 for the win

JOSE GALVEZ / Los Angeles Times

Terry Labonte displays the trophy he earned with Sunday's victory.

Darrell Waltrip leads the field through the esses

Budweiser 400

Change of Tires Gives Labonte Edge to Win

By SHAV GLICK
Times Staff Writer

RIVERSIDE—Terry Labonte led the first 20 and the last 15 laps of Sunday's Budweiser 400 at Riverside International Raceway, but in between fans were treated to one of the most competitive stock car races in the venerable old track's history.

It was also one of the cleanest races ever as 25 of the 42 starters were running at the end and only one car had a minor brush with the wall as a crowd estimated at 32,000 looked on.

Eight drivers led at times and during one 10-lap stretch in mid-race, the lead was swapped and re-swapped among Harry Gant, Kyle Petty, his daddy Richard Petty and Bobby Allison. Others who led were Tim Richmond, Darrell Waltrip and Bill Elliott.

A 25-second pit stop during which Dale Inman's crew changed all four tires on Labonte's Chevrolet Monte Carlo while the cars were racing at full speed under the green flag was a major factor in the win. Labonte was seventh at the time when he pitted on lap 67, but with fresh rubber all around, the Ice Man from Corpus Christi, Tex., began to run down the leaders one

Labonte quickly caught and passed Ricky Rudd and Neil Bonnett and, after Gant and the Pettys pitted, he had only Allison to catch.

On lap 80, fifteen laps from the end of the 400-kilometer race, Labonte made a daring pass on the outside of treacherous Turn 9—the same turn where he crashed and nearly ended his career in 1982—to get by Allison and pull away.

"I knew I could catch him, but getting by the Old Man is tough," Labonte said. "I knew I had to pass him as soon as possible before my tires started to go away."

In the final race of 1982, the Winston Western 500, a cut tire caused Labonte to crash hard in Turn 9. The accident broke his right foot and left ankle, fractured some ribs and caused extensive cuts on his face, necessitating plastic surgery.

Although he said at the time that he would have quit racing if his wife, Kim, had asked him to, Labonte now says the horrors of that day do not enter his mind anymore.

"The first time I raced here after that I thought about it, but not any more," Labonte said. "I think we're about even (with Turn 9) now."

At the end, Labonte's main concern was Gant, Mr. Second Place, who was closing fast but fell short

Terry Labonte

Geoff Bodine blows up

Ron Bouchard leads Neil Bonnett

Rusty Wallace leads Bill Osborne

The November 1985 Winston Western 500 Winston Cup race was won by Ricky Rudd over Terry Labonte and Neil Bonnett. Rudd picked up $37,875 for the win in front of a crowd estimated to be 60,000. Darrell Waltrip, finishing seventh, secured his third NASCAR championship,

Staff photo by David Schreiber

Darrell Waltrip (car No.11) leads Terry Labonte (44) through ess curves during early stages of Western 500 at Riverside International Raceway on Sunday. Waltrip finished seventh and won NASCAR points title; Labonte finished second behind race winner Ricky Rudd.

Harry Gant leads Bobby Allison and Dale Earnhardt

Derrick Cope

Dale Earnhardt

Bill Elliott

Ricky Rudd

Bobby Hillin Jr.

Ken Schrader

Tim Richmond

Buddy Baker

Waltrip, Rudd and Track Winners at Riverside

By SHAV GLICK
Times Staff Writer

RIVERSIDE—Darrell Waltrip won the Winston Cup championship, Ricky Rudd won the race and Jim Robinson the West Coast championship, but the biggest story Sunday at Riverside International Raceway was the huge crowd.

Oldtimers, who have seen every race since the track opened in 1957, claim the outpouring of fans was the largest for any stock car race ever held here. Perhaps it was because the venerable old road course is rumored to be closing, or perhaps it was the hoopla over the Waltrip-vs.-Bill Elliott points race.

Whatever, an hour before the race, traffic was backed up six miles to University Avenue in Riverside and it was taking an hour and a half to reach the track from there.

Track officials refused to announce a crowd for Sunday's Winston Western 500, the final event on the NASCAR schedule—but estimates ranged around 60,000.

One of the biggest cheers went up when Daniel Greenwood, president of the track, announced that the facility would remain in operation next season.

On the track, the tension over the championship ended quickly as Elliott, winner of 11 races and more than $2 million this season in his Ford Thunderbird, pitted on lap 7 with broken gear linkage in his transmission. By the time the Melling crew finished replacing the faulty part, Elliott had sat 32 minutes in the pits and lost 22 laps.

This enabled Waltrip, who entered the race with a 20-point lead despite having won only three races, to drive his Chevy Monte Carlo cautiously to a seventh-place finish to win approximately $440,000 in bonus money for his third Grand National title.

"Winning the first (championship) was great, the second was better and the third is definitely the

Associated Press

In the last race of the year, Ricky Rudd got his first win at the Western 500 at Riverside. He outdueled Terry Labonte over the final 23 laps.

best," Waltrip said after accepting congratulations from car owner and builder Junior Johnson. It was Johnson's sixth title in nine years, having three with Cale Yarborough in 1976, 1977 and 1978. Waltrip won in 1981 and 1982.

The part that broke in Elliott's car was a 1¼-inch long pin which goes in the shifter inside the transmission. It costs $8.

The pin was manufactured by Douglas Nash in Franklin, Tenn., which is Waltrip's home town.

didn't go our way. I guess I did say something to myself like, 'This just ain't my day.'

"The type of year we had, it was a great one, despite what happened today. The whole year has been memorable, day-by-day, no special day. All have been special."

Elliott had a 206-point lead over Waltrip after winning the Southern 500 Sept. 1 at Darlington, the day he won a $1 million bonus from Winston for winning three of four major 500-mile races. Only eight races remained on the 28-race schedule, but Elliott's luck suddenly turned sour and he failed to finish the next four races. This enabled Waltrip to catch up and make Sunday's race the championship decider.

The Ford-vs.-Chevrolet confrontation didn't materialize between Elliott and Waltrip but at the end another one developed between Rudd, in a Thunderbird, and Labonte, in a Monte Carlo.

Rudd and Ford won by holding off a daring Labonte challenge on the final lap, but the edge was determined in the pits by wily Bud Moore, Rudd's crew chief.

Riverside's 2.62-mile road is hard on tires and Moore made a move early in the race that paid off for Rudd. On the next-to-last scheduled pit stop, Moore had all four tires changed on the T-Bird, while Labonte's crew changed only two.

Late in the race, on the final pit stop, Labonte had a lengthy stop

Please see RIVERSIDE, Page 17

RIR reaffirms intention to race in '86

There will be racing in 1986 at Riverside International Raceway.

This announcement, made by RIR president Dan Greenwood, went out over the public address system at the raceway before the start of last Sunday's Winston Western 500. The news, which reaffirms a similar announcement made earlier this year, was greeted by cheers from the record crowd estimated at 60,000.

On the '86 schedule, said Greenwood, are two NASCAR races — the Budweiser 400 on June 1 and the Winston Western 500 in November — plus the SCORE Off-Road World Championships and Times IMSA race.

Motor racing

Katie Castator

ious, direct man who enjoys the spotlight, likes to needle the quieter Elliott, who admitted he'd rather tinker with his car than meet the public and endure interviews.

"I have to go to press conferences because he won't," Waltrip wisecracked last Wednesday at a news conference in Los Angeles.

the American Motorcycle Association. "The Ninth District Court of Appeals ruled in our favor in October. If the court had ruled against us we could have been shut down."

The motorcycle race, which was established in 1967 by the San Gabriel Valley Motorcycle Club,

caused the damage but the thousands of support people who took off across the desert after them.

A modified version started up again in 1983, even though the case was still unsettled.

"It just kept going to higher courts," Bell said.

Bell said the way the race is now run causes minimal damage since the route sticks to trails, sand washes and dirt roads. The field has been cut to 1,200 entries. All spots were filled in one month and there are 100 riders on the waiting list.

The 180-mile race starts with a bomb run. The riders line up abreast of each other and then funnel into the trail about three

In June 1986, Ron Esau won the Von's 200 Southwest Tour race after a tough battle with Duke Hienshell who ended up second. Randy Becker was third. In November, Hoenshell won the Motorcraft 300 event followed by Southwest Tour champ Ron Esau and Doug Taylor. Hoenshell took home $6920 for his win.

Esau survives bump-and-run race with Hoenshell, wins Von's 200

By KATIE CASTATOR
Sun Sports Writer

RIVERSIDE — Ron Esau of Lakeside survived a fierce battle with Duke Hoenshell of Orange on Saturday to win the Von's 200 NASCAR Southwest Tour stock car race at Riverside International Raceway.

Only the Las Vegas shows could match the bumping and grinding going on the last six laps as Esau relentless attempted to pass Hoenshell on some of the slower turns, espcially the eighth, on Riverside's snaky road course.

With his Chevrolet Camero scarred by tire marks, Esau finally pulled into the lead after the engine of Hoenshell's Pontiac Firebird started smoking on the eighth turn of the 48th and final lap of the 200-kilometer (125-mile) race, which was the third in the All-American Challenge Series.

How often did they bump? At least five times, Hoenshell said.

"I remember getting bumped a lot," he said. "I remember getting sideways. He was on my inside trying to pass and I wasn't going to give it to him. It was the best race I've ever been in. We both drove our hearts out and could have been side-by-side taking the checkered flag."

Esau covered the distance at an average of 98.442 mph for a $4,770 purse. He now leads in points for the series.

Randy Becker of Highland was in third the first three laps, held fourth place five more laps and then ran in fifth and sixth place until the first caution flag, when he ducked into the pit. He was still on the lead lap until the engine of his Camaro blew on the front straightaway after 38 laps. He fin-ished 22nd in the 35-car field.

Brian Jackson of San Bernardino, who ended in 19th place with his Camaro, had the best finish of the local drivers.

Race notes
Saturday's results for other area drivers were: **Walt Snow** of Grand Terrace (20th), **Dean Huss Jr.** of Bloomington (21st), **Rollie Jacobs** of Colton (26th), **Rick McCray** of Bloomington (30th) and **Bill Clarke** of San Bernardino (31st). ... Today's main event, the Budweiser 400, begins at noon. In Saturday's qualifying for positions 21th through 42, **Joe Ruttman**, a former Upland and Ontario resident, clocked the ninth fastest time of the field. But since he ran his Quaker State Buick into the dirt on the esses Saturday and was unable to run a qualifying lap the first day, he'll start 21st today. McCray (Stockman Race Cars Buick) qualified for the 31st spot and **Bill Osborne** of Rialto (Americans for Racing Buick) for the 42nd position. **Darrell Waltrip** of Franklin, Tenn., who qualified Saturday with a track record 117.006 mph, sits on the pole.

Duke Hoenshell: *"Our long time engine builder John Wilson was working at Fisher Engines and was building V6 engines.. He was all fired about the power they were making and with the weight advantage available for V6's, I thought I'd would build a new car designed for a V6. I t was basically the same as previous cars, just refined it a bit. Off to the track we went, tech went well; in practice it was overheating; took a while to figure it out. I was flat out through the esses; was hitting on the rev limiter everywhere; needed gears for the Jerico. Fixed that, dialed it in for qualifying, had the pole by 2 mph over the next guy and had the usual problems with officials who didn't like our chassis design. Really what they didn't like was our being faster than everyone else. So we went home added some chassis tubes and 150 pounds of lead, started last and won easily, but not by too much – didn't want to offend the NASCAR guys !!*

What's in the Stars for California's
DUKE HOENSHELL?

by Jim Hyneman

Upon meeting Duke Hoenshell, one's initial impression of this Southern California resident will be illuminated by his unassuming nature and easygoing attitude. He makes one feel comfortable, and that's a welcome attribute.

If you get to know Duke Hoenshell, you'll realize how accurate your first impressions were. He's a genuinely nice guy. You'll also discover he races stock cars and, in fact, relishes that part of his life with refreshing enthusiasm. He won't bore you with

The young California driver's pride and joy is his infant daughter, Elizabeth.

Photo: Frank B. Marmillo

Read the article on the attached DVD

Duke Hoenshell won the November 1986 Motorcraft. Carquest 300 Southwest Tour race, the last race of the season, followed by Ron Esau amd Doug Taylor. Esau won the championship.

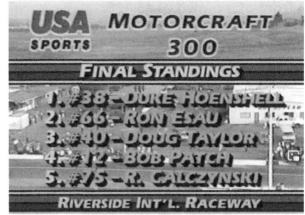

Watch the Motorcraft 300 on the attached DVD

Duke Hoenshell

Hoenshell comes from behind to win

By KATIE CASTATOR
Sun Sports Writer

RIVERSIDE — No one would have blamed Duke Hoenshell if he had gloated a little after coming from a start in the rear of the 42-car field to win the Motorcraft/Carquest 300-kilometer Grand American stock car race Saturday at Riverside Raceway.

After a wild qualifying lap of 116.118 mph Friday to win the pole position two miles faster than Jim Lee of Vista, Hoenshell had his qualifying time disallowed after a trial inspection.

He was told the frame of his Chevrolet Camaro did not meet the NASCAR Southwest Tour criteria. To race yesterday, Hoenshell had to add 150 pounds of lead to the frame and move to the back of the pack.

"I tried to use the penalty as a positive motivation," said Hoenshell, 29, of Orange. "I tried to turn all the negative into fuel and it gave us the fuel to win the race."

Hoenshell patiently maneuvered through heavy traffic and took the lead on the 36th lap. After a pit stop that put him back, he regained the lead on the 50th lap. He stayed in front through the 72nd and final lap to beat Ron Esau of Lakeside across the finish line by 8.1 seconds. Esau had clinched the Southwest Tour championship before Saturday's season-ending race.

Hoenshell won $6,920.

Bill Osborne of Rialto was 11th, the top finisher from a group of San Bernardino County entrants. Other county drivers were Dean Huss of Bloomington, 16th, and Brian Jackson of S.B., 39th.

Rod Hetrick of Yucca Valley (qualified fifth) and Randy Becker of Highland (qualified sixth) seemed to have the best chance of the local drivers. But the two collided on the first lap. The wreck took both cars out of the race.

"Both cars were probably going 130 to 140 mph because it was right after Turn 2 and that's a flat-out turn," said Becker.

Hetrick's right arm was reportedly in a splint. Becker was not injured.

Race notes

Dan Greenwood, president of Riverside International Raceway, made it official on Saturday, announcing that RIR will remain open through the entire 1987 season. He also said the first hurdle has been cleared in building a new track in nearby Perris. Today's Winston Western 500 was to have been the final race at the 30-year-old track, but a delay in opening another Southern California race facility has meant RIR will remain open another year.

Pole qualifier Darrell Waltrip picked up $49,000 for his win in the June 1986 Budweiser 400 Winston Cup race. Tim Richmond was second and Ricky Rudd third in front of a crowd of 45,126.

 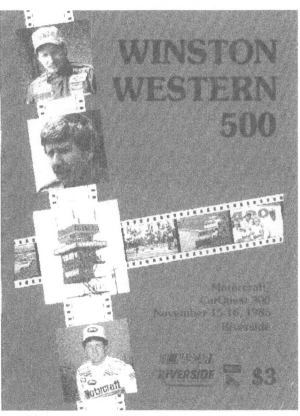

Morgan Shepherd: *"I drove at Riverside a few times, in my own car and for Rah Moc,*

Kenny Bernstein, Hal Needham and a few others. I got to fill in for Neil Bonnett and Harry Gant a few times to I guess I learned about road racing by racing on the roads, hauling moonshine, as a kid. My first time there; I'd only seen the track on TV and Neil Bonnett gave me a few tips like "don't worry about getting off the road" !! I saw Labonte's crash going into turn nine and had to slow down a bit for a while. I was privileged to drive in the last stock car race there, in 1988" Compiler's Note - Morgan's career spanned five decades in NASCAR, competing in 517 races with four wins. He was the oldest driver, at age 71 to start a NASCAR race; New Hampshire in 2011.

Waltrip wins pole in record time

By KATIE CASTATOR
Sun Sports Writer

RIVERSIDE — Darrell Waltrip rolled his trusty, 1981-model car out of storage, dusted it off and drove the 2.62-mile road course at Riverside International Raceway, Friday, in 1 minute, 20.57 seconds for the fastest qualifying lap in the track's history.

His average speed of 117.066 mph broke the track record of 116.938 set last November by Terry Labonte, and put Waltrip on the pole for Sunday's

driver from Franklin, Tenn., had to wait to celebrate, though. He ran his lap about midway through a marathon, 3-hour, 35-minute qualifying session that was stopped several times to clear debris and clean up oil.

Waiting to run was Geoff Bodine, a renowned hot-lapper. And Bodine's Levi Garrett Chevrolet was parked at the very end of the line on pit row.

"There was one guy left to beat me and he had to be last," Waltrip said. "I had to wait here until dark-thirty to find

He had run the second-fastest lap (116.757 mph) in his Folger's Chevrolet. The cars in line finally dwindled down to one and Bodine roared out of the pit and disappeared around the esses. Scant seconds later, he was in view again. His lap — 116.759 mph — beat Richmond's by a mere .002 of a second.

Neil Bonnett of Bessemer, Ala., who drives another Budweiser Chevrolet for the Johnson team, had the fourth-best lap (115.958). He was followed by two-time defending champion Labonte, who

DANIEL A. ANDERSON/The Sun

Riverside International Raceway record-setter Darrell Waltrip (left) is congratulated by team member Mike Hill on Friday.

Waltrip Pulls Out Riverside Win

RIVERSIDE, Calif. (AP) — A balky radio and Darrell Waltrip's Chevrolet started working again, just in time for his pit crew to warn him Sunday that he had to make up three car lengths in the final mile to win his first NASCAR stock car race of 1986.

With a daring push through the sweeping ninth and final turn at Riverside International Raceway, Waltrip powered ahead of Tim Richmond to grab the lead one lap from the finish of the Budweiser 400, and he held the lead through the last lap under a yellow caution flag.

Waltrip said his pit crew told him in either turn six or seven that the yellow caution flag was being put out.

"I knew if I stayed close to his bumper I had a good chance. I just inched him at the finish. We could have crashed, but Tim held his line," Waltrip said.

The frustrated second place finisher Richmond, who also drove a Chevrolet, could only watch Waltrip's tail-lights for the final lap of the race as a tow truck went out to remove the wrecked car of Terry Labonte on the first turn.

Waltrip averaged 105.083 for the 95 laps over the twisting road course. Waltrip's radio behaved poorly during the race, but came to life with 15 laps to go.

Richmond, still without a victory this year, said he had to be cautious in the final lap because a brush with another car had bent a fender against one of his tires. He also said that because of slower cars in the path, he had to slow down entering the final turn.

"I slowed down, and Waltrip made his move around me," Richmond said. "The slow cars got in the way."

"I out-drug him to the flag," Waltrip said of the dash to the finish. "We never touched. It was sanitary."

"This was just a great weekend for us. Terry (Labonte) and Richmond had the only cars that could outrun me. They were better on new tires, and I was faster on used tires, and that last series was just long enough," Waltrip said.

Ricky Rudd finished third, followed by Rusty Wallace, Dale Earnhardt, Richard Petty, Bobby Allison, Neil Bonnett.

Richmond battled Waltrip during the late stages of the 400-kilometer race and passed Waltrip on the 82nd lap. But Waltrip made up a one-second deficit on lap 94 and passed Richmond just before the start-finish line. The yellow caution flag was out because Labonte's car remained too close to the race course after a hard collision with a retaining wall.

Richmond and Geoff Bodine traded the lead for most of the first half of the race, but Bodine's car began smoking at lap 27 and he dropped out with a burned piston.

Midway through the race, Richmond's car developed handling problems and he went into the pits to take on four tires

Waltrip then opened the biggest lead of the race — about 15 seconds — over Labonte, who had won the race the last two years. At the halfway mark only 10 of the 42 starters remained on the lead lap.

The leaders bunched up on the 52nd lap, during the first caution flag of the race due to oil spilled on the main straightaway, where the fastest cars reached speeds approaching 170 mph.

When the car of Dave Marcis had to be towed from the apron of turn 2 of the 9-turn course, a second caution flag came out on lap 74. After the leaders went to the pits for their last load of fuel and new tires, Waltrip stayed in the lead, followed by Rudd, Richmond, Wallace, Earnhardt, Labonte, Richard Petty and Harry Gant

Harry Gant (33) and J.D. McDuffie (70) spin out on Turn 9 Sunday at Riverside, bringing out the yellow flag with two laps to race. The impending caution allowed Darrell Waltrip to slip past Tim Richmond.

Waltrip completes pass, wins Bud 400

By KATIE CASTATOR
Sun Sports Writer

RIVERSIDE — Darrell Waltrip tried his razzle-dazzle, criss-cross, passing move on Turn 9 in the final lap of the 1983 Winston 500 at Riverside International Raceway.

That time he and leader Tim Richmond collided and went spinning off into the infield mud. Bill Elliott, in third place moments before, maneuvered around the debris and raced to the checkered flag for the victory.

Waltrip put the same move on leader Richmond on Turn 9 in the a momentarily irked Richmond.

Waltrip, of Franklin, Tenn., thus scored his first victory of the 1986 Winston Cup Series, averaging a speed of 105.083 mph over the 95 laps in his Chevrolet Monte Carlo.

He collected $40,000 in prize money and promptly dedicated the win to Frank Cannon, his recently deceased bassett hound. Waltrip named his dog after the TV character portrayed by William Conrad because of an uncanny resemblance between the two.

"It's been a sad weekend for Stevie (his wife) and I," said Wal-

had to put him to sleep. He's been to every race track I've run but Riverside. I guess he won't make it here now."

To back up a bit, several incidents contributed to Sunday's spectacular finish. For openers, Richmond, pushing through slower traffic on Turn 9 of the 91st lap, bumped J.D. McDuffie and bent the fender down on his tire.

Waltrip who had been running only a second or two behind, began to close in.

Then, on Lap 94, Terry Labonte, who was running in third

came out while Richmond an Waltrip were snaking through th esses.

Waltrip's temperamental ra dio, which hadn't worked at th beginning of the race, ha crackled to life with just 15 laps t go. Lucky for Waltrip, it contin ued to stay fixed to the end.

"They called me on the radi on Turn 6 or 7 (to tell him the ye low flag was out)," Waltrip saic "They said, the track was clea and to race hard."

NASCAR rules allow drivers t race to the yellow flag, and that' what Waltrip did. Coming fror

Richard Petty leading Dale Earnhardt

Sumner McKinght

Glen Steurer

Ricky Rudd

Chad Little

Ruben Garcia: *"I had nine starts in Cup races at Riverside from 1984 through 1988 plus a few more in Winston West. I had learned the track pretty well before my first Cup race in 1984, running with SCCA in Super Production and battling with the likes of Willy T. Ribbs. Got a few tips from Ray Elder too. My most memorable moment – 1985; running in ninth, ahead of Richard Petty until the syncro in my trans started to go. Still hung on for fourteenth. Everyone remembers my big crash in 1988; we had changed motors a couple of times and one of the crew guys forgot to tighten the steering shaft. Car was working well when, on lap 29, entering turn nine, I pulled on the wheel and it just spun around in my hands – bam, straight into the wall. Fortunately, no one was injured but the race was red flagged for almost a half hour as they fixed the wall."*

216

Pole sitter Tim Richmond won the 1986 Winston Western 500 Winston Cup race and collected $50,955 in prize money. Second went to Dale Earnhardt, who had already clinched the championship, with Geoff Bodine in third. Track president Dan Greenwood announced that the track would be open for the 1987 season and a new track would be built in Perris.

Reprieve for Riverside Raceway

RIVERSIDE (AP) — Dan Greenwood, president of Riverside International Raceway, announced Saturday that the track will remain open through the entire 1987 season and that the first hurdle has been cleared in building a new track in nearby Perris.

Today's NASCAR Winston Western 500 was to be the final race at the 30-year-old track, which will eventually be demolished to clear the land for development of living units and a shopping center.

But, with what Greenwood called a "very good chance" of the new facility being opened by 1988, it was decided to keep the Riverside track open through next season.

He said Saturday that sanctioning agreements already have been signed for NASCAR stock cars races on June 21 and November 8 next year.

The former Los Angeles Olympics official said that the city of Perris, located about 12 miles south of the Riverside track, last Monday approved an agreement with track officials to annex those portions of the 490-acre site that are not currently part of the city.

"We've just crossed the start-finish line of a marathon and we've got about 23 miles to go," said Greenwood.

"I would say it will take nine months at best to get all the approvals needed."

The proposed facility would start with a 1¾-mile tri-oval and would eventually include a road course, a drag strip and other recreational facilities, including the

The Associated Press

Dale Earnhardt, who has already has wrapped up the Winston Cup title, qualified for the seventh position at the start of today's Winston Western 500 at Riverside.

veteran Benny Parsons led second-day qualifiers Saturday for the Winston Western 500 with a fast lap averaging 115.163 mph.

Parsons earned the 26th starting position for Sunday's 500-kilometer race with a lap that would have put him in the 16th position if he had done it in the opening session of qualifying on Friday.

Ken Schrader's was second quickest Saturday in a Ford Thunderbird at 113.734, followed by

mark of 117.691 set by Darrell Waltrip only minutes before.

Those two will lead the 42-car field when it starts the 119-lap race at 11:15 p.m.

The race is the season finale and a battle for second-place in the Winston Cup championship.

Richmond, $30,000 richer after winning the pole, will be chasing another $225,000 today.

Dale Earnhardt already has wrapped up the Winston Cup title

Richmond's Wild Pole Ride Nets Him $30,000

By SHAV GLICK, Times Staff Writer

RIVERSIDE—Tim Richmond knew what he had to do to earn the $30,000 Busch Pole bonus for winning the most Winston Cup poles Friday. So he went out and did it.

He had to break a Riverside International Raceway track record of 117.691 m.p.h., set only an hour earlier by Darrell Waltrip.

If he couldn't better that in one tour around the eight-turn, 2.62-mile road course, the $30,000 would go to his Hendrick Motorsports teammate, Geoff Bodine.

Richmond, driving a Chevrolet prepared by Harry Hyde, drove so hard that he bent an intake valve while downshifting, but he still managed to bring the car home at a record 118.247 m.p.h.

This won him the bonus and put him on the pole for Sunday's $404,000 Winston Western 500, the final race of the 29-race NASCAR season.

"The first three-quarters of the lap was a fast one, but the finish was neither safe nor smooth," Richmond said. "I definitely let it all hang out.

"When I downshifted to third in Turn 9, it seemed like an eternity getting from nine to the finish line. The engine was popping and backfiring and I wasn't sure what I'd

done until I got up through the esses (turns 3, 4 and 5) and I saw the people cheering me."

It was Richmond's eighth pole, the same number that Bodine has won, but Richmond won the tiebreaker because he had seven second-place finishes to six for Bodine.

"What can I say?" asked Bodine, who could muster only 116.858 m.p.h., good for fourth position. "It's disheartening. We tried our best. We gave it everything we had, but obviously we didn't have enough. I thought it was a good lap, a darn good lap, to say the least."

This will be the first time in 13 Winston Cup races at Riverside that neither Waltrip nor Terry Labonte will start from the pole. Not since Cale Yarborough was the fastest qualifier in the June, 1980, Hodgdon 400 had the two-driver monopoly been broken.

"If we get beat, somebody will have to run one heck of a lap," Waltrip said as he climbed out of Junior Johnson's car for the last time as a qualifier. Next year, Waltrip will become a third member of the Hendrick Motorsports team with Richmond and Bodine.

When Richmond ran his "heck of

a lap," it prompted Waltrip to make another statement.

"You know what you're looking at, don't you? You're looking at the future of 1987, that's what."

Only Ricky Rudd, the defending Winston Western champion, broke up the Hendrick combine-to-be as he edged Bodine for the third spot with a 116.911 lap.

With Waltrip moving to the Hendrick team next season, Labonte will take Waltrip's seat with Junior Johnson.

Waltrip's record lap had broken his own mark of 117.006 set last June. In 28 races (one race did not have a pole qualifying because of rain), 23 qualifying records were broken this year.

Twenty-five cars qualified Friday, with an additional 15 being added to the field today after a 9 a.m. qualifying session.

Among those still not in Sunday's race are Hershel McGriff and Chad Little, the two drivers contending for the Winston West championship.

A surprise in the 25th spot is Al Unser, three-time Indianapolis 500 champion, who qualified at 113.438 in a Pontiac. It is Unser's second stock car race this year, his having

driven at Watkins Glen, N.Y., in another road race.

Duke Hoenshell of Orange won the pole for today's Motorcraft/Carquest 300, the final event of NASCAR's Southwest Tour, but was disqualified in a post-time trial inspection.

Hoenshell's Chevrolet Camaro did not meet construction criteria, according to Bob Sweeney, NASCAR western operations director of competition. However, Hoenshell will be permitted to start at the rear of the 40-car field, but with an additional 150 pounds of ballast.

"I'm just grateful they're letting me race. I'll be coming through, you can count on that," Hoenshell said.

His qualifying speed of 116.118 m.p.h. was nearly two miles faster than Jim Lee of Vista, Calif., who will now start on the pole with a 114.395 effort. Alongside Lee will be Million Dollar Bill Elliott, the Dawsonville, Ga., veteran who collected a $1-million bonus last year for winning three superspeedway races.

Although Hoenshell will race today, he was ordered to rebuild the frame before his next Southwest Tour event.

Richmond hits the big time with Winston win

By Bill Center
Staff writer

Copley News Service

Lights. Camera. Action. This is the stuff of movies, which is exactly what Tim Richmond has in mind.

Moody young race driver with a penchant for crashing hooks up with an over-the-hill mechanic down on his luck.

The "odd couple" goes on to become the hottest thing in racing.

Roll 'em.

There's only one catch. No one would believe it. But the story is true.

When Richmond won Sunday's season-ending Winston Western 500 by 1.95 seconds over NASCAR points champ Dale Earnhardt before a record turnout of some 70,000 at Riverside International Raceway, he put the finishing touch on a season that was too good to believe.

famed country-western song "Thanks For The Ride, Harry Hyde."

"They all said we'd never do anything together," said Hyde of his association with Richmond. "I was over the hill and he was nothing. We had two strong wills and nothing else."

But, Richmond admits, Harry's will was stronger. It took the sting out of the driver and forced him to "go with the flow."

Over the last half of the 1986 season, the Richmond-Hyde team won seven of the last 16 races and claimed seven poles. In one 12-race span, Richmond finished first or second 10 times.

Eventually, he climbed from 10th to third on the points, finishing just six points behind the runnerup — a margin that cost him $80,000.

Over the weekend, Richmond capped his fairy tale rise by dominating the events over RIR's 2.62-

ed for the pits as the engine on Elliott's Ford let go to bring out the yellow.

Geoff Bodine, who was leading his 54th and last lap — and Earnhardt both preceded Richmond into the pits.

But Richmond was first back onto the track, followed by Earnhardt and Bodine, who has lost three other races this season (two to Rick Hendrick teammate Richmond) because of bad pit work.

Although there would be two more caution periods over the final 15 laps, Richmond would never yield the lead, although once he swapped paint with Earnhardt as the two leaned on each other for position through RIR's famed esses. "We did get together," Richmond admitted. "We don't mind that."

Not at all. Earlier in the race, Richmond had leaned on Benny Parsons leaving pit row, taking away a tire mark in his left door

Tim Richmond has fun with some champagne after winning the Winston Western 500 at Riverside International Raceway. Miss Winston Denise Lowry is on the left.

Waltrip, Rudd and Bodine

Tim Richmond

Winston Western 500

Motorcraft/ CARQUEST 300

NOVEMBER 15 & 16, 1986

RIVERSIDE INTERNATIONAL RACEWAY

Allison leads Hillin and Kulwicki

Earnhardt leads Ruttman

Rick Wilson

Ruben Garcia

In June 1987, Kevin Riniker won the Vons 200 Southwest Tour race, followed by Roman Calzinski and Troy Beebe. In the November Motorcraft 300, Ken Schrader won followed by Duke Hoenshell and Jim Lee.

Riniker first when it counts at Riverside

By JIM LONG
Sun Sports Writer

RIVERSIDE — Strange. Ron Esau has a wild, screwy ride full of long leads, long pitstops and long deficits, but almost pulls off a dramatic victory.

Jim Thirkettle hangs around, dangerous as always, and gets a lead his engine can't keep.

And the guy whose race is constant, but uneventful for 45 of the 48 scheduled laps — Riverside's Kevin Riniker — ends up winning the Vons 200 in his own backyard.

Strange, indeed. But true. Riniker earned the checkered flag in the NASCAR Southwest Tour event Saturday at Riverside International Raceway, outlasting Esau, Thirkettle and two other men who led the 125.76-mile race.

"I heard every squeak in that car," said Riniker, recalling his thoughts on the final lap. "I just wanted it to stay together."

He was the only leader in the 42-man race that fortunate.

Esau — the pole-sitter and defending champ — zipped in front and held the lead until he made a pit stop during a yellow flag.

The El Cajon man spent 51 seconds in the pit — much too long — and lost his lead to Highland's Randy Becker on Lap 20. Unofficial counts had Esau back in 10th place thanks to the trouble.

But Esau charged hard while Becker was losing his lead to Sepulveda's Roman Calcyznski on Lap 27.

By Lap 34, a charging Esau was back in front. But he lost his lead again on Lap 41 when his left front tire blew just before he went into Turn 9 — the huge loop just before the start-finish line. He spun out and went an estimated 100 mph in reverse, just missing a wall.

That allowed Sylmar's Thirkettle to take over the front spot. But engine problems became obvious three laps later, as his car smoked and left oil on the track. Eventually, he withdrew.

Riniker had his first Southwest Tour victory, although it came unexpectedly.

"I was hoping for a third-place finish," said Riniker. "Then Ron is sliding off the track and Jim is smoking. We were pretty lucky."

Getting his victory at Riverside was especially sweet for Riniker.

His father (and crew chief), Gene, raced in the first Vons 200 at Riverside in 1967, when Kevin was 6. He often races at Riverside and nearby Orange Show Speedway in San Bernardino.

Riniker conceded that he might have had an advantage over the others by racing on his "hometown" track.

"Being the local guy from Riverside, I had a lot of people behind me," said Riniker. "Definitely the greatest moment of my career."

Riniker won $5,524 and moved up to No.7 in the NASCAR Southwest Tour standings.

Calcyznski, the Southwest Tour leader, finished second, only to be disqualified after an inspection revealed he used too large an engine; his car was over the 358-cc limit at 359.048.

Modesto's Troy Beebe moved up to second place and earned $2,800, while Becker got third and $2,000. Greg Scheidecker of Redlands was fourth and earned $1,400.

As for Esau and Thirkettle, they finished sixth and ninth, respectively.

Race notes

Among the other San Bernardino County racers, Chino's **Rick Greaney** was eighth, **Walt Snow** of Grand Terrace was 15th, San Bernardino's **Alan Brown** 29th, **Brian Jackson** of S.B. 35th, and Highland's **Glen Cummings** 39th ... Cummings was put in the starting grid after No.6 qualifier **Ed Ash** crashed in a morning practice session. Ash was not injured.

Schrader Gambles on Mileage—and Wins

Ken Schrader gambled on gas mileage and won Saturday's NASCAR Motorcraft/Trak Auto 300 Grand American stock car race at Riverside International Raceway when leader Troy Beebe broke a shock with two laps remaining.

Schrader's Thunderbird carried a three-second lead into the final lap around the 2.62-mile course and

finished second in a Camaro.

The NASCAR Winston Cup Series veteran from Fenton, Mo., who started fourth in the 42-car field and got to the front by skipping a second pit stop for gas and tires, won $7,600 from a purse of $47,000. He averaged a record 98.850 m.p.h.

A fifth-place finish gave Mike

Schrader finishes strong at 300 Grand American

Ken Schrader inherited the lead one lap from the end and went on to win the Motorcraft-Trak Au-

300 Grand American Saturday

The June 1987 Budweiser 400 Winston Cup race was won by Tim Richmond, in front of a father's day crowd of 55,000 fans, collecting $36,450 for the win. Second was Ricky Rudd with Neil Bonnett in third.

Richmond drives home point at RIR: He's back

By JIM LONG
Sun Sports Writer

RIVERSIDE — All that's needed is a country-western composer with an interest in stock car racing, and we'd be all set.

The Ballad of Tim Richmond, we'd call it.

ALAN WARREN/The Sun

THE WINNER: Tim Richmond lets out a shout after winning the NASCAR Bud 400 Sunday at Riverside Raceway. Richmond returned from a life-threatening bout with double pneumonia only last week.

Rusty Wallace won the November 1987 Winston Western 500, followed by Benny Parsons and Kyle Petty. The win paid $47,725. A pit row accident injured four crew members.

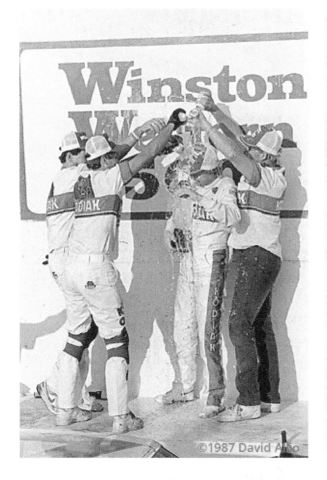

VICTORY TOAST: Driver Rusty Wallace (left) of Charlotte, N.C., gets a hug from pit crew member Jimmy Makar after winning the Winston Western 500 stock car race at Riverside International Raceway Sunday.

Wallace Gets the Win, but Not the Cheers
Riverside Crowd Thrills to Bitter Duel Between Earnhardt and Bodine

By SHAV GLICK
Times Staff Writer

RIVERSIDE—For 27 years the Winston Western 500 has been listed as a road race on the NASCAR schedule, but Sunday it was more than that.

For one memorable 20-mile stretch in mid-race, Geoff Bodine and Dale Earnhardt turned the twisting 2.62-mile course into a short track—banging and leaning on each other as if they were swapping paint on a banked bullring back in the Carolinas.

Both driving Chevrolets, Bodine and Earnhardt switched places seven times at the front of the 42-car field during that short stretch. And when they weren't passing, they were running side by side through tight turns that weren't meant for two cars at a time.

Both cars were predominately yellow, but before they were

4 Members of Elliott's Crew Injured In Pit Row Accident at Riverside

By SHAV GLICK
Times Staff Writer

RIVERSIDE—Four members of Bill Elliott's crew were injured and hospitalized in a pit row accident Sunday during the Winston Western 500.

Chuck Hill, 22, and a neighbor of Elliott's in Dawsonville, Ga., was the most seriously injured in the five-car crash. His spleen was removed and minor tears to his liver were repaired in an operation at Riverside Community Hospital.

Hill's hip was also dislocated and his right arm broken. His condition was listed as critical but stable.

Steve Colwell, 35, the crew's jack man from Blairsville, Ga., had a broken jaw, lacerated chin and fractured right knee.

Butch Stevens, 36, a tire carrier from Charlotte, N.C., had three fractures of his knee.

Dan Elliott, Bill's younger brother, had a bruised right shoulder and bruised right leg. Elliott and Hill were both changing tires when the accident happened.

The accident was triggered when the engine blew on Hershel McGriff's car on lap 8, bringing out the first caution flag of the race. All of the leaders immediately raced into the pits for fuel and a change of tires.

Elliott, in fifth place, was one of the first in. His car was already up on the jack when Mike Waltrip, who was pitted nearby, slowed to stop at his pit. Before he could turn in, he was hit from the rear by Jim Robinson.

The impact caused Waltrip's Chevrolet to spin sideways, hitting Elliott's crew members and blocking pit row.

Surprisingly, Elliott's Ford was not hit.

Bobby Hillin and Joe Ruttman tangled while trying to stop, which caused race officials to close pit row while they tried to extricate the cars.

All of the cars were able to continue although some were noticeably battered.

When Elliott pitted during the remainder of the race, members

Irv Hoerr: *"Buddy Baker had just become a commentator and offered me a ride in the fall 1987 race due his and my Oldsmobile connections. The car didn't seem to have any brakes after the first few laps, Kenny Schrader hit me on the approach to turn one and I lost about ten spots. Still I started 18th and finished 22nd."* Compiler's Note – Irv had a few more NASCAR starts with two top ten finishes, won two IMSA American Challenge Championships, the 1992 IMSA GTO Championship and 1992 and 1996 GTS-1 Championships and had numerous Trans Am wins.

Bobby Allison

In the last Southwest Tour race at Riverside, Ron Esau won the June 1988 Motorcraft / Carquest 300, followed by Mike Chase and Troy Beebe.

Pruett, Esau take victories at RIR

By KATIE CASTATOR
Sun Sports Writer

RIVERSIDE — Two more "lasts" were recorded Saturday in the final weekend of racing action at Riverside International Raceway.

Scott Pruett, a 28-year-old road racer from Roseville, Calif., captured the 12-car International Race of Champions series event. It was the third — and last — win in five Riverside starts for Pruett, who also recorded the first win of his career at RIR in a three-hour endurance race back in 1984.

Ron Esau, a 33-year-old from Lakeside, Calif., won his fourth and last race at the legendary 2.62-mile road course by taking the Motorcraft/Trak Auto 300, a Southwest Tour stock car event.

The final "last" of the weekend is scheduled for today, when the winner of NASCAR's Bud-

dirt. When he attempted to pull back on the track, the car spun wildly. But he got it back under control only to T-bone NASCAR's Dale Earnhardt after the latter blew his engine and was parked across the track in Turn 6.

"Maybe he (Guerrero) didn't see me go up underneath him," said Pruett. "We barely made contact. I knew it was close."

Said Guerrero of his collision with Earnhardt: "When I got back on the track there was a lot of oil where Earnhardt had blown his engine, and there was nothing I could do."

Pruett's next victim was Robinson. He got underneath him on Turn 7 of the 21st lap and pulled into the lead.

Pruett completed his winning run in 46 minutes, 34 seconds at an average speed of 98.182 mph. He led Robinson over the finish line by 2 seconds. Unser Jr. placed third.

In June, 1988, the Budweiser 400, the last Winston Cup race at Riverside and also the last pro race of any kind to be held at Riverside, was won by Rusty Wallace in front of an estimated crowd of 75,000, Terry Labonte was second and Ricky Rudd third. The win paid $49,100. The pace car led more laps than anybody; with eight cautions totaling one third of the race, making it the third slowest NASCAR race ever held there.

Riverside winner overcomes error

By Tom Higgins
Knight Ridder News Service

RIVERSIDE — Rusty Wallace held off Terry Labonte and Ricky Rudd in a furious, controversial Budweiser 400 finish Sunday to become the last NASCAR Winston Cup Series winner at historic Riverside Raceway.

The 2.62-mile road course soon is to be razed and turned into a shopping center.

Wallace, driving a Pontiac, overcame an error by officials to score his third straight victory on a road layout.

As the field restarted on the 85th of the 400-kilometer event's 95 laps following a yellow flag, a spectacular tangle sent the cars of Neil Bonnett, Ken Schrader, Dave Marcis and Sterling Marlin spinning off Turn 9. The yellow showed again but not before the leaders had passed the flag stand.

Under NASCAR rules, this meant they could race back to the line. Wallace, Rudd, Labonte, Phil Parsons and Dale Earnhardt were in the process of doing that when Wallace and then Rudd suddenly, inexplicably slowed on the long, downhill backstretch. Earnhardt and Parsons shot by, apparently taking the lead spots.

However, an official had erroneously ordered the pace car onto the track too soon from its position in Turn 8. That was the reason Wallace and Rudd braked.

"Since it was our screw-up, the decision was to put the cars back in line like they were," NASCAR spokesman Chip Williams said. "We've apologized to the crews on pit road."

The ruling placed Wallace, Rudd, Labonte, Parsons, Earnhardt and Kyle Petty in line for the restart on Lap 91.

Wallace surged away in a frantic dash to the finish, pulling to a lead of about five car lengths.

On Lap 94, Labonte muscled past Rudd's Buick for second place. He was followed by the Chevrolet of Earnhardt, who bumped Rudd. Rudd came right back with a bump of his own in Turn 6 to regain third place.

It was now a question of whether either Labonte or Rudd had the horsepower to run Wallace down. Neither did, and Wallace won by 1.30 seconds.

Earnhardt took fourth place, and Parsons was fifth in an Olds.

The race was red-flagged to a halt on Lap 32 after a Chevrolet driven by West Coast veteran Reuben Garcia went out of control, plowed through and over a guardrail along the homestretch, slashed through a steel fence and smashed down a concrete wall at the edge of the main grandstand. Miraculously, neither Garcia nor any spectators were seriously injured.

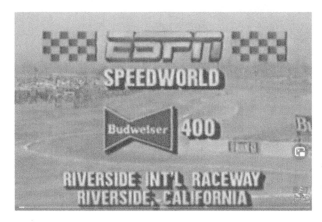
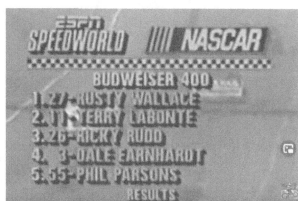

Watch the Budweiser 400 on the attached DVD

Eventual winner Rusty Wallace leads the pack during the 400 Sunday at Riverside International Raceway.

Bobby Allison

Chad Little

Is This the Year That Riverside Finally Closes?

Dale Earnhardt was named winner of the Jerry Titus Memorial Award for 1987 at the annual banquet of the American Auto Racing Writers and Broadcasters Assn. last Saturday night, but no sooner had the cheering subsided for the Winston Cup stock car champion than talk centered on this year's racing season.

The Titus Award, named for the late racing driver and journalist, is given to the driver who polls the most votes in the AARWBA's annual All-American team balloting.

For Southern Californians, the 1988 season figures to be bittersweet, filled with nostalgia and disappointment as Riverside International Raceway—possibly the most famous road racing course in America and one of the highest regarded in the world—finally closes its gates.

There have been false alarms before about the 30-year-old raceway yielding to the Inland Empire's building boom and becoming a Moreno Valley shopping mall, but this time the signs are strong.

NASCAR has dropped the Winston Western 500 race in November at Riverside, after a run of 26 years, and replaced it with a race on the mile oval at Phoenix International Raceway.

The final major event scheduled at the old racing facility east of Riverside is the SCORE International world closed-course off-road championships, Aug. 13-14.

Before that, racing fans will get their final looks at the nine-turn course during an International Motor Sports Assn. Camel GT program April 30-May 1, the International Race of Champions June 11 and the Budweiser 400 NASCAR race June 12.

For the first time since the International Motor Sports Assn. series began at Riverside in 1979, the event will not be sponsored by the Los Angeles Times and it will not include the prototype GTP cars such as Porsche 962, Ford Mustang Probe, Corvette GTP, Nissan ZX or the Jaguar XJR-7 that won last year's race with Hurley Haywood and John Morton driving. Only GTU and GTO cars will be featured this year.

The race, as yet unsponsored, will be called the Riverside Grand Prix.

The biggest disappointment to area racing enthusiasts is that there seem to be no signs of another racing facility on the horizon in Southern California. Many sites have been mentioned as possibilities—Corona, Perris, Lake Elsinore, San Bernardino, San Diego County, Simi Valley and the Palmdale-Lancaster region—but no ground has been broken and there are no plans in the works.

NASCAR officials, who have said it is imperative to have a West Coast date on the Winston Cup schedule, have given up on a Southern California site for 1989 and are planning to use the mile oval in San Jose, on the Santa Clara County Fairgrounds property.

□

Riverside: Cut down in its prime

By NATE RYAN
Sun Sports Writer

SUN PHOTO

Riverside International Raceway, a twisting, eight-turn road course, was open for 31 years. It closed in 1988 to make room for a shopping mall.

Los Angeles Times

Motor Racing / Shav Glick

Stock Cars to Make Last Stop at Riverside

230

Chapter Two - The SCCA Trans Am

Founded in 1966 as the Trans American Sedan Championship to showcase "pony cars", this was SCCA's second effort into pro racing; the first being the USRRC. Spearheaded by John Bishop, who would later found IMSA,, using FIA rules, there was initially only a manufacturers championship (a driver's championship was added later) with over and under two liter categories, There were ten races held at Riverside from 1966 to 1986.

SAME OLD LES — Les Richter l o o k s as big to drivers who race sedans on his road course at Riverside International Raceway as he did to NFL quarterbacks a few years ago as a linebacker for the Rams. Cars racing Richter's Trans-America sedan championships Sept. 18 aren't as small as the Mini-Minor (No. 5) and Hino Contessa (No. 51), but even big cars look tiny when Les is on the scene.

The first Trans Am at Riverside, the last race of the season in September, 1966, was a four hour enduro. 7000 spectators saw pole qualifier Jerry Titus win in a Mustang followed by the duo of Bob Tullius and Tony Adamowicz in the Group 44 Dodge Darts. Australian Frank Gardner won the under two liter category in a Ford Cortina. 34 cars started, 24 finished. Note: This first race featured a Le Mans start

Fords gain victory in big engine test

RIVERSIDE (UPI)—Neither poor start nor a minor accident could slow down Jerry Titus' drive Sunday as he claimed the Trans-American Sedan Championship and its $5,000 purse at Riverside Raceway.

Titus, from Canoga Park, at the wheel of a Mustang, covered 135 laps or 351 miles to win the four-hour endurance test.

His official time was four hours, one minute and 14 seconds as he averaged 87.297 miles per hour.

Second place went to Bob Tullius of Falls Church, Va., who also completed 135 laps, as did third place Ron Dykes of Pacific Palisades, in another Mustang. Titus' victory enabled Ford Motor Co.

to claim the U.S. Manufacturer's big engine title. Ford and Plymouth were tied going into Sunday's final race of the season, but Ford prevailed with 46 points in seven events to 39 for Plymouth.

There was one serious accident along the course when Dale Maher, of Santa Barbara, spun out and his car rolled. The vehicle was demolished, but Maher escaped with only a cut finger and a few bruises.

Titus, the top qualifier on Saturday, was in the pole position but he actually started last in the 38-car field when his engine stalled.

Bob Tullius - Dart

Mustang Trio Leads Qualifiers for Sedan Races at Riverside

BY SHAVENAU GLICK
Times Staff Writer

RIVERSIDE — The Ford Mustangs, led by the Southland driving duo of Jerry Titus and Don Pike, took charge of the $5,000 Trans-American Sedan Race Saturday by winning the first three qualifying positions for today's four-hour race at Riverside International Raceway.

Titus broke the 2.6-mile track record for sedans with a one-lap clocking of 1 minute 41.9 seconds, an average speed of 91.854 miles per hour. Pike, who held the old record of 89.471 m.p.h. set last May, came second at 1:42.5 (91.217 m.p.h.)

Chrysler-Plymouth entry currently tied for the sedan manufacturers lead with Ford, qualified both its cars in the eighth and ninth positions. Today's race is the last of the Trans-Am circuit.

In the Trans-Am, competition is not among drivers, but among cars. The race will begin at noon, with a LeMans start, in which the drivers race across the track—on foot —to their cars parked on the backstretch at Riverside Raceway.

'Little LeMans'

under-two liter champion ship, the track will be f of little BMWs, Volvos, at Abarths, Hinos and ni Coopers trying to more miles in the fo hours than their mo powerful rivals.

The Trans-Am has be called the "Little LeMa for Little Sedans," and offers an unusual oppor nity for the day-to-d freeway driver to wat how professionals dri cars just like the o parked in the garage home.

Leading qualifiers:
1. Jerry Titus (Canoga Park), 1966, 1:41.9, 91.854 m.p.h.; 2. Don (Hawthorne), Mustang, 1:42.5; 3. Dykes (Pacific Palisades), Mus 1:43.7; 4. Pete Cordts (South San

Pete Cordts – Falcon

Jerry Titus - Mustang

Charlie Rainville - Barracuda

TITUS WINS SEDAN RACE AT RIVERSIDE

BY SHAVENAU GLICK
.Times Staff Writer

RIVERSIDE—Jerry Titus took a 5-day-old Mustang and overcame two irritating delays to win the Trans-American Sedan championship for Ford in Sunday's final race at Riverside International Race-back onto the track, Titus was in seventh position two laps behind Pike.

Jerry kept roaring up the Esses, putting pressure on the lead driver until he finally overhauled Dykes (who regained first place when Pike pitted for fuel) on the 95th lap.

Titus Triumphs In Trans-Am Race

By BRUCE GRANT
Sun-Telegram Auto Editor

RIVERSIDE — Jerry Titus flooded his carburetor, then swamped a field of 39 cars yesterday to win the Trans-America sedan race at Riverside International Raceway.

He had better than half a lap lead over second-place finisher Bob Tullius, in a Dodge Dart.

The under 2-liter winner was Horst Kwech, in an Alfa Romeo was forced to run over a cement-filled course marker tire. The pit stop to replace the screw-in cartridge lasted two minutes and 10 seconds.

The victory was worth $1,200 for Titus, who said the money will come in handy to help pay for the car he hopes to drive in next month's Times Grand Prix here.

The order of finish:

Jim Law: *"I had been doing pretty well in regionals with my much modified Saab, courtesy of the Culver City Saab dealer and Swedish car expert Ingvar Lindquist. Dick Guldstrand wanted to race something, recuperating from a bad crash, and convinced me we could do OK in this new Trans Am thing and paid the entry fee. Turns out we were pretty outclassed in the D Sedan category by Fiat Abarths but finished, completing 93 laps and made $50"*

Pete Brock – Hino Contessa

233

In September 1967, the Mission Bell Trophy 250 was won by David Pearson in a Bud Moore Cougar with Ed Leslie second, also in a Cougar. Third went to Bob Johnson in a Penske Camaro.

WELCOME
TO THE
2ND ANNUAL

MISSION BELL
"250" FOR TRANS - AMERICAN SEDANS

We are especially happy and proud to extend a warm welcome to you today. Look around you and you'll see why. For the past two months we've been extremely busy on one of the most ambitious improvement projects yet undertaken here at Riverside Raceway. And we're proud, because most of it has been aimed directly at you, the spectator, to provide you with more comfort and convenience as you watch today's Mission Bell 250 and companion features.

Viewing is nearly 90 percent better through the Esses; some of the access roads have been improved and you'll find additional drinking fountains plus two new sanitation units of the permanent type located on the inside of the Esses. And adding to that, we've built four new oasis rest areas with drinking fountains, shade trees and benches. These are the first of many such conveniences planned for the near future.

Unfortunately, time did not permit the completion of two more planned changes. The new Turn One is in and paved, but the necessary retaining walls still have to be built so we are using the "old" turn today. And the new and beautiful main entrance, although in its beginning stages, still is not completed.

Yes, we're indeed proud of the new look at Riverside but far from satisfied. Once again, I wish to renew my pledge that we shall continue with these improvements in the months to come until they no longer are necessary.

Meanwhile, thanks for coming. We look forward to seeing you again soon as the "Good Season" of premier races continues here at Riverside. Please enjoy today's activity.

Les Richter
President & General Manager
Riverside International Raceway

Pearson Leads 1-2 Win For Cougar

The start of the Riverside TransAm race saw David Pearson storm his Bud Moore Cougar into the lead ahead of pole-winner Jerry Titus in the Terlingua Mustang. (Cam Warren photo)

By Ron Hickman
Area Editor

RIVERSIDE, Calif., Sept. 17 — David Pearson made his second effort in the TransAm series a winning one as he took the Mission Bell 250 in a Bud Moore Cougar by an 82-second margin over teammate Ed Leslie in the second factory Cougar.

Early in the race Pearson ran second to pole-sitter Jerry Titus' Shelby Mustang, but Titus' retirement after 17 laps cleared the way for Pearson.

Bob Johnson finished third, a lap and two-thirds behind Pearson, in the Roger Penske Camaro. Fourth place went to Milton Minter's Shelby Mustang.

Under-2-liter honors went to Bert Everett, who raised the Porsche total to a virtually untouchable 70 points. Everett trailed Monty Winkler's Alfa GTA for most of the early going taking the class lead on Winkler's pit stop and never relinquishing it thereafter. Later problems slowed Winkler to a sixth in class and left Alfa with 52 points.

The early practice sessions established clearly that two causes would combine to make a shambles of last year's qualifying record of 1:41.9 set by Titus — improvements to the cars and tires and changes to the course resulting from the Riverside International Raceway's $300,000 improvement program.

COURSE FASTER

While the majority of the changes to the raceway are in the area of spectator convenience, new paving in the apexes of turns two and four have shortened them up and reduced lap times somewhat. The old turn 1 was still in use pending the relocation of the barrier walls.

Both Titus and Pearson turned

(Continued on page 14)

LATE NEWS

● Carroll Shelby, concerned about the one-point lead Mercury now has over his Mustang team in the TransAmerican Championship, is said to be talking with A. J. Foyt about driving a Mustang at the finale in Kent, Wash., Oct. 8. Cougar will have their first team, Parnelli Jones and Dan Gurney, in their cars.

● "A significant increase in power" is reported for the 1968 version of the famed Offy engine.

● The Ford strike has further hindered development of the Group 7 racing Calliope, and the car will probably not see a race track this season. The same is said to be true of Shelby's King Cobra.

● Carl Haas is the new North American distributor for Lola Cars, replacing John Mecom Jr. Haas will relinquish his deal with McLaren Cars.

● Lodovico Scarfiotti has signed with Porsche for the 1958 European Mountain Championship and Group 4 competition.

● Lamborghini is seriously considering a concerted racing effort, possibly as early as next year.

● All American Racers will have only one entry in the U.S. and Mexican Grands Prix.

● Charles Parsons may have a new Lola 3B for the last three CanAms.

David Pearson

Early in the race, the star performers at the Riverside TransAm sedan championship stayed close together. Titus had just passed David Pearson to take over the lead, followed by Ron Bucknum's Mustang, the Cougars of Ed Leslie and Allan Moffat and the Camaro of Bob Johnson.   (Martin Greenberger photo)

Ronnie Bucknum

The Monty Winkler/Horst Kwech Alfa GTA team disintegrated when Kwech rolled his car in practice and Winkler suffered from a holed piston. Winkler ran ahead of the Porsche contingent, here represented by Terry Hall, until he experienced his mechanical misfortune.
(Cam Warren photo)

The September 1968 Mission Bell 250 was won by Horst Kwech in a Shelby entered Mustang, collecting $1500 in front of a crowd of 13,300. Second went to Peter Revson in a Javelin with Craig Fisher third in a Firebird. Fred Baker won the under two liter category in a Porsche.

RIVERSIDE RACEWAY'S

3rd MISSION BELL 250

OFFICIAL PROGRAM $1.00

TRANS-AM SEDAN CHAMPIONSHIP
SEPTEMBER 8, 1968

Field for Mission Bell 250 Labor Day Race Gets Bigger

By RYAN REES
Sun-Telegram Auto Racing Editor

The glittering list of drivers and machines for the Mission Bell 250 road race at Riverside International Raceway Labor Day weekend glows brighter each week.

Points Leader Mark Donohue is entered, so are Jerry Titus and George Follmer, Peter Revson, Dan Gurney, Parnelli Jones, Davey Pearson (last year's winner), Cale Yarborough, Sam Posey and Ronnie Bucknum.

The Mission Bell 250 is for the fleet pony cars of the Trans - American series. The autos pitted in this race feature Chevrolet Camaros, Ford Mustangs, American Motors Javelins, Pontiac Firebirds, Dodge Darts, Mercury Cougars, and Plymouth Barracudas.

Also entered in a separate division will be under - two-liter cars featuring Porsche, Cortina, Alfa Romeo BMW, Mini - Cooper, Volvo, Renault and Saab entries.

Donohue has won eight of the previous 10 Trans - American races in his Camaro to sew up the driving title, however, Titus, in second place, is not conceding a thing and will be out to clip Donohue's tail with his Mustang.

COMPETITION PRESS & AUTOWEEK

Vol. 18, No. 37   September 28, 1968

Horst Kwech Gets Mustang Its Third TransAm Win; Mark Breaks, Revson 2nd

By Ron Hickman
Area Editor

RIVERSIDE, Calif., Sept. 8 — A funny thing happened amidst the sweltering 103 degree heat at Riverside today. They had a TransAm sedan race and neither Mark Donohue nor Jerry Titus won.

Horst Kwech, in the second factory Mustang, stood by in a strong third place right from the start and saw Titus and then Donohue break in front of him. With this formidable opposition gone, Kwech breezed home 40 seconds ahead of Pete Revson's Javelin, whose bid for a win got started too late for him to make up the disadvantage.

Craig Fisher showed that the Firebirds are a force to be reckoned with by placing third another 40 seconds behind Revson after starting at the rear of the grid without a qualifying time.

ALFA WINS

Jon Ward's Camaro was fourth, trailed by under-2-liter winner Vic Provenzano, who went long and hard at what appeared to be an insurmountable group of Porsches which gradually withered and died in front of his Alfa GTA.

It marked the third over-2-liter win for Mustang against nine for Camaro, and the second for Alfa compared with 10 for Porsche.

During qualifying it appeared the same tune was about to be played on a new piano, as Donohue captured the pole with a 1:33.6 lap to become the first sedan driver to lap the 2.6-mile Riverside circuit at an even 100mph, knocking 2.5mph off the record set by Titus last year at a 1:36.0 (97.550mph). Titus cut a 1:34.3 to sit with Donohue on the front row. George Follmer, Javelin, and Kwech made up the second row, with Revson joining the group of those who had qualified faster than the previous lap record in the fifth spot.

Dick Guldstrand, now a car builder on his own, qualified the Camaro he had built for Sam Conigliaro in the sixth position, next to Revson.

At the rolling start Donohue got the edge on Titus and led into turn

(Continued on page 10)

Horst Kwech, Mustang (2), leads George Follmer, Javelin (4) through Riverside's turn seven. Running a steady race, Kwech inherited the top spot when Titus and Donohue dropped out. Kwech campaigned an Alfa Romeo GTA earlier in the season and gained that marque's initial under-2-liter Trans-Am win at War Bonnet (Okla.), May 12.   (Richard George photo)

TRIUMPH RACERS SWAMP COMPETITION IN PORTLAND

Jack Scoville, of Corvallis, Oregon, edged Jerry Barker, of Redondo Beach, California, to lead a Triumph Spitfire charge through the first five places of the G production class at the Oregon Grand Prix. Scoville, the defending Northern Pacific Divisional Champion in G production, currently tops his division in national points.

Gary Blodgett, of Portland, Oregon, also brought laurels to the Triumph banner. Blodgett, driving a TR4A, diced with L.T. Rockie, of Portland, for the class D production honors. When the checkered flag dropped, Blodgett was 12 seconds ahead of Rockie's TR4A.

The next Triumph outing for Scoville and Blodgett will be at Cotati, California, for the National Championship Road Races.

Titus Shatters Riverside Record in Trial Run

By RYAN REES
Sun-Telegram Auto Racing Editor

Jerry Titus is out to make his last ride for Mustang an impressive one as he shattered the 2.6 mile course record yesterday in a trial run for the Mission Bell 250 at Riverside International Raceway.

Titus roared around the road course in a clocking of 1:34.1 for an average speed of 99.469 mph. The old course record was 1:36.0, or an average of 97.521 mph.

Titus' racing mate, Horst Kwech also broke the track record with a time of 1:35.0 for 98.526 mph.

Titus set his mark in nine lap sprint while Kwech was out for 11 laps.

Titus said after his record-breaking run that he thinks the low qualifying mark will probably be a full second lower than his time yesterday.

Titus will be making his last appearance in a Mustang as he is going into business for himself and will drive his own Pontiac Firebird in the next Trans-American race at Kent, Wash.

He said his car is being built in Canada and is to be brought to Riverside for testing before the Kent race.

Titus is well-known at the Riverside Raceway. He lives in Reseda and has had little trouble with the Riverside layout.

Titus said the hot weather may be a factor in the Mission Bell.

The Mustangs have not exactly set the world on fire with their dependability record on the Trans-Am circuit this year.

The hot weather would make things tough on all the cars that will be running at speeds close to 140 mph on the back chute.

The most varied field of any Trans-Am race this season will be on the starting grid for the race tomorrow.

A Cougar and a Barracuda have been entered for the Mission Bell. Neither has run a Trans-Am race this season.

In addition, there will be

Mark Donohue's Camaro, Craig Fisher's Firebird and the factory Javelins with George Follmer and Peter Revson behind the wheel. There will be also independent Mustangs and Camaros entered.

The under -two - liter division features Porsches 911s, Alfa Romeos, Lancias, BMWs, Lotus Cortina and Mini-Coopers.

In all, there are 37 entries with 20 of them in the American sedan class.

Qualifying should begin this afternoon about 1:30 with more qualifying tomorrow morning.

A special salute to Mustang racing will feature a trip around the circuit by more than 500 Mustangs at 10 a.m. The Pacific Southwest Conference of

Mustang Clubs is sponsoring the round-up.

A similar round-up for Javelins will also go around the road course at 1 p.m.

The Southern California Sport Car Club region will begin preliminary races at 10:30 with the Mission Bell 250 getting under way at 1:30 p.m.

A complete list of entries for the Mission Bell 250 is as follows:

Car No. 1: Jerry Titus, Encino, Ford Mustang Group II; 2. Horst Kwech, Mustang Group II; 3. Peter Revson, New York, '68 Javelin; 4. George Follmer, Arcadia, Calif., '68 Javelin; 5. Malcolm Starr, Clifton, N.J., Ford Mustang Group II; 6. Mark Donohue, Media, Pa., Sunoco Camaro '68; 7. Tony Adamowicz, Wilson, Conn., Porsche 911; 8. Ken Deckman, Alburn, Wash. '67 Camaro; 9. Ray Wolff, Inglewood, Calif., '68 Mustang; 10. Philip Halbert, Garden Grove, Calif., '68 Ford

Mustang;
14. Bert Everett, Doylestown, Pa., 67 Porsche 911; 16. Frank Search, Hayward, Calif., '68 Camaro; 17. Dick Guldstrand, Manhattan Beach, Camaro; 18. Jerry Grant, San Diego, '68 Camaro; 19. Dick Richards, Pasadena, '67 Ford Mustang; 20. Fred Baker, Mount. Minn., Porsche 911; 21. Pete Harrison, Long Beach, '66 Porsche 911; 22. Bob Bailey, Burnt Hills, N.Y., '68 Porsche 911; 23. Del Taylor, Denver, Alfa Romeo; 27. Dale E. Mahar, Ventura, Calif., '66 Barracuda; 35. Carl Fredricks, Inglewood, '68 BMW; 36. Wilbur Pickett, Daytona Beach, Fla., Porsche 911; 41. Browne C. Goodwin, Culver City, Calif., Lancia '67; 51. Don Peake, Los Angeles, '68 Lancia;
55. Jon Ward, Saugus, Calif., '68 Camaro; 63. Noel Armstrong, El Paso, Tex., '67 Alfa Romeo; 64. Tony Settember, Mill Valley, Calif., '67 Camaro; 66. William Maier, San Leandro, Calif., '68 Mustang; 71. Bruce O'Neil; Peter Buschbaum, San Francisco, '66 Porsche 911; 77. Craig Fisher, Montreal, Canada, '68 Firebird; 78. Ronnie Bucknam, La Canada, Calif.; 79. Ford Mustang; 79. Mark Waco, Tarzana, Calif., '67 Cougar; 81. Rob Colonia, Woodland Hills, Calif., Mini Cooper; 88. Dennis Duncan, Long Beach, Lotus Cortina; 91. Vic Provenzano, Van Nuys, Calif., '66 Alfa Romeo.

Kwech Drives Mustang to Mission Bell 250 Victory

By RYAN REES

After winning the Mission Bell 250 Trans - American race yesterday, Horst Kwech told reporters "I made up my mind to beat George to Turn One even if I had to get roughed up."

The Australian with an Austrian name, was explaining a minor collision between his Mustang and the No. 4 Javelin driven by George Follmer at the start of the race.

Both cars started from the second row and made a mad dash for the first turn to get in line behind the pole sitters—Mark Donohue and Jerry Titus.

Kwech won the duel with Follmer and took over a solid third place seat that later proved to be the winning pocket.

Titus blew the engine on his Mustang on the 15th lap near Turn Six just after he had overtaken Donohue for the lead.

Donohue took over the lead again and proceeded to run away from the rest of the field until the 50th lap.

He had lapped everyone on the track except Kwech and then on lap 56 he pitted for a brief talk with his crew. Two laps later he again rolled into the pits and turned off the engine with high oil pressure.

Follmer left the race on lap 37 with

a blown engine as he neared Turn Nine.

That left Kwech in first place with Peter Revson second in a Javelin about a half minute behind him.

After a pit stop, Kwech held only a scant 10 second lead on Revson but then Revson had to pit for gas and Kwech drew away to take a comfortable lead throughout the rest of the race.

Revson tried to catch the flying Aussie for several laps but said his water and oil temperatures prevented him from putting on as much pressure as he would have liked.

He settled for a comfortable second place finish — the seventh red ribbon for the Javelin team in the 11 Trans-Am races.

Craig Fisher in his Firebird started at the back of the pack after failing to post a qualifying time Saturday when he had a bad engine.

However, yesterday he moved through the field of cars with relative ease and when the leaders fell out, he moved into third spot — a long distance behind Revson.

After the race, Kwech said his engine ran perfectly all through the race although he did experience some difficulty with his differential in the early going.

"I started cutting back sooner on the turns and then I didn't have any trouble at all," he said.

Asked how he felt when Titus, his teammate went out, Kwech said "I was

a little tense. We haven't been too reliable this year. But the engine just kept running good and I didn't have any trouble."

He said the second best part of the race, aside from seeing the checkered flag, was seeing Donohue go into the pits the last time.

"Mark doesn't usually break and it was a real pleasant surprise today when he did," he said.

Donohue had broken down in only one other race, and had won eight of the previous 10 races. Titus won the other two.

Kwech's finish put the Mustang team ahead of the Javelins by six points with the Kent, Wash. race next month the last chance for the American Motors' entry to overtake the Ford team.

Fred Baker won the under - two - liter division in the race with his Porsche 911. Baker won the last under-two-liter division in the Denver, Colo. race to give him two straight wins on the Trans-Am circuit.

Vic Provenzano in an Alfa Romeo was second in the foreign car division.

A crowd of 11,566 saw the 22 cars roar away from the starting grid. Twenty - two cars were still running at the end of the race—80 laps later.

Time of the race was two hours, 28:08.6 for an average speed of 84.699 miles per hour.

The blistering heat took the toll on many drivers with some cars switching drivers during pit stops.

Kwech said he had a two gallon jug of ice water but that ran out "real soon."

The heat reached 123 degrees in the cockpits of the cars with the crowd sweltering in 106 degrees around the track.

The top 22 finishers were: Kwech, Mustang, first; Revson, Javelin, second; Fisher, Firebird, third; Jon Ward, Camaro, fourth; Baker, Porsche, fifth; Malcolm Starr, Mustang, sixth; Provenzano, Alfa Romeo, seventh; Jerry Oliver, Camaro, eighth; Ronnie Bucknam, Mustang, ninth; Pete Harrison, Porsche, 10th.

Wilbur Pickett, Porsche, 11th; Del Taylor, Alfa Romeo, 12th; Don Peake, Lancia 13th; Bruce O'Neil, Porsche, 14th; Ray Wolff, Mustang, 15th;

Mark Waco, Cougar, 16th; Ken Deckman, Camaro, 17th; Browne Goodwin, Lancia, 18th; Dennis Duncan, Lotus Cortina, 19th; Bob Barker, Mustang, 20th; Bob McGinty, Camaro, 21st, and Bob Bailey, Porsche, 22nd.

San Jose Looks Good

SAN JOSE (UPI) — The play of all three Spartan quarterbacks and the offensive running and defensive play of Walt Shockey featured San Jose State's first full scrimmage of the season Saturday.

Through the early laps of the race Donohue and Titus were never very far apart, and both led the race. Titus parked his Mustang in turn six at the end of 15 laps with a sick engine. Donohue was out at the end of 61 laps with the same malady.   (Richard George photo)

Vic Provenzano, Alfa Romeo GTA (97), passes Dennis Duncan's Lotus Cortina on his way to win the under-2-liter class and place fifth overall at the Mission Bell 250 held at Riverside Raceway, Sept. 8. It was Alfa's second win on the TransAm circuit. (Fritz Taggart photo)

A crowd of 14,335 saw Mark Donohue in a Penske Camaro win the October 1969 Mission Bell 250, the last race of the season. He was followed by teammate Ronnie Bucknum with Jerry Titus third in a Firebird.

Mustangs-Camaros To Battle At Riverside's Mission Bell 250

RIVERSIDE - Although Roger Penske's Camaro racing team has won two Trans - American sedan championships in a row, it still rates as an underdog to Ford Mustang in the Mission Bell 250 at Riverside International Raceway Oct. 5.

The $15,000 Mission Bell 250 is the 12th and final event on the 1969 Trans-Am calendar and it will be the first major race held on Riverside's

Last year, Donohue completely dominated the Trans-Am series, winning 10 of the 13 events, but still lost to Mustang at Riverside. It was also a Mustang that won the first Mission Bell 250 in 1966 and David Pearson's Cougar that set the race record of 94.715 miles per hour in 1967.

Ford's strong four-car Mustang team with Parnelli Jones, Dan Gurney, George Follmer and

Sears Point Trans-Am last weekend. Donohue's two - second win over Jones gave the Camaro team an insurmountable lead in the point standings.

Despite that, however, the Mustang team is under heavy pressure from its Detroit offices to win the race at Riverside for the simple financial fact that Southern California is the biggest market for Mustang sales in the country.

Parnelli Blisters Course and Tires

BY SHAV GLICK
Times Staff Writer

RIVERSIDE — Roger Penske credits a more efficient pit crew and superior tire wear — plus Mark Donohue's driving talents—for winning the Trans-American Sedan series championship for his Camaro team.

The racing rivalry of the Camaros and the Mustangs reaches its final phase today in the Mission Bell 250 over Riverside International Raceway's newly-paved 2.5-mile course. And as usual Penske has the same factors going for him.

Parnelli Jones, the 36-year-old semi-retired racing driver, posted the fastest qualifying time Saturday, blistering his Mustang around the nine-turn track at an average speed of 102.970 m.p.h.

Jones, however, was heats up the tires much more than we expected. The way they banked and widen the turn, it's almost like a super speedway turn now."

Mustangs qualified third and fourth, with Follmer at 101.152 m.p.h. and Peter Revson at 100.940. Also under the old track record were veteran Jerry Titus, in a Pontiac Firebird, at 100.334, and Donohue's Camaro teammate, Ronnie Bucknum, at 100.027.

Al Unser, fresh from a dirt track championship car win at Sacramento last Sunday, drove the third Mustang of Bud Moore's entry, and placed it seventh on today's starting grid despite unfamiliarity with its handling.

After Unser had spun twice on the course during practice, Parnelli looked

COMPETITION PRESS &
AUTOWEEK

Vol. 19, No. 41   October 25, 1969

Donohue Survives Rough Riverside

By Ron Hickman
Area Editor

RIVERSIDE, Calif., Oct. 5 — The Mission Bell 250 brought a crashing climax to the end of the 1969 TransAm series.

To the sounds of the crashing, Parnelli Jones was doing a slow burn in the pits with a shattered radiator on his Bud Moore Mustang while Mark Donohue's Penske Racing-prepared Sunoco Camaro was taking its seventh checkered flag.

Donohue ran the 250 miles in 2.36:35.5 to average 95.76mph and augment the Penske coffers by $3500.

Donohue took the lead for the first time after early leader Jones pitted for tires, relinquished it to George Follmer on his first pit stop, and took over for good as Follmer crashed his Bud Moore Mustang

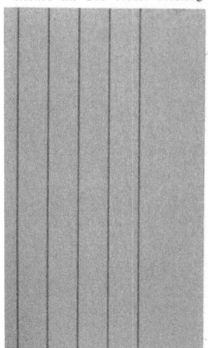

spectacularly into the end of the pit wall after a wheel broke when he was coming out of turn nine.

FOLLOW ORDERS

The only car on the same lap with Donohue at the finish was the blue Camaro of teammate Ronnie Bucknum, who spent the last dozen laps with Mark right on his tail, but Donohue under orders not to pass so that both cars could finish on the same lap.

Third place went to the T/G

Racing Firebird of Jerry Titus, a lap in arrears of Donohue but only 13 seconds behind Bucknum. During the closing laps Titus managed a steady erosion of Buknum's margin but ran out of time at the finish.

Peter Revson, a lap down on Titus, was the first Mustang to finish. One lap further in arrears, Rusty Jowett's Camaro was the top independent to finish.

The top under-2-liter car was Alan Johnson's Porsche 911, 10th

(Continued on page 19)

George Follmer, after spinning off on turn 7 at Riverside International Raceway, sets his Mustang in motion to get back into the race as Mark Donohue, Mission Bell 250 winner, passes him.   (Fritz Taggart photo)

Mark Donohue in Camaro wins Mission Bell 250

RIVERSIDE (UPI) — Mark Donohue looked ahead today to a third year of victorious Trans American sedan competition after he captured the $15,000 Mission Bell 250 at Riverside International Raceway for his sixth win in the 12-race series.

The Media, Pa., driver averaged 95.785 miles an hour in scoring his win that widened the Camaro lead in the final race of the 1969 series. Teammate Ronnie Bucknam of La Canada, Calif., finished on the same lap after Donohue slowed down.

Donohue last year captured 10 events in a 13-race series. His win Sunday brought him a $3,500 purse.

The series ended with the Camaro drivers scoring 78 points to 64 for Mustang and 34 for Firebird. Porsche won the under 2-liter class with 81 points.

The crowd of 14,335 saw Donohue and Parnelli Jones engage in a bumping match that eventually forced Jones out

Davis named Pac-8 back of the week

Watch the AMC Javelin Trans Am film on the attached DVD

Tony Adamowicz Pit Stop

Ron Grable pits his Javelin for tires and fuel. Grable finished sixth, three laps down, at the final round of the 1969 TransAm series at Riverside, Calif., Oct. 5. (Autoweek photo)

RACING AND AMERICAN RACEWAYS INCORPORATED

As many of you racing fans know by now, Riverside International Raceway was purchased in part earlier this year by American Raceways, Inc., a Detroit-based firm headed by businessman Lawrence H. LoPatin.

With the acquisition of Riverside, A.R.I. now manages five major tracks either in operation or under construction. Those with racing schedules already established include Riverside, Atlanta International Raceway and Michigan International Speedway. Texas International Raceway, a $7 million facility at College Station, Tex., is nearing completion and will hold its first race--a Can-Am-- next month.

The fifth track, Eastern International Raceway, in New Jersey was only recently announced and will not be in use until sometime next year. Major racing dates, however, have already been approved for the track.

By joining A.R.I., Riverside becomes a part of the most dynamic concept in the history of auto racing--a concept which promises to be a major force in the future of the sport. Auto racing has become "big league" in the best sense of the term and it requires big league plants in order to accommodate both its fans and its participants.

Spectator comfort and driver safety are the two prime considerations of A.R.I. facilities and that accounts for the many changes you see here today. We are proud to be a part of the American Raceways concept and we look forward to enjoying with you the exciting future of auto racing.

Jerry Titus charges his '68 Firebird (13) toward a third place finish at the Riverside TransAm. Here he's chased through turn 7 by race winner Mark Donohue's Camaro (6) and Miles Gupton's Porsche 911 (57). Gupton was seventh in under-2-liter. (Fritz Taggart photo)

THE GOODYEAR Tow
er, Riverside's most fami
iar landmark, has found
new home. The 60-foot, 6
ton steel structure wa
moved three weeks a
from the start-finish lir
to its present location b
hind the permanent gran
stands in the Esses.

The move was initiat
to make room for
$160,000, two-level pres
radio and television co
plex. The Goodyear Tow
will now serve for crov
control.

The move marked t
second transplant of t
tower in its brief histor
Originally the air contr
facility for the old Los A
geles International A
port, the tower was or
moded by a huge 170-fc
structure when L.A. Int
national unveiled its "
age terminal" in 1961.

W h e n Richter learr
that the city of Los An
les planned to destroy
old tower, he submitted
sealed bid of $1. It was
highest and only offer
city received.

Richter and Hord
mantled it in L.A. a

255

Attendance was 16,500 for the Mission Bell 200 in October 1970. For the first time there was a separate under two liter race. Pole qualifier Parnelli Jones in a Bud Moore Mustang earned $5750 to win the over two liter event, recovering from a spin that put him back to ninth. He was followed by teammate George Follmer with Mark Donohue in third. Fourth went to Swede Savage in the All American Racers Barracuda with teammate Dan Gurney, in his only Trans Am start at Riverside, in fifth.

In the under two liter race, a 35 lap, 90 mile event, Bert Everett won in an Alfa followed by Horst Kwech in another Alfa and Don Pike in a BMW in third.

Jeff Kline: *"My first pro race - In a 1300cc Alfa GTA jr. It was a factory prepared car, alloy body, twin plug head. Cost $5800 at the time. I qualified mid field, finished seventh. Won $250. Racing Sports Cars had me listed as the youngest driver in the race."*

Sam Posey and Peter Revson had a post race altercation

Jim Trask: *"Embarassing story now – October 1970; money was tight so my dad went to Riverside without my brother and I. My birthday was October 3rd and the day after the race my dad said; I've got a present for you and handed me a Bell Star helmet that said Gurney on the side. I was a big Gurney fan. Turns out it was Dan's last race and the newspapers mentioned Dan's helmet had been stolen. So my dad called AAR, said he had the helmet. The receptionist asked where he found it and he said; "in the seat of a racecar. He returned it anonymously - no questions asked !! I am privileged to say I had it on my head, albeit for a short time"*

Gurney Wants Helmet

SANTA ANA, Calif. (AP) — Dan Gurney wants the helmet he wore in his last race as a memento and asks whoever took it to please return it.

After driving in the Mission Bell 200 at Riverside International Raceway last Sunday, the star of 15 years competitive driving announced it was his last race.

As he was being interviewed, somebody took the helmet from his car, Gurney said Thursday. And the headgear had his name written on it in bold letters. A thorough search failed to turn up the helmet and one of the pit crew recalled seeing a "distinguished gentleman," taking it from the car.

NEWSWORTHY — The "distinguished-looking gentleman" who lifted **Dan Gurney's** helmet from his car the day Dan announced his retirement as a race driver has had a change of heart. He returned it anonymously with a note which ended, "All my nerve was expended when I obtained your helmet, therefore, none left to sign this letter."

Parnelli Survives Crash to Win; Gurney Fifth in Farewell Race

BY SHAV GLICK
Times Staff Writer

RIVERSIDE — It was Dan Gurney's swan song as a race driver, but the day was upstaged by Parnelli Jones.

The "Gurney for President" fans among the 16,500 at Sunday's Trans-Am sedan series finale at Riverside International Raceway had moments to cheer when their hero briefly led in the 200 mile race, but it was the mad dash of Parnelli from ninth (after spinning off the course) to first which captivated the crowd.

Shortly after his Plymouth Barracuda finished fifth in the Mission Bell 200, Gurney said the words everyone had predicted he would say: "I quit."

"I have always felt that part of being a successful race driver is in knowing Dan held the lead for two laps.

Jones, who had won four earlier Trans-Am races to help Ford sew up the manufacturer's championship, started from the pole and appeared to be on his way to a wire-to-wire win when trouble occurred on the sixth lap. He was about to lap two slower cars when it happened at the approach to Turn 9.

"The driver in car No. 44 (John Silvia) waved me by on the left," explained Jones later. "Just as I started to move, another car (Clay Priola, in No. 30) moved up on No. 44. This caused him to slide and he hit me broadside."

Goes Off Track

The impact sent Parnelli's orange-colored Mustang spinning off course, to disappear behind the hay bales protecting the The Chaffey College car, No. 0 with Dick Guldstrand at the wheel, completed 12 laps before blowing an engine moving up through the esses.

"It was a magnificent experience for the kids," said enthused Chaffey racing car technology instructor Sam Contino. "The car blew an engine Saturday and the students worked all night putting in an engine we had for a training class at school. They learned more here in a couple of days than they could have learned in a month in class."

Jones drove the 200 miles in 2 hours, 40.3 seconds at an average speed of 99.771 m.p.h. and earned $5,750 for his fifth Trans-Am win.

Sunday's results:

MISSION BELL 200 (79 laps)—1. Parnelli Jones (Torrance), Mustang, 79 laps, $5,200; 2. George Folimer (Arcadia), Mustang, 79, $3,050; 3. Mark Donohue (Media, Pa.), Javelin, 79, $2,300; 4. Swede Savage (Santa Ana), Barra-

Congratulations from **MINILITE** to
BUD MOORE ENGINEERING and

MUSTANG

1970 TransAm Champions

Drivers: Parnelli Jones, George Follmer

Owner: Bud Moore   Team Crew Chiefs: Bobby Jones, Glenn Sewell

Crew Members: Ed Blanton, Marion Newman, Cecil Moore, Daryl Moore, Lane Powell, Ed Stevens, Cap Chastain, Bill Delaney, Forrest Leonard, Morse Cody. **Team Manager:** Bud Moore **Ass't. Team Manager:** Kenneth Myler **Builder:** Bud Moore Engineering **Scoring & Timing:** Don & Ruth Nixon - Mr. and Mrs. Henry

Minilite is proud that every competitor of the eleven race series who received manufacturers points was using Minilite wheels! Points are based on nine points for the winning make of car, six points for the second place auto (provided it is not the same make as the winner), four points for the third place, two points for fifth place and one point for sixth place. *Only the highest finishing car of each make gets points for the first six positions.*

The October 1971 Trans Am, now the Mission Bell 200 and shortened to 79 laps or 200 miles, was won by pole qualifier George Follmer in a Roy Woods American Racing Associates Javelin, collecting $6700. He was followed by teammate Vic Elford with Jackie Oliver third in a Penske Javelin.

George Follmer (69) and Vic Elford in their ARA Javelins cruise the Riverside circuit holding the same positions in which they finished, giving the Roy Woods team a 1-2 sweep in the last TransAm of 1971. (Bob Mangram photo)

John Ryals: *"I got recruited to help a friend of a friend, John Ware, with his Camaro. While by no means a pro (I was only 21), I put together a pit socket with a spring and modified the lug nuts for our pit stops, something I learned from watching NASCAR. The pit stops all went well and, for some reason, I then took the fuel cans over to refill them. Sure enough, I come back to see a flat shredded tire lying in our pit. John had put a wheel off, flattened a tire and came in for an unscheduled stop and, me, the tire guy, wasn't there to help. We finished twelfth in spite of that !!"*

Story from the Pits: *"Mustang racer Bob West pulls in on the last lap; screaming through his helmet - "I'm out of gas". His crew chief, behind the pit wall yells back – "one more lap to go" They went back and forth a few times before Bob figured it out and roared out of the pits. He made it around one more time and finished seventeenth."*

Marshall Robbins: *"I ran fifth, made $1900. The first Camaro. One lap up on Mo carter in another Camaro. My first and only time at Riverside, loved that long straight and turn nine. Didn't so much like to heat, dust and smog"*

Arcadia's Follmer wins Trans-American 200

RIVERSIDE, Calif. (AP) — Jackie Oliver had more ground to make up and more than pride at stake in the Mission Bell 200-mile Trans-America sedan race.

Oliver qualified only 12th in the 35-car field for Sunday's 10th and final Trans-Am circuit race. His was the only factory American Motors Javelin in the race, the same car which a month before had captured the national team title.

In front were the likes of George Follmer and Vic Elford. Not only that but Oliver had taken over the car late Saturday without any practice when Donny Allison suffered a broken wrist in a freak practice-lap accident.

Allison had actually been a substitute driver for Mark Donohue who is the Javelin team's No. 1 driver.

But Oliver pulled his car through traffic and into third behind Follmer of Arcadia, Calif., and Elford of London.

And it proved itself in Follmer's hands, too, because that was the model he—and even Elford—drove. But theirs were privately owned and not part of the factory team.

The victory was worth $6,700 to Follmer, a tire dealer, and Elford gathered $4,800. Follmer led virtually all the way so the only true drama was with Oliver, the veteran driver from Walton-on-Thames, England.

The small bore category race, now called the Two Five Challenge, with engine sizes under 2.5 liters, was won by John Morton in a Brock Racing Datsun 510 followed by Bert Everett in an Alfa and Mike Downs in another Brock Datsun.

Horst Kwech leading John Morton

Jeff Kline: *" Bert Hornbeck had a BMW 2002 that was basically a regional car and he asked me to drive it at the 1971 Trans Am. It was pretty slow, but we finished eleventh. I managed to stay out of the front runners way but It got pretty uncomfortable toward the end;my shoes were melting and there was a pool of hot oil at my feet."*

Watch the Datsun produced video about the 1971 season on the attached DVD

A view of the garage

Buzz Dyer: *"I got started in the Trans Am, crewing for Ron Grable and later, Bob Tullius. I bought Grable's Dodge Dart, then moved up to a Javelin. My only Riverside race, in '71, didn't turn out well; developed an oil leak and retired after 32 laps. Most memorable was Follmer and Parnelli, using more dirt than road to get through the esses."* **Compliers Note – Buzz had a great career in the Trans Am with numerous top ten finishes. Now retired in Nevada, he's watching his son Tom making a name for himself in IMSA**

George Follmer won the 1972 Trans Am championship but there was no Riverside round. In the Under Two Five Challenge, the last year for that series, the October race was won by John Morton in a BRE Datsun 510, collecting $2900. Second was Peter Gregg also in a 510. Bert Everett in an Alfa was third.

 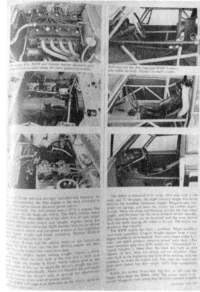

The January 1972 Road and Track had an in depth article covering the two five challenge. Read the entire article on the attached DVD.

Morton Takes Trans Am Sedan Race

RIVERSIDE — John Morton made it look easy at Riverside Raceway yesterday, winning his fifth straight 2.5 Trans Am sedan race.

Morton, a 30-year-old race car builder from Torrance, had a 41-second lead on second-place Peter Gregg after the 127-mile grind and took home first money of $2,900.

The victory was the sixth in 11 races for Morton, as he piloted his BRE Datsun 510 to a 50-lap average speed of 93.27 m.p.h.

Organizers of the 2.5 series decided after Morton's win that it would be the final race of the year, due mainly to Morton's dominance.

Gregg, who will also drive in today's Times Grand Prix Can Am event, had a 57-second lead on third place Bert Everett. Gregg won $1,575 and Everett $1,050.

Morton was expected to receive a strong challenge from Horst Kwech and Bobby Allison (of NASCAR fame), but Kwech pitted twice early, finishing out of the top 10 and Allison dropped out after 11 laps when he broke a rod on his Datsun 510.

Morton took the lead on the third lap, lost it momentarily on lap 40 when he pitted and was passed by Walt Maas, but recaptured it a lap later after Maas ran out of gas.

Bob Williams of Santa Monica won the pole position yesterday for today's 20-lap Super Vee race, which starts at noon prior to the 2:05 running of the Times Grand Prix.

Williams, driving a Volkswagen owned by San Bernardino's Frank Maka, toured the 3.3 mile road course in 1:27.65, a speed of 104.324 m.p.h.

Elliott Forbes-Robinson of LaCrescenta is next to Williams with 104.253, while John Woodner of San Rafael in third at 104.158.

The two drivers who are fighting for the series championship, Bill Scott and Harry Ingle, are fourth and ninth respectively. Scott, who holds a philosophy doctorate from Yale, has a 14-point lead over Ingle, who lives in Charlotte, N.C.

The winner of the year's final Super Vee race gets 20 points, runner-up 15, third place 12 and fourth 10.

Maka who will field three cars, qualified sixth. Morton, winner of the 2.5 Trans Am sedan race yesterday, drives the third of Maka's cars, which he qualified 10th.

2.5 Trans Am Sedan Results
(31 cars started)
1. John Morton, Torrance (Datsun 510), 93.279 m.p.h., $2,900; 2. Peter Gregg, Jacksonville, Fla. (Datsun 510), $1,575; 3. Bert Everett, Doylestown, Pa. (Alfa Romeo), $1,050; 4. Bob Stevens, Richmond, B.C., Canada (Datsun), $700; 5. David Burns, Redwood City (Alfa Romeo), $500; 6. Carl Fredricks, Inglewood (BMW), $400; 7. Corky Bell, Arlington, Tex. (Datsun 510), $300; 8. Dave Redding, Poway, Calif. (Datsun 510), $250; 9. Jim Ethridge, Los Angeles (Alfa Romeo), $200; 10. Tex Guthrie, Scottsdale, Ariz. (Ford Cortina), $150; 12. Lee Midgley, Hemet (Alfa Romeo), $75; 16. Charles Burns, Montclair (Vega), $75.

Pace Lap - Morton on the pole, Kwech second

Charlie Theriot hits the wall in turn six

Don Pike, Horst Kwech and John Morton

Watch this 1972 Trans Am video on the attached DVD

After a multi year gap the trans Am returned in October 1980 with Greg Pickett winning in a Corvette and collecting $5300. Second went to Roy woods with Mark Pielsticker in third.

Woods bags Trans-Am pole

motor racing

Associated Press

RIVERSIDE — Roy Woods of Oklahoma City, Okla., averaged 106.580 miles per hour in a Camaro Friday to earn the first starting position in today's 200-kilometer Trans-Am event at Riverside International Raceway.

Woods broke a 10-year-old record for factory cars of 103.673 mph, set by Parnelli Jones in a Mustang.

Also bettering the old mark was Greg Pickett of Alamo with 104.210 mph in a Corvette. Another Corvette driven by Phil Currin of Gainesville, Fla., was third in qualifying over the 2.547-mile road course with 103.450 mph. Mark Pielticker of Orinda was fourth among the qualifiers with 103.200 mph in a Monza.

George Follmer of Huntington Harbor, Woods' teammate in an other Camaro, was told by Sports Car Club of America officials his car wasn't legal for Trans-Am racing. After day-long conferences Follmer was told that if his crew makes a suspension modification and other required changes, Follmer can start 30th in the 30-car field today.

In a preliminary qualifying session for Sunday's Can-Am race at Riverside, another track record was broken as Lola driver Geoff Brabham of Tustin toured the course at an average of 127.994 mph, breaking a mark of 125.994 set last year by Keke Rosberg of Finland.

Rosberg, driving a Spyder, was second fastest Friday at 126.130

mph. Follmer was third in a Woods-Frisselle Frissbee with 125.020 mph. Qualifying for Sunday's race continues today.

Cardinal 500

MARTINSVILLE, Va. — Geoff Bodine led an assault on Martinsville Speedway's Late Model Sportsman qualifying record Friday and won the pole position for his division's half of Sunday's $112,595 Cardinal 500 Classic double-header. Bodine turned in a fast lap on the .525-mile track of 92.699 mph in a Pontiac.

SCCA championships

BRASELTON, Ga. — Dave Frellsen of Evanston, Ill., skidded off the Road Atlanta race course in a light rainfall Friday, but charged back to capture the GT-2 class national title in the national Sports Car Club of America championships.

ing.

Greg Pickett of Alamo, Calif., driving a Corvette, won his second straight Trans-Am by 10 seconds over Roy Woods of Oklahoma City, who drove a Camaro. Woods, who was a familiar figure in Southland racing in the late 60s while a graduate student at UCLA, was to have sponsored both cars for Follmer. After first saying he would withdraw his sponsorship after Follmer was ousted from the Frissbee, Woods changed his mind and said he would sponsor John Morton's efforts today.

100 m.p.h. Average

Pickett, who won last Sunday in Laguna Seca, averaged 100.99 m.p.h. for the 200 kilometer (49 laps) race around Riverside's 2.547 mile road course.

Again after a couple year gap the Trans Am returned in September 1983 with pole sitter David Hobbs winning in the DeAtley Canaro. Second was teammate Willy T,

Ribbs with Paul Newman in third, driving the Bob Sharp 280ZX. Hobbs picked up $8650 for the win

Meguiar's, Riverside's fall classic, set Sept. 23-25

Meguiar's Grand Prix Weekend, Riverside Raceway's traditional fall racing classic, runs Friday through Sunday, Sept. 23-25, with total cash prizes of more than $100,000.

The weekend is comprised of three main races: the Trans-Am, the Super Vee and the Rabbit/Bilstein. All races take place on the 2.5-mile Riverside Raceway course located 54 miles east of Los Angeles at U.S. Highways 60 and I-15E.

Among the competitors in the 101.88-mile, 40-lap Trans-Am will be England's David Hobbs, actor Paul Newman, Tom Gloy, Elliott Forbes-Robinson, top woman racer Lynn St. James and Greg Pickett.

Some of the racers in the 61-mile, 24-lap Super Vee contest will be Ed Pimm, Price Cobb, John Andretti and Chip Robinson. These cars are scaled-down versions of Formula I cars, with highly-modified 1500cc VW engines and drivetrains.

In the Rabbit/Bilstein race, veterans Karl and Paul Hacker, Peter Schwartzott, Mark Behm and Ed Mautner will be some of the top contenders. The race is 50.9 miles, or 20 laps, long. VW Rabbit economy sedans are driven.

Practice and qualifying begin at 10 a.m. Friday and last until 5 p.m. Practice, qualifying and three California Sports Car Club regional races are scheduled 8:30 a.m. to 5 p.m. Saturday.

On Sunday, warmups begin at 9 a.m. Regional races start at 11:45 a.m. The Super Vee race is at 1:30 p.m. with the Rabbit/Bilstein race beginning an hour later. The Trans-Am starts at 3 p.m.

Friday admission is $5 for adults. Children under 12 get in free. Weekend general admission tickets cost $12 and are good for gate admission both Saturday and Sunday. Parking is $10 per vehicle.

Tickets are on sale at the Riverside Raceway ticket office, 22255 Eucalyptus Ave., Riverside, and at all Ticketron outlets. For more information, call (714) 653-1161.

The event is sponsored by Meguiar's, makers of car-care products. The Trans-Am race is round 11 of the 12-race, 1983 SCCA Trans-Am Series sponsored by Budweiser. Robert Bosch sponsors the Super Vee Series, and Bilstein sponsors the VW Rabbit Series.

Vic Manuelli followed by Paul Newman and Irv Hoerr

Paul Newman, David Hobbs and Willy T. Ribbs

Hobbs Wins Trans-Am Battle and Maybe the War

By SHAV GLICK, *Times Staff Writer*

RIVERSIDE — David Hobbs was only slightly exaggerating when he said after Sunday's Trans-Am race, "The combined age of the first and third finishers is greater than the age of the rest of the field."

Hobbs, 44, was a wire-to-wire winner, and Paul Newman, 58, was third in the 11th of the 12-race Budweiser Trans-Am "muscle car" series at Riverside International Raceway. Willy T. Ribbs, Hobbs' Camaro teammate, caught Newman three laps from the finish of the 40-lap race to finish second.

The win, coupled with points leader Tom Gloy's failure to finish, virtually clinched the championship for the versatile Hobbs, who doubles as a TV commentator when he's not driving. Hobbs has 146 points to 129 for Gloy and 126 for Ribbs with only one race, Oct. 8 at Las Vegas, remaining.

Hobbs, who first raced at Riverside in 1965 in a Lola T-70, had not won in 15 starts before this year but now he has two in a row here. He co-drove a turbocharged Porsche 935

David Hobbs

with John Fitzpatrick that won the Times 6-hour IMSA race last April.

"Driving a Camaro is quite a change from the Porsche, which has ground effects and sticks to the pavement through the corners," said Hobbs. "These (Trans-Am) cars have no ground effects at all and slide through the corners. The contrast in driving techniques is total."

Hobbs and Ribbs got off the line one-two and raced that way for 17 laps before Ribbs tangled with a lapped car and cut a tire. With the help of a yellow flag that

Hobbs managed to pass them all but one, but he never came close to challenging his DeAtley teammate. Hobbs, who slowed the last several laps to conserve his heated tires, won by 11.6 seconds. Hobbs averaged 100.826 m.p.h. for the 1 hour 37.63 seconds he took to negotiate the 101-mile race around Riverside's 9-turn, 2.54-mile road circuit.

Hobbs said the happiest moment of the race, excluding taking the checkered flag, was when he saw Gloy's broken car sitting by the side of the road on lap 34. Gloy was third at the time his car quit.

"There's no use being coy about it," said a happy Hobbs. "When I saw him, I knew it meant I was a lot closer to the championship, so you bet I was pleased. He probably felt the same way last week."

Gloy, who passed Hobbs for the points lead a week ago after Hobbs failed to finish, dropped out with engine failure. It was only the second time Gloy had not finished in 11 races.

A crowd estimated at 17,000, including Newman's wife, Joanne Woodward, gave the gray-haired, blue-eyed actor a big hand as he drove his Datsun 280ZX into the winner's circle with the Camaros. It was Newman's highest finish this year.

"Gentlemen, I just feel lucky to be alive," said an exhausted Newman at the race's end. Asked if this might be his last year of racing, Newman looked over at his wife, paused a moment and said, "Who knows? Every year about this time I say it'll be my last, and then I come back. Maybe 70 will be a good year to quit."

One of the most impressive performances was by Richard Wall of Arcadia, who started at the rear of the 38-car field as an added entry in a rented Camaro and finished 17th. Wall had crashed his own car in practice Saturday.

Two-time Trans-Am champion George Follmer, who had planned to make his debut in a new Corvette, failed to get it finished and withdrew.

Rabbit/Bilstein Cup race, his brother Paul won 20-lap race with Peter Schwartzott second in pb finish with Karl Hacker.

David Hobbs: *"My main recollection of Riverside is that it was my last-ever win, so it has a special place in my heart," Hobbs recalled. "I loved that track. I drove in a lot of different cars there – IROC, Formula 5000, Can-Am, a Lola T-70, IMSA Camel GTP, including Bruce Leven's Porsche 962. There was something about Riverside that made for great racing, it had challenging corners – Turn 1 and the Esses were terrific."*

David Hobbs in the DeAtley Camaro leads Elliott Forbes Robinson in the Huffaker Firebird

Tom Gloy: *"Riverside; 1983 - Here we are the factory Ford team but have no engine pieces. Ford SVO is working like crazy to manufacture new parts like blocks and heads. To keep the program going we're scouring under workbenches and in shops for blocks and heads left over from the late 60's and early 70's, paying stupid money for any piece we can find and most of them end up being cracked or unusable but it's all we can do.*

This story begins at a hotel pool back east a few months before. Also at the pool are a couple SCCA officials who will go unnamed. We won a couple of races but were not in the hunt due to the lack of parts. They suggest to me that we build a couple of 335 cu inch engines and run them under 305 cu inch weight which they will monitor. Their plan was to make us more competitive for the rest of the year.

So I had a couple built. we debuted one at Riverside in my car; supposedly a secret between me and these SCCA guys. We ran practice and qualifying and did not sit on the pole!

When I arrived at the track on race morning, I was approached by the DeAtley team people who said they heard we were running an illegal engine. I was completed blindsided, as it had to be the SCCA who let out the secret. We switched back to a 305 before the race and my faith in "secret" deals ended that day.

That's my sad story. It was a good idea; we were not going to win with it but it would have helped while we awaited new engine parts which did not arrive until the next year." **Compiler's Note – Tom Gloy was 1979 Atlantic Series champ, won the Trans Am championship in 1984, had wins in IMSA GTP and GTO and had 6 starts in Indy Cars including the Indy 500.**

In the October 1984 Trans Am, Darin Brassfield won the 40 lap, 100 mile event in a Corvette, followed by Wally Dallenbach Jr, in a Camaro. Third was Willy T. Ribbs in a Jack Roush Capri.

CON KEYES / Los Angeles Times

Darrin Brassfield drives his DeAtley Corvette to an easy victory in the Trans-Am race Sunday at Riverside International Raceway.

Brassfield wins at Riverside

RIVERSIDE (UPI) — Darin Brassfield of Los Gatos won Sunday's Trans-Am race and Michael Roe of Ireland won the Can-Am race in the Riverside Grand Prix Festival at the Riverside International Raceway.

Skipping a year, the Trans Am came back in May, 1986, the first race of the season. While Wally Dallenbach had the pole in a Protofab Camaro. Paul Newman led for a while before being sidelined with engine problems. The 100 mile event was a Roush sweep, won by Scott Pruett in a Roush Capri followed by teammate Pete Halsmer in a Roush Merkur, Third was Chris Kneifel in a Roush Capri.

Roseville's Pruett overpowers Trans-Am

Pruett takes Riverside day after 3rd place IMSA effort

By BILL CENTER
Copley News Service

RIVERSIDE — It started as a race, but the opening Trans-Am event of the season ended up a commercial for Mercury Sunday.

Roseville's Scott Pruett, flying in overnight from North Carolina and starting from the back of the 37 car field, came from far off the pace in a Capri to lead Mercury teammates Pete Halsmer and Chris Kneifel to a 1-2-3 sweep at Riverside International Raceway.

Paul Newman led 18 of the race's 40 laps before the engine on his turbocharged Nissan Turbo ZX let go in the 26-degree heat. The sport Camaros of pole-sitter Wally Dallenbach Jr. and Jim Miller required much earlier with electrical problems.

The sweep was truly satisfying for Jack Roush, who owns all three of the leaders.

"We docked another one," said

Roush after Kneifel recovered from an early race tangle with Miller and Pruett and Halsmer survived a bumped mid-race duel that cut second from a cape.

Down eight seconds to Newman at the time, Halsmer was trying to hold onto second 25 laps into the race as Pruett, having come from 36th on the 37 car grid, was making tracks toward the front.

But just as Pruett and was getting past the new turbocharged Merkur driven by Halsmer, Newman's Nissan was slowing in a cloud of smoke down RIR's long back straightaway.

"Everything was fine," said Newman, who had taken the lead on the eighth lap with a nifty outside move on Halsmer going into turn nine.

"I knew Pruett was coming. I was started to miss. I thought it might clear out, but it got worse the, I just shut it off."

There was no shutting off Pruett

however.

Given a big assist by Halsmer who set up and qualified Pruett's Capri Sunday while Pruett was finishing third at an International Motor Sports Association GTO race at Charlotte, the winner sprinted through the majority of the Trans-Am field and was steadily moving up on the front-runners.

After starting next-to-last on the grid, Pruett was 16th after one lap, 11th after two laps and cracked the top five when Kneifel and Miller spun on lap seven.

"I made a move on Miller and it didn't work out," said Kneifel, who had started outside of Dallenbach on the front row. "The result was I inched places with Pruett at the back of the pack."

Pruett had survived a long night just to get to the starting grid. It forced the ride in mid-week, he arrived from Charlotte at 1:30 a.m. Sunday and didn't reach his hotel until 2. Then he had to report early in the

track to get his Sports Car Club of America license.

"Halsmer did a good job setting the car up," said Pruett. "That part really went good.

"My strategy was to feel the car out and move steadily toward the front and see what happened. If there was a chance to go for the lead, I'd go for it."

He saw his chance when he came up on the rear bumper of Halsmer after 23 tours of the 3½-mile circuit.

And Indy 500 veteran Halsmer knew he was in trouble.

While preparing both cars, Halsmer came to the conclusion that the turbocharged Capri was still a little stronger than the team's new Merkur's.

"We made really good progress with the Merkurs this weekend, but they are not perfect cars this race," he said. "These cars are our future, but we're still probably two or three races away from getting them where we want them.

But the Merkurs are also turbocharged, making it hard for Pruett's Capri to make a pass on RIR's long straights.

"If my brakes hadn't been going away, he never would have passed me," said Halsmer.

Much to the chagrin of car owner Roush, Halsmer and Pruett became engaged in a nasty little duel for second for three laps as Newman too slowed up front.

"We had some confusion out there," said Halsmer. "There was only one pit board for all three cars. I didn't know if they wanted me to move over and let Scott by (Roush claimed no such command was ever given) and Scott didn't know if we were racing for second or the lead."

Actually, they were racing for both. For just as Pruett eased ahead of Halsmer, Newman's car expired.

Once in front, Pruett had too much car for either Halsmer or Kneifel, who had climbed all the way back to third from 16th after his spin.

Pruett

"This is a good series," said Pruett. "In IMSA there are only two guys we have to battle in our class. Here there were five or six more tough people.

Pruett is a Roseville High graduate.

Scott Pruett: *"I loved racing at Riverside. It was my first Trans Am race (1986), and I won it coming from the back of the field. In fact, I joined the SCCA that morning. I also was very fortunate to win the last IROC race at Riverside (1988), during their final NASCAR weekend"*

Pruett Flies in From East, Soars to Riverside Win

Mercurys Finish 1-2-3 as the Opposition Falters in Trans Am Series Opener

By PAT RAY
Times Staff Writer

RIVERSIDE—Jack Roush gave another demonstration of why his Ford Motor Co. cars have dominated both the Trans Am and International Motor Sports Assn. circuits Sunday at Riverside International Raceway in the opening event of the SCCA 1986 Bendix Trans Am series.

Sunday's race started out as a battle among the Camaros of Wally Dallenbach Jr. and Jim Miller and the Nissan turbos of Paul Newman and Jim Fitzgerald and Roush's Ford entries. But by the time it was over, it was all Roush's Ford-made Mercury cars, as they wound up 1, 2, 3.

The winner was Scott Pruett of Roseville, who didn't even arrive in Riverside until 2:30 Sunday morning.

Pruett, 26, had competed in a Roush Mustang Saturday in an IMSA race at Charlotte, N.C., and if he was suffering from jet lag it sure didn't show as he roared up from his 31st starting position.

Chasing Pruett across the finish line was Indy veteran Pete Halsmer of Anaheim in the Mercury Merkur XT4Ri with another Indy veteran Chris Kneifel, who survived an early off-course spin to finish third. Pruett and Kneifel were in Mercury Capri cars.

Pruett, who had been battling with Halsmer for several laps, finally got by on lap 36 and suddenly found himself in the lead when Newman, who had led since lap 8, slowed with engine problems and left the race.

The sudden fortune came as a surprise to the winner.

"I thought Pete and I were fighting for second and that somebody else was way in front," Pruett said afterward. "After that things went really well, although I was getting a little tired since I only had about four hours of sleep last night."

Pruett was also quick to praise teammate Halsmer, who did the basic setting up of the car while Pruett was in North Carolina.

"Pete really had it close," Pruett said. "All we did was make a couple of minor changes this morning." As pleased as they were with Pruett's victory, Roush and the rest of the Mercury crew were even more happy with the showing of turbocharged Merkur, which is scheduled to replace the 3-year-old Capris this season.

"It's hard to believe that this car performed as well as it did considering that everything, including the engine, is new," a happy Halsmer said.

"We had been fighting a miss in the engine and just before the race we decided to take a chance and change to colder spark plugs. I guess we were lucky because it cured about 80% of the problems.

"Other than a slight problem with the brakes midway in the race I had no problems."

Kneifel had to earn his third-place finish the hard way.

"I guess you could say that I did things in reverse of Scott. He started in the back and went to the front while I started in front, went to the back and then had to fight my way back," he said.

Kneifel, who started on the front row, had his troubles on the seventh lap when he was running second behind Miller's Camaro. The pair tangled in Turn 7 with both of them spinning off the course.

"He (Miller) was holding me back and I decided I had to make a move. Unfortunately we both ended up in the same place at the same time," he said.

It was more unfortunate for Miller, who returned to the race after a pit stop, but dropped out shortly thereafter with electrical problems.

At that, he lasted longer than his teammate Dallenbach, who had started on the pole. Wally's ride was fast, but short.

He jumped into the lead at the start but got only as far as the back straight where his Camaro went dead with electrical problems, failing to complete a lap.

With Camaros and Kneifel out of the way, Newman, who had started third, took over the top spot and appeared on his way to his first Trans Am victory as he began to pull away from Halsmer, who was helping unintentionally to keep Pruett back.

Just as Pruett finally got past Halsmer, Newman's engine went sick and he coasted around and into the pits.

"Everything was fine, the tires were holding up great until the engine began to miss," a dejected Newman said. "I thought it might clear up, but it just got worse, so I shut it off and coasted down the back straight."

With their last competition eliminated, the Mercury trio was home free.

Chris Kneifel: *"I loved Riverside, especially that long, long straight. Good rhythm to it and fast in an Indy car. Could have done without the smog though. When CART changed the chassis rules to a one piece cockpit, I could no longer fit (I'm 6'6) but I found a ride in the Trans Am. Driving for in my first race for Jack Roush, I finished third in '86, a sweep with teammates Scott Pruett and Pete Halsmer. I'd' have been farther up but a brief encounter with Protofab Camero driver Jim Miller forced a pitstop.*

Trans Am Series

Dallenbach Wins Pole; Kneifel Also Out Front

By PAT RAY, *Times Staff Writer*

RIVERSIDE—Defending series champion Wally Dallenbach Jr. saved his best for a time when it counted Saturday and as a result will start on the pole in today's opening race of the 1986 SCCA Bendix Trans Am series at Riverside International Raceway.

The 22-year-old driver from Basalt, Colo., posted a 1-minute 21.45-second (112.417 m.p.h.) lap in his new Protofab Camaro to earn the top starting position for today's 100-mile event over the 2.54-mile short course at Riverside.

For his pole-winning run, Dallenbach won $1,000 and one point in the Trans Am series.

Alongside Dallenbach will be Chris Kneifel, who replaced Dallenbach on the Jack Roush Mercury Capri team after last year's winning combination split up—Dallenbach and Protofab leaving Ford to go with Chevrolet. Kneifel qualified at 111.117 m.p.h.

Paul Newman in a Nissan 300ZX

role in today's race, and Dallenbach believes he has an edge there.

"The heat will definitely be a problem for all of us," Dallenbach said, "but for tire wear I definitely think my car will be easier on them than the Capri."

While Dallenbach and his crew were able to overcome the usual new car problems, Pete Halsmer and his turbocharged Mercury Merkur XT4i are still having problems and wound up sixth in qualifying, but is still optimistic.

"We're still having some teething problems with the new car, but it is settling down for us, and I think overall the getting-acquainted process between myself and the XT4i is going quite well," he said.

Halsmer also qualified seventh in a second Capri, but if Scott Pruett drives it as expected today, it will have to start at the back of the pack.

Pruett finished third Saturday in

278

Chapter Three - IROC

The International Race of Champions was a made for TV spec series developed by Les Richter, Roger Penske and Mike Phelps. Run with a field of twelve top drivers from different disciplines in racing, it became dominated by the oval track stars. Riverside held the most IRIC events from 1973 to 1979 The series stopped in 1980 and was reborn when the next generation Camaro came along in 1984

Debuting as the 1974 season in October 1973 with Porsche RSR's, the series soon converted to Camaros,all built at Penske's Reading PA facility by a staff overseen by long time Penske employee, Jay Signore. In 1977, Banjo Matthews built the latest incarnation, a tube frame, fiberglass body more or less stock car. The next iteration, also built by Banjo Matthews was a Winston Cup car in disguise. Starting grids were determined by draw.

The 1974 season kicked off with three races in October, 1973 at Riverside, 30 laps on the 2.6 mile course, in conjunction with the Times Grand Prix can Am, Mark Donohue won the first riverside race followed by Bobby Unser and Peter Revson, the next day, George Follmer won with David Pearson second and Emerson Fittipaldi third. The third race was won by Mark Donohue again, followed by Bobby Unser and Emerson Fittipaldi. The series was televised on ABC until 1980, and then tv shows were split with CBS.

Motschenbacher Tabs Peter Revson

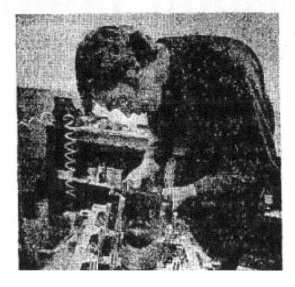

BY AL CARR
Times Staff Writer

SANTA ANA—A veteran road racer thinks that Peter Revson will be the point leader in the International Race of Champions this weekend at Riverside International Raceway.

He also thinks that USAC drivers Bobby Unser and A. J. Foyt may break their cars or their engines in their impatience to go too fast too soon.

Lothar Motschenbacher, a German immigrant who

in the RPM. He's a good driver, but very fast and determined. He will break the engine before he breaks the car. His attitude is win or break the engine. He has a thorough knowledge of Riverside. He also is familiar with the Carrera. He is Mark's teammate in the Manufacturers' series."

4. Bobby Unser—"He's extremely fast. But he might be too hard on the car. Will the car hold up, as fast as he is? It's not so much that he is not used to road racing. He's a great driver and will get used to it in a hurry. He has done well in the Pike's

Donohue's actions overshadow Follmer

RIVERSIDE — While Mark Donohue captured races and the attention, George Follmer went about his business and dramatically reaffirmed his position as one of America's greatest active race drivers.

Follmer, a vastly underrated professional driver from Arcadia, was the top

U.S. Auto Club star Bobby Unser, one of the pleasant surprises of the IROC, matched Follmer's point total with two seconds and a sixth, but Follmer was awarded the top spot because of his win in the second heat.

Also qualifying for the IROC final were Donohue,

Hulme spun in yesterday's third heat when he had sixth place overall clinched. Fittipalid and Follmer were put at the back of the grid in the first heat for missing a driver's meeting. Unlike Follmer, Fittipalid never recovered from the setback.

(Finishes in three heats, plus total points; top six

A.J. Foyt, Roger McCluskey, Bobby Allison, Denis Hulme, Emerson Fittipaldi, Gordon Johncock, Richard Petty, Peter Revson, George Follmer, David Pearson, Mark Donohue and Bobby Unser.

Daytona awaiting IROC showdown

RIVERSIDE — The heat races are history in the first International Race of Champions, and everyone agreed the three 75-mile runs at Riverside International Raceway last October provided some of the closest racing competition seen during the year.

Now the six winners, based on points earned at Riverside, head for Daytona International Speedway and the final race February 15.

The championship event will be 85 miles around Daytona's 3.81-mile road course for a purse of $75,000 with the winner getting $35,000. George Follmer, Bobby Unser, Mark Donohue, Peter Revson, David Pearson and A. J. Foyt are the six drivers who earned starting positions for the Daytona race.

The complete four-race series will be shown on ABC-TV on four consecutive weekends beginning Jan. 27. Goodyear is furnishing identical radial racing tires for all cars running in the series and will be a prime sponsor of the nationwide telecast.

George Follmer's performance in the first three IROC events should convince people the 39-year-old veteran is one of the world's most talented drivers.

Follmer tied with Bobby Unser for the most points in the three Riverside races with 29, but it was George who put on the show. He had a net gain of 23 positions in the three races while Bobby showed a gain of only 13.

Follmer's best showing came in the second race when he started in ninth spot and came on to win. In the first race he started 12th and finished fourth and in the third race he started 12th and finished fifth.

It surprised absolutely no one that Unser was USAC's big winner in the first three IROC events. Bobby improved his position in every race.

Unser started a little slow in the first race, moving from fifth to second for a gain of three positions. He got with the program in the last two, gaining five spots in each race. Bobby moved from 11th to sixth in the second race and seventh to second in the last one.

Seldom, if ever, has a race driver had a weekend such as Mark Donohue enjoyed at Riverside last Oct. 27-28. Donohue won two of the three IROC events run that weekend, won his sixth con-

secutive Can-Am race, was crowned Can-Am champion and announced his retirement as an active race driver.

Mark's last appearance in competition will be the final IROC race at Daytona, and many people think he will go out a winner.

The only blemish on his Riverside weekend came in the second IROC race when a sticking throttle forced him to the sidelines after only seven laps. He finished 12th in that race. The other two IROC races, and the Can-Am, were fairly easy victories for Donohue.

Mark's retirement as a driver does not mean he and Roger Penske are parting company. Donohue will continue in charge of the Penske rac-

ing operation, but as team manager instead of number one driver.

Peter Revson came out of the first three IROC events tied with Donohue with 25 points. Revson had a net gain of seven positions in the three races, with his best effort coming in the second race when he started 10th and finished fourth.

Peter dropped one spot in the first race going from second to third, and picked up two in the third race from ninth to seventh.

He has proven to one and all this year that given equal equipment he can run with the best. The final event in the IROC should be no exception.

NASCAR's representative in

the IROC final is David Pearson, who had to overcome a disastrous finish in the first race to make the Daytona trip.

Pearson was going well in the first race, but a leaking transmission seal forced him to the sidelines after 28 laps with a ninth place finish.

A second place finish in the second race a drive from 11th to fourth in the third race gave David 24 points and a place in the final.

A. J. Foyt was a late arrival in the IROC, because he didn't think it was fair to ask the oval drivers to compete against the best road racers in the world in four road course events.

"I'm surprised Bobby, David and I came out so well," commented Foyt after the three races at Riverside. "For myself I just played it cool. I figured it would take more than 20 points to get to Daytona and that's the way I ran."

Well the Texan cut it pretty close, beating Formula I ace Emerson Fittipaldi out of the sixth spot by just one point, 22 to 21.

"Riverside was just the heat races," Foyt said, "now we're going to Daytona to run the feature. This is where the money is, and it's the one people will remember."

Squire selling pitching book

WALNUT — Ron Squire, former head baseball coach at Mt. San Antonio College, has purchased the rights to his book, "How to Develop the Successful Pitcher."

Squire, who coached MSAC to a state championship in 1965, reports he has copies of his book available at his

home for $5.25 tax included.

"The book has been selling especially well to parents who want to help their sons with pitching," Squire said. "Many of the area coaches also use it for their players and assistants."

Copies of the book are available by telephoning Squire at (714) 595-7889.

Bobby Allison: *"When I got invited to the IROC deal, I went out and bought a Porsche 911 so I could get accustomed to driving it on the roads back home. When we got to Riverside I felt I was ready and during practice the only one quicker was Mark Donohue, and he was the guy who set the cars up. We drew for cars and when I went down pit road to qualify, mine started missing. I came in and told the mechanics what was wrong, that it wouldn't shift properly. All the mechanics were from Germany and one of them said to me, 'It can't be the car's fault, it was made in Germany. It must be your fault." Needless to say, I ran last. The next day Bobby Unser drew that car and he finished last, too. By some strange luck, I drew it again for the third heat. It was still a turkey but Roger Penske told me I had to go with it. On the first lap it started smoking, but I wouldn't come in. The longer I went, the more it smoked and I knew it was making the Porsche people mad, but I was mad, too, so I just kept driving around and around with smoke pouring out. I proved what I'd told them all along, that that one car was lousy. I went right home and sold my Porsche as fast as I could."*

IROC cars sold for $208,000

RIVERSIDE, Calif. (UPI) — It was a scene which would have delighted Ralph Williams, seeing $208,000 worth of used cars sold in a 24-hour period.

Shortly after the final event of the unique International Race of Champions at Riverside International Raceway ended Sunday, eight of the 15 Porsche Carreras used in the IROC races went on sale.

Buyers representing racing teams and individual drivers shelled out $26,000 per car. Some of the buyers casually made their choice on the basis of color, while others had kept logs of the races and knew which of the cars had the best finishing record.

"I was surprised there were no arguments over any particular car," said Steve Beizer, an Atlanta Porsche dealer who handled the sales.

The cars were identical in every aspect except their color, an attempt at equalizing the effect of the machine on the outcome of the race. All were insured by Lloyds of London (at a $25,000 premium price) and protected by a "wreck rule" during the race, which penalized drivers who caused damage to cars by reckless driving. There were no major mishaps, no serious damage to the cars, and no claims filed with Lloyds, rate organizers happily announced.

"We were very happy with the way the drivers took care of the cars," said Les Richter, a director of Penske Productions.

When the sale began, the black car in which George Follmer won the second race and in which Mark Donohue won the third race was the first to be sold. After that, the white Porsche Donohue drove to victory in the first event was sold.

Beizer said most buyers indicated the eight Porches would be raced in next year's Camel GT sports car series and in endurance races on the East Coast.

IROC organizers are keeping the other seven cars until the fourth and final event in the series is held next February at Datona Beach, Fla. Follmer, Donohue, Bobby Unser, Peter Revson, David Pearso and A. J. Foyt, the six finalists from Riverside, will drive the remaining cars in that race.

Bobby Allison: *"They took me to a hospital in Riverside, took my clothes away and gave me one of those front side only smocks. Then they took some X-rays and put me in a room and told me to wait for the doctor. It hurt more when I laid down so I sat up. About two hours later, I was still waiting when some friends from back home came to see how I was. I told them if I had my clothes, I'd leave. I was tired of waiting. They told me the clothes were out in the hall, so they got them for me and I got dressed and left. I guess it was about 5 o'clock then. About an hour later, I was back in my motel room and the doctor called."Where are you?' he said. I told him he ought to know because he'd called me. "He said to get on back to the hospital, the X-rays showed I had a broken back and he hadn't released me. "I told him, 'You had me and you lost me and I ain't coming back." The doctor said it would take about 30 days to heal, that I'd better take it easy. All afternoon it had been eating on my mind that if I made it back to the track the next day, I'd get the black car for Sunday's race. In those days the cars weren't really equal and we all knew the black one was the best. And being I was the first one out Saturday, I'd get to start on the pole Sunday. I was hurtin' pretty good but I couldn't pass it up. I showed up the next day and won, wire to wire. "It was hurtin' so bad that I couldn't fly home for four or five days, but it would have hurt a whole lot more if I hadn't won the race."*

For the 1975 season, now using Camaros, the October 1974 run in two heats. Bobby Unser won the first heat, followed by Foyt and Andretti. The second heat had an hour delay due tor cleanup from Fittipaldi's crash. Allison won with Bobby Unser second and Foyt third..

FITTIPALDI WINS IROC AFTER CRASH AT START

Allison wins heat in Champions race

Watch the 1974 race on the attached DVD

In 1976, the first race in October 1975, supporting Formula 5000 the Bobby Unser won the first race followed by AJ Foyt and Mario Andretti. Bobby Allison won the next day, followed by Al Unser and A.J. Foyt

Watch the video of Bobby Uunser's 1975 crash on the attached DVD

In 1976, on the F5000 weekend, Cale Yarborough won, folowed by A.J. Foyt and Jody Scheckter

MEET THE IROC DRIVERS

1978 - Mario Andretti, Linda and Elouise (Hurst), and Emmerson Fittipaldi   *MORMILLO PHOTO*

1977 - Neil Bonnett, Bobby Allison, and Chris Economaki   *PATRICK PHOTO*

1978 - David Hobbs, Bobby Allison, and Cale Yarborough   *MORMILLO PHOTO*

1977 - Al Holbert and Richard Petty   *TAKACS PHOTO*

1977 - Al Unser and Johnny Rutherford   *TAKACS PHOTO*

1979 BUDWEISER GRAND PRIX WEEKEND — **27**

TAKACS PHOTOS

MEDIA GUIDE

Williy T. Ribbs: *"At the 1978 IROC race, I stopped in on Friday to watch practice and qualifying. Practice was completed for the day so me and a friend went into the IROC garage to see Jody Scheckter. Jackie Stewart saw me walk into the garage and scurried over to Les Richter about fifty feet away. Les promptly walked over and told me to get out - It was for IROC drivers only !!"* **Compiler's Note - Willie T was the 1976 Dunlop Formula Ford Champ in the U.K, drove in NASCAR both in the Cup Series and Craftsman trucks, won 17 Trans Am races, had 4 wins in IMSA GTO driving for Gurney and 46 starts in Indy Cars.**

1988 Winston Cuop weekend was the last pro race at Riverside. Scott pruett won.

Pruett, Esau take victories at RIR

By KATIE CASTATOR

dirt. When he attempted to pull

Chapter Four - Off Road Racing

Off road races at Riverside were the second longest running events in track history, eclipsed only by NASCAR. Early off roader Brian Chuchua, a Fullerton Jeep dealer, organized early off road races in the Santa Ana River near Riverside Raceway. Then Ed Pearlman, founder of the National Off Road Racing Association (NORRA) and organizer of the first thousand mile off road races in Baja Mexico, put on a Ford sponsored Off Road Fair and NORRA race in 1970. In 1978 the Western Racing Association put on the Riverside Roundup Off Road Race in conjunction with the High Desert Chili Championship, using much of the infield.

Unique Off-Road Race at RIR

RIVERSIDE — Imagine all the spectator thrills of a Baja off-road race being condensed into one area and a single afternoon, with comfortable and safe, full-scope viewing!

A dream? No, a reality —

on a lengthy Baja-type run. They'll just have to cover less ground in bucking the hazards. Which means the slam-bang thrills will come thick and fast, making for the best kind of spectator interest!

Bit O' Sports

Racers) Team, motion picture star Jim Garner, and famed

Redlands downed Banning in its opening scrimmage, 8-

Armenta Dies

BREA — Funeral services are today at 11 a.m. in Brea Mortuary for Sixto Armenta, former Sunset League manager and umpire, who died Sunday. Armenta had lived and worked in Colton

RIVERSIDE — A course hewn from the barren hills adjacent to RIR's Turn 9 will test such off-road veterans as Parnelli Jones, Jim Garner, Bill Stroppe and conductor Ray Coniff. Recent rains may turn it into a mud bath, but the sponsoring Ford Motorsports Assn. insists it will start at noon Sunday. Many of the same drivers will be in the Westward Ho 200 Saturday.

Actor Garner Fifth Fastest in Dune Race

RIVERSIDE — Actor James Garner steered his Olds-powered Banshee through a two-mile course of water, sand and swamp to post the fifth fastest

OFF ROAD—The Western Racing Assn. presents the Riverside Roundup Saturday and Sunday at Riverside International Raceway with the High Desert Chili Championships thrown in. Main event on the 2.4-mile road course is the Celebrity Stampede, a 10-lap race for $20,000 with a LeMans start featuring Malcolm Smith, Rolf Tibblin, Fritz Kroyer and Danny and Marty Letner. There are 109 entries in 11 classes. Final events are divided between Saturday and Sunday. The chili contest is Saturday ... Nancy Reader, rookie of the year in the sprint buggy division of the SoCal Inde-

By 1973, Mickey Thompson, longtime competitor in the Baja 1000 and other SCORE events (and founder and president of SCORE, which stood for Short Course Off Road Events) realized spectators only had one chance to see a racecar in most off road races and wanted to bring the Baja 1000 experience to the public. Capitalizing on the previous off road events, and convincing Les Richter, he put together the first actual short course race at Riverside, the AC Delco RV Spectacular, in October 1973. The first event had a seven and a half mile course with high speed straights, jumps. mud holes and sand pits, driving competitions with RV's and trailers and an aerobatic flyover. Cash prizes were offered to spectators driving trailers and motorhomes, showcasing their low speed handling and maneuvering talents. To add to the party atmosphere there were also square dancing contests, a rock concert and fireworks. 284 drivers and 42 motorcyclists entered the richest offroad event ever held. But with bad timing, attendance was light, 13,297. That was the first weekend of the energy crisis producing long lines at gas stations combined with a boycott staged by L.A. area gas stations to protest supply problems.

Mickey may have found money-maker

Deke Houlgate

Motor sport today

Everybody will know after this weekend if Mickey Thompson was right about his hunch that people will pay money to see off-road racing.

A special interest group is quite anxious to find out. It is made up of the operators of the nation's road racing courses. If Mickey's Delco RV Spectacular pans out, he may have created a sorely needed new source of revenue for them.

It's no secret that many of America's best loved racing facilities are in financial trouble or are coping with money problems of one sort or another.

The list is topped by Ontario, which has an impossible debt payment schedule. Second in line is Texas World Speedway, which is the only...

Successful operators, like Bill France at Daytona and Talladega, Mal Currie at Watkins Glen and Les Griebling at Mid-Ohio, are also interested in Mickey's new concept, because they pay taxes all year long on facilities they only use a few weekends. Finding a new type of spectator event that makes a profit would be like adding a new prop under the entire race track economy.

Off-road racing, like so many other motor sports, began as an enthusiast affair. First there were rock hounds, building special vehicles so they could explore remote areas. Then came sportsmen who just liked to drive these freaky machines. Next were the more enterprising sportsmen — call them hustlers, if...

sport to a ticket-buying public.

Mickey is not the only off-road racing enthusiast who believes the sport is a thrilling spectacle that can be sold as entertainment, but he is the first to bet a quarter of a million dollars that it is. That's his investment at Riverside this weekend.

His concept is that the most likely customers are those who are hung up on recreation vehicles — campers, motorcyclists...

A season of racing in Europe hasn't changed George Follmer any. He still doesn't speak anything but English. He's just as outspoken now as when he went away. And he'd rather collect money than prestige.

Follmer is in that delicate state known as negotiations for next season. This weekend he will drive for the UOP Shadow team in his final formula 1 race of the season. For the rest of the year he will be a Can-Am driver, ca-

The other drivers are world champs Jackie Stewart, Emerson Fittipaldi and Denis Hulme from formula 1; Mark Donohue and Peter Revson, American road racing stars; Richard Petty, David Pearson and Bobby Allison from NASCAR, and USAC championship drivers Gordon Johncock, Roger McCluskey and Bobby Unser.

Anybody trying to figure a winner off press clippings might eliminate Follmer right away as a contender in that company. But actually there is a strong case for his chances.

First, of that group nobody has logged as many miles at Riverside as Follmer has. With the single possible exception of Dan Gurney, the one-time insurance salesman has more experience at Ri-

Last weekend was the first he has taken off since March.

In fact, Follmer has enjoyed very favorable comment in the European press this year. He has been driving a car not considered good enough to win, he has been learning circuits from scratch, and he has been getting adjusted to the high level of skill that is commonplace in formula 1. Despite all this, "the press has been good to me over there," he said.

Follmer right now is a holdout. Holdouts are celebrated in most of sports but not racing, because salaries of drivers are seldom discussed. Hardly ever is there a contract that lasts longer than a single season, and injury clauses are about as rare.

"It's only a question of coming to terms right now."

Motor Homes, Campers, Trailers To Compete in Area Road-E-O

Nine skilled drivers of recreational vehicles will leave Riverside International Raceway at least $500 richer on Oct. 7.

They will be the nine class winners in the Mickey Thompson RV Road-E-O, an entertaining and educational safedriving event held as part the Mickey Thompson Delco RV Spectacular.

The first is a straight-line problem, driving the right wheel track between two rows of balls that allow only four inches of clearance.

Then the contestant will be directed to back from a 20-foot wide roadway into a simulated campsite space, with only the assistance of his passenger, directing him to back up while standing behind the vehicle.

and roll dancing and motorcycle demonstration riding.

For information about any of these activities or entry forms for the RV Road-E-O, contact SCORE International, 2701 E. Anaheim St., Wilmington, Cal. 90744, (213) 437-0466.

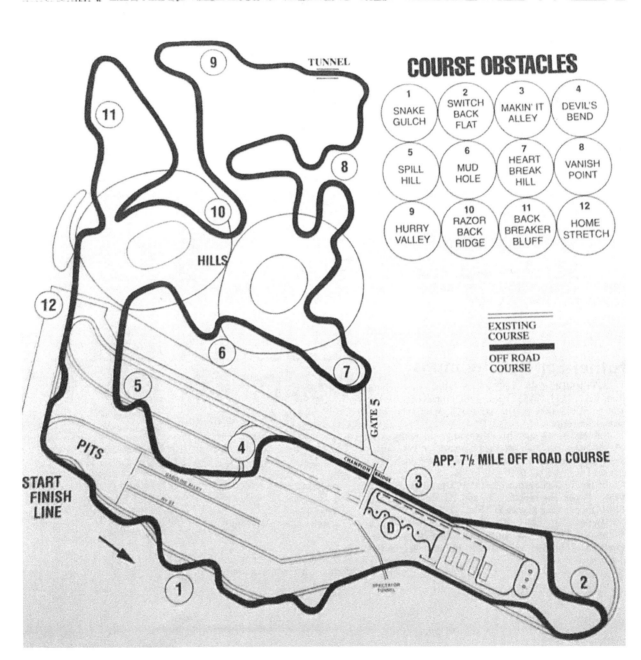

TUNNEL

COURSE OBSTACLES

1 SNAKE GULCH	2 SWITCH BACK FLAT	3 MAKIN' IT ALLEY	4 DEVIL'S BEND
5 SPILL HILL	6 MUD HOLE	7 HEART BREAK HILL	8 VANISH POINT
9 HURRY VALLEY	10 RAZOR BACK RIDGE	11 BACK BREAKER BLUFF	12 HOME STRETCH

EXISTING COURSE

OFF ROAD COURSE

HILLS

GATE 5

CHAMPION BRIDGE

APP. 7½ MILE OFF ROAD COURSE

PITS

START FINISH LINE

SPECTATOR TUNNEL

293

HI-JUMPER — Fritz Kroyer flies his dune buggy in practice for Mickey Thompson's Delco R-V Spectacular off-road race to be held at Riverside Raceway October 5-7. Over 200 motorcycles and 4-wheel-vehicles will compete for the richest purse in off-road history, $200,000. The race will be the first opportunity for spectators to view the grueling Baja-type racing from grandstand seats.

Rick Mears and Bobby Ferro

Father-Son Duo Triumphs

RIVERSIDE, Calif. (UPI) — A father-son combination from Bakersfield, Calif., captured the professional four-wheel vehicle race Sunday at the Delco RV Spectacular off-road racing competition.

Bill Mears, 43, and his 21-year-old son, Rick, averaged 44.250 miles per hour in their Sandmaster VW single-seat dune buggy in the 132-mile race over Riverside's 6.6-mile course. They won $11,000.

In the 72.6-mile motorcycle race, a pair from Santa Ana, Calif., Bryan Farnsworth, 36, and Al Baker, 22—won 56.017 m.p.h. on a Kawasaki 250cc.

Myron Van Ells, 41, Garden Grove, Calif., in Hi-Jumper 2,000cc VW single seat dune buggy, won the sportsman fourwheel vehicle race of 66 miles in 48.9 m.p.h.

Bakersfield Driver, 21, Wins Off-Road Race

BY SHAV GLICK
Times Staff Writer

RIVERSIDE — When Rick Mears was a teenager in Bakersfield he wanted to race motorcycles, but his mother was afraid he'd get hurt.

Rick's father, Bill, built him a sprint buggy instead and Rick, now 21, showed his appreciation Sunday by winning Mickey Thompson's inaugural Delco Recreational Vehi-

place and halfway through he was the only serious challenger to Mears.

During Saturday's race Ferro had the ignition stick and his car crashed through a fence and lit on Highway 60, on the north side of the course. The buggy was demolished but his crew worked all night rebuilding it for Sunday's start.

Don Rountree, Satu-

Father-son combination collects top prize in RIR off-road race

Doug Drosper of Los Altos leads the pack
...his Sandmaster Bustler bounced over the bridge at RIR

Matlack's pitchi brings Mets ev

Rountree Easy Winner of Off-Road Qualifier

Special to The Times

RIVERSIDE — Veteran off-road racer Don Rountree of Riverside was an easy winner in Saturday's qualifying race for today's $50,000 Mickey Thompson-Delco RV Spectacular at Riverside International Raceway.

Rountree, 33, drove his Sandwinder dune buggy to a 35-second win over Rich Mears, 21, of Bakersfield, who was in a single seater Sandmaster Bustler. Each qualifying heat was

practice Friday, Rountree became the favorite and he drove like it. Rountree had finished second overall to Jones in the Mint 400 and won the single-seat class.

A field of 114 professionals and 88 amateurs bucked and slid their way around the 7½-mile course in a series of races. Attrition was swift as cars broke wheels, shocks and engines as they leaped from one bump to another

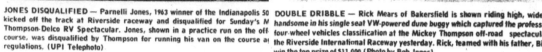

JONES DISQUALIFIED — Parnelli Jones, 1963 winner of the Indianapolis 50 kicked off the track at Riverside raceway and disqualified for Sunday's M Thompson-Delco RV Spectacular. Jones, shown in a practice run on the off course, was disqualified by Thompson for running his van on the course a regulations. (UPI Telephoto)

DOUBLE DRIBBLE — Rick Mears of Bakersfield is shown riding high, wide handsome in his single seat VW-powered dune buggy which captured the profess four-wheel vehicles classification at the Mickey Thompson off-road spectacula the Riverside International Raceway yesterday. Rick, teamed with his father, Bi win the top prize of $11,000.(Photo by Bob Jones)

In 1974, with help from Walker Evans, Thompson redesigned the course, shortened it to three miles and put most of the action packed obstacles in front to the spectators. The San Bernardino Sun reporter called the second annual AC Delco World Championship the "best organized weekend of racing I have ever seen. The races started on time and ended on time"

Balch captures off-road championship

RIVERSIDE, Calif. — Sherman Balch of Union City held off the Hall of Hemet charge of Rodney at Riverside International Raceway to win the four-wheel drive main event of the AC-Delco World Championships of Off-Road Racing.

The triumph is expected to be worth over $6,000 in prize money and contingency money to Balch and his sponsor, Archer Brothers Jeep Parts of Hayward.

Balch and Hall dueled with each other in both the qualifying race Saturday and yesterday's one hour, 15 lap main event over Riverside's 3.2 mile dirt road course.

Driving a Jeep CJ5, Balch started yesterday's main event on the pole position by virtue of winning Saturday's qualifying run. He lost his lead to Hall only once, trailing for a couple of laps. Once he regained the lead Balch opened up a 20 second lead over Hall at one point. At the finish Balch was still nine seconds in front of Hall, last year's winner in a Ford Bronco.

Balch also had to battle Hall in the qualifying race. Balch also had to battle Hall, in the qualifying race, taking the checkered flag 17 seconds in front of Hall. On one turn during the last lap Hall actually bumped Balch trying to pass him on a turn.

Balch's victory yesterday was his first major one since he captured the top prize in the Mint 400 at Las Vegas two years ago. Earlier this year in the Baja International he was on his way to a high finish when mechanical problems...

Clyde King still coaches

PRACTICE RUN — Race drivers Parnelli Jones (right) and Mickey Thompson watch as Gary Gabelich, holder of the world land speed record, now a novice driver in the $170,000 Mickey Thompson AC-Delco World Championship Off-Road race, puts his two-seater Sandmaster Buggy through its paces in early practice this week at the Riverside International Raceway course. The championships will be held starting tomorrow through Sunday.

(UPI Telephoto)

Walker Evans, Mickey Thompson and Sal Fish

RACING ACTION

If there's one thing we can't stand, it's a race driver who babies his vehicle. Lou Fuentes gives a lesson in the art of stunt flying to a Baja Bug. This kind of action was common at Mickey Thompson's recent SCORE off-road event at Riverside Raceway. Pat Brollier used the trusty Hasselblad loaded with Ektachrome X and a 500mm lens.

Race Action: SCORE at Riverside!

OFF-ROAD

VEHICLES AND ADVENTURE

JANUARY 1974   75¢
34510

Trail Blazing:

JEEP CHEROKEE!
'74 LAND CRUISER 4-SPEED!

SPECIAL SECTION - NEW PRODUCTS for '74

PROJECT BACKYARD RETURNS!

The 1975 AC Delco World Championship, run again on Labor Day weekend, had a purse of $50,000 plus $130,000 on contingency awards. New was that Sal Fish was now president of SCORE after leaving Hot Rod. Mickey Thompson won the new stock class Volkwagen event. Second was Johnny Johnson followed by Rick Mears. Walker Evans won the big truck, Class Eight category in a Chevrolet owned by Parnelli Jones. For the main event, a crowd of 41,500 saw Roger Mears hang on with a broken transmission to win, with Bobby Ferro second.

Mickey Thompson

Frank Arciero

BEHIND THE WHEEL—World famous motorcyclist Malcolm Smith will drive a dune buggy at Raceway.

$182,500 off road race
Ferro Riverside choice

By ALLEN WOLFE
Staff Writer

Last month, 200 drivers participated in the lottery-type draw for starting positions in the AC-Delco World Off Road Championships, which begins today and runs through Sunday at Riverside International Raceway.

As it turned out, Bobby Ferro extracted the lucky No. 1 pill out of the bin—thereby winning "first off the line" honors.

That's tantamount to spotting the Pittsburgh Steelers 21 points in a game against the Pop Warner All-Stars—the point being that Ferro hardly needs the advantage.

Over the last eight years, the 38-year-old, bushy-haired driver from Sherman Oaks has compiled one of the most enviable records in off road racing, if not all of racing. His victories are virtually

Arnett-built Sandmaster around the specially-prepared 3.5-mile Riverside layout in three minutes, 34.37 seconds, the fastest 4-wheel vehicle to participate in the special practice session.

The "course" that Ferro and the remainder of the huge entry field will encounter is unlike any in existence. Normally, the off road veterans have to contend with what nature presents them—sand dunes, hills, barrancas, mud holes, cactus, sand washes and oppressive 100-degree temperatures—far from the appreciative eye of spectators.

But Riverside is different. For one, the 3.5-mile, 18-turn artificial layout features many of the same obstacles found in nature, but less than 70 miles from downtown Los Angeles. For another, almost 90 per cent of the circuit, utilizing portions of the

BOBBY FERRO
A hard charger

Race format calls for a full day of practice rounds today beginning at 9 a.m. Qualifying heat races and 14 class races are scheduled Saturday from 10:30

MIDGET RACING—The full midgets of the U.S. Racing Club battle twice this weekend—tonight at Speedway 605 with an eight-event program and again Saturday night at Orange Show Speedway in Ben Bernardino, sharing the card with late model stock cars. Jim Laari of Garden Grove, winner of the main event at Lancaster last week, goes for two-in-a-row Saturday night when the National Midget Racing Association invades Pearson Speedway in Prazosville, some 100 miles north of San Bernardino on Highway 395.

STOCK CAR RACING—The Eddie Gray Memorial, a 40-lap sportsman main event named in honor of the late West Coast stock car champion, will be held Saturday night at Saugus Speedway. Oren Prosser, winner of $6,000 in the Saugus 200 three weeks ago, returns for the 14-event card that also includes limited stocks and Figure-8s. Limited stocks race Saturday night at Speedway 605. Ascot Park offers street stocks Sunday afternoon and Figure-8s and a demolition derby Sunday night. Oval stocks, powder puffs, street stocks and Figure-8s duel Saturday night at Corona Raceway.

SPRINT CAR RACING—

Bernie Mayer's hard work pays off in pole position for off-road race

By PAUL HAGEN

RIVERSIDE — Bernie Mayer thought he was ready for Saturday's off-road race at Riverside International Raceway. Two weeks ago.

He wasn't really set until 2 a.m. Saturday.

"We had the car all ready," Mayer said, shaking his head at the memory. Then we brought it out here for practice. I got in sure my head a little, and crawled into the redmist hate of a

sawhorse tower.

"It crumpled the whole side and we had to work on it another week to get it ready. Then Friday the transmission broke, so we had to work until two in the morning to fix that."

All the extra work paid off. Mayer and co-driver John Burner, both of Colton, started in the sixth position, then forward to an easy win in their class at the SCORE AC-Delco world championships of off-road racing.

That pole then put them on the pole

in today's main event. Saturday's qualifying also witnessed by an estimated crowd of 20,000.

The other two San Bernardino County drivers to win a pole position were motorcyclist Ron Rollen of Fontana, who won the Class II race Larry Roessler of Bloomington was third in the Class II cycle event, and Mel Tyree of Redlands was second in the Class 9 race for single-seat buggies. Both could challenge Roessler.

Mayer, who did all the driving

in the 16-person 1300cc buggy was quite concerned with Friday's transmission problem than the earlier accident.

"Last year we raced here with a Sandito stock, 4-speed transmission," he explained. "That gets us in effect only two gears to work with, which is a disadvantage on a course like this with a lot of tight turns.

"We had a Webster 5-speed transmission in it, but when it

Continued on E4, C4-2.

Bernie Mayer
...pole sitter

Malcolm Smith to Drive Dune Buggy at Raceway

Off-road racing became a professional sport with the first Mexican 1000 in 1967 and the winner was a motorcyclist named Malcolm Smith.

Experts say he probably is the greatest all-around motorcycle rider of all time and Smith is still in the top ranks of off-road racers but now in a dune buggy. With the relatively new challenge of a four wheel vehicle he is one of the favorites in the 3rd annual SCORE "AC-Delco World Championships" of off-road racing Sept. 5-7 at Riverside International Raceway.

Now a Riverside businessman with two motorcycle companies occupying three buildings and employing 14 people, Smith finds it difficult to evade his image as a motorcycle racer even though he is now a winner on four wheels.

The Canadian-born celebrity proved his claim as one of the world's best dune buggy drivers early this year when he won SCORE's "AC-Delco Parker 400."

Perhaps Smith is best known as the star of the full length Bruce Brown film documentary, "On Any Sunday," a movie released in 1971 which glamorized the burgeoning sport of motorcycling. That same year he won his fourth Gold Medal for the united States in the International Six Day Trials.

Many of the top competitors, including Mel Tyree, Bud Feldkamp, Rolf Tibblin, Andy DeVercelly, Roger and Rick Mears — both Mears brothers are former overall winners at

Costa makes bid at SCORE

By ERNIE CASTILLO
Daily Press Sports Editor

RIVERSIDE — Andy Costa considered his next off-road race will turn out better than his last

Costa, from Hesperia, along with co-driver John Ridley of Apple Valley will pilot one of the more than 230 vehicles entered in the SCORE AC-Delco Championships at off-road racing this weekend, their first race since multiple-loss came at the July 4 Frontier 250 in Barstow.

Costa is the racier and best driver of the Datsun 1600 mini-pickup that is one of a dozen entered in that class (7) which had practice runs this morning.

Saturday, the Class 7 preliminary race will begin at 12:30 p.m. while Sunday it joins classes 5, Baja Bugs, and 8, production two wheel drives at the first main event at 11 a.m.

At the Frontier, Costa had been forced out after completing just two of the required six laps, despite a rugged desert terrain that ran from Barstow to Lucerne Valley and back.

Among the problems were a bad fuel pump, a broken motor mount, a blown head gasket, a blown radiator hose, a flat tire and a tire jack that left and shorted out the truck's wiring.

But they plan on having things turn out better this time especially since the course repeatedly since the Frontier — Rift, a 3.5-mile road that is

complete with hills, gullies, tight turns and sand puddles doesn't have the marathon ranks that intense most off-road race entries. The faster time will be a clue for a tight vehicle the short first said.

"I came here to see at just 60 and said 'Man I have to run in that speedometer and so I go here," Costa said late Thursday during opening day of practice. "Not to really. Ready for this one."

"Costa knows his truck, especially since he's a mechanic at the local Datsun dealership in Victorville. He must of the work on the $12,000 vehicle has been done by Chuck Smith his head mechanic.

"It has a new engine when

has been run only 10 minutes, which said before Costa took the first tour around the course last week. We saw it completely apart after the Barstow run and there's going to be some more work done on it before the actual race.

"We've been working on it this and night and weekends. Heck, we just got it put back together last night."

Despite the rush job, the vehicle easily passed inspection and seemed to be running smoothly as Costa pushed it around the course. And when a Ford Courier shot in his class, pulled up by his bumper to challenge him, Costa ran his vehicle full throttle, opening up a large lead and grinning when he looked

back to his rear-view mirror and saw the Courier wrapped around an off drum.

"This buggy is ready," he said.

SCORE race

Among the top names entered are both Costa also in one in the Riverside motocross league of the San Diego and some recent Baja competition in this form. Andy Smith, San international and late. Rolen finishing the overall winners of a recent events, including the Baja 500 and the last Mexican Thompson, the point system known who was the founder of SCORE

Your car vehicles will compete in the registered classes with a total sum of $182,000 coming from all it's of a car entry of various types with a starting eight race in VWs. Many events begin in 10 a.m. Sunday.

Your fill of this later is available at SCR for 40 cent includes free overnight camping. A Sunday ticket costs $5. Children under 6 (and is free with an adult.

Spectators chased the water truck to cool off in the heat

Unusual cars turned up - A Brubaker Box above and an Edsel below

By 1976, the event was named the SCORE Off Road World Championship and had grown to 273 entries in 15 classes and a crowd of 30,000. Prize money consisted of a purse of $60,000 and an additional $65,000 in contingency awards. This became a true weekend event with Friday practice, Saturday qualifying and main events on Sunday,

Mechanized Mayhem At Riverside

By ART PARRA

Mechanized mayhem, a combination of rodeo and demolition derby, gets top billing in motor sports activity this weekend. It is in the form of the Fourth Annual SCORE Off-Road Championships at Riverside International Raceway. Preliminary action begins Friday and the finals take place Sunday after three days of torrid racing.

True off-road racing is point-to-point trajectory across rugged open terrain, using trails, abandoned roads and dry washes. It is rare finding more than thirty-percent of an original entry finishing the grueling grind. Man and machine are put through hours of torturous beating, often becoming airbourne in spectacular spills.

Off-road racing is rarely viewed by spectators. It is usually limited to other contestants watching opponents drop off like fumigated insects.

Such is not the case at River-

Champions of every other class will be in action.

Mitch Hayes, Rodney Hall, Larry Minor, Walker Evans, Al Baker, Mel Tyree and Don (The Beachcomber) Johnson of drag racing fame are also in the 300-plus entry field.

A prize fund of $60,000 cash plus an additional $65,000 in contingency money makes the classic one of the richest ever offered. It is enough to attract all the major factory teams in both autos and motorcyles. There will be a total of 15 racing classes taking part.

Friday will find each class practicing for half-hour periods from 8 a.m. until 6:15 p.m. followed by qualifying runs Saturday starting at 7 a.m.

Sunday finds the first of seven 40-minute races beginning at 11 a.m. Admission for all three days is $10, including free overnight camping Saturday. Sunday only admission is $8.

California 500 Near

The California 500, a prestigious USAC automobile race offered at Ontario Motor Speedway is only two weeks away. The western counterpart to the Indy 500 for USAC championship cars is the third jewel in the so-called Triple Crown encompassing the famous Hoosier track and Pocono in Pennsylvania.

It has been a long span since the last California 500 as the 1975 edition, sixth in the series starting in 1970, was held in March. When Ontario Motor Speedway officials resumed management of the facility, one of the first things they did was restore the racing date to the original Labor Day weekend date. The Seventh Annual California 500 will be staged Sunday, Sept. 5.

Three former winners are already in the field and a fourth will be running. Since the start of the classic, no driver has been successful at scoring a

repeat victory. Jim McElreath won the inaugural, followed by Joe Leonard (1971), Roger McCluskey (1972), Wally Dallenbach (1973), Bobby Unser (1974) and A.J. Foyt (1975).

Foyt, defending king of the OMS, has filed his entry while McCluskey and Dallenbach are also listed. Unser's Cobre Tire Team is definately going to participate but at this writing an entry hasn't officially been entered. Incidently, Unser holds the track qualifying mark of 201.374 set in 1972. This isn't expected to be challenged but there will be a real battle for the pole position.

Foyt, who experienced an encounter with the wall at Trenton last Sunday, has hopes of becoming the first Ontario repeater. Says Super Tex, "I'd have to say the 1975 California 500 was probably the most perfect race I've run in my career. If I can get another performance out of the car, crew and weather we will be in the winner's

Ferro tops qualifiers for RIR off-road feature

RIVERSIDE (AP) — Hollywood stunt driver Bobby Ferro, the biggest winner in off-road racing, will start in the pole position today in the feature unlimited dune buggy main event of the SCORE World Championships of Off-Road Racing at Riverside International Raceway.

Ferro, 28, of Sherman Oaks, Cal., averaged 42.2 mph on his fastest lap around the 2.5-mile obstacle course today to become the fastest four-wheel driver during a marathon series of 42 two-lap qualifying races.

Fastest overall was a motorcycle rider, Terry Clark, 23, of Lancaster, Cal., who was clocked at 43.691 mph on the 50-turn course. Ferro will start on the front row of the 25-mile

dune buggy feature with the Pikes Peak Hillclimb champion, Rick Mears, 23, of Thousand Oaks, Cal., who qualified at 41.981 mph, and Malcolm Smith of Riverside, who averaged 41.978 mph.

Rick's older brother, Roger Mears, 26, of Bakersfield, Calif., will start on the pole for the two-seat dune buggy main event with Dow Hadaway of Sun Valley, Calif., riding as navigator. Mears, who won the single-seat race the last two years and who is qualified fourth fastest in that race, averaged 40.146 mph to turn fast time in two-seat buggy qualifying.

The first of eight 10-lap races will begin at 11 a.m. Sunday.

Others expected to give

Ferro a run in the featured Class 1 race include Mickey Thompson, who brought off-road racing to Riverside three years ago, and Parnelli Jones, Thompson's biggest off-road rival.

The Class 1 race is scheduled to begin at 4 p.m. Twenty-one San Bernardino County competitors are entered, with the largest county contingent in Class 9 — small-engined single-seat vehicles. Seven county representatives are scheduled to go in that race, including Mel Tyree of Redlands, who won the class two years ago.

The Class 9 race gets underway at noon. It is the second race on the schedule.

Ferro threat in off-road race

The names of Parnelli Jones and Mickey Thompson appear first on the marquee, but the real super star of the 4th annual SCORE World Championships of Off-Road Racing Aug. 22 at Riverside International Raceway may turn out to be Bobby Ferro.

The Sherman Oaks movie stunt driver will be going after the only major off-road racing victory that has eluded him, as well as his fourth straight win this season.

Ferro, the intense young scrapper who was "discovered" by actor James Garner and sent to race driving school, will drive a Sandmaster Hustler dune buggy on the 2.5-mile obstacle course against none other than Jones and Thompson plus at least half a hundred other drivers of single-seat dune buggies.

Nobody could have predicted last November that Ferro would be on a winning streak at this time, because

racing carreer would be over.

That wasn't Ferro's game plan at all. When he woke up after coming out of a 10-day coma, he demanded, "Let me out of here," threw a bedpan at a nurse and walked out, notwithstanding his fratured skull and injury to his back, thought to be immobilizing.

His comeback ride came in the Laughlin 300, when he finished second. Since then the victory parade has been his first-ever win in the Mint 400 and Baja Internacional and a repeat in the Firecracker 250.

Not one with a reputation for caution, Ferro said he has been driving much more carefully since his skiing accident. The man who is noted for passing dune buggies in Baja by leaping over them as often as he drives around them is said to have developed a new smoothness that if anything has made him even faster.

Ferro, however, has had no success worth bragging about

during practice. His Sandmaster buggy cartwheeled so far that Ferro blacked out, and when he came to he was on the shoulder of the Palm Springs Freeway outside the raceway grounds.

The 28-year-old former desert motorcycle racing champ and decorated Vietnam veteran doesn't regard Riverside as a "jinx" track any more than the elusive Mint 400 win an impossible task. As far as he is concerned, nothing goes wrong with his dune buggy, the packed grandstands of Riverside International Raceway will cheer him in the winner's circle and not anyone by the name of Parnelli or Mickey.

Tickets are on sale at the raceway, all Ticketron outlets and SCORE headquarters, 20944 Sherman Way, Suite 115, Canoga Park, CA 91303. Information (213) 999-2250.

Evangelical F

Rick Mears Evens SCORE With Brother Roger

BY SHAV GLICK
Times Staff Writer

RIVERSIDE—If one Mears brother doesn't win in SCORE's World Championship of Off-Road Racing, the other one does.

Rick, 23, driving a Chenowth dune buggy owned by the racing doctor, David Sauers, won relatively easy in the unlimited single-seat class against a strong field of 35 starters as 31,750 looked on Sunday at Riverside International Raceway.

Then Roger, 29, made it look like a TV rerun as he, with 42-year-old Dow Hadaway riding along, won the unlimited two-seater class in his Hi-Jumper buggy. Roger also won the single-seat class for VW-powered vehicles under 1200cc.

The Mears sweep only continued the domination they have had ever since Mickey Thompson put on the first off-road race at Riverside in 1973. Rick won the main event that year and Roger won the next two in 1974 and 1975.

It was a $15,010 day for the Mears. Rick won $3,524 from the $60,000 purse and another $1,300 in contingency money from the $120,000 put up by manufacturers. Roger collected a combined $5,414 in the VW race and another $4,772 in the two-seat race. Payoffs are determined by the number of entries in their class.

Both feature races proved tough on favorites as the chuckholes, switchbacks and hay bales sent cars spinning off course, into one another—and even over one another.

It used to be said of Parnelli Jones that "if he doesn't break, he'll win, and if he doesn't win, he'll break for sure" when he was off-road racing's Bronco-buster. So it was a surprise Sunday when he finished an uncharacteristic fourth in his plastic-bodied buggy built to look like a Chevy Blazer.

Second, 41 seconds back of Rick, was Dennis Keefe, a plumbing contractor from Lancaster, followed by John R. Johnson, an off-road veteran from Lemon Grove.

Johnson was bumped completely off the track in the first turn when Mickey Thompson, in his V8-powered buggy, thundered past. The entire field passed before Johnson got back in the chase.

Thompson after thrilling the crowd and his fellow

Walker Evans, who drove a 3,800-pound truck against the 1,400-pound buggies in the two-seater race, found himself in a wild first turn encounter that sent him into the hay to sit while the field thundered past. Evans finally extricated the truck, which looked like a dinosaur among the low-profile, hole-hopping buggies, and worked up to ninth before a flat tire ended the chase.

Mitch Mayes, showing no effects from three accidents during the year in which he broke and rebroke his collarbone, was an easy motorcycle winner. Mayes, who wrenched his knee Friday and competed with a swollen knee against doctor's orders, averaged 43.2 m.p.h., fastest of the day. Mears' winning speed was 40.454. Sunday's results:

SINGLE-SEATERS—1. Rick 3. Bobby Stone (Huntington Mears (Bakersfield), Chenowth. Beach).
40.454 m.p.h.; 2. Dennis Keefe 4-WHEEL-DRIVE MODIFIED (Lancaster), Funco; 3. John John- —1. Don Barlow (Fillmore)-Coco son (Lemon Grove), Chenowth; 4. Corral (Santa Paula), Ford Bron-Parnelli Jones (Torrance), VPJ co, 34.983; 2. Ray Russell (Tulare) Blazer; 5. Malcolm Smith (River- Dennis Harris (Roseville), Jeep; 3. side), homemade special; 6. Bill Steve Mizel (Mill Valley)-Max Ja-Silverthorn (Lemon Grove), Chen- miesson (Torrance), Ford Bronco.
owth; 7. Ivan Stewart (El Cajon), PRODUCTION UTILITY VEHI-Funco; 8. Clyde Jennings (El Ca- CLES—1. Stan Gilbert (Cypress), jon), Chenowth; 9. Don Rountree Ford pickup, 36.840; 2. Frank Ves-(Riverside), Sandwinder; 10. Mark sels (Los Alamitos)-Charlie Haga Steele (Huntington Beach), Funco. (South El Monte), Ford F-100; 3. John
TWO-SEATERS—1. Roger Feeney (Altadena)-Scott Harness Mears (Bakersfield)-Dow Hada- (South El Monte), Blazer.
way (Sun Valley), Hi-Jumper, 4-WHEEL-DRIVE PRODUC-37.536; 2. Tim Crabtree (Holtville)- TION—1. Sherman Balch (Union Earl Stahl (La Mesa), Chenowth; City), Jeep, 34.927; 2. Lonnie 3. Marty Letner-Jay Gillman Woods-Dennis Betscher (El Ca-(Downey), Hi-Jumper; 4. Lester jon), Chevy pickup; 3. Kurt Larson-Scott Taylor (Topanga), Stracker (Lakeside), Ford Bronco.
Funco. VW-ENGINED SINGLE SEAT-STOCK VW SEDANS—1. Dennis ERS (1200cc or less)—1. Roger Hamilton-Richard Phipps Mears (Bakersfield), Hi-Jumper, (Blythe), 30.416; 2. M. Van Ells- 38.322; 2. Rolf Tibblin (Escondido). Donna Van Ells (Garden Grove);

Hi-Jumper; 3. Malcolm Smith (Riverside). Homemade Special; 4. Ken Crossman (Thousand Oaks), Hi-Jumper; 5. Mel Tyree (Redlands), Hi-Jumper.
TWO-SEAT FOUR-WHEEL VE-HICLES (1200cc or less)—1. Bernie Mayer (Colton), Hi-Jumper, 36.879; 2. Steve Hobert (Huntington Beach), Funco; 3. Michael Lund (Huntington Beach), Lundco; 4. Russell Welch (El Monte), Funco.
PRODUCTION 2-WHEEL-DRIVE CARS—1. Robert Weston (Lynwood), VW sedan, no time; 2. Frank Ball (Lemon Grove), Datsun; 3. Gordon Poff (Seal Beach), VW sedan.
MINI-PICKUPS—1. Bud Belveu (Northridge), Datsun, 31.750; 2. Bruce Daley (Tucson), Datsun; 3.

Jim Conner (La Canada), Datsun; 4. Andy Coste (Hesperia), Datsun; 5. Jim Baldwin (Corpus Christi, Tex.), Toyota.
MOTORCYCLES: Open—1. Mitch Mayes (Palmdale), Husqvarna, 43.271; 2. Jack Johnson (Las Vegas), Husqvarna; 3. Terry Clark (Lancaster) Kawasaki. 250cc—1. Mike Bell (Lakewood), Husqvarna, 41.500; 2. Gary Jones (Hacienda Heights), Jones Islo; 3. Bob Rutten (Covina), Husqvarna. 125cc—1. Bobby Jones (Fillmore), Honda, 41.819; 2. Dave Carlson (Anaheim), Honda; 3. Michael Stearns (El Cajon), Husqvarna.
BAJA BUGGS—1. Bill Johnson (Sylmar), 37.187; 2. Doug Ellsworth (Mountain View); 3. Nick Nicholson (Spring Valley); 4. Mark Hansen (Escondido).

Phil Caliva rolled his VW and was caught by an L.A. Times photographer

In 1977, B.F. Goodrich became the sponsor and 40,000 fans showed up to see the 243 entrants battle for a total of $200,000 in prize money and contingencies. The highlight of the weekend was the $18,000 Challenge of Champions Invitational Race on Saturday, won by Marty Letner.

Lon Petersen: *"In 1980, I was 32, thought I'd jump into the big time. I had over 30 class wins; bought a new Yamaha 365 Mooshock. Stiff competition as this short course series and Mickey Thompson's promotion attracted all the hot shoes from all over the west, most of them young and fearless. I got a good start and led all the way; winning by a motorcycle length"* Compiler's Note – Petersen went on to driving rally cars, winning the California Rally Series numerous times and scoring a couple of National Championships.

Off-road title races near

RIVERSIDE — Off-road racing enthusiasts eagerly await the start of the invitational $18,000 Challenge of Champions Saturday at 2 p.m. at Riverside International Raceway, but there are a few drivers who would just as soon bypass the first 300 yards of that race.

In that short space a starting grid 18 cars wide will converge on a blind, downhill, left-hand corner that will allow only two cars at a time to go through without crashing.

The Challenge of Champions is a highlight of B F Goodrich's SCORE Off-Road World Championships Saturday and Sunday, the only event of its kind in 1977 to be held in front of spectators sitting in comfort and safety in protected grandstands.

The concept of the "Challenge" race is quite different from ordinary off-road racing as well. The well known crosscountry marathon, with its hours of torture for driver and car alike, is essentially a race across

USAC championship circuit driver Rick Mears of Phoenix. Dead center are San Marcos' Bob Rodine and 1963 Indianapolis 500 winner Parnelli Jones of Palos Verdes in positions 9 and 10.

"The biggest thing to me is getting out of the hole," commented Ivan Stewart of Lakeside, recent winner of the Baja International, starter No. 7. "My aim is to get there (to the first turn) first."

Long Beach speed king Mickey Thompson is a long distance from where he'd like to be on the grid, far from the pavement in the No. 4 starting position. His heavy, V8 powered buggy is at the same disadvantage as Jones' Chevy Blazer — lacking the quick response on a soft dirt surface that the lighter VW-powered buggies enjoy.

"I think all the VWs will out accelerate Parnelli and me in the first 30 yards or so," Thompson said, " and then I'm afraid they will sur-

Champion short course driver Jim Taber of Woodland Hills, starter No. 6, disagrees. "If the ground is wet, Mickey and Parnelli will get the jump on us, but if the dirt is dry the VWs will beat them to the turn.

"I'll say this about the first turn, it will separate the men from the boys. You'll find out who the race drivers are."

Gary Gabelich will come out of his involuntary retirement to co-drive a four-wheel-drive Ford Bronco in the "truck race" Sunday (3 p.m.) that is the spectator favorite year after year in the $200,000 event. His co-driver will be car owner Mike Edwards, a Santa Monica bail bondsman.

The Long Beach stunt driver holds the listed two-way record of 622.407 mph in a rocket car and was the first to top 200 mph in a drag boat.

In the "truck race," which includes separate racing categories for production and modified four-wheel-

309

MICKEY THOMPSON — THE LONG BEACH SPEED KING
warms up his radical V8-powered dune buggy for Riverside event, Aug. 27-28.

Letner Gets Victory as Parnelli Falters

BY SHAV GLICK
Times Staff Writer

RIVERSIDE—Off-road racing's Challenge of Champions looked more like a Challenge for Survival as 18 cars and drivers charged off the starting line together Saturday, heading for a lane only two cars wide.

The results were predictable.

Three cars spun out in the first couple of hundred yards, six more tangled in a Destruction Derby-like crash in the first turn—and Parnelli Jones came flying out of the debris in the lead before the survivors had finished two laps around the two-mile obstacle course at Riverside International Raceway.

"I was in the middle and those buggies got the jump on me in the first ten yards," said Jones, who was in his big yellow Blazer that looked like a dinosaur among the nimble little buggies. "They closed up right in front of me, so I decided I'd make my own hole."

Tire marks all over the side of his Blazer gave an indication of how close they were racing. A crowd of about 20,000 were on their feet most of the race, most of them cheering for Parnelli.

But, like what happened so many times when Jones was driving Indianapolis championship cars, he took the lead and appeared to be headed for a win when his car suddenly stopped. It happened Saturday on the fourth lap of the 10-lap race as he was headed for Thompson Ridge. The Blazer spun on the asphalt and wouldn't budge. A broken U-joint did it in.

Marty Letner, a 25-year-old roofer from Downey, inherited the lead in his Chenowth and never gave it up to win the $11,000 first prize in the main event of SCORE's World Championship of Off-road Racing that concludes today. A fast-closing Malcolm Smith, this year's Mint 400 winner, finished second for $5,000 and Fritz Kroyer, who won the Mint twice in 1970-71, collected $3,000 for third.

Letner is the son of former NASCAR Pacific Coast late model stock car champion Denny Letner, who drove Chevrolets and Dodges in the late 1950s against such old-timers as Lee Petty, Joe Weatherly and Fireball Roberts. The elder Letner, 49, finished seventh in the race his son won.

"I was running about sixth off the start and really got nerfed going into that first turn," said young Letner. "One guy hit a bump, bounced across the track and took (Bud) Feldkamp out. I was about an inch or two from getting it myself."

Letner apparently slid into Bob Radine, knocking his car into Roger Mears, who spun halfway around only to see Parnelli's big Blazer coming straight at him.

FLYING LOW—Driver Pancho Weaver has all his wheels off ground as he negotiates a jump during running of off road races Saturday on Riverside International Raceway course
Times photo by Ben Olender

buggy race (Class 9) with brother Rick second. It was only the second time in their long career they had finished 1-2. The other was at Ascot Park.

The two of them also raced together most of the way later in the unlimited two-seater race (Class 2), with Rick winning in a Funco when Roger, in the PJ Blazer, had engine failure about 30 yards from the finish. Roger had led most of the way in the "old" Blazer, not the one Jones drove in the Challenge of Champions.

Mickey Thompson, who broke three ribs in a practice crash last week and had two more spills in qualifying Friday, drove one of his most impressive races in the Challenge of Champions. Caught behind the first-lap melee, he was 15th when the field got sorted out but he pushed the heavy V8-powered MT Challenger buggy to sixth place. It was one of the few times the 49-year-old father of SCORE racing had finished a race.

Nearly all the Challenge of Champions cast will be back today for the Class 1, unlimited single seaters, race at 4 p.m. Bud Feldkamp will start on the pole, but back in 46th position after being unable to qualify Friday, will be defending champion Rick Mears.

Mears Still Master of Riverside

BY SHAV GLICK
Times Staff Writer

RIVERSIDE—Roger Mears continued his mastery of Riverside International Raceway's off-road course Saturday by winning the $20,000 Challenge of Champions against 18 other winners of major SCORE races.

It was the 31-year-old Bakersfield driver's seventh win here in 13 races since 1973 when Mickey Thompson and SCORE first took off-road racing out of the wilds of Baja and put it on a closed course with spectators. After his brother Rick won the first single-seat championship race in 1973, Roger took over and won in 1974 and 1975 and repeated again last year. Rick also won in 1976 to make the Mears Gang domination complete.

Mears' crew changed the engine on his Funco and he came back to win the 1200cc single seat and today he will drive the same car in the feature unlimited single seat championship race and another Funco in the 1200cc two-seat race.

He has already won close to $20,000 in prize money.

After today's race Roger will move down Highway 10 to Ontario Motor Speedway to take his rookie test Tuesday for his first U.S. Auto Club championship car race—next Sunday's California 500.

Par 5 of the 13 laps in the Challenge race over a 1.3-mile course dotted with pot holes, jumps, bumps and a careening ride down 35 m.p.h. Thompson Ridge, Mears and Bob Rodine battled in a twin reminiscent of the Mears-Parnelli Jones battle of 1974.

"I think this one was the toughest of all," said Mears, who drove with a badly gashed elbow, the result of a morning accident in the unlimited two-seat class race. "Rodine put more pressure on me for a longer time than even Parnelli. Even when he dropped back late in the race I couldn't see where he was for the dust so I had to keep driving as hard as I could."

Rodine, a building contractor from San Marcos, led the first lap after winning the half-mile drag race from the start to the first corner, then gave way to Mears on the second go-round. Rodine appeared ready to try to regain the lead toward the end of the seventh lap when his VW-powered Chenowith suddenly dropped back with a flat left rear tire.

"About that time I knew the chase was over," Rodine said. "I just hoped no one was close behind me while I limped around."

The only challenger for second place at the time, Norton Tarx (who won the two-seat race earlier in the day), crashed in the hay bales and dropped out. Rolf Tibble, 41-year-old former world motocross champion from Norway and Emeralda, finished third.

Only 19 cars started the Challenge race as Bob Gordon, who was to drive one of the big Parnelli Jones Blazers, broke an axle in the two-seat race. Frank (Scoop) Vessels finished fifth in the other Blazer. Malcolm Smith, winner of the Mint 400 and Baja 500 and one of the private favorites, also dropped out on the first lap with a broken axle on his Funco.

Mickey Thompson, in a V8-powered M/T Challenge that looks like a sprint car, thundered around the first lap in third place, scattering dust and dirt behind him like a turbocharged plow. The more nimble buggies started catching him in midrace, however, and Thompson ended up eighth.

The 1200cc race was the day's best as Mears and Glenn Walker Harris of Camarillo swapped the lead back and forth until Harris rolled into some hay bales to avoid a course flagman on the track two laps from the end. Harris' misfortune, to front of the grandstands where most of the estimated 20,000 were sitting, permitted Mears and also Brian Herbst to pass and finish 1-2.

Will Chamberlain failed to show up for practice and was scratched from today's Jeep Celebrity race. Ricky Nelson withdrew because of a newly scheduled engagement and Tracy Donahue and Martin Milner were added to the field. Kent McCluskey, former Baldwin Park High and Citrus College football player (as Kent McWhirter) was more than two seconds faster than any other driver in practice. First prize is $20,000.

Saturday's results.

(results listings — illegible)

KEN NORTON IS ALMOST KO'D IN AN AUTO RACE

BY SHAV GLICK
Times Staff Writer

RIVERSIDE—What must go down as one of the wildest and wooliest days in the long history of racing at Riverside International Raceway ended Sunday with SCORE'S world

In 1978, a sun burned crowd of more than 40,000 saw Roger Mears win a record $23,050. In the celebrity race, boxer Ken Norton made headlines by cartwheeling off a jump. The race was won by Dick Smothers with James Garner in second. Garner said of Norton," For a guy who hasn't raced much, he's totally out of control". Third place went to Martin Milner who survived a rollover in front of the grandstand. Marty Letner won the Class One race followed by Bob Rodine, Fritz Kroyer, Bud Feldkamp and Danny Thompson. Walker Evans, who also built the Jeeps for the Celebrity Race, won the truck class.

Jim Tabor (No. 117) walked away from Riverside crash and will run in Bombero.

Mears SCOREs 3rd weekend win at Riverside...

MERGING LANES—No, no, no, it's not the Sepulveda entrance to the San Diego Freeway at 5 p.m. It's the start of the unlimited single-seat race in the off-road championships at the Riverside International Raceway Sunday. After the jamup, the race had to be restarted

Times photo by Christopher Hardy

Volkswagen driven by John Wright of Encinitas lands hard in class 5-1600 race Saturday.

Mears brothers race off with a big SCORE

By JIM MATTHEWS
Sun Sports Writer

RIVERSIDE — It was a brotherly conversation between the two Mears Saturday, good-natured and friendly.

The younger Rick, the winner of the Indianapolis 500 last Memorial Day, had just spent a battering few minutes at Riverside International Raceway in a Volkswagen-powered Funco dune buggy to win the SCORE Challenge of Champions.

And brother Roger, a consistent winner in off-road events, came in a not-too-distant third. Between them, the Bakersfield duo took home most of the purse.

They had good reason to be jovial.

"Twenty thousand dollars? You mean you got $20,000 to win," said Roger, 32. "I wouldn't have let you pass me if I'd known that."

"I wouldn't have run into my own brother for any less than that," deadpanned Rick.

They both laughed and grinned into the cameras in the press trailer — Rick wearing brother Roger's spare driving suit because "mine didn't have Goodrich (the overall race sponsor) on it."

Roger wearing his own suit was content with a beer and the $4,000 check he'll take home for third place.

The format of the Challenge is simple. Twenty of the top off-road drivers are invited to put up an entry fee of $1,000. In the past, the winner took home the entire bun-

die. But this year, Pepsi put up matching funds and the drivers entered voted on how the pay-off should progress.

The breakdown was $20,000, $6,000 and $4,000 for the first three places, respectively. But it was money earned by the two Mears. As they sat talking after the race, Rick showed brother Roger his blistered hands.

"I usually don't get blisters in a 300-miler," smiled the 27-year-old

Rick as he sipped a beer. The blisters caused him to withdraw from another race later in the day, and it made him a dubious entry for today's Class 1 event.

"It's rougher than I like," said Rick, who grew up on off-road courses before graduating to championship cars. "When it's that rough, it cuts some of the racing out because you can't run side-by-

(Continued on D-6, column 1)

OFFICIAL
PACE CAR

Jeep Cherokee

In 1979, 323 entries showed up to compete for the $225,00 purse. A crowd of over 40,000 watched Rick Mears win the Challenge of Champions with Marty Letner second. Actor James Brolin won the celebrity race and Walker Evans won the Class Eight truck race.

The Jeep Celebrity races attracted a variety of celebrities. The list includes Ted Nugent, Vicki Carr, Patrick Duff, Dick Smothers, John Schneider, Ken Norton, Martin Milner, Tanya Tucker, Dan Haggerty, James Garner, James Brolin, Larry Wilcox and Denver Pyle

UPI Telephoto

'In your face'

Singer Vikki Carr has her own way of rewarding actor Patrick Duffy of TV's "Dallas," who finished ahead of her during a celebrity off-road race. Carr, who was married last week, "shares" her cake with Duffy. Tulare's Ray Russell and TV's John Schneider were second in the race.

Roger Mears, Bill Mears and Sal Fish

Rick Mears captures big Riverside event

RIVERSIDE, Calif. (AP) — Rick Mears, winner of the Indianapolis 500 last Memorial Day, captured the Challenge of Champions event in the $225,000 SCORE Off-Road World Championships at Riverside International Raceway on Saturday.

Mears, of Bakersfield, Calif., earned $20,000 for his victory in the 18-mile race which highlights the seventh annual Off-Road Championships. The 27-year-old Mears drove a Funco Volkswagon to an average speed of 41.639 miles per hour.

ons was Marty Letner of Downey, Calif., in a Hi-Jumper Volkswagon. The second-place finish was worth $6,000 and Letner also won the two-seat unlimited race, worth $3,265.

Mears' brother, Roger, who won the challenge race last year, finished third this time. Roger, 32, led the first four laps of the event even though he began experiencing problems with his Funco Volkswagon after just one lap around the 1.5-mile obstacle course.

Six races encompassing nine clases were run Saturday with six more races encompassing eight classes scheduled Sunday.

Actor Dan Haggerty of Grizzley Adams fame, practicing for Sunday's celebrity race, was involved in an accident but was unhurt. However, his vehicle was damaged to the extent that it had to be withdrawn.

The Challenge of Champions was sponsored by Pepsi with the entire competition sponsored by B.F. Goodrich.

Now sponsored by Bridgestone, the Bridgestone - SCORE Off Road World Championship posted $45,000 in prize money in 1980 for the 348 entries. A new track, two miles in length, designed by Bob Rodine and Dennis Keefe, more accurately replicated desert conditions. The featured Pepsi Challenge of Champions invitational was won by Marty Letner who collected $25,000 for the win who also won the Class One race. There was also now the J.D. Heavy Metal Challenge for trucks, won by Ivan Stewart who also won the Class Eight race after favorite Walker Evans broke.. Roger Mears won Class Three and Class Seven and Lon Peterson won Class Thirty.

OFF-ROAD SUPERSTAR — SCORE Baja 1000 winner Walker Evans is thre odds-on favorite to win the J.D. Brand Heavy Metal Challenge, a new feature of the Bridgestone SCORE Off-Road World Championships Aug. 22-24 at Riverside International Raceway.

World's fastest off-road truck racer favored in heavy metal challenge

RIVERSIDE — There have been a lot of glamour names in off-road racing, from Parnelli Jones to Rick Mears, but the closest a fellow ever got to becoming a legend was Walker Evans.

The world's fastest and toughest truck driver is favored to win the new J.D. Brand Heavy Metal Challenge feature of the eighth annual Bridgestone SCORE Off-Road World Championships Aug. 22-24 at Riverside International Raceway.

Why shouldn't he? He beat everybody in the long distance haul from Ensenada to La Paz driving a 3,800-pound Dodger truck, which is not your everyday race car.

Evans, the king of the truckers, is still doing amazing things as the 1980 off-road racing season reaches its midpoint. Last month he drove to victory in a 250-miler near Barstow, then hopped into J.D. Brand's Lear Jet and flew all night to a race near Buffalo, N.Y.

Without either practice of qualifying, with no sleep after a bone-bruising 10-hour race the night before, he finished second in the race over a course he had never seen before.

Evans is one off-road racer who has been a winner both in the long distance races from town to town and on the short courses in front cheering fans where the action is wheel-to-wheel. At Riverside he has won four out of the last five years.

"You race in Baja," Evans said, "and you hope that all nine pit stops are set up all the way down the penninsula when you get there. That's what it took for me to get to La Paz, and I never knew that everything was going to work out. It's an incredible logistics problem."

On the other hand, racing around Riverside's man-made Baja simulation track, two miles around, for 20 minutes or so at speeds up to 85 miles an hour is a different sort of problem.

"You just go pedal to the medal all the way," Evans said. "It's fun, but you can't take a 3,800-pound truck and start and stop the car as quick as you can a dune buggy. You go just as fast in top speed as a dune buggy, and that's 80 to 85 miles an hour along Thompson Ridge on a 30-degree slope. It's wild."

Wor has gotten around to other areas of motor sport about desert racing's folk hero, Evans, and he finds it difficult to be anonymous in places where he now spends his days off — like gasoline Alley at Indianapolis in May.

Evans' interest in other forms of auto racing has led to speculation that he might like to make the same sort of diversification that the Mears brothers, Rick and Roger, have. Not true, Evans said.

"Maybe a few years ago, but not now," he said. "I like to get involved in all kinds of racing, but I really love off-road. This will be my 11th year and I love to perform, if people in the stands like to see me, they should know I get just as excited racing for them."

Also featured at Riverside will be the Pepsi Challenge of Champions and races for all 18 classes of SCORE International competition — motorcycles, cars, four-by-fours and dune buggies. As for the fans, they can enjoy free overnight parking to capture the true off-road racing flavor.

a race

maiden score, returns to the saddle for the De Anza at 116 pounds.

Midwest Invader Cross Flags, stakes-placed at Ak-Sar-ben this summer, got the feel of the Del Mar track in the Graduation Stakes and should be much tougher in the De Anza. The

Anthony earns top PBA seed

WAUKEGAN, Ill. (AP) — Earl Anthony won five of his last six matches to seal the top-seeded position going into tonight's finals of the $90,000 Waukegan Open on the Professional Bowlers Association tour.

Anthony's victories Monday night included a final game 207-172 victory over Guppy Troup.

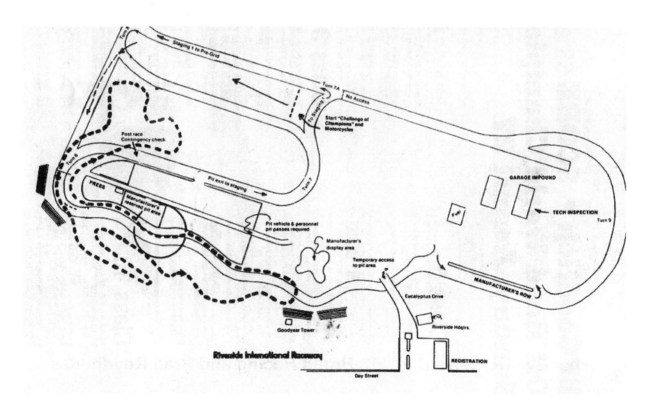

Riverside International Raceway

A Special Brand of Racing

Brad Roydhouse's Team Comes With Top Drivers, Vehicles

By TOM HAMILTON
Times Staff Writer

RIVERSIDE — Brad Roydhouse said he wanted to "make a splash" when he arrived Friday for the SCORE Off-Road World Championships at Riverside Raceway. It looked more like a tidal wave.

Roydhouse, owner of J.D. Brand Racing team, arrived with a fleet of vehicles and equipment that had everyone buzzing Friday. Roydhouse made his entrance in a gold Rolls Royce. His partner was driving a new Ferrari. Two BMWs followed.

But it was his race cars and equipment that drew the most attention. His crew opened four trailers revealing three trucks, a Bronco and a new, $45,000 Class I car (unlimited single-seater).

"I have about a half a million dollars wrapped up in the cars and equipment," said the 33-year-old from Pompano Beach, Fla. "But I couldn't buy the advertisement I'm getting here."

Roydhouse owns a retail parts store in Florida and a car perparation shop in El Cajon. He is a relatively new to off-road racing, making his debut at Riverside last year.

Roydhouse also has a pretty impressive stable of drivers here — Dan Gurney, Frank (Scoop) Vessels, Glenn Harris, Gary Paige, Cam Thieriot and Ray Cunningham.

Harris, a 22-year-old from Camarillo, will be driving the newest car in the J.D. Brand Racing Team. It's a 160-horsepower magnesium-bodied buggy that he'll drive in Class I and the Challenge of Champions.

"We just got it Thursday afternoon and I'm really looking forward to driving it," said Harris. "I feel really lucky to be driving for the J.D. Brand team. They do everything first class."

Harris then pointed to a small, black cap on the top of the engine and said, "That's the only VW part on the car. Most of the components on the car were only developed this year."

The car characterizes the J.D. Brand Team. Roydhouse bought his retail store in Pompano Beach three years ago from John Dietrich (thus the name, J.D. Brand) and started reading the trade magazines.

"We really don't have many big off-road races on the East Coast, so I decided to bring a car out here to Riverside last year and check it out," he said. "The sport is a state of art here.

"The drivers and their crews are so professional. I decided to open a shop in California and put together the best racing team around."

Roydhouse concentrated on truck drivers and has lured Gurney out of retirement to join his team along with Vessels and Paige. Roydhouse will even get into the act himself, driving a Bronco in Class 3 and 4.

If that's not enough, he's put up $25,000 for the J.D. Brand Heavy Metal Challenge on Sunday where 27 trucks will vie.

Eventually Roydhouse would like to promote off-road races on the East Coast where he also owns a construction company.

"I love this sport because it's different than any other type of racing," he said. "The people are different . . . everyone's so friendly. There is a charisma about the people and the sport."

Roydhouse is hoping his luck as a driver will change this weekend. He broke down in both the Mint 400 and the Baja Internacional and did not finish either race. Sometimes money doesn't buy everything.

Locals are part of SCORE weekend

Gurney looking to SCORE in off-road

What Ever Happened to J.D. Brand Racing and Brad Roydhouse

Roydhouse claimed to be an auto parts manufacturer based in Florida. He spent a lot of money for a few brief years but the government caught up with him as drug smuggling was his primary business.

Federal agents seize 200 acres bought illegally by drug suspect

United Press International

Federal Drug Enforcement agents in New York have seized 200 acres of land they suspect was bought with illegal drug money earned by a man arrested in Fort Lauderdale.

The confiscation in Bridgewater, N.Y., was the first such seizure in New York state under a 1978 federal drug law.

U.S. District Judge Neal McCurn signed a seizure order late Tuesday covering the property, on which rest five homes and a helicopter pad worth about $700,000.

About 30 heavily armed plainclothes officers converged on the property, owned by the family of Brad Roydhouse — a fugitive charged with drug-smuggling. The property allegedly was bought with money that came from the illicit sale of marijuana.

U.S. Attorney George Lowe said Roydhouse was arrested Jan. 31 in Fort Lauderdale in possession of 2,800 pounds of marijuana. He was released on bail, but failed to make a court appearance and is now a fug owned by Roydhouse, was seized under a federal drug law. The government freezes ownership, preventing the property from being sold while an investigation continues.

"The land seizure was the first one ever in New York state," said Lowe.

Production four-wheel-drive winner Roger Mears plows along the lower edge of Thompson's Ridge at 85 mph while Brad Roydhouse fights to keep the muck from pulling his vehicle off the track. Off-chamber turns, haybales and concrete walls make safety equipment doubly important.

Four Abandon Cruiser Used In Drug Hauls

Palm Beach County sheriff's vice agents yesterday were searching for four persons who reportedly abandoned a 55-foot cruiser believed to have been used to ferry a shipment of marijuana from the Bahamas to the Fort Pierce area.

The boat was boarded and searched Sunday by U.S. Customs and vice agents who say they found more than an ounce of marijuana residue.

One agent said the boat docked in the North Palm Beach Marina at about 8:30 a.m., Sunday. The captain paid for one day of dockage. At about 2 p.m., reportedly after receiving a phone call in a public booth, the captain and his three companions were picked up in a white van driven by a woman.

The captain was identified as 29-year-old Brad Roydhouse, of 405 SE 20th St., Fort Lauderdale. The other three were identified only as a man and two women.

The agent said the captain registered at the marina as Roydhouse and was identified by photographs shown to marina personnel.

"The boat was definitely used to bring in a large load of marijuana to the Fort Pierce area," the agent said. "The boat was seen in that area at about 2:30, Sunday morning, before it came here."

The agent said the four thoroughly cleaned and polished the cruiser before they left the marina. A load of garbage taken from the boat contained marijuana residue, the agent said.

"They even shampooed and vacuumed the carpets," the agent added. "Even so, we still found more than an ounce of marijuana and lifted some fingerprints from the helm and controls."

He said what was first believed to be blood stains on the carpeting is now believed to be stains made by the marijuana.

The boat, owned by the W.P. Investment Corp., based in a Nebraska city, reportedly is one of at least two boats operated on a charter basis by Roydhouse out of Port Everglades. The agent said it left port on May 23 with Roydhouse and the other three persons on a voyage to the Bimini Island. It was due back in port Thursday. Coast Guard officials were alerted when it failed to return.

— SALLY SWARTZ

U.S. Goes After Drug Defendant's Alpine Area Land

The U.S. Attorney's office Thursday filed two civil forfeiture motions in U.S. District Court in an effort to seize property it claims is connected with money received in drug deals.

The office hopes to acquire an Alpine condominium and three parcels of undeveloped land adjacent to the Cleveland National Forest owned by Brad Allen Roydhouse, a fugitive from Florida wanted on federal marijuana smuggling and trafficking charges. The office claims the properties were purchased with profits from drug deals.

Police nab 4, seize marijuana

Three men and a woman were arrested today and held on $500,000 bond each after Fort Lauderdale police seized 2,800 pounds of marijuana — worth $750,000. Police said the suspects were nabbed as they were unloading 46 bales of the drug from a boat in the 2100 block of Northeast 19th Avenue. The boat, a 21-foot Mako, and a van were seized. Arrested were Joseph Lee Woodall, 28, 1516 NE Third Ave.; Brad Allen Roydhouse, 33, and his wife, Sharon Lynn, 23, both of 530 NE First Terrace; and Charles Martin Kalinosky, 23, 3001 NW

Dan Gurney in the J.D. Brand Class Eight Ford

Jim Meyer: *"I made the knock-off hubs and axles for that truck before the Baja 1000 in 1980. I also set -up/organized the pits for the team. There were some pretty good guys involved, but whole deal turned out to be a bit shady. I commuted back and forth from my shop in Paramount to their nice new facility in El Cajon. Seemed that money was no object; anything we needed and a lot of stuff we didn't we just bought. We parted company under less than friendly terms (hell, I had to hitch a ride home from LaPaz ;-). I did get paid for the axles and hubs, but ended up getting stiffed for of my time organizing, supplying and setting up the pits and my expense money. By cousin, a big shot in the DOJ said; "just write it off"* !!

Press Day at Dodger Stadium 1980

Auto racing

Gurney returns to Riverside

Dan Gurney, who ended a 10-year retirement from racing last January, has joined the off-road fraternity with his entry in the eighth annual Bridgestone SCORE Off-Road World Championships this weekend at Riverside International Raceway.

Gurney will drive a Ford pickup for the J.D. Brand team in the J.D. Brand Heavy Metal Challenge feature race that pays a record $25,500 purse. A Riverside Raceway legend in stock cars, the 49-year-old Gurney will be making only his second appearance in an off-road event this weekend.

Roger Mears, who has lived in the shadow of his more famous brother, Rick, will try to set SCORE and raceway records for earnings by racing in six events, including the J.D. Brand Challenge, with a total payoff of more than $45,000. He is favored to win the Pepsi Challenge of Champions.

The total purse for the two days of racing on the two-mile simulated Baja course is $250,000. The $30,000 Pepsi Challenge for unlimited single-seaters is set for 4:30 pm Saturday with the Heavy Metal Challenge scheduled Sunday at 3:30.

Mears favorite at Riverside's Off-Road Championship

Roger Mears, whose public recognition factor comes mainly from his family relationship to brother Rick Mears, has a good chance to write his name into the record books in the Bridgestone SCORE Off-Road World Championships Aug. 22-24 at Riverside International Raceway.

On that weekend Mears has an excellent chance to win more than $45,000 in prize money, and if he does he will elevate himself, SCORE International and the sport of off-road racing into the front ranks of professional motor sport.

Only six other automobile races in North America pay more prize money than that to the winner. Headed by the Indianapolis 500, which paid a record $318,020 to Johnny Rutherford in May, the other top racing payoffs are the Daytona 500, $102,175; Pocono 500, $73,755; Ontario California 500, $72,900 and Charlotte World 600, $55,400.

The possibility of a big payoff to the older Mears brother became apparent this week as Mears reported his intention of racing six times during the Riverside off-road weekend.

He's favored to win the Pepsi Challenge of Champions, and he has a good shot at the J.D. Brand Heavy Metal Challenge race for pickups and other utility vehicles. Prize money totals more than $50,000 in these two races alone, with the winners expected to take home $30,000-plus.

Mears is also entered in the single-seat unlimited class race, in both the production and modified wheel-drive and Baja Bug VW races.

The veteran Bakersfield driver, who has expanded his racing activities to include Indianapolis cars, is a threat to win all six races he enters at Riverside, and he has proven that he's capable of such an ironman stunt.

In 1978 Mears won three of five races he entered at Riverside, including the Pepsi Challenge, to set an all-time record for off-road race winnings at $22,530. In fact, he was just a shade under the all-time raceway purse record of $24,400 set by Darrell Waltrip when he won the Winston Western 500 stock car race last January.

Last year in the SCORE Riverside classic Mears raced six times, winning twice and collecting $15,811 in prize money.

To reach the $45,000 figure, Mears will have to log 72 racing laps on the rugged two-mile course and almost as many in practice.

In addition, his variety of racing machinery — ranging from the Tracy Valenta single-seater to Mike Moore's Budweiser Jeep, from the Ford pickup to the modified VW — will have to perform flawlessly.

It's a lot to ask of either driver or racing equipment prepared by four separate teams.

There will be at least 20 other drivers in each of Mears' six races trying to prevent him from making off-road history. In fact, the entry list, already past the 100 mark, won't stop till it nears 400, SCORE International officials predict.

Tickets are on sale at SCORE International, 31332 Via Colinas, Suite 103, Westlake Village, Ca 91361, the raceway, 22255 Eucalyptus Ave., Riverside, Ca 92508, and all Ticketron outlets. Information: 213-889-6487 and 714-653-1161.

Crawford flips, but he survives

By RICK HOFF
T-A Sports Writer

RIVERSIDE — Triumph nearly turned to tragedy for an Escondido driver at the Bridgestone SCORE Off-Road World Championships at Riverside International Raceway.

The weekend of racing started on a good note for Monte Crawford. He won Saturday's first race for 1650cc dune buggies in a Chenowth-powered racer, pocketing $2,304 for his efforts. But in yesterday's final race for single-seaters, Crawford flipped his machine end-over-end less than 100 yards from the start.

Crawford was taken to Riverside Community Hospital for observation and was later released. After the race was re-started, following Crawford's mishap, Marty Letner of Downey went on to collect his second win of the weekend. Letner won Saturday's $100,000 Challenge of the Champions, giving him a winning take of $39,261 for the two races, a new all-time record for off-road racing in a single event.

Yesterday's feature race was the J.D. Brand Heavy Metal Challenge for pickups, won by Ivan "Iron Man" Stewart of Lakeside. Stewart, a winner of six Baja 500's, a Baja 1,000, three Mint 400's and SCORE's man of the year award, led the race from start to finish to bring home $17,700.

The weekend's only other double winner other than Letner was Roger Mears, who won the mini-pickup race on Saturday before coming back to take the production four-wheel drive event yesterday.

Lee Wheeler of Valley Center placed third yesterday in the race won by Mears while driving a Ford.

Other North County finishers during the weekend of racing included Bob Rathos of San Marcos, who placed fifth in the Challenge of Champions and 13th in the open single-seat race; Mickey Garrison of Carlsbad, 13th in the 1650cc dune buggy race; Crawford, seventh in the Challenge of Champions in addition to his 1650cc win; Robert Knight of Escondido, 12th in 1650cc Baja Bugs; Randy Fleming of Escondido, 14th in the 125cc motorcycle race; Mike Herbst of Escondido, eighth in class for motorcycle riders over 30; Bob Risley of Escondido, 15th in class for riders over 30; Dave Garig of Vista, second in open motorcycles and Wally Schmutz of Leucadia, ninth in open class for single-seaters.

THE DUST WAS FLYING YESTERDAY IN THE SCORE OFF-ROAD RACE IN RIVERSIDE

(top, middle) **The first start** of the last race of the weekend had Monte Crawford tumbling end-over-end at the point where the course narrows from 400 to 50 feet wide. (bottom) **On the restart** of the final event, Jerry Whelchel flipped on the opposite side of the track from Crawford's earlier tumble.

The Challenge of Champions

New Bargain Buggy Dusts Off Big Boys

Marty Letner's Homemade Racer Wins $75,000 Riverside Feature

By SHAV GLICK
Times Staff Writer

RIVERSIDE—While some of his big bucks competitors were spending as much as $75,000 on tricked-up racing buggies for Saturday's Pepsi Challenge of Champions, Marty Letner was home in Downey building a car in his backyard.

Letner's girl friend had given him the money to build the car and Saturday the investment paid off.

The Sand Hawk, as he calls the ugly-looking machine, cost about $10,000. When Letner ran away from an invitational field in the Challenge race, highlight of the opening day of the Bridgestone SCORE off-road championships at Riverside International Raceway, he collected $25,000.

"Not a bad return on her money, was it?" said a smiling Letner at race's end.

This was the 28-year-old driver's second Challenge win since it started four years ago. He won the inaugural in 1977 and finished second last year to Indianapolis 500 winner Rick Mears.

All the big names—Roger Mears, Bob Rodine, Bob Hannah, Danny Thompson, et al—ate Letner's dust during the 12-lap race. He got off the line first in the mass start and was never challenged. Late in the race he lost his front shocks and slowed but when Dennis Hamilton got close with two laps to go, Letner pulled away and won by 10 seconds.

LETNER PICKS UP ANOTHER $5,321

His $30,321 Total Is All-Time Record for an Off-Road Event

By SHAV GLICK
Times Staff Writer

RIVERSIDE—That $10,000 Marty Letner's girlfriend loaned him to build a backyard racing dune buggy paid another dividend Sunday.

After winning $25,000 in Saturday's Pepsi Challenge of Champions in his homebuilt Sand Hawk, Letner came back Sunday to win another $5,321 in the Class 1 race for unlimited single seat vehicles. The $30,321 total is an all-time record for off-road racing in a single event.

Letner, 28, was the only double winner of the two-day Bridgestone SCORE off-road racing championships at Riverside International Raceway. Marty's father, Danny Letner, is a former West Coast NASCAR stock car champion.

Stewart a Runaway Winner

Ivan (Iron Man) Stewart, 35-year-old San Diego construction foreman, was a runaway winner of the Heavy Metal Challenge for Grand National pickup trucks after perennial winner Walker Evans failed to reach the starting line. Evans' truck lost a driveshaft before the race when a pinion flange failed.

"I was happy to win but I was disappointed Walker wasn't in the race," said Stewart, who had Charlotte Corral, the wife of his sponsor, as a passenger.

Stewart has won six Baja 500s, the Baja 1000, Mint 400, three Parker 400s and has been SCORE's Off-Road Man of the Year twice—usually driving nimble, lightweight buggies. Last year he switched to the big trucks because "I wanted to see if I could beat the best, and Walker Evans is the best."

Evans had won the truck class three years in a row here and five of seven times it had been run. Sunday the stage was set for a showdown of the two premier drivers. Evans in a Dodge running on Goodyears and Stewart in a Ford running on Goodrichs.

"I don't know if we would have beaten Walker," said Stewart, "but I know we could have. If he'd stayed in, I guarantee you one thing. One of us would have broke."

The two-mile course with its 14 turns, deep chuckholes and slippery off-camber runs along Thompson Ridge took its toll of machinery during the two days.

A Punishing Course

"Running 25 miles on this course is much more punishment than running the Baja 500," said Stewart, who credited a stint at Bob Bondurant's driving school at Golden State Raceway for smoothing out his racing techniques.

"I'd never done well here at Riverside on such a tight course," said Stewart. "I realized after racing in the Coliseum last year that I needed some help so I enrolled in Bondurant's school. It really helped me, especially on the tight turns."

Stewart, apparently blessed with more horsepower than his rivals, easily beat the field to the first turn and from there on it was only a question of finishing. At one point he was 40 seconds ahead of Jim Jacobus of Sierra Madre, who finished second in another Ford. Stewart won $17,300 from J.D. Brand, sponsors of the race.

Most of the other favorites such as Dan Gurney, Roger Mears and Frank (Scoop) Vessels, had a variety of problems and dropped out early.

Gurney, driving in his first closed course off-road race, was fifth coming out of the mass start and looked smooth as he bounced from one bump to another in the 3,600-pound truck. On the second lap, just after passing Turn in front of the jammed grandstands, the Ford suddenly stopped, leaving Gurney and his driving companion, Judy Smith, sitting alongside the road.

Gurney: 'I Enjoyed Myself'

"It felt like the ignition quit, or the gas line was severed," said Gurney, 49, who has won many stock car and champ car races here at Riverside. "I really enjoyed myself. I had the best seat in the house to watch the start of the race. It was fantastic to see all the leaping

On the restart, Letner followed motocross champion Bob Hannah through the narrow funnel where the drivers reach the main course. Hannah failed to finish a lap and by the time Letner was back at the finish line he was in front. Steve Kelley, then Dennis Hamilton and finally Brian Harber mounted minor threats but none came close enough to attempt a pass. Kelley crashed, injuring his neck, and was taken to the hospital for X-rays. Hamilton's car started smoking and finally quit. Harber, the lesser known of the Tracy Valenta team that originally included Hannah and Mears, finished second.

It's just as good as Baja; Uh-huh! Uh-huh! Uh-huh!

The thrill of off-road racing are normally witnessed by a few hearty folks who venture into the depths of Baja (that's in Mexico, south of California, in case you're a newcomer) or the Mojave desert. Nevertheless, every year the biggest spectator attraction at Riverside, Calif., International Raceway is the Off-Road World Championships. From convenient grandstand seats, spectators see the sport's best drivers compete on a specially-constructed two-mile course that features virtually every kind of bump, berm and hog that would be encountered on a long-distance course.

Off-road racing has come a long way from the days of claims and counterclaims that led to the first Baja 1000. Before the grandstands of off-road racing got started in 1967, motorcyclists and dune buggy drivers would boast of individual record times in making the trip from Ensenada to La Paz. However, with the inaugural Baja 1000 credibility was given to the times, and sanctioning organizations brought safety to the sport.

Usually the Baja race is a destination-type event from Tijuana, Ensenada or Mexicali south to La Paz. This is how it will be run again in 1981, although officials have hinted at running the race backwards — from La Paz to Ensenada. But this year marks the 8th time the event has used a "loop route" centering around Ensenada. This cuts some of the logistics problems associated with running the full length of the Baja peninsula. In turn, this makes it more economical as well as more convenient for the racers, their families and pit crews.

Taking a loop route and really tightening it until the racers have to run several laps over the same terrain changes off-road racing from a lonely sport of participants-only into a spectator sport. That is what has been

happening for eight years at Riverside.

Part of off-road racing's tremendous growth can be seen in its major influence on the automotive aftermarket. Many of the products that were created for racing have found their way into street and recreational applications. This could be seen in the Riverside spectator parking lot, where thousands of machines closely resembled those actually racing. And not the least of this aftermarket equipment was safety-oriented. There were massive roll bars, beefed-up suspensions, better braking systems and tires designed to take the tortures of off-road driving.

Yes, safety is part of this motoring sport. And this safety spills over into the crowd. Even though the speeds don't approach 200 mph as they do on so many clean, paved racing circuits, anytime a vehicle goes in a direction the occupants don't like, they are happy the machine can take the beating instead of their bodies. That's racing safety.

One look at Riverside's off-road course and everybody understands the beating machines have to take. When the drivers lined up for one of

continued

Read the 1980 edition of Driver magazine on the attached DVD

334

Unknown captures main event at Riverside off-road spin-off

RIVERSIDE (AP) — Mike Gillman of Orange, an unknown in major off-road racing, won the main event Sunday in the Bridgestone SCORE Off-Road Racing Championships at Riverside International Raceway and promptly donated his $16,500 in prize money to charity.

Gillman, 26, also donated the $500 he won Saturday in the qualifying race for Sunday's Pepsi Challenge of Champions, making the total $17,000 for the Cystic Fibrosis Foundation of Orange County.

Gillman was known previously only to a small number of enthusiasts who follow "short-course" off-road racing. Major off-road racing, with the exception of this ninth annual event, is held on the desert over long distances

triple for the weekend.

Earlier in the day, Mears, older brother of 1979 Indianapolis 500 winner Rick Mears and an Indy qualifier himself (bumped from the field on the final day of time trials in May), won the four-wheel drive race overall and captured the four-wheel drive production title in his Jeep.

Mears had won the mini-pickup race on Saturday in a Toyota prepared by Cal Poly-San Luis Obispo students. His two wins brought his nine-year total of Riverside off-road victories to 15, a track record.

Another crowd favorite, Johnny Johnson of Lemon Grove, won the 1600 cc Baja Bug modified VW race with his wife, Linda, serving as co-driver. The Johnsons first became a

The 1981 Bridgestone Score Off road Championships ran on a a new one and a half mile track, The Challenge of Champions, no longer an invitational, now was open to the sixty who registered first with two thirty car qualifying heats; the top fifteen in each going for the Sunday main event. and a. And there were classes fir three wheelers, sponsored by American Honda. Winners included Mike Gillman, who collected $16,500 for winning the Challenge of Champions, Ivan Stewart in Heavy Metal Challenge, Roger Mears in Class Three with his Jeep and in Class Seven, driving the Cal Poly San Luis Obispo SAE entered truck.

Rocker Ted Nugent Ready to Roll

By SAM McMANIS, *Times Staff Writer*

Anyone who has heard Ted Nugent sing knows that the hard-driving rock 'n' roll star thrives on high decibel sounds.

His hit records such as "Cat Scratch Fever" and "Wang Dang Sweet Poontang" are ear-piercing, push-it-to-the-limit music.

It should be no surprise, then, that the 32-year-old singer/guitarist is drawn to another high-decibel activity, off-road racing.

And he's doing surprisingly well. In his one experience in off-road racing, other than celebrity races, he finished seventh in a 20-car field in a 260-mile race out of Barstow last April.

This Sunday, he'll race his Class 9 single-seat racing car in the Bridgestone SCORE Off-Road World Championships at Riverside International Raceway.

"I like the anonymity of being just another driver," Nugent says, "just a normal guy."

Who's he kidding? Given Nugent's wildman appearance and his reputation as a manical performer, it's difficult to think of him as normal. He concedes he's a striver. "I'm extremely aggressive in everything I do, on stage or in a race."

Recording star Ted Nugent shows he's equally at home in a racer as on a concert stage. Nugent will drive a buggy in this weekend's $300,000 Bridgestone SCORE World Championships at Riverside.

Harness for His Hair

While checking his race car at Tracy Valenta's racing headquarters in Rosemead, Nugent looked better prepared for a war than a race. "The Motor City Madman," as his fans call him, was dressed in combat fatigues and a cap which served as a harness for his waist-length brown hair.

When greeted by a reporter, Nugent's eyes bugged out and he said, "Hi, I'm Ted Nugent, From Earth."

Some doubt whether he is from this planet. Especially when he appears on stage with nothing more than a loin cloth and a guitar. But nobody connected with off-road racing questions Nugent's capabilities as a driver.

Said Ron Walker, chief mechanic for Valenta's racing team: "He surprised me and a lot of people with his ability. He's an excellent driver, who's in top condition."

Nugent takes pride in his health, saying his hectic life as a rock star hasn't taken its toll. "When I'm on the road, I'm in excellent shape," he said. "What I do in a two-hour show would kill most men. Concerts are excellent preparation for off-road racing."

Abuse at Barstow

After nine hours and various mishaps during the Barstow race, Nugent couldn't believe the physical abuse his body had taken.

". . . I had an acute spinal condition on lap four. I was screaming my brains out. It would've made a great rock 'n' roll song. I had a 'wango-tango' headache of 'gonzo' proportions," said Nugent, using terms often found in his songs.

"The physical abuse my torso received in the Barstow race was the most oppressive attack on my being that I've had. I could start a small farm in my mouth."

Nugent talks about as fast as he plays guitar. And he's just as intense off stage, too. He seems to be living in a different time zone than most people, but Nugent says he simply has a tremendous zest for life.

He says he doesn't take drugs, although many people perceive his antics as drug-induced.

"I think 999 out of a 1,000 rock stars do drugs," Nugent said. "I happen to be the one that doesn't. It's easy for me to stay away from it because I see all of those saps bump into walls and make complete fools of themselves.

"They can't enjoy life like I do, and I feel sorry for them."

Writing and Performing

Writing and performing music comprises most of Nugent's life. But he's devoted most of his spare time to hunting and racing off-road vehicles.

Growing up in Michigan, Nugent wanted to hunt in places where a normal car wouldn't take him. So, he bought a four-wheel-drive truck and began studying off-road engines.

Nugent: "Certain engineering procedures in racing vehicles could well be adapted to a civilian four-wheel-drive. My cars literally became race vehicles."

He began following the off-road circuit. When he mentioned his desire to race in a magazine interview three years ago, Parnelli Jones called ed and taught him how to race. And promoter Mickey Thompson asked Nugent to compete in a celebrity race.

He finished third to Fred Dryer and Bruce Jenner in a 1979 celebrity event at the Coliseum. The next year, he won.

An Offer to Turn Professional

That led to an offer by Valenta to join his racing team and compete in professional desert races. Nugent was inexperienced and, at first, balked.

"My only experience in racing had been in Detroit and New York rush-hour traffic. So I figured I'd apply the same basic approach to off-road racing," he said. "I love going over the terrain and running other cars out of the way."

Nugent also enjoys the outdoors and is a strong supporter of the National Rifle Assn. He has 40 handguns and takes about six months every year to hunt and race cars.

How does he find the time to take half-a-year off?

"I don't need to work," he said. "I've sold 15 million albums and I could've quit five years ago. I'm a millionaire. I scheduled my concert tour short so I could race Sunday. I was in Canada two days ago and 45,000 people came.

"I really want to race in this one (at Riverside). The main thing is to finish and try to stay in one piece."

Nugent said Columbia Records, his label, hasn't required him to take out more life insurance. "They already have a lot of insurance on me. I hope they don't need it."

Bridgestone sponsors off-road championship

Bridgestone returns to Riverside International Raceway August 7-9 as the sponsor of the richest short course off-road race in history, the 9th annual Bridgestone-SCORE Off-Road World Championship.

Featuring over 300 competitors in 22 classes of racing and a total estimated purse of over $300,000, the event marks the highpoint of Bridgestone's involvement in off-road racing, begun last year when the company took on the Riverside sponsorship for the first time.

Since then, Bridgestone has more than doubled its number of sponsored drivers, bringing the current total to 42. Among those on hand at the Riverside spectacular will be Bob Rodine and Dennis Keefe, entered in the $40,000-plus Pepsi Challenge of Champions, as well as a number of class leaders of the 1981

professional kart racin interests that merged the 1981 Grand Prix, wh Bridgestone introduced t first annual Bridgeston Pro-Kart Challenge to t weekend's activities Long Beach.

And racing is n Bridgestone's only area sports involvement. Ever winter since 197 Bridgestone has served a major sponsor of the Gl Campbell Los Angel Open, sister event to t Bridgestone Golf Tou nament held each Octob in Japan.

The 14-year-o Bridgestone Tire Compan of America has grown fro sales of slightly more th half a million dollars 1967 to a current figure excess of $200 million, wi over 1,100 deale nationwide. Based Torrance, Calif Bridgestone offers complete range passenger tires — cluding the ne

Ted Nugent

Ted Nugent

Hall & Fricker, just a pair of crazy racers

They're not as famous as Laurel & Hardy or Olsen & Johnson, but the funniest team in off-road racing is Hall & Fricker.

"Hey, Fricker," Rod Hall of Reno is likely to say when he greets his co-driver the weekend of Aug. 7-9 in the Bridgestone-SCORE Off-Road World Championships at Riverside International Raceway, "Where'd you leave your pitchfork? You look like you just finished baling the hay."

Fricker, who is not a farmer and doesn't look like one, is Hall's old high school buddy from Hemet, Calif. If you know him, you can imagine his reply.

"Don't come near me, cowboy. I'm getting used to staying right side up, and I don't want to get in a race car with you this weekend. I think I'll go fishin'."

The truth is that the odd couple of the desert, Hall and Fricker, can't leave each other alone. Hall, short and stocky with a cigar—sometimes lighted—permanently attached to his mouth, would give up off-road racing if his 6 ft. 3 in buddy, Fricker, decided to quit, as he is always threatening to do.

They are known for their multiple victories in such races as the SCORE Baja 1000, Mint 400 and SCORE Baja International. They are also known by folks in the sport for their entertainment value.

Hall has never crashed his side of his Dodge truck as hard as he crashes the passenger suite. And he complains about it.

"Fricker, can't you steer your side any better?"

On those occasions when the perennial four-wheel-drive champs fall out of a race, it's rarely for mechanical reasons (Fricker carries a little black bag that magically makes everything right again), but they don't ever seem to crash either, according to Hall.

"Crash? No, there was this bush, and it just sort of reached out and grabbed us."

Off-roaders have built one Hall & Fricker anecdote into one of the legends of the desert. It happened during a race at Barstow a year ago.

Leading their class in a tough race, but not by much, their transmission started to fail with less than 100 miles to go. The Dodge was losing power,

and there was this hill they couldn't climb.

"I guess that's it, Rodney," Fricker said. "End of the line."

"No, it isn't," Hall said. "And here's what I want you to do."

They turned the truck around, bashed out the rear window glass and pulled loose one of the roof lights so Fricker could sit in the bed of the truck and shine it out the back.

Hall, with Fricker clinging to the rollbar with one hand and pointing the light with the other, backed up the hill, then down through a valley and up the

last hill before the finish line. That's how they took the checkered flag for another victory, locked in reverse and zigzagging as fast as their truck could back up.

Meanwhile, SCORE International president Sal Fish reported that the entry filed by Mike Moore

of Midland, Tex., for Rick Mears, the 1979 Indianapolis 500 winner, has been withdrawn due to a racing conflict Mears will have on Riverside's off-road race weekend.

Tickets are on sale at the raceway and SCORE International. Information 714-653-1161 or 213-991-8504.

JUMBO JUMPER—Rick Grumbein of Tempe, Ariz., demonstrates the fine art of teaching an elephant-on-wheels to leap off the ground. Action like this returns to Riverside International Raceway on Aug. 7-9 for the ninth annual Bridgestone-SCORE Off-Road World Championships.

Thompson, son crash race cars

RIVERSIDE (AP) — Fritz Kroyer, of Northridge, Calif., and Steve Casagrande, of Littlerock, Calif., won the two qualifying races for the $40,000 feature in today's windup of the ninth annual Bridgestone SCORE Off-Road World Championships at Riverside International Raceway Saturday.

Kroyer, a two-time Mint 400 victor but winless in all his previous 17 races here, swept to an easy victory in the Pepsi Challenge of Champions qualifier after early leader Mickey Thompson of Bradbury, Calif., crashed on the second lap of the 12-lap race.

Kroyer averaged 45.822 mph on the 1.5-mile obstacle course in his Chenowth VW single seat unlimited, admittedly taking it easy to conserve his car for the big money event Sunday.

Casagrande, a veteran of the two-seat unlimited class, said he was driving his first single-seat race. He scored an easy win in his Chenowth VW at an average speed of 46.755 mph.

Thompson's spectacular crash came on the second lap of the first qualifying heat after a restart made neces-

When the qualifying race was restarted, Thompson roared into the lead and was well out in front, with his son Danny, who lives in Sunset Beach, running second a few feet behind. When his front suspension collapsed, Thompson spun and his son crashed into him, retiring both from the race. There were no injuries in either accident.

Another winner was Roger Mears of Bakersfield, older brother of 1979 Indy 500 champ Rick Mears. Roger drove to victory in the mini-pickup race at the wheel of a Toyota prepared by student members of a Society of Automotive Engineers chapter at Cal Poly-San Luis Obispo. The winner's average speed was 37.503 mph.

It was the 14th victory in the nine years Roger Mears has been racing here. He will compete twice more today in the four-wheel-drive race and in the Heavy Metal Challenge for pickup trucks.

Craig Verendes, 29, of El Cajon, received the only injury of the day when he fell from his three-wheel motorcycle during a practice run. Medics said he appeared to have separated a shoulder, but he declined medical

339

260 entries turned out for the 1982 Bridgeston Score Wotrld Championship. Roger mears won the Challenge of Champions, the Mini Metal Challenge and the Class One race, giving him eighteen wins at this event. Walker Evans won the Heavy Metal Challenge. A side note; three racecars were stolen from a Riverside motel parking lot after the event, two belonging to Jeff Probst and one belonging to Bob Gotdon.

Challenge of Champions race set

The Challenge of Champions, featuring off-road racers Roger Mears, Glenn Harris, Mike and Scott Gillman, and Larry Ragland, will highlight the Bridgestone SCORE Off-Road World Championship at Riverside International Raceway Aug. 7-8.

Racers will line up 30 abreast in open-wheel race cars, ready to race for a purse estimated at $35,000 over Riverside's Baja-style badlands course.

The Challenge of Champions is the featured attraction in this off-road event, which includes competition with every type of four-wheel vehicle; trucks, four-wheel-drives, sedans and modified Volkswagens as well as motorcycles and three-wheel all-terrain cycles.

The competition begins Aug. 7 with two qualifying heats. The main event will be flagged off on Sunday.

The Challenge racers have only 12 laps to win wheel-to-wheel around Riverside's 1.5-mile circuit of ruts and ditches.

Racers will start side-by-side on a wide chute that narrows to 30 feet a few hundred yards away.

It Sure Wasn't an Off Day for Roger Mears

By TRACY DODDS, *Times Staff Writer*

It was all Roger Mears Sunday in the 10th annual Bridgestone SCORE off-road races at Riverside International Raceway.

It was Mears in the Modified Four-Wheel Drive class, Mears in the Datsun Mini-Metal Challenge for small pickups and Mears in the SCORE Challenge of Champions for unlimited single-seaters.

His last two victories were back-to-back in two of the three featured events.

In the other featured event, Walker Evans of Riverside won the Pernod Heavy Metal Challenge, driving his '82 Dodge to an easy 34-second victory.

Mears, who like his brother Rick is also an Indy car driver, was all aglow with his big day in the dust, thinking it not at all strange that these races were being run in the rutty, bumpy, banked dirt trailing up one side and down the other side of a perfectly good race track.

"I like the challenge of going against the dirt with the terrain changing in front of you all the time," Mears said.

Beats Scott Gillman

Mears had to beat Scott Gillman to win the unlimited single-seater race. These are just 10-lap races, and Mears passed Gillman halfway through the eighth lap, taking the inside of a turn while Gillman got caught on the outside, behind a slower car.

The unlimited single-seated victory gave Mears a total of 18 victories on the Riverside course, adding to the record total that he had going into this weekend's events. His three victories this weekend paid him at least $18,950.

He had to coax his car to the finish line in his last race, saying, "C'mon baby." The fan belt had gone with two laps to go.

"I was just supposed to win this one, that's all there is to it," Mears said. "When they break at the finish line, you're meant to win it."

A Dream Race

Mears called his victory in the mini-trucks a dream race. That one he won going away. "You wish all the races could be that way," he said.

Evans, however, who won going away, would have liked more of a race for his amusement as well as the crowd's. He was disappointed when his top competitor, Ivan Stewart, broke down and went out early.

"People don't come out to see a runaway," he said. "That's what it really boiled down to. The track is so muddy at the start, but it was just getting to the point where we could really make a race of it, and he went out.

"That's too bad."

It was too bad for Scott Gillman that his right front tire was slowly deflating late in the race, and he was feeling the effect of that when Mears passed him going into the switchbacks. Mears, who had passed Mike Gillman on the third lap, was waiting for just such a break.

The Gilmans dominate closed-course dune buggy racing. Mike Gillman won the Challenge of Champions here last year. He won the Class 10 division for one- and two-seat 1600cc unlimited buggies Sunday.

There were also breakdowns for drivers in the mini-trucks, but they had no effect on Mears' victory in that class.

Spencer Low, who was heading for a third-place finish, rolled into the wall with just yards to go.

Josele Garza, the Indianapolis 500 Rookie of the Year in 1981, made his first off-road start in the mini-truck race and moved up from eighth place—after getting his Ford squeezed out between Datsun team drivers Mears and Mike Mosely at the start—to third place after passing Low on the fourth lap. He was still in third place on the sixth lap when his right rear tire went flat.

"I had a fast pit stop to fix the tire," Garza said. "Not as fast as an Indy pit stop, but pretty fast."

He ended up fifth, and the truck's owner and usual driver, Dick Landfield, was pleased with his showing. "Josele can have my ride anytime," he said.

Mears wins Riverside Off-Road

RIVERSIDE (AP) — Hopping from truck to car, Roger Mears of Bakersfield scored three victories worth $18,950 Sunday in the 10th annual Bridgestone SCORE Off-Road World Championship at Riverside International Raceway.

Mears, the older brother of former Indianapolis 500 winner Rick Mears and an Indianapolis driver himself, added to his success at Riverside with his 16th, 17th and 18th all-time wins, all of them scored in this event. He won the races for modified four-wheel-drive vehicles, mini-pickups and unlimited single-seaters.

Trailing in the featured SCORE Challenge of Champions after a wild start that saw 29 drivers start side by

Mears wins three races in off-road

Hopping from truck to car, Roger Mears of Bakersfield scored three victories worth $18,950 Sunday in the 10th annual Bridgestone SCORE Off-Road World Championship at Riverside International Raceway.

Mears, the older brother of former Indianapolis 500 winner Rick Mears, won races for modified four-wheel-drive vehicles, minipickups and unlimited single-seaters.

Mears needed only the first lap to take the lead in the Datsun Mini-Metal Challenge for minipickups, passing Guillermo Valdez of El Monte to take the lead and pull away in a Datsun.

Valdez, driving a Ford Courier, protested against a Mazda driven by Steve Kelley of Rolling Hills Estates on technical grounds

Race aids in marketing and testing of tires

As sophisticated as marketing has become, there is nothing like an auto race to stir up enthusiasm among tire customers.

It's on that theme that the Bridgestone Tire Company of America, Inc., plays out its continued sponsorship of the 16th annual Bridgestone SCORE Off-Road World Championship at Riverside International Raceway Aug. 7-8.

The premiere spectator off-road race in the country, a sort of Wild West happening that draws upward of 50,000 fans each year, provides Bridgestone with several benefits, the company believes.

Primarily, the race is the cornerstone of a retail customer sales promotion that offers a Ford Ranger as the grand prize in a super sweepstakes.

Bridgestone dealers offer channel ticket coupons, with both the super sweepstakes and discount coupons heavily advertised in local media to create a fresh source of traffic into retail outlets.

Not the least of its sponsorship benefits is the opportunity for Bridgestone to test an experimental new tire in action during the Riverside race as proof that it does indeed use the sport of off-road racing as a testing ground.

To develop the new tire, Bridgestone started with its stock Desert Dueler steel-belted radial design, a tire that has been proved in cross-country competition from the forbidding Baja California peninsula of Mexico to the washboard terrain of Nevada.

Greg Higham, national product manager for passenger and light truck tire sales, describes the basic features of the Desert Dueler as "outstanding

super cross-country handling response combined with maximum impact resistance." The high performance features are an aggressive tread pattern and stiff bead area.

But short course racing at Riverside makes different demands on tires than motorists or even competitors find in the desert. There are no rocks, the ground is harder, and traction is the most important winning ingredient in short course racing.

So the modified Desert Dueler, the new "Riverside tire," has a more open tread design plus a softer compound for additional traction.

All of Bridgestone's 12 contracted factory drivers will have the option to race on the new tire at Riverside. The factory stable includes Sam Gibert of Cypress, Calif., a many-times champion in his class for drivers of stock automobiles, and Baja Bug champ driver Malcolm Vinje of San Diego, Calif.

Many of the fans in the grandstands looking out over a sea of banners strung around the course and cheering for their favorite drivers will already have visited their local Bridgestone dealer, either to try to win the specially prepared $9,750

Ford Ranger or to acquire discount coupons that save them money on tickets to see the race. Dealership traffic is the final element of the event promotion, creating enthusiasm at the retail level, according to Harold L. Brown, vice-president, sales.

"We are proud of our products," Brown said, "and we are equally pleased with the success of our efforts to get recognition for them through aggressive sports promotion."

Bridgestone is the official tire of the Long Beach Grand Prix and is directly involved in the Bridgestone Pre-Kart Invitational race that weekend. It is a sponsor of the World Speedway Motorcycle Finals and of major motorcycle motocross events. Bridgestone has also been a long-term sponsor of the Glen Campbell Los Angeles Open golf tournament and women's world championship tennis doubles competition held in the U.S. and Japan.

Bridgestone Tire Company of America, Inc., is now 55 years old. Since it began operation in 1967, it has grown from a staff of 12 to more than 366 employees. Sales in 1981 ap-

proached $270 million, and the company now has more than 1,600 dealers in the U.S.

Based in Torrance, Calif., Bridgestone offers a complete range of passenger car and light truck tires, as well as heavy duty truck, giant off-road vehicle, motorcycle and kart tires.

NEW TIRE DESIGN—Even off-road racing has become so specialized that there is a new tread design being introduced by the sponsoring tire company at its 16th annual Bridgestone SCORE Off-Road World Championship Aug. 7-8 at Riverside International Raceway. Left, pickup truck driver Danny York of Canoga Park,

Calif., shows how the open tread of the new Bridgestone designed strictly for short course spectator racing events differs from the stock Desert Dueler model he uses in Baja California racing. Right, engineer Mark Dundick checks heat buildup of the open tread design with a pyrometer (heat gauge).

Pictured at left are Chris Blanke of Minden, Nev., Don Kennedy of Stockton and Scott Taylor of Belvidere, Ill., making their way around a corner while Jeff MacPherson of North Tustin gets trapped by an out-of-control buggy. More action will be seen at the Bridgestone SCORE Off-Road Championship at Riverside International Raceway Aug. 7-8.

249 entries battled the rain for the Bridgestone Score Off Road Championships in October, 1983. The move from August to October had more to do with conflicting events

than weather but the cooler, though sometimes wet October date was welcomed. For the first time, the race was broadcast on NBC. Roger Mears win the Class One race; Walker Evans won Class Eight and Ivan Stewart won Class Seven.

Roger Mears and Josele Garza, two stars of the Indianapolis 500 who have equally large followings in off-road racing, will battle each other in mini-trucks at the Bridgestone SCORE Off-Road World Championship Oct. 1-2 at Riverside International Raceway.

Mears, who teams with garza on the CART-PPG Indy car circuit with both sponsored by the Machinists Union, will drive a Nissan in the Nissan Mini-Metal Challenge, while Garza will pilot a Ford Ranger.

The two crowd-pleasers have impressive off-road credentials.

Mears of Bakersfield is the all-time SCORE Riverside victory leader, with 18 wins in 34 starts including 3-for-3 in 1982. He has raced in all 10 previous SCORE Riverside world championships.

Indianapolis 500 superstars Mears, Garza to clash in Oct. 1-2 Bridgestone SCORE mini-truck battle

Relatively, Garza is a novice. The driver from Mexico City took a ride last year in Orange County auto dealer Dick Landfield's Ranger on a lark. In his maiden race Garza was battling for third place with veteran Steve Kelley when a tire flattened, dropping Garza to fifth in the finishing order.

Proving his performance was no fluke, Garza entered Mickey Thompson's Off Road Gran Prix at Pomona last April and burst through the pack to lead. Despite terminal mechanical woes, he held on grimly to edge veteran Ivan Stewart in the mini-truck feature. Garza's truck self-destructed a few feet past the finish line. He had won by inches.

The Nissan Mini-Metal Challenge for foreign and domestic mini-pickup drivers is no two-man battle, as the race has attracted factory-backed teams. Entries are coming from Toyota, Dodge, Chevrolet and Mitsubishi.

Toyota, which also serves as SCORE International's officials truck, has a team led by Ironman Ivan Stewart of Lakeside and New Zealand's road-racing star Steve Millen.

Walker Evans of Riverside is preparing two Dodge mini-trucks for himself and Camarillo's Glenn Harris to drive. Multiple Baja 1000 winner Johnny Johnson of Lemon Grove heads the Chevy S10 effort, while veteran John Baker of Santa Fe Springs will race his Mitsubishi.

If there is a sentimental favorite, however, it could be Guillermo (Willie) Valdez of Baldwin Park, who has pushed his way past the toughest competition ever seen in mini-truck racing to beat the factory teams. Valdez flew the Mexican flag on the tailgate of his Ford Ranger all the way to the winner's circle in the June Pomona race.

STAMPEDE!

Ivan Stewart of Lakeside (front left) leads a thundering herd of heavy pickups into the first turn in recent competition. This year's Skoal Heavy Metal Challenge will pit large pickups like these against four-wheel-drives in a Bridgestone SCORE Off-Road World Championship feature race Oct. 1-2 at Riverside International Raceway.

Evans Is Battered, but Not Beaten

By SHAV GLICK, *Times Staff Writer*

RIVERSIDE—For many years, Rod Hall and his four-wheel-drive cohorts have been crying for recognition, claiming they could run with the more glamorous pickup trucks in SCORE's off-road races at Riverside if they were only given a chance.

Sunday, they got it in the Skoal Heavy Metal Challenge, and they sort of proved their point—but the winner was the same guy who's been winning here since Mickey Thompson held his first closed-course capsule of Baja in 1973.

Walker Evans

Walker Evans, truck driver nonpareil, fought off a midrace challenge by Hall to win the main event of the 11th annual Bridgestone SCORE Off-Road Championships, but not before his freshly-painted Dodge pickup was battered and bent.

Hall, after dogging Evans for half of the 12 mile race, pulled his 4WD Dodge alongside Evans after exiting a 180 degree corner—and then his truck quit cold. From then on Evans cruised along uncontested and was an easy winner.

"I'd been quicker in all the corners and was making my move to pass Walker when I stood on the gas, and all of a sudden I quit moving," said a disappointed Hall, who also was a winner back in the 1973 inaugural. "The engine was still going strong so I guess it must have been something in the drive train. I feel like we showed we were as fast or faster than the pickups."

Evans was not pleased with Hall's move and even after winning was hot about the incident.

"I don't relish having a guy drive through the side of me, especially a driver with the experience Rod (Hall) has," said the Riverside veteran. "I almost didn't get through the turn."

Hall countered by claiming Evans had drifted wide in the turn and he took the inside line.

"We were going down the road side by side," Hall said. "I'm sorry if he's upset. I'm not perfect, but then there was only one perfect man, and we all know what

quarter-mile dash for the beginning of the course. Darrel Jorgenson, in a black home-built machine with a huge rear wing, leaped from the line on top, closely chased by Don Adams and Evans. Then they all came together.

"I was in the middle, just behind them," Evans explained. "Adams was on my left and the black thing on my right when I got sandwiched. My truck must have popped 20 feet in the air but when it came down, for some reason it landed flat and I was ahead."

When Evans came around the next time, one side of his Dodge had a big black tire print and the other side had a crunched fender. From then on the only challenge came from Hall as the two big Dodges roared down Thompson Ridge together like rolling thunder.

The Nissan Mini-Metal Challenge for mini-pickups was won by Ivan Stewart, Evans' chief truck driving rival for a decade. Stewart and Steve Millen, a former pro rally driver from New Zealand, finished one-two in team Toyotas after a fender-banging battle with Evans, defending champion Roger Mears and Johnny Johnson. It was the third time in six races this year the two have finished one-two.

Only five of the 18 starters finished as the course was strewn with broken equipment. Josele Garza, one of the pre-race favorites, failed to start as his Ford broke down on the parade lap.

Stewart took the lead with a bold move when five cars attempted to squeeze through a hole that wouldn't take more than two. Millen and Evans were leading when they went for the inside and Stewart, moving from third place, took the lead by sweeping past on the outside.

"I saw the jam on the inside, so I just went around the outside and passed everyone," Stewart said.

Mears, who later won the unlimited single-seater race to keep his winning streak intact at Riverside, dropped out when he was hit by Johnson and blew a tire. Johnson also managed to put a large dent in Stewart's winning Toyota, but caused only cosmetic damage.

Mears had won at least one race in the last nine SCORE programs at Riverside but was down to his last chance in his single-seat Chenowth.

"I was scared when I got here," said Mears, who is now more involved with Indianapolis cars than off-road vehicles. "I wondered if this would be the year I would not win. Then the Checkbook Challenge was canceled Saturday and I dropped out of the Mini-Metal. I had to win that last one."

Gillman Brothers Are Taking Their Act On the Road

By TOM HAMILTON, *Times Staff Writer*

Move over Mears brothers, here come the Gillmans. Mike and Scott Gillman, the most successful team in off-road racing during the past two years, are bringing their driving act to the pavement.

The Gillmans spent the week at Laguna Seca in Monterey preparing for their debut in an IMSA series race in Portland on July 31.

The Gillmans are hoping to follow in the footsteps of the Mears brothers, who graduated from off-road racing and are successful drivers in the CART Indy car series.

The Gillmans entered off-road racing in 1980 after enjoying successful careers as motorcyclists. Scott was a factory rider in 1979 and his older brother, Mike, was a desert racer who competed in the Big Bear Grand Prix at Riverside among other events.

It wasn't long before the family team became the best short-course racers in off-road. They also created a lot of goodwill by donating their winnings to the Cystic Fibrosis Foundation.

In 18 months, the Gillmans donated $100,000 to the charity and while honored at a dinner last October, Barbara Boyle, executive director of the chapter said, "This is the largest single individual donation in the history of our foundation.

"All I can say about them (Gillmans) is they have done more to save a child's life than any person in history."

Accolades aside, the Gillmans have gone back to school to launch a new chapter in their racing careers. Mike, 27, and Scott, 23, entered Jim Russell's British School of Racing at Laguna Seca to become familiar with the four-cylinder, fuel-injected Toyota Celica they will be driving in four IMSA races this year.

"The car is a lot more than we expected," Mike said. "We plan on splitting the time behind the wheel with most of the races going either three or six hours. The class up here is more or less a refresher course of the Bondurant school we went through last year."

The Gillmans participated in the Bob Bondurant School of Driving at Willow Springs and impressed everyone by turning lap times that were faster than their instructor.

They returned to Willow Springs 10 days ago after completing a deal with Dan Gurney and Toyota to test drive their new car.

"We actually were driving a couple of the celebrity cars from the Long Beach Grand Prix, but they gave us a pretty good indication of what to expect," Mike said. "Everything happened so fast.

"We've been trying to get into road racing for over a year. We put this together in less than a week. Scott and I keep pinching ourselves and asking if this is really happening."

Gurney watched the Gillmans race at Mickey Thompson's Off-Road Championship Gran Prix last month in Pomona and was impressed. He offered the brothers the opportunity to compete in four IMSA races—Portland, Elkhart Lake, Atlanta and Daytona.

"This is a great way to get into road racing because you get so much time behind the wheel in an IMSA race," Mike said. "We plan on splitting the time, driving between an hour and twenty minutes to an hour and 45 minutes before switching."

The duo will split their earnings with Gurney, who is providing six mechanics and preparing the car for each race. IMSA races offer a winner anywhere from $3,000-$8,000.

"We'll continue to drive with the logo, 'Driving Hard

to Conquer Cystic Fibrosis' on the car and donate all of our earnings to Cystic Fibrosis," Mike said. "This is a great opportunity for us. We're with a top team, have top equipment and hopefully are doing everything right.

"You couldn't ask for a better guy to be involved with than Dan Gurney. He told us, 'Be consistent and smooth.' He also said, 'You have time to learn, don't rush things and don't become discouraged if you don't win right away.'"

One thing is certain. The Gillman's racing schedule is booked solid. They return to the area on Friday to prepare for Thompson's final race at the Los Angeles County Fairgrounds on Saturday night.

Mike is second in the points standings for the unlimited, 1600cc class where he trails leader Brian Harber by half a point. Scott is seventh in the unlimited, single-seat class. But the final race is a double points event and both drivers have a chance to win the series.

On Tuesday, the Gillmans depart for Portland to help promote the race and then prepare and qualify. The following Monday, they depart for Dallas to drive in a High Desert Racing Assn. event.

"We only have one conflict with off-road racing and that's next month at Saddleback," Mike said. "But we're so far ahead in the series there that missing one race shouldn't hurt our chances of winning."

Mike and Scott Gillman, champions of off-road racing, spent the week at Laguna Seca in Monterey preparing for their debut in an IMSA series race in Portland on July 31.

Photos: DEBORA ROBINSON / Los Angeles Times

Scott Gilman, airborne, of Anaheim Hills loses control while scrambling for an early lead in last year's Bridgestone SCORE Off-Road World Championship. Gillman and his brother, Mike, will be back for this year's competition.

The 1984 SCORE Off Road World Championship boasted a guaranteed purse of $68,180 plus almost double that in contingency awards. The officials decided to add an additional quarter mile to the track on saturday to improve spectating. There was a brief rain on Saturday but Sunday dawned sunny, got to 100 degrees, then turned to rain and wind, blowing away many of the banners, signage and even some tents. 16,000 fans scrambled for cover and the races were delayed for an hour and a half. Scott Gilman won the Challenge of Champions, Rod Hall won the Heavy Metal Challenge, Ivan Stewart won the Mini Metal event and Walker Evans won Class Eight.

Evans ready to motor past SCORE field

By KATIE CASTATOR
Sun Sports Writer

RIVERSIDE — Walker Evans enjoys racing anything with a motor. At his mountain retreat near Park City, Utah, he keeps five snowmobiles. But shucks, that's nothing. His next door neighbor, Parnelli Jones, has at least 15.

"When the girls are off skiing, we go snowmobiling," Evans said. "I've got a snowmobile that goes about 90 mph so it's a real thrill."

Evans will go off the beaten track again today when he races in two classes of the Riverside SCORE Off-Road World Championship at Riverside International Raceway.

Evans, whose residence and business (Walker Evans Enterprises, builders of state-of-the-art vehicles) are in Riverside, started out as a general contractor, a natural choice of careers since it was his father's profession.

"But lo and behold, I always had this other trait," said Evans, 44, a Riverside resident since age 7 when his family moved to the Inland Empire from Michigan. "I liked to compete in automobiles, anything that had a motor on it got my heart started."

It took about 10 years of racing drag boats, John Crean-James Garner team. Then one race, the guy who was supposed to drive got sick. Evans filled in and the rest is history.

In 1979, he was the first to win the Baja 1000 overall title in a pickup truck. He even beat all but one motorcycle entrant, who finished about six or seven minutes ahead of Evans in the Ensenada to La Paz run. Then last year, he won overall honors in the Pernod Barstow Classic. Both races cover rugged terrain and favor the dune-buggy type, open-wheel race cars.

It's evident Evans has been on the move on the off-road circuit. And he had no intention of playing the tortoise to John Baker's hare Saturday at RIR.

After all, you can't count on a guy like Baker underestimating his competition and taking a snooze midway through the race. So in the interest of competitive justice, Evans filed a protest, one that was upheld by SCORE and disqualified Baker's Mitsubishi truck.

Actually, the whole affair smacked of a good old-fashioned family feud. Evans entered his Dodge Ram in today's Nissan Mini Metal Challenge (class 7) at the SCORE race. The Dodge Ram and Mitsubishi are essentially the same truck

Harris Was in a Hurry to Get Off Road

Driver Won a Trophy Before He Was Old Enough to Get License

By TOM HAMILTON, *Times Staff Writer*

Everybody at Camarillo High School knew Glenn Harris. He was the only student in school who drove his off-road racing vehicle to auto shop and then spent most of day working on his car.

He was the wheeler-dealer who used to tune up his counselor's car and then surprised his classmates by graduating a year early. He was also the guy who came back to class one Monday with a race trophy—and he wasn't old enough to have a driver's license.

"I was one of those guys who lived in the auto shop and spent every dime I earned on my car," Harris said. "I washed dishes to earn the money for my first motorcycle. I was motorcycle crazy."

Harris' motorcycle career was over practically before it started. He broke both of his arms in his first season of motocross racing and vividly remembers the day he decided to pursue an off-road racing career.

"I came home for dinner with a broken wrist, and mother told me she wouldn't take

thought I was doing pretty well after one loop. By the time I got to the finish line, there wasn't a car in sight. I thought everybody had finished an hour ahead of me, packed up and gone home. I couldn't believe it when they told me I had won."

Harris has been winning off-road races for nearly 10 years. He's won major desert races such as the Mint 400 and the Parker 400. In the past four years, he's concentrated on short-course races and recently won his class at Mickey Thompson's Off-Road Championship Gran Prix in Pomona.

The 26-year-old is among the favorites in the Nissan Mini Metal Challenge today in the 12th SCORE Off-Road World Championship at Riverside International Raceway. Harris will compete in a Mazda. He will also drive an unlimited 1600cc Volkswagen for owner Jim Swift in the Class 10 series.

"I consider this race the Indy 500 of short-course races," Harris said. "I've been coming here since 1976 and this is my favorite

has a quarter-million dollar setup.

"I've learned how to become a business man as well as a racer," Harris said. "Everything I've done, I've learned myself. When I'm not racing, I spend most of my time on the phone with sponsors. The phone bill is usually about $400 a month."

Harris' business sense comes naturally. He was among seven children in a successful family that includes a younger brother who portrayed the young boy in the film "Airplane" who torments pilot Roger Murdoch, a.k.a. Kareem Abdul-Jabbar.

"My family and my wife (Gina) have been so supportive in my racing career," Harris said. "I've finally reached the point where I can support myself through racing and the future looks great driving the Mazdas."

Off-Road Notes

Action begins today at 9:15 a.m. with the three-wheel ATV race and concludes with the Skoal Heavy Metal Challenge for pickup trucks in which **Walker Evans will defend his title against rival Rod Hall**

Rain Delay Helps Ivan Stewart, but It's an Off-Day for Mears

By TOM HAMILTON, *Times Staff Writer*

The basic elements of off-road racing are enough to challenge the best driver. Tales of rocky terrain, sand pits and dry deserts are as famous as the drivers themselves.

But when a downpour turns a course into a quagmire that is better suited for mud wrestling, the odds against simply finishing a race—much less winning—are increased.

The elements could not have been worse for the estimated 250 drivers who competed in the 12th SCORE Off-Road World Championship Sunday at Riverside International Raceway.

A lengthy downpour stemming from tropical storm Norbert off the coast of Baja California delayed the race for an hour and a half and reduced the 1.4-mile course to a hazardous mudslide. Drivers scrambled for spare mud tires on a day that began with 100-degree temperatures and then saw the estimated 16,000 fans scramble for cover.

The winners—make that survivors—on a long afternoon were Ivan Stewart, Rod Hall and Scott Gillman. Stewart completed a remarkable season by winning another mini pickup race in his yellow and white Toyota in the Nissan Mini Metal Challenge.

Metal Challenge. Hall was also awarded the Strohs Cup for the best performance of the day.

Gillman won the Bugpack Challenge of Champions for unlimited single-seat cars and ended five years of frustration at Riverside. Gillman gave an assist to Canadian driver John McPherson for loaning him four rain tires.

Roger Mears, who has won more world off-road titles (19) at Riverside than any other driver, was shut out. He dropped out of the mini truck race on the eighth lap with transmission problems and then failed to finish in heavy metal race with steering problems. It marked the first time in 11 years that Mears had failed to win a race at Riverside.

"I guess it just wasn't my day," Mears said. "I had a feeling when it started to rain we would be in trouble. When the rain came, we lost our advantage."

Stewart said the rain delay gave his crew the necessary time needed to change his truck's transmission before he won his race. The delay also gave him an edge over Mears.

"Roger had the edge judging by the practice sessions, but the rain turned things around," Stewart said. "I got some tips from Jack

A messy SCORE victory for Hall at Riverside

By KATIE CASTATOR
Sun Sports Writer

RIVERSIDE — The difference was mud, lots of the slippery, sloppy, gloppy stuff.

Rod Hall of Reno, Nev., took full advantage of the dirty, mudhole conditions to beat out archrival Walker Evans of Riverside for first place in class 8 and a winner's purse of $1,920 in Sunday's SCORE Off-Road World Championships at Riverside International Raceway.

Evans, who drives a two-wheel-drive Dodge, got less traction than Hall did in his Dodge 4X4. On top of that, he lost his power steering early in the race.

Last year, Hall broke an axle and finished second to Evans. "It's almost like evening the score," said Hall, no pun intended.

Sunday, the last three races were run after an hour's rain delay. Consequently, when the cars weren't getting stuck in the mud in the switchbacks, they were sliding into each other — and just plain sliding into something.

"On the ess turn where the mud was this deep, I just accelerated right by them (2X2s)," said Hall, indicating about two feet between his hands. "It wasn't horsepower, it was just traction that pulled us by there."

Hall saw five cars get ahead of him at the start of the race, but charged ahead of the pack before reaching the switchbacks.

"I thought I had a bad start, everybody going around me," Hall said. "They must be 20 years younger or 10 percent crazy. They sure have a way to get around you. We had to go to Plan B, and that was be smart and see if we could work our way back up front."

The Nissan Mini Metal Challenge (small pickups) and Bugpack Challenge of Champions also followed the deluge which lasted about 30 minutes. Drivers were running without fenders and with smashed-in hoods and, in the bugpack group, occasionally without a front wheel.

Team Toyota dominated the class 7 Mini Metal race with the same one-two finishing combination of 1983: Ivan "Iron Man" Stew-art of Lakeside defended his title and Steve Millen of Irvine took second place.

Scott Gillman of Anaheim finished first in the Bugpack Challenge followed by Frank Arciero Jr. of Laguna Hills.

Roger Mears, who was a favorite to win one of the three classes he entered (7, 8 and bugpack) had equipment trouble in all three.

"When it started raining, I figured we'd have trouble in the mini-truck race," Mears said. "The shifter was a problem at the start, but I thought I could close in on Ivan. But Glenn Harris got stuck in the mud before the first turn and I didn't see him. Our

(Please see Off-road, C-7)

Pancho Weaver of Huntington Beach (401) whips his Bronco around one of Riverside International Raceway's switchback turns, which are famous for jamming up race vehicles. Action like this is expected at the SCORE Off-Road World Championship on Friday and Saturday.

EAPING HIGH — G.T. Gowland of Palm Desert leaps his
ehicle off a jump en route to an 8th-place finish in the 1-1600
lass during race on 1.5-mile course at Riverside Raceway.

John Nelson

John Clark Gable, 24-year-old son of the late Clark Gable, will be at Riverside this weekend in the Off-Road World Championships.

For 1985, a new sponsor renamed the event as the Turbo Wash SCORE Off Road World Championship. A crowd in the 40,000 range saw 315 cars in 33 classes competing. It was another hot August day. Walker Evans won the Heavy Metal Challenge.

Highly Successful Off-Road Racer Bob Gordon Finally Wins the Big One

By JOHN PENNER

Until recently, the Turbo Wash SCORE Off-Road World Championships—the World Series of off-road racing—has been the one major event that has escaped Bob Gordon.

At age 27, Gordon drove in his first ever off-road race, finishing second to renowned driver Walker Evans in the 1976 SCORE Parker 400. Since then, Gordon has won nearly every major off-road event.

In his first nine years of racing in the world championships, which have been held at the Riverside Raceway for the past 13 years, Gordon has been among the top five finishers on four occasions. After several years of believing he had taken the fastest car into the competition but constantly coming up short, he and his crew were beginning to doubt whether he would ever win it.

Earlier this month, Gordon, who lives in Orange, finally won that elusive title with a victory in the Bosch Bash, a world championship event for single-seat vehicles limited to 1600cc engines.

"Riverside is the grand-daddy of them all," the 37-year-old Gordon said. "You wait all year for it. It's like the Indianapolis 500 (of off-road racing). And now we feel like we've broken the jinx."

During his 10 years competing at Riverside, Gordon has been frustrated by a string of bad luck and — on two occasions — even sabotage.

In 1979, he was leading the race for Class 2 unlimited cars, when his Chevy Blazer broke its rear axle on the final lap.

Then in the 1982 Bilstein Challenge of Champions, the Riverside race for single-seat unlimited vehicles, Gordon was even more unfortunate. He was well out in front with three laps to go when his car's distributor cap fell off, dropping him to a 30th-place finish.

"Someone tampered with the car before that race," he claimed. "We had the fastest qualifying time going into the race. So I guess whoever did it figured I would be the best guy to get."

He believes the car was tampered with because the distributor cap usually fell off during the parade lap, and when he checked it, he discovered that the two clips which held it in place had been removed. He used tape to secure the cap, but it wasn't sitting enough

---

to hold during the race.

To make matters worse, later that evening he had his truck, trailer and race car stolen from outside his hotel room. Since insurance cannot be obtained on a trailer or a race car, it cost Gordon $50,000 to replace them.

Gordon also ran into difficulties at Riverside the day before his Bosch Bash victory. He was leading the Challenge through most of the race until a shock absorber broke, forcing him to settle for second.

But Gordon and his crew switched the shocks with a similarly equipped car which he would be racing the following day. And this time he ran the course without a hitch.

Gordon said that throughout Sunday's race, especially near the end, he couldn't help but think that a disaster of some sort was imminent.

"I was holding onto first with two laps left," Gordon said. "So I figured something was going to go wrong. I was coming onto lap

---

times."

Dave Houlgate, public relations director of SCORE, believes Gordon's problems have been due to an inferior car.

"There's always an element besides the driver you have to consider in racing, and that's the car," Houlgate said. "I would call (Gordon) one of the top drivers in off-road racing, but I think that at Riverside he just hasn't been in the appropriate vehicle."

Gordon's victory at the world championships climaxed an already impressive list of wins. His desert victories include the 1976 Mint 400, the 1977 SCORE Parker 400, the overall four-wheel title in the 1979 Mexicali 250 and the 1980 SCORE Baja International.

He has also won several short course events, such as the Mickey Thompson Formula One Gran Prix Championship in 1983, the four-race Off-Road Championship Gran Prix at the Pomona Fairgrounds in 1983 and 1984 and the unlimited main event race at Pomona earlier this year.

Gordon is a fixture in the business world as well. His company, Gordon Fred, supplies Los Alamitos and Bay Meadows race tracks with nearly all of the feed for the horses. He also owns Thoroughbred Feed Company, which is the main supplier to Santa Anita, Hollywood Park and Del Mar.

"Racing is just a hobby," Gordon said. "There are a lot of other guys who have had two or three good years, and so they quit their businesses in order to race full-time. But my business is too successful to quit and go racing."

In the last year, Gordon's 16-year-old son, Robbie, has become

---

interested in off-road racing. He will make his competitive debut next month at Frontier 500 in Nevada, where his father will also compete.

Despite finally accomplishing what had been his ultimate goal for the last 10 years, Gordon says that he has no intention of giving up the sport in the near future.

"I'm going to keep racing as long as I'm able to," he said. "One goal I have is, I'd still like to be the overall points champion at the end of the year, and this upcoming race (the Frontier) carries a lot of points.

"And I would also like to win the championship of both races at Riverside, the Class 1 and Class 10."

Gordon only hopes it won't take him another 10 years to accomplish those feats.

'Riverside is the grand-daddy of them all. You wait all year for it . . . And now we feel like we've broken the jinx.'

—Bob Gordon

Riverside Takes On the Look of Baja for Off-Road Program

Riverside International Raceway will, once again, become a little bit of Baja this weekend for the 13th annual Turbo Wash SCORE Off-Road World Championships.

A 114-mile course of simulated

In the Bilstein Challenge desert cars, drivers will include Arciero, Vince Tjelmeland, LeDuc and Larry Minor, making rare appearance in something other than a truck.

After practice Friday, racing

354

Photo / JEFFREY FORD

Huber of Apple Valley will drive his mini-pickup at Riverside Raceway this weekend

25,000 attended the 1986 SCORE Off Road Championships, braving the heat, winds and ever present dust. There were 316 entries in 34 classes. This was supposed to be the last as the track would soon be a shopping center and industrial park. Who

knew, we had two more years left !! Walker Evans won the Heavy Metal Challenge. Roger Mears won Class Seven but ended up second in the Mini Metal Challenge after a flat tire dropped him behind winner Glen Harris.

Evans shows mettle, wins SCORE Challenge

By KATIE CASTATOR
Sun Sports Writer

RIVERSIDE — On a day marred by fights, collisions, penalties, appeals and 100-plus degree heat, Walker Evans of Riverside defended his title in Four Wheeler Magazine's Heavy Metal Challenge for his 11th career victory in the SCORE Off Road World Championships at Riverside International Raceway.

He may be the last off-road racer to take a checkered flag at the 30-year-old plant, which is scheduled to close at the end of the 1986 season.

"This is the toughest one I've had to run, and I'm the most pleased with it," said Evans, who kept his Dodge pickup ahead of a charging Steve Kelley of Rolling Hills, who collided with Rodney Hall of Reno in the first lap.

Also along for the ride in the Evans' Dodge was Phyllis Evans, Walker's wife.

"Phyllis didn't ride one practice lap with me and they warned her the track was rough this year," Evans said. "After our parade lap, she wanted me to pull over and let her out, but I told her it was too late. Now she's glad she didn't get out, but she's going to feel it tomorrow."

Other highlights in the 14th running of the event included:

• Glenn Harris of Camarillo overcoming a stall problem (six times stalled out) in his Mazda pickup to win the Nissan Mini Metal Challenge;

• Frank Arciero Jr. of Laguna Hills winning his first race (Class 10, stadium buggies) at Riverside after 12 years of trying — and that was after he and brother Albert reportedly visited Kevin Pence's compound and physically objected to being run into the wall by Pence's truck in an earlier race for Class 1 desert racers;

• Roger Mears winning his 20th SCORE title.

Mears, the 39-year-old driver from Bakersfield, first won here in 1974 after a wheel-to-wheel battle with Parnelli Jones. Beating the legendary Jones was the thrill of the young driver's career, and remained his No.1 career highlight until Sunday when he took the lead at the start of Class 7 desert trucks and held it for an easy win.

The Class 7 event isn't supposed to be the weekend's glamour race.

But off-roading doesn't pretend to be a glamour sport, either. Saturday and Sunday, the race-

See SCORE/C2

Walker Evans
Riverside resident

Baja Bugs and Class 11 Action

Off-Road Racing Veteran Bob Gordon Will Compete Against His 17-Year-Old Son, Rob, This Afternoon at Riverside Raceway

By TOM HAMILTON,
Times Staff Writer

When 17-year-old Rob Gordon asks his father, Bob, for the keys to the car, it usually means it's time for a pit crew to go to work.

The Gordons are off-road racers and will be among the field today in the SCORE Off-Road Championships at Riverside International Raceway.

Bob, who owns a feed company in Los Alamitos that supplies the horse racing tracks in Southern California, has three race cars. He will drive in the unlimited single-seat, unlimited two-seat and 1650cc classes.

ORANGE COUNTY

Rob, a 17-year-old senior at El Modena High School, will race in the 1650cc class.

It will mark the third time the two have competed against each other in a race.

Rob was credited with the fastest lap time at the Parker 400, but he hit a rock on the second loop, suffered two flat tires and a broken front suspension, and limped home for 10th place. Bob, showing the skill and expertise that comes with years of racing, kept a steady pace to finish second.

The two met again at the Lucerne 250, where Rob finished second but was penalized 15 minutes for failing to stop at a crossing. Bob, despite an early problem with a flat tire, finished fourth.

"Rob has made some mistakes that come with youth," his father said. "He has no fear at all. He's driving as fast as anybody in the sport. But he's also got some things to learn."

Still, Bob said he was surprised to find that his son was five minutes ahead of him in his off-road racing debut at the Parker 400.

"I came into the pit area for fuel after the first loop and asked if anybody had seen Rob," Bob said. "The crew told me, 'Don't worry about Rob. He was here five minutes ago.'

"He probably would have won the race, but he got impatient. He

'Rob has made some mistakes that come with youth. He has no fear at all . . . But he also has some things to learn.'

—Bob Gordon (above) talking about son Rob (below).

rider, but his father had other ideas.

"I watched kids break their necks in three straight races in the Golden State series that Rob was competing in and said, 'That's it,'" Bob said. "I prefer seeing a roll cage around him.

"Nobody wants to see their kid get hurt. He had a lot of ability in motocross. But it seemed like when Saddleback Park closed, he was no longer as sharp in the races and was starting to get hurt."

Now, the only hurt for Bob Gordon is watching his son finish five minutes ahead of him at a checkpoint.

Mears wins off-road in Riverside

RIVERSIDE (AP) — Roger Mears of Bakersfield, Calif., won his 20th SCORE Off-road World Championship victory in the Desert Challenge race for compact pickup trucks at Riverside International Raceway on Sunday.

Mears, 39, won the day's opening race in a Nissan Hardbody. It was his 41st start in the 14 years of the event, which on Sunday was run with the temperature well over 100 degrees and dust from the improvised dirt track permeating the atmosphere.

Mears, older brother of Indianapolis 500-winner Rick Mears, said the track was "rougher than I've ever seen it. A driver has to use his judgment out there and I think that's good all the way around."

Mears had some minor mechanical problems with the transmission dropping out of gear.

"I was talking to the truck at the end," he said. "The transmission

Racing roundup

Mario Andretti wins

LONG POND, Pa. — Everyone who knew Mario Andretti's racing history at Pocono International Raceway, including Andretti himself, was waiting for something to go wrong.

"Believe me, I was worried," the jubilant Andretti said Sunday after running away to one of the sweetest victories of his illustrious racing career in the Domino's Pizza Pocono 500.

It took the 46-year-old Andretti 14 tries to win the 500-miler on the 2.5-mile tri-oval located just 30 miles from his home at Nazareth, Pa.

And the long wait weighed heavily on the man who has won virtually every important race in the world at least once.

engine problems doomed him to an 11th-place finish.

That cost him the lead in the CART-PPG championship series, with Mario moving on top 96 points to 91.

"I'm glad my father won. It means a whole lot to him. But I wish we could have held on," said Michael, who was in third place before his engine let go just 14 laps from the end of the 200-lap race. "We have to start finishing races if we hope to have any chance at winning the championship."

The elder Andretti picked up $102,843 for averaging 152.106 mph in a race slowed by seven caution flags.

Andretti, earning the 47th victory of his career and second of the season in his Cosworth-powered Lola, added, "I was elated with the performance of the car."

There were several crashes in the race, the most serious a one-car

Elliott, whose car is owned local businessman Harry M grabbed the lead for good on I and held as much a a 10-second on the field before an accident second turn of lap 171 brought caution flag out and bunched field.

Kyle Petty hit the wall, bro out the caution flag. The Richard Petty was not in seriously.

The race restarted on lap Pole-sitter Benny Parsons, in t place behind Elliott, hit the w the second turn of the first lap the restart. Parson was shake but treated and released at t field care center.

The yellow flag came out out not until after Elliott Richmond staged a furious ch the start-finish line. Richmon at the end of the lead lap just of Elliott when Parsons' ac occurred.

When the race restarted

ATV racer to make comeback at Riverside

Concern for safety of all-terrain vehicle riders has kept Honda spokesman Mark Weixeldorfer of Chula Vista busy.

The combination of a speaking schedule and a recent elbow injury have prevented "Wax" form participating in many of this year's races. However, Weixeldorfer will make a comeback of sorts Aug. 15-17 in the 14th annual SCORE Off-road World Championship at the Riverside International Speedway.

Weixeldorfer, 1985 winner of the open 3-wheel ATV class at the Riverside event, hopes his luck will continue to hold

Teenager hopes to SCORE in quad class
Apple Valley's Chappell, 16, is off to fast start in his sport

By KATIE CASTATOR
Sun Sports Writer

SAN BERNARDINO — David Chappell is a compact 5-foot-7½, 150-pound, wide-eyed 11th grader at Apple Valley High School, a second-section trumpeter in the school band, and — most important of all — a licensed driver these days.

But even before turning a legal 16 on June 7, Chappell found an outlet for his driving ambitions on an off-road bike.

At age 13, he was racing three-wheelers in All-Terrain Racing Association events. And winning. At age 14, he changed to the new quad (four-wheel) racer and ran in a Mickey Thompson Off-Road Gran Prix Championship event at Pomona.

He was illegal, but nobody then knew — not even Chappell until he later tried to enter a SCORE race and was told he had to be 15 with his parents' or guardians' consent.

The consent was easy. His parents also race. Dave Sr. is "maxed out" on ATCs, according to his son. His mother is the ATRA Powder Puff champion in a suspended 350 odyssey. And his 12-year-old brother races Chappell's old quad.

If the family has a star racer, though, it's David. In 1983, he became the ATRA points champion in the quad class.

This year, he won by a margin of 5 minutes, 45 seconds in a 20-mile ATRA race in June near Lucerne, and followed that with two more ATRA wins.

Moving up against tougher competition, he raced in SCORE's Great Mojave 250, running in first place for 150 miles.

"Then the nozzle on the extra gallon fell, the coil burned and a shock broke," he said.

"Next year, I intend to really go for it."

This Saturday, Chappell will go for a win in Class 24 (250cc quads) of the SCORE Off-Road Championships at Riverside International Raceway. He'll be racing his Suzuki against Honda and Suzuki factory drivers with pit crews and extra parts.

Since Chappell's father may have to work this weekend, his son could be a one-man show — mechanic, crew chief and rider. Plus there will be no extra parts if it breaks.

Last year was the first for quads in off-road competition. The SCORE championships at Riverside featured 14 in that class.

This year the class will split into two — 250cc and open quad classes — and entries are expected to nearly double. Most riders, however, won't file for entry until late registration on Friday.

The reasons for the growing popularity of the quad racer, essentially a three-wheeler with an extra front wheel, are pretty obvious. Like the three-wheeler, it's a less expensive vehicle to buy and maintain (Chappell's '86 model cost $2,500), and it offers more stability than the three-wheeler with about the same speed (75-85 mph).

"The quad is also the latest type of recreational vehicle which has become suitable for competitive purposes," said Steve Kassanyi, race steward for SCORE. "And it's true, they seem to be more predictable and safer."

It's a good place for a young racer to begin his career. While Chappell is one of the youngest, most of the riders are only in their late teens and early 20s.

Chappell is serious about his racing, as long as he can keep his parents interested in sponsoring him — paying the $185 to $300 entry fees, tires and rims, fuel and parts.

This weekend's event will cost the family $500 minimum.

Sometimes Chappell stretches the family budget, but his success makes it worthwhile, especially when he doesn't break down.

"My dad's getting a little bummed by all the expenses, though," Chappell said. "I'm working for him now and will be putting more of my own money into it."

Last September, Chappell ran at Ascot in the qualifying for last month's Mickey Thompson race at the Los Angeles Coliseum. He finished fourth for a spot in the field. Plus he came home with a plan.

His parents' home is located on five acres in Apple Valley between Hesperia and Lucerne. So he had plenty of room to develop his idea, and the equipment to do it since his father is a tractor operator.

"I took my dad's tractor and went up on top our hill and built my own half-mile track," he said. "I designed it after the Ascot track. It has doubles, a big straight off a jump, three jumps, one after the other, a bunch of whoops and burms."

Of course, that's off-road lingo for creative torture for man and machine.

To keep in shape, Chappell practices an hour each day and jogs 10 miles.

"I also work out — pushups and situps," he said. "And I play a lot of racquetball and work out at the racket club. I do everything there but aerobics."

Chappell plans to race in the Mickey Thompson show at Orange Show Speedway in September.

"If I had the money, I'd build a truck or buggy and race that," he said. "I'd like to race professionally. If I put all my skill into it, I could make it happen."

Danny Thompson

Al Arciero

Bob Gordon

Some Unusual Vehicles

In 1987, Stroh's Beer became the sponsor – The Strohs Score Off Road Championship. Possibly the last fir sure (so we thought at the time, 3012 entrants, 34 classes and $210,000 in prizemoney and contingencies. Danny Thompson won the Jeep Mini Metal Challenge while Frank "Scoop" Vessels won the Hungus Heavy Metal Challenge; his first Riverside win.

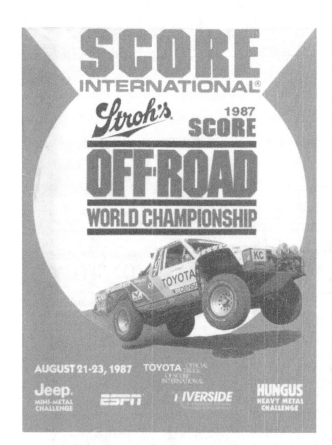

George Wins Ultra Stock to Highlight Big Weekend

By SCOTT HOWARD-COOPER,
Times Staff Writer

RIVERSIDE—A weekend of milestones got off to a good start for Greg George of Colton Saturday with a victory in the Ultra Stock division at the 15th Stroh's SCORE Off-Road World Championships, his third title in as many years. After not even making it past the first lap the previous six years, it appears that his fortunes have changed for good.

"It [the Volkswagen] is basically a desert car. "It's never run a short course before, and I've never run a short course before. I thought, let's take it out and run it and see how it does."

The Class 1, the final event of the day, was a race of attrition more than anything, especially from the seventh lap on. First, George, driving with three wheels on the ground and one dangling after an accident, spun while in second

Thompson Wins Mini-Metal Challenge

By SCOTT HOWARD-COOPER
Times Staff Writer

RIVERSIDE—Danny Thompson's pre-race notion was way off. But his post-race emotion was right on.

"I thought there'd be five or six stadium tracks on top of each other at the end," Thompson said of Sunday's Jeep Mini-Metal Challenge, the featured event in the 15th Stroh's SCORE Off-Road World Championships at Riverside International Raceway. "But it didn't end that way. I was surprised. But happy."

It didn't end that way because Thompson, driving his bright yellow Chevy, ran away with the title, his first, on the second day of the two-day event that his father, Mickey Thompson, started 15 years ago.

Ivan Stewart finished second in a Toyota, Sherman Balch was third in a Nissan, Steve Millen took fourth for Toyota and Al Unser Jr. finished fifth in his Jeep.

The eight-lap race on the specially constructed 1.5-mile course might as well have started at the midway point, when Thompson took the lead and Stewart started his pursuit. Before that, the top two spots belonged to Glenn Harris and

Mazda and Millen, but Millen rolled to allow Thompson to climb into second and, a little later, Harris dropped out with engine problems.

Thompson, coming off a second-place finish at the Coliseum off-road event, took advantage of the opportunity. Almost immediately, he built a 14-second cushion over Stewart, who then started to come back on the leader before falling far behind.

Thompson may have needed a couple breaks to land in first, but the way he was driving proved luck had nothing to do with the championship.

"I thought somebody was right on me, so I kept running hard," he said. "We don't have any mirrors, so it's hard to look back and see who's there. You try to look if you have the opportunity on a corner to see if anyone's close. Finally, my pit told me I was in good shape."

It was the type of race, Thompson said, where you could sneeze and fall back three places, especially in the first few laps. The Costa Mesa resident, whose lifetime ambition still is to race Indy cars, had no such problems. Only a nose for the finish line.

"I didn't sneeze," he said. "I was holding my breath."

By now, Al Unser, the four-time Indianapolis 500 champion, might take to crossing his fingers before off-road races. After failing in two previous attempts to make finals in stadium events at the Silverdome in Pontiac, Mich., and the Rose Bowl, he ran into more problems Sunday in what has become a very unforgiving rookie year on the circuit.

For starters, he missed the morning practice session with engine troubles. Then, when it came time to race five hours later, he lasted two laps before dropping out with more mechanical difficulties.

Frank Vessels had reason to be in a much better mood—a Chevy-powered win in the Hungus Heavy Metal Challenge, the other featured race of the weekend. It was his first victory at Riverside.

"Of all the wins I've had, this is the most exciting," Vessels said. "I really wanted this one."

The Class 4 title for Frank Arciero Jr. of Laguna Hills capped a big weekend for the Orange County family. He also won Stadium Class 1 Saturday and Stadium Class 10 Sunday. His brother, Albert, from Anaheim, took the title in Desert Class 1 Sunday.

"This is the kind of weekend you dream about," Frank Jr. said.

Larry Ragland won the Jeep Desert Mini-Metal Challenge, beating a field that included many

from the stadium starting line was a come-from-behind win, passing Roger Mears, who got stuck in the stadium feature the fifth lap and out-powered the rest of the way.

"I've lost so many races in the desert car," Ragland said. "Three years in a row here, leading by a sizable margin, broke." Finally, I beat...

The day's other winner was Steer Law in a Nissan in the showroom stock mini-pickup. Michael Leslie in a Jeep in Class 2 for four-wheel drive mini-pickups. Danny Ashcraft in the Class 2 division; 18-year-old Robby Gordon in Class 2 for unlimited two-seat vehicles; Hohn Hagle in Class 10 for 1650cc vehicles; Cook in Class 34 for four-wheel single-seat ATVs, 360cc unsuspended; Steve Grier in Class 44 for four-wheel single-seat ATVs, 500cc; Don ... Class 3 for four-wheel drive vehicles with 105-inch wheelbases; Larry Schwacofer in Class 2 unlimited production mini-pickups; Jerry Lee Daugherty in Class 2 unlimited four-wheel drive vehicles.

Crash wrecks Mears' chances at win

Arciero takes advantage to record triumph at Off-Road Championships

By KATIE CASTATOR
Sun Sports Writer

RIVERSIDE — Roger Mears could see the number in the record books. In fact, he could even taste his 21st victory at Riverside International Raceway. It cut clear through the grit that coated his tongue and teeth — a powerful, sweet taste.

Then before he could savor it, it was gone. Evaporated. And the legendary off-roader from Bakersfield was looking at the world upside down from inside his Chevrolet V-8-powered yellow Chenowth as it lay on the huge, scoop-shaped wing on its top with wheels grinding uselessly against the open

"Have you thanked me yet?" Mears asked.

"Thank you very much, Roger," Arciero obliged.

Mears was driving for car owners Karol Van Zant and Jack Warye, who have tried a half dozen times to win at Riverside with the Chenowth, which out-horsepowers everything on the track, but has stability problems. Thus the wing this year.

"They make little changes every year, so in a few years it should be great," Mears said. "I'll come out here in a wheelchair and win the sucker."

This time it was the brakes. And Mears probably ran it a little too fast knowing he had a problem.

day in the race for classes 5, 5-1600, 1/2-1600, Ultra Stock and 11. He was entered in the Ultra-Stock category.

"I first came out here in 1976, and I never got past the first lap until three years ago," George said. "I finally figured out you don't win on the first lap. You have to survive it."

He won in Class 1 in 1985 and '86.

"Now I've won Ultra-Stock. I'm on a roll," he said.

It's a busy weekend for George, who planned to attend his class reunion at Chaffey High School in

John Courts

COME TO RIVERSIDE AND BE A PART OF HISTORY...

WATCH INDY 500 WINNER AL UNSER AND HIS SON AL JR. BANG FENDERS WITH OFF-ROAD RACING'S BEST DRIVERS IN THE JEEP MINI-METAL CHALLENGE...

FEEL THE GROUND SHAKE FROM BRUTE V-8 POWER OF THE BIG TRUCKS IN THE HUNGUS HEAVY METAL CHALLENGE...

TASTE THE DIRT AS OPEN CHASSIS BUGGY AND ULTRA-STOCK DRIVERS STAND ON IT CHARGING DOWN THOMPSON'S RIDGE...

THE TOP MOTORCYCLES, ATV'S AND ODYSSEYS WILL BATTLE FOR CLASS CHAMPIONSHIPS...

Photo by Paul Leedy

SEE THE BEST RIVERSIDE OFF-ROAD TRACK EVER...BIG TIME WHOOP DE DO'S...HELMET-SLAPPING WASHBOARD...FAST STRAIGHTS...AND TURNS TIGHT ENOUGH TO MAKE YOU PUCKER!!!

DON'T MISS THE EXCITEMENT OF THE STROH'S/SCORE OFF-ROAD WORLD CHAMPIONSHIP. THE LAST TIME AT RIVERSIDE... BE THERE!!!

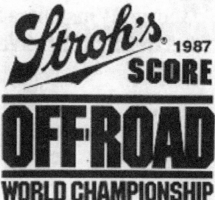

Stroh's 1987 SCORE OFF-ROAD WORLD CHAMPIONSHIP
AUGUST 21-23, 1987

EVENT SUPER TICKETS @ $35/ea. ($47 Value) (includes 3-day event general admission, event pit pass and reserved seat in rows 97-40 at turn 6 on Sunday). Not available at gate.		$
3-DAY EVENT GENERAL ADMISSION @ $25/ea.		$
PIT PASS @ $10/ea.		$
SUNDAY ONLY GENERAL ADMISSION @ $15/ea. (Can enter track anytime after 9 a.m. Saturday)		$
*RESERVED SEATS @ $10/ea. (rows 1-96 at turn 6 on Sunday)		$
*RESERVED SEATS @ $12/ea. (rows 97-40 at turn 6 on Sunday)		$
*MUST ALSO HAVE GENERAL ADMISSION TICKET.		
CT	add handling charge per order	$ 2.00
	TOTAL	$

ORDER NOW! REDUCED PRICES IN EFFECT UNTIL AUGUST 99.

Children under 13 admitted free when accompanied by an adult. However, they must have a reserved seat ticket in order to sit in the grandstands at turn 6 on Sunday. NO Saturday only tickets will be sold.

If rows 97-40 are sold out, rows 1-96 will be substituted and a refund of $2 will be made. Open seating in the Turn 6 grandstands on Saturday; reserved seating only on Sunday.

Coolers that exceed 14" in length will not be permitted in the grandstands. Also, no glass containers will be permitted.

Mini-bike or motorized cycle riding not allowed on raceway premises.

Name _____

Address _____

City _____

State _____ Zip _____

Phone ( ) _____

☐ Master Card ☐ VISA   Expiration Date _____

Card No. _____

Cardholder's Name _____

IMPORTANT: Any ticket orders received after August 14 will be held at the Will-Call Booth at Riverside International Raceway.

Where to Buy Tickets

Use the attached coupon and order your tickets directly from SCORE International at reduced prices. Tickets may also be purchased prior to the event at Riverside International Raceway and TicketMaster, as well as on race day at Riverside.

All tickets available from:

SCORE International
31356 Via Colinas, Suite 111
Westlake Village, CA 91362
(818) 889-9216

Riverside International Raceway
22255 Eucalyptus Avenue
Moreno Valley, CA 92388
(714) 653-1161

For Sunday General Admission Tickets & Sunday Reserved Seat Tickets:

TICKETMASTER

EVENT TO BE RUN ON DATE SPECIFIED. RAIN OR SHINE. NO REFUNDS OR EXCHANGES ON TICKET PURCHASES.

EVENT SCHEDULE

FRIDAY - August 21st
- Spectator gates open 7:00 a.m.
- A full day of practice for all classes.
- FREE Overnight Parking

SATURDAY - August 22nd
- 7:00 a.m. to 11:00 a.m. - Practice sessions for all classes.
- Championship racing starts at Noon.
- FREE Overnight Parking

SUNDAY - August 23rd
- 7:00 a.m. to 11:00 a.m. - Practice sessions for all classes.
- Championship racing starts at NOON, including the HUNGUS HEAVY METAL CHALLENGE and the JEEP MINI-METAL CHALLENGE.

TOYOTA OFFICIAL TRUCK OF SCORE INTERNATIONAL

Stroh's OFFICIAL BEER

HUNGUS HEAVY METAL CHALLENGE

Jeep MINI-METAL CHALLENGE

ESPN

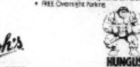

Last, Last Race at Riverside Scheduled

Al Unser and his son, Al Unser, Jr., who staged auto racing's most exciting duel for a national championship two years ago, plan to race each other gagin in the historic "last, last race at Riverside" the weekend of Aug. 21-23.

They are matched in the featured Jeep Mini Metal Challenge, the main event of the Stroh's SCORE Off Road World Championship. The 15th annual off-road classic is said to be the last major event before Riverside International Raceway closes its gates on a 31-year history in American motor sports.

It will be the first appearance ever of the famed father and son in the Stroh's sponsored event, which down through the years has featured many of the other great names of this and other eras—a virtual hall of fame roster including Dan Gurney, Mickey Thompson, Parnelli Jones, Rick and Roger Mears, Malcolm Smith and Josele Garza.

In the Jeep Mini Metal Challenge Roger Mears, Ivan Stewart, Steve Millen, Mannie Esquerra and Glenn Harris are expected to race against the Unsers.

Competition will be staged on the traditional 1.5-mile man made off-road track designed to simulate the thrills of racing in Baja in an area where spectators may watch in comfort.

This will be the first time Stroh has presented SCORE's Off Road World Championship.

On behalf of the race sponsor John Hellwig, vice-president marketing services, said, "We at Stroh's are very pleased to be associated with the premiere event in off-road racing and to be a part of history" as presenter of Riverside's final race.

Sponsorship of the Jeep Mini Metal Challenge and the two Stroh Jeep Comanches to be driven by the Unsers are being provided by Jeep Corporation.

Walter Voss, manager of competition activities for Jeep Corporation, commented: "We are happy to be sponsors of the Mini Metal Challenge, which we feel will be one of the major highlights of the Stroh World Championship. This race to us is the Indy 500 of off-road racing."

Mears Guns For Win

Roger Mears of Bakersfield, Calif., will see a different race course when he lines up to gun for his 21st win in the 15th annual Stroh's SCORE Off Road World Championship August 21-23 at Riverside International Raceway.

The "Oklahoma Land Rusch" start that has been a featured attraction in the event since 1980 has been changed. The old "Land Rush" had all the race vehicles starting side by side and charging full speed across a quarter-mile plain pockmarked with ditches and mounds before funneling into a sharp left turn.

The new course will start the same way, but racers will go halfway before turning left to dodge a pond, then veer right and head uphill toward the main grandstand area.

"I liked the old way, but it got kind of nasty at the end of that long rush," Mears said. "Most guys would get cazy when they hit the holes and dips. You had to use your head to slow down. It's hard to second guess how the new start is going to be."

Mears, 40, will be racing both his desert and stadium racing Nissan trucks in an attempt to add to his record of 20 wins in the off-road spectator racing classic. He has won more races at Riverside than any other driver, including greats like Dan Gurney, Richard Petty and perennial winner Hershel McGriff.

Mears has been racing on the Riverside off-road course since the event began in 1973 and has won at least one featured race in 11 of the 14 years. He has been able to win almost every time the course was changed and with every different starting format.

"I remember when we used to line up on the pavement in turn 8 and change down the road course into turn 6," Mears said. "Cars were really crashing when they

Father's-Son's Compete in Off-Road Championship

Al Unser and his son Al Unser Jr. may headline the Stroh's SCORE Off Road World Championship Aug. 21-23 at Riverside International Raceway, but the father-son duel to watch may be the matchup of off-road veteran Bob Gordon and his teenage son Rob.

Bob Gordon, 39, and Rob, 19, of Orange, California, have been a major contending force in the HDRA-SCORE desert series as well as Off-Road Championship Gran Prix stadium racing. Between the two Gordons, they have won four major desert races overall since last September and have won or placed second five times in the stadium series.

At Riverside Bob will race against his son in the highstakes 1650cc stadium car race and possibly in the unlimited single-seat stadium car class. Bob will also try to defend his title in the desert car race driving the same car in which he and son Robbie won the SCORE Parker 400 and the HDRA Gold Coast 300 overall and the SCORE Baja International with Tim Crabtree of Holtville, California co-driving with Bob.

"Robbie has been the fastest guy, both in the desert and in the stadiums," Gordon said of his son. "He's going to be very tough to beat at Riverside."

A year ago Bob Gordon won his second title in 20 starts since his first race at Riverside in 1976. The younger Gordon, however, will be making his third start. His best finish was fifth in the 125cc motorcycle class in 1985.

Bob Gordon feels the 1650cc and unlimited stadium car races will be the toughest to win.

"If we have no mechanical problems, run hard and get through the first lap without any problems, then Robbie or I will be in good shape to win," Bob Gordon said. "In the stadium clases, a lot of cars get taken out on the first corner."

Gordon is referring to the "Oklahoma Land Rush" start at Riverside, in which 30 to 40 cars line up to start side-by-side and funnel into a narrow turn preceded by a series of bone-crunching whoop-de-doos. The rest of the

1.5-mile course includes a series of switchback turns, jumps, mud and a high-speed off-camber hillside known as Thompson Ridge.

"Most of the desert racers back off before heading into that first turn, which gives an advantage to us stadium guys who also race in the desert, like Frank Arciero, Jr., his brother Al, Robbie and myself," Gordon said. "We are a lot more aggressive in that first turn. We just go for it."

Gordon's company supplies horse feed to Santa Anita, Hollywood Park and Los Alamitos race tracks. Rob plans to pursue his racing career by attending the Bob Bondurant School of High Performance Driving this summer, then start as a freshman at Santa Ana College.

Tickets to the Stroh's SCORE Off-Road World Championship are on sale a tall Ticket Master outlets, Riverside International Raceway and SCORE International. Information: 818-889-9216 or 714-653-1161.

In 1967, Carl Yazstramski won the batting title in the American League with a .391 batting average.

Walker Evans

Frank Vessels

Cameron Steele

Mike Lesle

Even in off-road, Unser stays on the right track

By KATIE CASTATOR
Sun Sports Writer

RIVERSIDE — Driver: Al Unser, Albuquerque, N.M. Status: Rookie.

Rookie? Those crow's-feet don't belong to a first-year driver.

Unser, 48, got them from squinting down a glare-hazed strip of asphalt the past 31 years. The four-time Indianapolis 500 winner certainly earned those creases and the salt in his pepper-dark hair, and his impressive list of credits: 303 Indy-car races, 39 wins, 30 seconds and 26 thirds.

Yet he is a rookie, and undoubtedly the most famous one in this weekend's 15th annual Stroh's SCORE Off Road World Championship at Riverside International Raceway. Some would say Unser is taking a step down moving from a low, sleek Indy-car into the cab of a pickup.

Unser says: "Why not? It's racing. It's fun. So what's the difference?"

No apparent difference when

Al Unser
Off-road racing rookie

it comes to winning. Unser remains one of the drivers to beat in Sunday's Mini Metal Challenge, for his racing instincts aren't a rookie's.

"I'll tell you, Al is a real race-car driver," said Roger Mears,

See UNSER/C2

Frank Arciero

Robby Gordon

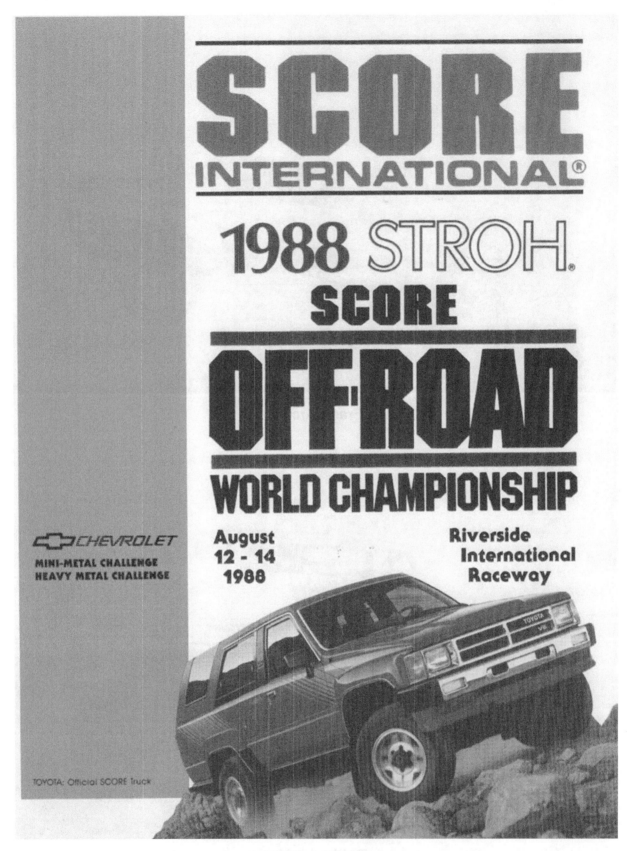

SCORE INTERNATIONAL®

1988 STROH.

SCORE

OFF-ROAD

WORLD CHAMPIONSHIP

CHEVROLET
MINI-METAL CHALLENGE
HEAVY METAL CHALLENGE

August
12 - 14
1988

Riverside
International
Raceway

TOYOTA: Official SCORE Truck

1988 would be the last off road event at Riverside. Bulldozers were already at work, removing pieces of the track. Stroh's was now the sponsor and a record $325,000 in prize money and contingencies were offered. A crowd of 20,000 saw Robby Gordon win the Heavy Metal Challenge and Ivan Stewart win the Mini Metal Challenge, his seventh win.

CHEVROLET
MINI-METAL CHALLENGE
Team Chevy Looking to Repeat

They're billed as those light-weight, high tech little trucks that defy gravity, flying over the dirt. At the STROH SCORE Off-Road World Championship, the Chevrolet Mini-Metal Challenge will be a featured event of the final race ever to be held at historic Riverside International Raceway.

The Chevrolet Mini-Metal Challenge this year will actually include two separate races, one for three desert classes of mini trucks and the other for the super trick racing machines of the stadium circuits.

And, while this is the first year for Chevrolet to be the title sponsor of the Mini-Metal Challenge, the Red Bowtie is a familiar sight to Riverside fans.

Last year, as a matter of fact, Team Chevy captured the two Mini-Metal Challenge features along with the Heavy Metal Challenge as well.

And, both Team Chevy racers in the Mini-Metal Challenge are back to defend the titles they won last year. Danny Thompson, son of off-road pioneer Mickey Thompson, won last year's stadium race while Phoenix businessman Larry Ragland drove the Team Chevy colors to victory in the desert challenge.

In last year's stadium challenge, 1986 champion Glenn Harris in his Mazda jumped to the early lead followed by Toyota racer Steve Millen, Thompson, Dodge's Walker Evans, and Millen's Toyota teammater and four-time Mini-Metal Challenge champion Ivan Stewart. Harris led into the fourth lap, when he stood his Mazda on its nose in the first switchback, and Thompson, who was pushing him hard, got around. Millen had given up second place on the second lap when he rolled after the switchbacks. Thompson built up a big lead and sailed uncontested to the win. Stewart picked up some ground near the end but still finished second and Sherman Balch patiently pulled his Nissan Desert Runner into third place at the end.

Another former Mini-Metal Challenge champion, Roger Mears, took the early lead in last year's desert challenge. He was chased immediately by eventual winner Ragland. On the third lap, Ragland lost control in the turnaround at the north end of the course and lost about five seconds to Mears. He caught back up to Mears and passed him on the fifth lap at the south end of Thompson's ridge and outpowered Mears all the way to the finish.

Class 7S was won by Nissan's Spencer Low, who, like Ragland, won his first race at Riverside. Mike Lesle, in his STROH-sponsored Jeep, led from start to finish to take Class 7/4X4, finishing fifth overall in the race for desert mini-pickups.

All of last year's challengers will be on hand this weekend to shoot at the defending champions along with a pot full of other talented factory and non-factory racers.

In the desert race, also in the starting field which could grow to as many as 20 by the time the green flag goes down, will be Paul Simon in a Ford and Rob MacCachren of the Stroh/Jeep team in Class 7S and Siman's brother David in a Ford, Jim Conner in a Nissan and Jerry McDonald in a Chevy in Class 7/4X4.

Also in the starting grid for the stadium race are, among others, Roger Mears, Jr. in a Nissan and MacCachren and Albert Arclero racing in Comanches for the Stroh/Jeep team.

It appears like all the ingredients are there for a hot time in the final Chevrolet Mini-Metal Challenge! at the Riverside International Raceway.

Danny Thompson brought his flashy Chevy S-10 home first in last year's Stadium Mini-Metal Challenge.

Gordon, Stewert Win to Close Down Riverside

Evans Misses 5th Heavy-Metal Title, but Finishes 2nd in Mini-Metal Challenge

By PAT RAY
Times Staff Writer

RIVERSIDE—It was fitting that the final day of the final racing program at Riverside International Raceway Sunday produced something new and something old in the featured events of the 16th annual SCORE Off-Road World Championships before a crowd estimated at 20,000.

The new was the victory by 19-year-old Robby Gordon in the Chevy heavy-metal challenge for full-sized trucks. The old came in the co-featured mini-metal challenge for the small-sized trucks when veterans Ivan (Ironman) Stewert of Lakeside and Walker Evans of Riverside ran 1-2.

Gordon, who earlier won the race for desert dune buggys, got off to a slow start in his 1966 Ford when a tangle at the start eliminated Evans, the favorite who was seeking his fifth heavy metal title.

"The start was a wild one and I decided to play it cool and I was a lot farther back than I wanted to be," Gordon said. "We had to pass everybody in our class but we got some breaks and things worked out good."

With Evans out, he got another break when last year's winner, Scoop Vessels, broke the front end on his Chevy and dropped out while leading on the first lap.

Gordon followed early leader Jack Johnson for four laps before finally overhauling him and moving away to an easy win in the 10-lap race.

Veteran Rod Hall of Reno finished second in a Dodge four-wheel drive Dakota while Johnson, who said he lost his power steering in his Nissan FWD after two laps, held on for third.

Evans, the 49-year-old driver who designed the course used for this event, took his misfortune with grace.

"All weekend our truck was one of the fastest, but what happened at the start is just one of those things," Evans said.

"Everything was going fine at the start, but then the guy next to me got out of shape and into me, breaking a wheel and damaging the whole side of the truck."

Evans couldn't, however, resist a little jibe at Gordon: "It's bad enough being beaten, but by a kid who isn't even old enough to buy me a beer is too much," he said with a chuckle.

While Evans was having his problems in the event he has dominated for most of this series, Stewert was driving to his fourth mini-metal title in his Toyota in the last six years.

Stewert took the lead at the start and was never headed in the 8-lap event on the 1.5-mile series of jumps, humps and assorted bumps.

"Everything worked out just perfect," said Stewert, who also won this race from 1983-85. "We were strong off the start and that is a must here.

"I saw somebody coming up behind me. I knew it was a Jeep. It could have been Al [Arciero] or it could have been Rob [MacECachren], but when he kept coming that hard I knew it had to be Walker.

"I decided to go a little harder and I saw I could keep him back so I wasn't too worried."

Glenn Harris finished third in a Mazda with MacCachren fourth and Steve Millen, Stewert's Toyota teammate, who was forced to stop to change a tire, losing a lap, getting back to fifth.

"I wondered what happened to Steve," Stewert said. "I expected to see him."

Stewert, who has a total of eight world championships, feels that this will help the rest of year.

"We haven't won but we are leading the Mickey Thompson stadium series, but this should help us to finish strong and win the title," he said.

Although Evans luck was good, and then bad, Roger Mears' was just bad.

Mears, the all-time winningest driver in the Riverside Off Road Championships with 20 victories in this series, failed to finish a race over the weekend. In fact, in two of the three events he was in, he failed to complete a lap. In the other, he was running fourth behind Stewert in the mini-metal event when his engine blew.

Stewart gets a win for the road at Riverside

By CINDY ROBINSON
Special to The Sun

RIVERSIDE — It's hard to say goodbye to a legend, but Ivan "Ironman" Stewart came up with a good way Sunday in the SCORE Off-Road World Championships, the final day of the final event held at Riverside International Raceway.

Stewart pulled into the lead during first lap of the Chevy Mini Metal Challenge and went on to win the race ahead of Walker Evans.

This was the 42-year-old Stewart's eighth victory at RIR, but first since 1985. He is now tied with Marty Lefner with the third-most victories in the SCORE event, two wins behind Evans. Roger Mears has the most with 20.

"I came out of the start really strong," said Stewart, who drove a Toyota. "We were concerned about the engine overheating."

As it was, Stewart took the lead and never gave it up.

As for Mears, the all-time RIR victory leader had perhaps his worst run of luck ever at the track. Sunday's Stadium Class 7 race not only was the first event he finished all weekend, it was the only one in which he completed more than one lap.

"It's been a bad week," said Mears, who came in second. "Everything seemed to happen to us. During practice, everything I took out didn't seem to make a lap either."

Larry Ragland repeated as the winner in Desert Class 7, driving a Chevy S-10. His only real competition, Mears, dropped out before the second lap with a busted gearbox.

"I passed him (Mears) early and he never appeared," said Ragland. "Roger and I would have had a really good race. As it was I was just cruisin' at the end.

"I felt like I could go all day long at that speed. It was a shame for the spectators that it didn't turn out to be a better race — but I'll take it."

Ragland is from Phoenix, which is a strong contender to host the 1989 SCORE Championships.

"It's a shame not to come back here," Ragland said. "It's a great course. But, they (Phoenix International Raceway) are really in an expansion mode. It should be good out there."

Corona's Mike Lesle, driving a Jeep Comanche, won his event, the Class 7 4x4 Mini Truck, which was run concurrently with the Desert 7 race.

Desert racing champion Scott Douglas won the 7S class, driving a Ford. It was sweet revenge for Douglas since he finished second last year to Spencer Low, who was runner-up this year.

"I was stuck in the middle of the pack," said Douglas. "The truck is pretty well torn up. Everybody took a shot at us."

He didn't win by much, but Douglas said that didn't matter, because "We won the last one."

Dwaine Walters, who ran away with the Challenger class event driving a T-Mag off-road buggy, wore his father's driving suit. "I don't race often enough to buy a suit," he said.

Walters almost raced a little too much for his own good Sunday. His day nearly ended after his morning practice run.

"We got hit and had to pull the whole car apart. We had to go into town to get the parts at a store in Redlands. The guy was kind enough to open up for us on Sunday morning."

The third event during Sunday's final race day at RIR matched Desert classes 1, 2 and 10. Ron Gordon was the overall winner. Craig Watkins won Class 10 in a Raceco and Jim Stiles got the win in Desert 1, also in a Raceco.

Stiles is a desert racer; the SCORE event is an exception for him. After winning Sunday, he said he still prefers the desert.

"The car I have is definitely desert," he said. "In the desert you can relax; here you have to go all-out when the green flag drops. This is pretty rough on the equipment. I had the lead at the start and by the turns, I was covered by mud and couldn't see."

Gordon, from Orange County, was the final winner at RIR, taking the day's last event, the Class 8, for his second victory of the day.

• • •

At precisely 4:57 p.m. Sunday, Riverside International Raceway officially closed its gates. The 31-year-old track will be torn down, beginning today, to make room for a regional shopping center.

The last big SCORE at Riverside

By KATIE CASTATOR
Sun Sports Writer

This is it once again.

This weekend's 16th annual Stroh's SCORE Off-Road World Championship is absolutely, positively the last race at Riverside International Raceway before it closes for good.

"For the last three years, we've heard, 'This is it — the last ever,'" said Steve Millen, a member of the Toyota team that has dominated the truck classes the

Dirt, mud, sheetmetal, and tempers — all have flown at the storied plant. Millen, a transplanted New Zealander, has seen almost everything but the checkered flag there, largely because of teammate Ivan Stewart of Lakeside.

Stewart, the 43-year-old, six-time champion at Riverside, won the Mini Metal Challenge in 1983 and '84. Millen took second both years.

"As I recall, Steve Millen and I raced back and forth for the lead both years," Stewart said.

history as the last driver to win at Riverside. At least, I think this is the last race. Do they have another car race after this?"

It appears not. This really is it.

Stewart is not mourning the loss of Riverside, however. "It really doesn't upset me," he said. "I've had a lot of fun at Riverside. But it's progress. It's got to go and we've got to go somewhere else."

The off-road racing veteran of 16 years raced the inaugural off-road championship in 1973 and hasn't missed one since.

Metal class for mini pick-up trucks. Those three years, Stewart also was the sports truck points champion of Mickey Thompson's off-road stadium series.

He's leading in points in the stadium series again this year.

Thompson, the founder of SCORE who was killed by two gunmen last May, initiated his concept of short-course, off-road racing at Riverside.

"I remember Mickey standing in the back of a pick-up truck at a drivers' meeting before the first

Off-Road World Championships Are Riverside International Raceway's Last Show

By PAT RAY,
Times Staff Writer

RIVERSIDE— When the curtain drops on the Stroh's SCORE Off-Road World Championships and Riverside International Raceway this afternoon, it will close one of the most popular off-road racing programs ever.

The layout of the course, which combines the best of desert and stadium racing, was designed and built by Walker Evans, a 49-year-old Riverside resident who is the sport's biggest winner.

"Mickey [Thompson] built the first one in 1973," Evans said Friday during practice for the 16th and final race of the series. "The next year, however, I volunteered and built it for the second race.

"Funny thing is, that first one is almost identical to the way we will go in the last one. There have been a few minor changes, but mostly it is the original."

When asked whether he thought it would be possible to duplicate a course such as Riverside, Evans was not too confident.

"It's possible, of course, but it is going to take a place with the elevation variations that we have here, and it is going have to be within 50 or 60 miles of Los Angeles," he said. "You probably can get the fans to go once, but if

they are not entertained as well as they were here, then you are in trouble.

"The thing that makes Riverside so unique is that it's a near perfect mix of desert and stadium racing. On the stadium courses you're lucky if the top speed is 50 m.p.h. Here, we will hit up to 90. It gives you room to stretch your legs."

Evans will compete in both of today's feature truck races. He will be in the Chevrolet Heavy Metal Challenge in his full-size Dodge Dakota and then will return in the Mini Metal Challenge in one of three Jeep Comanche mini-pickup trucks.

His top rivals in the Heavy Metal race are Scoop Vessels in a Chevy, Robby Gordon in a Ford, Steve Kelley in another Chevy and four-wheel drivers Rod Hall in a Dodge and Jack Johnson in a Nissan.

In the mini metal chase, Evans will face the Toyotas of Ivan Stewart and Steve Millen, the Mazdas of Glenn Harris and Jeff Huber, the Nissans of Roger Mears and his son as well as his two Jeep teammates Al Arciero and Rob MacCacheren.

Racing today is a far cry from when Evans started in 1969, finishing third in the Baja 500 in a Jeep Scrambler. From 1970 through 1977, Walker won all but one Baja 500 he entered.

"Back then, it was a lot different from today," Evans said as he looked over a vast array of transporters and support vehicles that he uses to haul the Dodge and the four Jeeps. He also has a crew of 10 full-time workers and another 15 who do it on race weekends just for the fun of it.

"Back in 1970, I drove the truck I raced to the starting line. It had a lot of stock things on it. Today, we have vehicles to pre-run the course that are five times more sophisticated than the machine I won that race with," Evans said.

"The old days were fun, and there wasn't the pressure to win. When sponsors put up the kind of money they are these days, they expect performance. I'm lucky in that I have grown up with the sport and it doesn't bother me as much as some of the new people. With the advent of stadium racing, a sponsor can say, 'We've heard how fast you can go with our car, now prove it,' and that is pressure."

Practice today begins at 7 a.m. The opening ceremony is scheduled for 11:45 a.m. with the first race at noon.

□

Frank Arciero Jr. of Laguna Hills, who last year became the first person to win four races in the annual Stroh's SCORE Off-Road

World Championships, began Saturday where he left off, racing to an easy victory in his Stadium Class 1 buggy in the main event of the 16th and final running of the races at Riverside.

Arciero took a big early lead and coasted to a 14-second victory over runner-up Wes Elrod of San Jose. Robby Gordon and his father, Bob Gordon, finished third and fourth, respectively.

At first, officials disqualified Elrod, Robby Gordon and fifth-place finisher Art Schmitt for course violations. However, after a review, the officials decided to let the original finish stand.

"It had to be the best start I've ever got here," Arciero said. "For the first few laps I ran hard to make sure nobody was gaining on me. After that I just cooled it, trying to conserve the car."

This year, Arciero will have only one more chance for a victory. He will compete in the Stadium 10 buggy class today after finishing third in his heat earlier Saturday.

The Gordons took both heats for Class 10.

Other winners Saturday were Terry Fowler in motorcycles, Rodney Gentry in ATVs and Ultrastock driver Greg George of Cucamonga, who took the race for his class and several other desert car classes.

Roger Mears

Farewell, Riverside.
Goodbye, competition.

The Stroh's/SCORE Off-Road World Championship at historic Riverside International Raceway was the last event ever for the 31-year-old racing facility. Jeep's final tribute to Riverside came in the form of victories.

Mike Lesle led Jeep's efforts by taking on Riverside's short but brutal course in his four-wheel drive Jeep Comanche. In an all-out effort, Lesle easily outdistanced his competition from Ford, Chevy, Mazda, and Nissan without suffering a single mechanical failure. Jeep and Lesle are currently in the lead for the Class 7-4x4 Manufacturers Title.

Jeep also wrapped up the top spot in Class 3. Don Adams, driving with his son Doug, piloted their Jeep Wrangler to the top spot in the class. Walker Evans fought it out in the Mini Metal Challenge to bring his Comanche stadium truck in for a strong second-place finish that rounded out Jeep's impressive performance for the day.

With these victories, Jeep has said its farewell to Riverside and, in the process, said goodbye to the competition.

Mike Lesle's victorious Jeep Comanche is based on stock models.

Only in a Jeep.

Jeep is a registered trademark of the Jeep Eagle Corporation.

Buckle up for safety.

Official Sponsor 1988 U.S. Olympic Team

Jeep's farewell to Riverside left the competition behind.

Development wins race

ALAN WARREN/The Sun

A car in Sunday's 1988 SCORE Off-Road World Championship competes in the final race held at the Riverside International Raceway, which will be demolished to make way for a 640-acre commercial and residential development. Stories and photos in Inland Empire/B1 and Sports/C1

1988 SCORE Championship Video

Watch this on the attached DVD

Off-Road Track at Riverside Is One of a Kind

Each time a race is held at Riverside International Raceway there is justifiable speculation that it may be the last of its kind at the 30-year-old facility, which is scheduled to close at the end of this year.

Most of the races, such as the Times enduro for IMSA Camel GT sports cars, NASCAR's Winston Cup stock cars, or the Trans-Am sedans, can readily be carried on at other facilities once the bulldozers move in at Riverside, but it is doubtful if another site can ever be found to match Riverside for its off-road racing course.

Built by veteran truck driver Walker Evans in 1974, it has been modified over the years to give the impression of a Baja 1,000 or a Mint 400 crammed into two miles of bumps, jumps, spins and the legendary Thompson's Ridge.

"There is no other facility for off-road racing like Riverside," said Sal Fish, president of SCORE International, which will present its 14th annual world closed course championship race there Aug. 15-17. "I can't think of any other place that allows the heavy-metal pickup trucks to go 100 m.p.h. or the nimble lightweight Baja racers to do their thing on the same course.

"The course winds through great spectator facilities without losing any of the flavor of true Baja-style off-road racing. There's nothing artificial about what the drivers do there."

Two of the most competitive and entertaining races in Riverside's storied past were off-road events.

In 1974, the year after Mickey Thompson had brought racing off the desert into a closed course, Roger Mears and Parnelli Jones, the retired 1963 Indianapolis 500 winner, went side by side or nose to tail for nearly 50 miles in unlimited single-seaters before Mears pulled away in his Cloud Hopper buggy.

"This was real professional racing," Jones said when it was over. "I'm only racing for fun these days. If I'm going to do this sort of thing, on a closed course, I might as well gas up my stock car, or my midget, and go racing for money again. This was the same thing."

The victory was one of 19 for Roger Mears in 40 off-road races at Riverside. From 1974 to 1984, the older Mears brother won at least one SCORE race every year. He will compete in three races this year in an attempt to start a new string, driving a new Nissan-backed Hardbody pickup in the Mini-Metal Challenge, his own desert truck in the mini-pickup class and a V-8 desert buggy in the unlimited single-seater class.

In 1983, when pickup trucks had replaced single-seaters as the glamour vehicles of off-road racing, Evans and Rod Hall put on a classic duel of Dodges,

Mears Wants Final Touch on Riverside's End

Quite possibly, nobody will miss Riverside International Raceway more than Roger Mears, who will help write the facility's final chapter this weekend in the Stroh's SCORE Off-Road World Championships.

As he has for the last 15 years, Mears will race and the chances are pretty good that he will win. He'll drive Nissan trucks in Sunday's Mini-Metal Challenge and the desert mini-pickup race. On Saturday, he will drive a single-seat buggy in that day's feature event.

His record of 20 victories in 15 SCORE off-road events cannot be topped, but the Bakersfield veteran would like to make it at least 21.

"Come to think of it, 23 would be best of all," he said Wednesday. "I guess that sounds greedy, but there is no point racing if you don't think you can win."

Not only is his victory mark safe, so is his other record. He has raced off-road 47 times at Riverside and if he starts all three scheduled events this weekend that figure will hit an even 50.

"Riverside has been good to us," he said. "If I had my choice of what off-road race to run, I pick Riverside every week. It has just the right combination, a cross between stadium racing and desert racing.

"It has the stand-on-it attitude of stadium racing, but those races are so short you can't depend on your driving ability to carry you. At Riverside, you have the time and room to set up the other drivers. Desert racing is wide open, no tight corners and plenty of room, but it is so long. Riverside is just right."

Of all his victories, Mears remembers his first one most fondly. He went wheel to wheel against Parnelli Jones in an open-wheel single seater in 1974 and came out a winner.

"I had just met Parnelli," Mears said. "He was my hero and I was just thrilled to have a car that enabled me to race with him. We had a good race. He bumped me a few times and I bumped him back and I think I gained some respect from him."

Another highlight occurred in 1980, when Mears drove a mini-pickup built by engineering students at Cal Poly San Luis Obispo to victory.

"I'll never forget the winner's circle," Mears said. "Here were all these college kids, so delirious over winning they were crying. It was a very emotional moment."

No doubt. But it may not match the emotion should Mears pull off another victory Sunday.

His famous racing brother, defending Indy 500 champion Rick, won the first off-road feature at Riverside in 1973 and nothing would suit Roger more than to win the last one.

Chapter Five - Drag Racing

From 1957 unti 1969, Riverside held all sorts of drag racing events, half mile and quarter mile. Culminating in the Hot Rod Magazine Chamionship race in 1965. The dragstrip utilized the back straight from turn nine to the bridge.The first race, running a half mile, was held on October 1957. Fastest was national champ Cal Rice

at 16.88 and 161 mph. in a Chrysler powered dragster. Then, in 1958 a combined half and quarter mile event was held, Also in 1958, the "Annual World Championships'" produced a big show with record setting Art Chrisman going over 160mph. SCTA also ran some events when the dry lakes were unusable, ending in 1962. An "East vs West" fuel meet, held the same day as NHRA's gas only Winternationals at Pomona in 1962, drew a large crowd, watching a number of dragsters exceed 180mph.

After a year and a half of drag racing inaction, Les Richter, negotiated a deal with Petersen Publishing; Motor Trend got the stock car race and Hot Rod got the drags, billed as the "Hot Rod Magazine Championship Drag Races". They ran unti 1969, effectively the last drag races held at Riverside, the exception being sand drags held in the infield.

1957

Riverside Drag Races Draw Big Field Today

Drag racing on a half-mile strip will be conducted today at the new Riverside International Speedway today, with about 100 entries expected from Southland points.

Runs start at 9 a.m. and continue throughout the day, with top eliminator being held around 4 p.m. Cal Rice had top speed last weekend during a two-day inaugural meet.

Riverside Drags Set at Speedway

Another program of drag racing on a half-mile strip is on tap today at the new Riverside International Speedway's track east of the Mission City.

Single runs start at 9 a.m. and continue throughout the day. Speeds up to 170 m.p.h. are forecast by officials on the longer

Cal Rice Enters Riverside Drags

Calvin Rice, 1955 National Hot Rod champion dragster from Santa Ana, is one of the early entries in Sunday's program of half-mile drag racing at Riverside International Raceway. Rice set the track record at 161 m.p.h. on Oct. 6 and was one of the more than 200 entries turned away due to the wet course preventing racing last Sunday.

Officials expressed confidence

Riverside Drag Races Cancelled

The drag races originally scheduled to be run Sunday at the Riverside International Race way have been cancelled, it was announced today by track officials.

Reason for the cancellation was given as "a necessary measure to get the track in shape for the sportscar races to be held November 16 and 17.

Drag races which were set for November 24 have also been cancelled in order to continue work of the new track.

Opening Day 1957

RIVERSIDE RACEWAY

—PRESENTS—

HOT ROD DRAGS

Saturday August 10th

TOP CASH PRIZES AND TROPHYS
DONT MISS THIS ACTION PACKED EVENT

The Safe Place To Race
Riverside, California

View this 1965 Video on the attached DVD

RIVERSIDE DRAG RACES TO AID BUILDING FUND

Norton AFB is sharing in a building fund campaign for mentally retarded children at the School of Hope at 24554 Sixth St. in San Bernardino, through the efforts of Rex Gilbert, warehouseman in the Directorate of Supply and Services.

Gilbert, who manages the Riverside drag strip on weekends, is donating half the profits from Sunday's drags, to show his personal appreciation to the school which made it possible for a younger brother to obtain specialized speech therapy, enabling him to later enter public schools.

A Nortonite since January of 1951, Gilbert also managed the Colton drag strip over a period of four years prior to taking over the Riverside strip in July of 1958.

The Riverside drag strip is known as one of the world's fastest. The present world's record for one-quarter mile was set there and still stands at 181.81 mph.

Cary Cagle of the Los Angeles police department, who is scheduled to compete Sunday, is presently one of four drivers who has turned 180 mph or better.

Special guests have been invited for the Sunday meet. Families of children attending the School of Hope have been asked to attend. In addition, all Norton airmen who are part of the Norton AFB Service Club tour (by bus) will honor guests.

———————◆———————

Moore, Thomas Win Surrey Tennis Matches

SURBITON, Eng. (AP) — Sally Moore of Bakersfield, Calif. and Gwyn Thomas of Shaker Heights, Ohio, reached the semifinals of the Surrey Lawn Tennis Championships yesterday.

Miss Moore defeated Mrs. Rosemary Deloford of England, 6-2, 6-0. She will meet Britain's Julie Lintern today. Miss Thomas' opponent yesterday, Deidre Catt of England, withdrew because of illness. The Ohioan will meet Britain's No. 1 player, Ann Haydon, in the other semifinal.

Chuck Gireth Takes Drag Strip Feature

RIVERSIDE, May 17 — Chuck Gireth of Altadena, driving the Gireth Brothers Isky Special of Altadena, turned 179.28 m.p.h. in 8.58s to defeat world champion Art Chrisman of Compton in the quarter-mile race yesterday at the Riverside Dragstrip Raceway.

Cyr Wins Trophy at Drag Meet

Ted Cyr of Escondido turned 179.28 MPH in 8.51 seconds to win the top time trophy at Riverside dragstrip yesterday.

Top gas eliminator was Tommy Ivo with a 145.39 MPH clocking in 9.58 seconds. Top fuel eliminator honors went to Art Chrisman who edged Chuck Gireth with an elapsed time of 9.19 seconds.

Riverside Drag Races to Benefit Retarded Children

San Bernardino County's Council for Retarded Children will benefit from a Drag Race of Champions the next three Sundays at Riverside International Speedway, it was announced by meet director Rex Gilbert.

A feature of Sunday's speedfest will be a $100 match race between two of the world's fastest dragsters, the Chrisman - Cannon machine that has turned 181 m.p.h. and Cyr and Hopper's Chrysler at 180.

A total of $450 in bonds will be offered Sunday, with five multi-

Riverside Speedway Has Drag Meet Today

Riverside International Speedway will have drag meet today on its quarter-mile strip, with a race of champions, between Chrisman-Cannon and Cyr-Hopper, featuring the day-long meet.

Don Van Vranken of San Bernardino has an open challenge for any Class B. roadster. He has been undefeated in his stock Chevrolet powered car by a B entrant.

Drag Racers Set Records

RIVERSIDE — The World Championship Drag Races will conclude here today at the International Speedway.

The Chrisman & Cannon Hustler set a record of 181.54mph
and 8.54 seconds in 1959

Drag Eliminations Start At Riverside

A series of monthly eliminations to name the 1961 Riverside International Raceway drag champions in both fuel and gas categories will start Sunday on the Riverside quarter-mile strip.

First invitation has been accepted by Ed Pinks of Los Angeles, driver of the fuel Chrysler Pink Dragon. Pinks has an ET of 8:51 for the Riverside quarter, and time of 180 plus mph.

Pinks holds victories over such nationally famous dragsters as Chris Karamasines of Chicago, Ron Stuckey of Kansas City and Art Malone of Tampa, Fla.

Expect 200 Cars at Riverside

They race two cars at a time, against time, or sometimes qualify singly against the electric timer. Then they are classified and race two at a time. They keep this up until everybody has been eliminated in heats but the final winner. There are trophies for the fastest laps in the various divisions, as well as for the winners.

Some cars run on gasoline and are called gassers. Faster than these are the "fuelers" who use some more advanced fuel that must have a lot of alcohol in it.

All races are on the straight. They are automobile racing's answer to the 100-yard dash you will see in any track meet. These cars will flick down the 440 straight in from 8.23 to 13.9 seconds. A man with a running start, if his name were Jesse Owens or Mel Patton or Ray Norton, would cover 100 yards in about the same that it takes a car like the Chizler to go the 440 from a standing start. Whoosh! He went thataway.

Paul Schissler expects around 200 drivers and 200 cars in action at Riverside Raceway Sunday. Some are ordinary stock cars and others are special-built dragsters with a long, low chassis, small motorcycle tires in front and huge truck tires in the rear. There's a class for everybody.

The audience gets into the act. Anybody who wants to see how fast his old car can run, or his new one, can pay $1 and they will time him for the quarter mile. They will give him his total elapsed time for the quarter mile, also his fastest m.p.h. en route.

Sunday's races lead up to the Golden Gate Cup to be run April 23. This contest was originated when drag racing first started and the man who originated, C. J. Hart of Santa Ana, is now race director at Riverside. Hart started the first drag strip in Southern California, on the air strip at Santa Ana.

Dozen Enter Quarter-Mile Drag Race

What had originally been planned as a challenge race between two cars, has snowballed into a possible dozen of the top cars for the first quarter-mile drags of the year at Riverside's International Raceway. Gates open Sunday, 8 a.m.

C. J. Hart, former Santa Ana drag strip operator, now in charge of the Riverside Drags, said yesterday he had received entries from the record holding gas dragster owned by Chet Herbert and driven by Lefty Mudersbach, as well as the Howard Can twin-Chevy job which has been a threat at almost all Western drag meets.

Art Chrisman has entered his Hustler I, the same car in which

Chicagoan Captures Drag Racing Honors

Chris Karamesines of Chicago won top time and top elapsed time honors at the Riverside drags Sunday afternoon before a crowd of 2,500. Karamesines had clockings of 8.10 and 183.67 mph, but lost the top eliminator award to Ed Pink, who was clocked in 8.69 and

Hot Dragsters At Riverside

RIVERSIDE— A collection of the hottest machines and drivers in the West will be pitted Sunday in the Gold Cup drag races on the quartermile back strip at Riverside International Raceway.

Trials start at 9 a.m. with the eliminations getting under way at 1:30 p.m.

Lou Canglose of St. Louis, Mo., is among the latest entries in his famous "Missouri Missile," fuel-dragster with top time of 185 m.p.h.

In danger of toppling is the Riverside drag quartermile record of 183 m.p.h., held by Chris Karamesines of Chicago.

Drivers include a topflight field of Double-A stars, among them, Glenn Stokey, Jack Chrisman, Lefty Muddersbach, Jim Nelson and Dode Martin. Muddersbach, Nelson and Martin gun twin-engine Chevvies, while Chrisman goes in the hot Howard-Cam Special.

Mickey Thompson, holder of the American land speed record, drives a Pontiac Tempest dragster.

Cyr-Ward Dragster Entered In Weekend Riverside Event

RIVERSIDE — Jim Ward of San Diego, Frank Cannon and Leland Kolb, three top western fuel dragsters, have entered the East-West Drag championships at Riverside Raceway Saturday and Sunday in hopes of getting a crack at the powerful eastern team.

Ward will pilot the C&W Special, a Chrysler-powered machine, which was built by Ted Cyr of Escondido.

Riverside Drag director C. J. Hart has announced that the top 10 westerners in Saturday's eliminations will go against the best from the east on Sunday.

The two-day competition gets under way at 9 a.m. Saturday and 11 a.m. Sunday.

Ward heads drag field

RIVERSIDE — Defending champion Jim Ward, driving the Ted Cyr Chrysler fuel dragster, heads a field of 200 drivers and cars tomorrow in the annual Riverside Gold Cup drag championships at Riverside Raceway beginning at 9 a.m.

Three 180-mph dragsters were late additions to the list of challengers for Ward. They are Norm Weekly of Compton, Don Yates who drives the Garen-Madden dragster of Compton, and Paul Marriette Jr. of Redondo Beach.

A serious threat in the eliminations is Lefty Mudersbach of Pico-Rivera who drives the Herbert Cam Special. He has turned 185 mph for the quartermile.

Fuel and gas dragsters will be running for a 40 per cent share of the gross gate, it was announced by racing director C. J. Hart.

See the "Hot Rod Story" video on the attached attached DVD

Unique Drag Meet At Riverside Track

A unique drag meet will be held at Riverside International Raceway at 10 a.m. today.

It's a special event for members of San Bernardino and Riverside area car clubs, who have formed the Inland Empire Racing Association.

"We want to do our racing on the drag strip, not the street," IERA spokesman Bob Bierma said. "Riverside Raceway has let the group use its drag strip for this purpose."

The association includes the Noblemen and Tyrants of Redlands, the High - Winders of Loma Linda, the Mystics of Yucaipa, and the T-Timers, Seagrams, Chessmen and Cherubs of Riverside.

"Seven other clubs are contemplating joining the association," Bierma added.

He said the IERA was conceived by Charlie Hooks of Riverside, "who is involved with the Police Advisory Council for Car Clubs. He got together with Roy Hord, track manager for the raceway, and set up the association."

While the races are open to members only, Bierma said, the members are allowed to bring one guest a year.

"We race street machines only," he pointed out. "That is, cars that can be licensed at the Department of Motor Vehicles.

"We don't want dragsters or anything like that. We want to keep it competitive. We don't want it to wind up with the same winner every time."

IERA members will serve as race officials — starters, timers, etc. Bierma, for instance, will man the fire truck. The raceway's safety equipment will all be made available to the association.

Clinic Today For LL Players

Little League baseball players from throughout the Inland Empire have been invited to attend a baseball clinic this morning. Originated by radio

Tom McEwen took top honors in 1966

Drags Slated at Riverside

Southern California drag racing enthusiasts will have a three-day festival of speed and competition June 17-18-19, when the third annual Hot Rod Magazine drag racing championships unfold at Riverside International Raceway.

Nearly 200 entries already have been filed according to event director Les Richter, with a total of more than 400 anticipated by the time activity gets underway over the quarter-mile strip on Friday, June 17.

First to file an official entry was popular Tom "Mongoose" McEwen, veteran

major eliminator categories.

In addition to McEwen, some of the other popular names already signed include: John Mar's Comet, Colt 45; Bobby Spears, the Glass Coffin II; Kay Sissell's "Six Tee," Dick Landy and the Green Mountain Boys.

Time trials are slated to lead off the action on Friday, June 17, with class champion-

The Mongoose (Tom McEwen and the Snake (Don Prudhomme) shared top speed honors in 1968.

Art Chrisman was often Top Eliminator

1967 - Don Prudhomme

Hot Rod Champion Set To Appear At Riverside Course

Adams Leads Riverside Raceway Field

CHRYSLER DRAGSTER HITS 161 MPH

RIVERSIDE, Oct. 6—Some 200 imported and domestic cars were timed here today as regular sessions of drag racing opened at Riverside International Motor Raceway. About 25 cycles also roared.

Drags slated Oct. 13 were rained out.

Top eliminator, according to the sanctioning NHRA, was the

Dragsters Aim for 200 m.p.h. at Riverside

BY BOB THOMAS
Times Auto Editor

Drag racing's 200 m.p.h. speed barrier is about to be broken claims one of the most likely young men to do it.

Don Prudhomme, 22-year-old dragster from Van Nuys who will attempt it himself

BLASTOFF—Class AA fuel dragsters like this one, driven by George Bolthoff of Encino, will seek top eliminator honors this weekend in Hot Rod Drag Championships at Riverside Raceway. More than 500 cars will compete in 76 classes during three-day dragfest on quarter-mile strip.

Randy Walls at the 1964 Hot rod Championships

 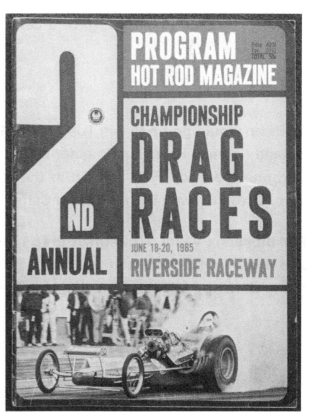

The Hot Rod Magazine Championship ran from 1961 to 1969,
The purse was $37,000

HOT ROD Magazine presented its own annual drag race known as the HOT ROD Magazine Championship Drag Races. From 1964 to 1969 HOT ROD's yearly meltdown was on par with NHRA's top events in terms of importance. Held at the historic Riverside Raceway in Riverside, California, the first HOT ROD Championship posted $37,000 in cash and merchandise, well beyond NHRA purses at that time. Conceived in conjunction with the NHRA, itself created through the pages of HOT ROD and its first editor Wally Parks in 1952, HOT ROD publisher Ray Brock and editor Bob Greene coordinated with NHRA for an early summer event to enhance their schedule. NHRA national records for Top Fuel, Top Gas—all of their top classes, could be set during the three days of racing. In that first year new Ford Mustangs were the prize in each class in addition to cash. A new Mustang was even given away in a special drawing to a lucky spectator.

Including a full field of Sportsman classes—something Parks was adamant about maintaining in all NHRA events, in 1965 the Factory Experimental cars made their first appearance, soon to become the Funny Car class. In Top Fuel Tom McEwen and Don Prudhomme dominated the 1965 race each hitting 211-plus mph in mid-7 second runs, but they were ultimately defeated by Nando Haase and John Smyser from Upland, California, in the final against Jim Warren. The 1965 event was also the subject of the HOT ROD Magazine-produced film *The Hot Rod Story-Drag Racing.*

Narrated by Dick Enberg, it gave a comprehensive overview of the sport up to that time.

McEwen would go on to win Top Fuel in 1966, with Mike Snively winning the class in Roland Leong's Hawaiian dragster with a 7.07 at 221.66mph the following year. Steve Carbone took Top Fuel in 1968 in the Atlas Oil Tool Special, and for its final year Larry Dixon Sr. won in the Howard Cams "Rattler."

For those six years some great drag racing brought to you by HOT ROD Magazine and those participants and spectators attending took place in the hot Riverside sun, going down in history as one of the most significant drag racing events of the day.

The Airoso Brothers B Gas Willys vs Dick Landy's Super Stock Dodge in 1967

Pushing dragsters up to the starting line in 1970

Nando Hasse Takes 1st BIG Drag Win

RIVERSIDE, Calif.—Nando Hasse of Upland, Calif. pushed his 354 cu.in. Chrysler-powered AA/fuel dragster to top honors June 20 in the second annual Hot Rod Magazine Championships with a 180mph run and an et of 7.70 sec.

For Hasse it was his first major drag racing triumph.

The 24-year-old district man for the Southern Counties Gas Co., turned back the fastest 26 class AA/fuel machines in the country, including Tom McEwen's Chrysler which had turned 211.76 earlier in the day. His 1320-lb. Rader Wheel spcl., put down the challenge of Jim Warren of Bakersfield, Cal. in the final round of the three-day meet.

For the win, Hasse picked up a

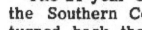

Bill Golden's Hemi Powered "Lil Red Wagon" AFX wheelstander. The first wheelstanding truck when introduced in 1965, toured extensively, running in the 11's at 120 mph.

Hurst Hairy Olds Funny Car – Twin Supercharged 425 c.i engines

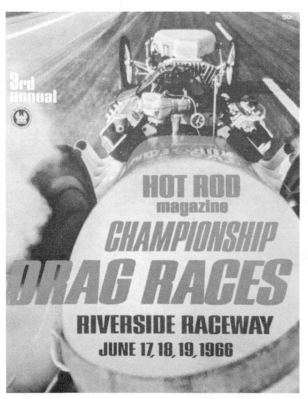

Watch this drag racing video on the attached DVD

BLASTOFF—Class AA fuel dragsters like this one, driven by George Bolthoff of Encino, will seek top eliminator honors this weekend in Hot Rod Drag Championships at Riverside Raceway. More than 500 cars will compete in 76 classes during three-day dragfest on quarter-mile strip.

$50,000 in Prizes Await Drag Racers at Riverside

By DAVE DANIEL

The final big drag race meeting of the West Coast season tops this weekend's card as Riverside Raceway presents the fifth edition of the Hot Rod Magazine drags.

Bob Russo, director of publicity for the RIR for the past several seasons who resigned, effective at the end of this month, promises to close out his position with the best-ever event.

More than $50,000 has been put up as prize and contingency money and as

near-desert facility today but things really get busy Saturday with practice and first eliminations and Sunday with final eliminations. Gates open at 8 a.m. all days.

As always, the exotic top fuel elimination category heads the list; but this time look for some real thunder as most of the big names from the East Coast are still around — just waiting for Riverside.

It used to be that the event was held in June and only Southern Californians

the gas rails have never benefitted from the extra hot air temperatures, but increased strip temperatures provide more bite when rubber is laid down.

The funny cars will be out in force as well as the local stockers and all the other classes for the big finale and you can look for Peterson Publishing Co. to go all-out in its coverage of the event. It'll be worth it.

Elsewhere on the motor sports scene finds Orange County Speedway back with its old moniker as least problems forced the management, headed by Ron Jones, to drop the name of Western Speedway.

The reason the name was changed in the first place was so the oval for the midgets wouldn't be confused with Orange County International Raceway, the ultra-modern drag strip.

Anyway, the midgets are back and so is the name and they go this Saturday night instead of Sunday afternoon.

Ascot Park hosts a 2:15 Sunday afternoon show of PRA Figure-8 stock cars featuring and defending champion Jerry Jones favored to take his second win in as many weeks.

Riverside Drag Racing Opens

Local Team Top Rated In 'A Fuel'

RIVERSIDE — A four-man team of Pomona enthusiasts has been installed as the top favorite in the weekend's Hot Rod Magazine Championship drag races at Riverside International Raceway.

The three-day meet got underway at 8 a.m. this morning. Class eliminations are set for tomorrow, followed by final eliminator runoffs on Sunday.

Norm Weekley and his three partners, all from Pomona, are among the 400 participants who will be competing in the $35,000 event. Their class A fuel dragster is recognized as one of the fastest in the nation and currently holds the national class record of 192.72 mph, set at the County Fairgrounds strip. Their best speed, not an official record, was 199.54 mph, with an elapsed time of only 7.71 seconds.

THE CAR, powered by a 392-cubic-inch Chrysler engine is a regular winner in the Southern California area, often beating cars with lighter

WEEKLY-RIVERO-FOX HOLDING DRAGSTER . . . vies at Riverside

Chapter Six - Other Series and Events

Every IMSA weekend included their signature small sedan series, the Champion Spark Plug Series. Winners include Jim Downing, Dennis Shaw, Joe Varde, Irv Pearce, Bobby Archer and Kal Showket and cars ranged from Pintos, Mazda RX-3's Renaults, Dodges and Hondas.

Geoff Koteles – *"I literally grew up at Riverside. Was there almost every weekend with dad, George, who was an instrumental player in SoCal SCCA and pro event administrator nand pretty serious competitor in IMSA's RS Series. I attended my first race driving schools there and first actual track time. Real shame it got bulldozed. I have a lot of memorabilia from there including a credential and program from the last ever event held there"*

Dave Wolin

Bill Shaw

John Norris

Jim Downing

Racing Sedans Pointing Toward Riverside Race

By SHAV GLICK, *Times Staff Writer*

Have you ever yearned to take the family car out to a winding country road and go so fast that the tires squeal on every turn?

Well, that's what happens when the RS (for racing sedans) cars race in the Champion Spark Plug Challenge series of the International Motor Sports Assn. They're the popular pocket-size economy cars of today —running on the same type of radial tires available at your local tire center. The only difference is that the tread may be shaved somewhat for better adhesion under racing conditions.

Forty or more of them—Mazdas, Datsuns, Toyotas, Ford Pintos and Mercury Capris, Renault LeCars, Hondas, Volvos, Chevrolet Vegas and AMC Spirits—will go at it Sunday at Riverside International Raceway as a preliminary to the Times/Toyota 6-Hour Grand Prix of Endurance. The 75-mile race, 23 laps around Riverside's 3.25 mile course, starts at 10 a.m.

For the first time since IMSA brought the RS class West, the points race is led by a pair of Southern Californians. Dave Lemon of Long Beach and Irv Pearce of Leucadia. Lemon, a veteran of Cal Club amateur racing, drives a Mazda RX-3,

precise) with nine cars on the same lap with the leader.

After his second-place finish at Daytona, Varde ran 10th at Sebring and far back at Atlanta. Downing, who won the RS race at Atlanta, is skipping this one to drive a GTU car in the 6-Hour endurance race.

"I expect Joe (Varde) to be tough at Riverside," said Lemon. "He's been having some developmental problems with his car but I expect them to be ironed out by Sunday."

New Category Added

The RS cars are one of the least expensive ways to go racing on a national level. A competitive car can be obtained for $20,000 to $25,000. The cars will be running for a $15,000 purse. And the spark plug company has a $40,000 year-end point fund for the top 15 drivers. Also, a tire company gives the series champion $10,000.

As an added incentive for fuel-efficient, front-wheel-drive cars, a new ProFormance category is part of the series this year. There are 10 ProFormance cars in Sunday's field, including Mazda

---

Hard-driving Joe Varde defends Champion title

If there's an IMSA race around, you won't find Joe Varde cooling his heels.

Last year, Varde won the Champion Spark Plug Challenge season championship, winning 6 of 14 races (including the '83 Riverside event) in his Dodge.

He also finished fifth in the Camel GTU standings, scoring two race victories. And, he occasionally hopped into a Kelly American Challenge sedan to run three races in one weekend.

And, to no one's surprise, there's a good chance Varde will be doing double duty at the Times/Nissan Grand Prix of Endurance.

At 10 a.m. Sunday, the Tampa, Fla., native will fire up his Dodge Daytona to defend his Riverside Champion Spark Plug Challenge title. And there were also indications he will come back later to drive a GTO car in the six-hour Enduro.

Los Angeles Times

Street Racing and Weekend Drivers Take to the Track

Tampa's Joe Varde Wins Champion Challenge Race

By RICHARD HOFFER, Times Staff Writer

Lining up (from left) before Father-Son Race Sunday are (rear) Chris Heckman, Al Unser, Bobby Unser, Bill Maers, Wally Dallenbach, Jack Brabham. (front) Geoff Brabham and Michael Chandler

Datsun Tip:

YARDMAN
Lawn Care Equipment
TILLERS

Showket Romps to Another Easy Victory in Champion Challenge Race at Riverside

RIVERSIDE—Kal Showket ran away from the field to win the 19-lap Champion Spark Plug Challenge at the Riverside International Raceway Sunday afternoon by more than 19 seconds. He was all alone, averaging 90.4 m.p.h. in a Dodge Daytona, while Dennis Shaw, who finished second, and Dave Jolly, who finished third, chased him in Mazda GLCs.

It was no contest. He admitted it was getting a little lonesome out there.

And Jerry Grant, Champion series coordinator, said that he expects the sanctioning organization, the International Motor Sports Assn., to legislate for more equality. Showket had dominated the same way in the first race of the series at Road Atlanta.

"IMSA is an intelligent dictatorship," Grant said. "They will find some way of handicapping the cars, just like you would handicap horses, so that we'll have some better show business."

Showket said: "IMSA saw the same thing you saw. They're watching us like a hawk. . . . What I'd like to see is for them to find more horsepower for the Mazdas rather than cutting us back."

The only challenge Showket was expected to come Sunday from

Pearce Survives Mishaps and Wins

Irv Pearce won the Warner Hodgdon Champion Spark Plug Challenge 75-mile race for racing sedans at Riverside International Raceway Sunday morning despite spinning out in a patch of oil in the seventh turn and leaning on the wall through the ninth turn.

Pearce, who started from the pole position in his Golden Eagle Racing AMC Spirit, jumped ahead of Dave Jolly in the first turn and held the lead until he had trouble with a slick track on lap 8.

"A car had dropped oil on seven, and that was slowing everybody down a little," Pearce said. "I finally thought I knew where the oil was, and I was trying to drive where the oil wasn't. But I guess that by the next time I came through, the other cars had spread it around a little more.

"The toughest part of the race for me was trying to get up speed again after I spun and gaining my composure to start really driving hard again."

After the spin Pearce dropped into fourth place, behind Jolly, William Spencer Jr. and Tony Garcia.

But Pearce kept at it and by the 14th lap he was running in second place. On the 16th lap Pearce passed Jol-

"I just let the car have its head. It's a heavy car."

Jolly added. "Yeah, it's lucky he drives a tank, that way he can just hit the walls."

Pearce's winning average speed was 87.922 m.p.h. He was timed on the backstretch at 127.47 m.p.h. on lap 20, the fastest top speed turned in for the sedans.

The victory was Pearce's second of the season. He's the first driver to win two races this year, so he moved into the standings lead with 50 points. Dave Lemon, who finished fourth Sunday in a Mazda RX-3, is second with 48 points.

— TRACY DODDS

*

John Paul Jr. won the Toyota Veteran/Rookie Race Sunday morning and Michael Chandler was second. But the winner among the veterans was Parnelli Jones, who finished third overall in the just-for-fun race in identically prepared Toyota Celicas.

Jones later took some ribbing about his off-road racing. He was one of several drivers who took a shortcut through the second turn.

"Wasn't that something," Jones said. "I saw all those other guys going crazy and I decided I might as well get

---

Downing, Mandeville are top contenders

Jim Downing and Roger Mandeville are competing together once again for the 1981 Champion Spark Plug crown at 10 a.m. April 26, during the Los Angeles Times/Toyota Grand Prix of Endurance. The 75-mile race has a record 50 sedans scheduled to start.

Last year, Downing and Mandeville were runners-up to series-winner Rob McFarlin. This year McFarlin is racing in a different series, leaving the pair as top candidates for his crown.

To date, Mandeville and his Mazda RX-3 are tied for first place in the point standings with Irv Hoerr and his AMC Spirit. Both drivers

have 37 points. However, Downing won the most recent Champion race in his home town of Atlanta, Ga., and now trails the two leaders by seven points. Downing could close the gap considerably if he and his Mazda RX-3 can win Sunday at Riverside.

Another Mazda RX-3 driver, Joe Varde, is third in points followed by two Spirit drivers, Amos Johnson and Leucadia's Irv Pearce.

At Atlanta, Downing, Mandeville and Varde finished in the first three places with Johnson and Pearce finishing fourth and fifth.

The race is open to compacts and sub-compacts running on street ra-

dial tires, including Capris, BMWs, Mazda RX-3s, Spirits, Datsuns, Toyotas, Pintos, Hondas, Renault's Le Car, Scirocco, Mazda RX-2 and Volvo.

Aside from Pearce, many Southland drivers are set to compete for the Champion Spark Plug Challenge's prize money. They include:

David Turner, San Diego, Mazda RX-2; Jim Jordan, Dana Point, Mazda RX-3; George Kotales, Newport Beach, Mazda RX-3; David Day, Garden Grove, Datsun 510; Dave Lemon, Long Beach, Mazda RX-3; Win W. Maynard, Long Beach, Capri; Bob Peckham, Torrance, Pinto; Dave Wolin, Palos

Please Turn to Page 8, Col. 1

From 1983 to 1985, the Renault Cup, a spec car series with as many as 50 Renault Le Cars and Alliances, battled it out for a championship. In 1985, Parker Johnston won at Riverside, folllowed by Scott Gaylord, John Norris and Mark Mitchell.

Renault Alliance Cup
RIVERSIDE
April 23

IMSA's Firehawk Series, for showroom stock cars on Firestone street tires, debuted in 1985 with a six hour endurance race on Sunday and a 100 mile compact sedan race the previous day. In the six hour, Tom Kendall won the sports class in a Nissan 300ZX with compiler in chief Dave Wolin winning the touring class in a Mitsubishi Mirage Turbo.

12 die in desert heat chasing Mirage.

It was one of those August days at Riverside. The beer lines were long. Engines were cooking. The heat was driving the crowd mad.

It was the IMSA/Firestone Firehawk six hour, showroom-stock enduro. Dave Wolin and his Team Mitsubishi Mirage Turbo' had gone from 6th to a 3-way shoot-out for 1st. In less than two hours.

Then he turned the car over to teammate Ron Cortez. And the rest, as they say, is history.

Cortez conquered Riverside with a solid lead for 1st. Final driver, Mike Rutherford, took the checkered flag with a minute and a half lead.

Team Mitsubishi's Mirage Turbo had put away 12 IMSA touring class cars: CRXs, MR 2s, GTIs, 200SXs and Corollas. 147 laps — nearly 400 miles — in just 6 hours.

You could say the Mitsubishi Mirage Turbo had gone through a 12-pack at Riverside 6 ways from Sunday.

Takes you where you want to be.*

Mitsubishi Mirage Turbo
Enduro Champion

For nostalgia's sake

Parnelli Jones, the czar of zoom, has been out of the driving business for some years. But this weekend, the 49-year-old alumnus of the Indy winner's circle will buckle up in a Camaro, owned by Les Lindley of Anaheim, for the six-hour Firestone Firehawk Enduro at Riverside International Raceway. This is the fifth race in a seven-race series sanctioned by the International Motor Sports Association (IMSA).

Jones said he wanted another turn around the ol' Riverside road course before it closes for good at the end of the 1986 season. It was at RIR that Jones picked up two or his many career victories: A 500 stock car race and a Times Grand Prix.

Volkswagen's Bilstein Cup Spec series for Scirocco's and Rabbits ran at Riverside from 1979 to 1987. Winners included Paul Hacker, Gary Benson and Al Salerno

Rabbit sedans will compete again for the Bilstein Cup in the Budweiser Grand Prix at Riverside, along with Super Vees and featured Can-Am cars Oct. 2-4

Super Vee's (VW Rabbits) will be racing as part of the Rabbit Bilstein Cup in the upcoming Meguiar's Grand Prix Weekend at Riverside Raceway.

In 1985, SCCA's fledgling Playboy Showroom Stock Endurance series debuted at Riverside with a field of 87 cars for a six hour race. Unfortunately, amateurish scoring produced no results until pro scorers Sylvia Wilkinson and Judy Stropus spent five days sorting out the results. Needless to say, the Playboy, later Escort series, never returned.

The Pro Super Vee series made numerous appearances at Riverside from 1971 to 1983. Winners included Elliot Forbes - Robinson,. Bob Lazier, Eddie Miller, Bob Earl, Michael Andetti and Ed Pimm.

The short lived Coors Racetruck Challenge made its one appearance at Riverside in 1988. Factory teams from Jeep, Nissan, Ford, Dodge, Toyota, Mazda and Mitsubishi battled for the championship. Jeff Krosnoff won at Riverside in a Nissan.

Trucks Make Debut at Riverside

Race trucks, motor racing's newest competitive vehicles, will make their Southern California debut this weekend at Riverside International Raceway as part of a six-event racing package staged by the Sports Car Club of America.

Although many of the competitors and most of the manufacturers are based in Southern California, the fast-growing SCCA series never came closer than Sears Point Raceway, north of San Francisco, in its first two seasons.

"Race trucks are like NASCAR sedans were in their early days, when the public related directly to the models on the race track," said Spencer Low of Arcadia, owner of last year's winning Nissan. "Pickups are the major item in the United States car market, and the owners seem to identify the same way with the race trucks as the stock car fans did. This has rubbed off on the manufacturers, who are giving full support to most teams."

Five makes are among the top seven leaders after two races.

Bobby Archer, who won in a Jeep Comanche two weeks ago in Dallas, is tied at 31 points with Mike Rutherford, who drives a Mitsubishi Mighty Max. Rutherford won the series opener at Sears Point.

Next comes John Norris of Culver City, in another Mitsubishi, with 28 points, followed by Steve Saleen of Brea, in a Ford Ranger, 21; Tommy Archer, Bobby's brother, in a Jeep, and Ray Kong of San Jose, who switched in midseason from Mitsubishi to one of Low's Nissans, 20 each; and Scott Sharp in a Dodge Ram 50, with 17.

The series is open to all 1987 and 1988 mini-trucks with standard cabs, short wheelbases, 4-cylinder engines, 5-speed transmissions and 2-wheel drive.

Max Jones, the 1987 champion from Long Beach, is running with

ters). On Sunday, preceding the race trucks, there will be 15-lap main events for Sports Renault and NASPORT cars and 25-lappers for the Russell Pro Series and the Western Formula Atlantic series.

Race trucks have added a new dimension to the art of racing—bump drafting.

That is not to be confused with stock car drafting, in which a trailing car can pick up a draft and slingshot past the leading car.

Bump drafting is coming up behind another truck and whamming it in the rear—deliberately. Such an act could be cause for disqualification in some forms of racing, but in race trucks, the guy doing the bumping is more often than not the teammate of the guy getting bumped.

Low explains the technique:

"It all started accidentally last year in Portland, which has a long straightaway and a tight chicane where you try to keep as close as possible to the truck ahead of you. The racing is so tight that guys got bumped now and then.

"When we started checking lap times, we couldn't figure out why one was quicker than the others

until someone said, 'Hey, that wa the lap where I got bumped,' so w went out and tried a few laps an found that both trucks in a bump ing situation had lap times betwee a second and a second and a ha faster than when running alone.

"At first, the officials frowned o it, but we convinced them that was for our benefit. Now it's get ting really wild. It's kind of lik dancing, you've got to both be i the right rhythm for it to work. you're not in rhythm, you can en up knocking your teammate side ways."

RUSSELL SERIES—Norm Breedlov whose father **Craig** once held the worl land-speed record, will bring a 20-poi lead into Sunday's Russell Pro race, thir of a 10-race series for the Mazda Cu championship. Breedlove, 25, of Tustin finished second to former snowmobi champion **Jim Noble** of Idaho Falls, Ida., i the series opener at Phoenix and then wo the second race at Firebird Raceway. H has 55 points to 35 for Noble.

STOCK CARS—Modifieds and sports man cars will race Saturday night a Saugus Speedway, with a train race as a added attraction. . . . Winston Cup driv **Davey Allison**, who sat on the pole for th Winston 500 at Talladega May 1, will tr his hand at short-tracking Saturday nigh when he drives in a Southwest Tour even at Madera Speedway.

The American City Racing League made its one appearance at Riverside in 1988. These were Sport 2000 cars, each sponsored by a city.

Team road racing series to debut

EXAMINER NEWS SERVICES

SACRAMENTO — The American City Racing League, the city-based, team road racing series, will make its Southern California debut at Riverside Raceway on the weekend of May 14-15.

The ACRL three-car Pro Sports 2000 teams, representing 13 cities throughout the western states, will be competing for a purse of $22,000. This will be the second SCCA Pro Racing weekend in the 12 event series for the ACRL City Team League Championship. The series opener will be held at Firebird International Raceway in Phoenix on April 16-17.

The drivers will be racing for a total series purse of $500,000, with over $22,000 at stake at Riverside. This ACRL professional road racing series features teams representing the cities of Phoenix, San Diego, Long Beach, Los Angeles, Fresno, San Jose, Oakland, San Francisco, Sacramento, Portland, Seattle/Tacoma, Spokane, Reno, Las Vegas, and Honolulu.

Each ACRL city is represented by a team comprised of three Sports 2000 cars. These 1,200-pound cars are powered by two liter, four cylinder Ford overhead cam motors. Chassis are manufactured by Lola and

Meanwhile, with ACRL at Riverside International

RIVERSIDE (AP) — Pole sitter Bob Lesnett of Team Oakland led the entire way to win the American City Racing League auto race during the Riverside Grand Prix Saturday at Riverside International Raceway.

Lesnett, the owner of team Oakland, was never challenged in the 25-lap, 63.6-mile race. He finished second in the series' first race in Phoenix, Ariz., in April, during which he also held the pole position, and leads the individual point standings with 203.

Peter Zarcades of Team San Diego passed Carlos Bobeda of Team Sacramento at the finish to take second place.

Dick Gamble of Team San Diego was fourth.

Team San Diego leads the series standings with 404 points, followed by Team San Francisco with 326, Team Oakland 322 and Team Los Angeles 276.

The series, run in Sports 2000 cars, resumes May 28 at Sears Point International Raceway at Sonoma.

Meanwhile, Mike Rutherford of Pittsburg, Calif., will have the pole position for Sunday's Sports Car Club of America 20-lap, 50-mile Racetruck Challenge Race.

Rutherford drove his Mitsubishi around the 2.547-mile Riverside short course at an average speed of 81.238 mph.

That made him the seventh-fastest starter and, under the SCCA's rules, the top 40 percent of the qualifers start in reverse qualifying order.

The road racing series features stock compact pickup trucks, modified only with required safety equipment.

Jeff Krosnoff of La Canada turned the fastest qualifying speed in a Nissan hardbody, averaging 81.624 mph. He'll start from the seventh position.

Veteran Trans-Am champion George Follmer of Huntington Beach and Indianapolis 500 veteran Pete Halsmer of Anaheim were among four drivers penalized by the SCCA for practicing on Thursday.

Riverside to host road race

SACRAMENTO — The American City Racing League, a team road racing series, will make its Southern California debut at Riverside Raceway May 14-15.

The ACRL three-car Pro Sports 2000 teams, representing 13 cities throughout the Western states will be competing for a purse of $22,000. This will be the second SCCA Pro Racing weekend in the 12-event series for the ACRL City Team League Championship.

This event will replace the previously scheduled IMSA event.

The first known vintage races were held at the 1959 Kiwanis Grand Prix

In 1979, VARA ran an event an as a support show to the Times Grand Prix Can Am

Otis Chandler, then the owner of the L.A. Times and the museum in Oxnard brought a Porsche 917 and McLaren out and battled with his son, Michael Chandler, future Indy car driver. Compiler's Note: the museum in Oxnard is now the Mullin museum.

Here. John Thomas in Otis Chandler's Porsche 917K takes to the dirt to try and get by Gary Arentz in the McLaren M8F. Otis was driving his ex-Penske 917/30 and had motored off into the distance. Thomas was playing wingman and determined to get into second so he could cover Otis' tail.

1985 Road and Track test of Vintage Cars
With Dan Gurney, Bob Bondurant and Phil Hill

Watch the video on the attached DVD

Vintage Car Races Bring Back Racers, Memories
Can-Am Reunion for Oldies, But Fasties

The Los Angeles Times Historic Sports Car Races—the first major vintage-car events ever to be in the Southland—are set for Saturday, April 21, as a companion feature to the Times Grand Prix of Endurance.

Vintage-car racing, long popular in Europe, had been the exclusive province of a relatively small group of collectors on the East Coast until the early 1970s.

In 1974, Steven Earle and a small group of enthusiasts started the Monterey Historic Automobile Races. The first year there were about 65 entries and an almost equal number of spectators. Today the Monterey event attracts some 200 entries and the spectators number in the thousands. The Portland Historic Automobile Races were added to the series in 1978.

Differing from the early club events, these races are designed with the spectators in mind, as well as the driver. The most desirable feature of this approach enables the spectator to see these beautiful restorations from every period of racing, from the early 1900s to the present.

Normally a car built during the last 10 or 15 years is not considered 'vintage'. However, there were many cars built during this period that had an historic impact on the sport. One of the groups is an Exhibition Class.

Cars built since 1965, such as the Otis Chandler Porsche 917-30, produced in 1973 and driven to a World's Closed Course Speed Record by Mark Donohue, will race in this class.

The exhibition group will include some of the Porsche's, Ferrari's, McLaren's and Lola's that appeared at Riverside during the late '60s and early '70s in the famed Can Am series.

In dividing the vintage cars into classes; period of manufacture and engine size are all important. However, a real effort is made to pair off cars with an equal performance potential where possible.

Winning the race is really a secondary consideration. As a matter of fact, there have been times when the sixth-placed won got a larger trophy than the winner. The cars are the real stars of the event, and the drivers are out for the fun of it.

A lot of the people who will exhibit cars April 21 are not professional drivers. Some have been so bitten by the racing bug that they have disqualified themselves from vintage-car racing and gone into the professional ranks.

One of the most popular machines of the early '50s was the Jaguar XK-120. No less than six of these sturdy machines will appear with a mixed bag of Healey's, "Gull wing" Mercedes, Allards, an Arnolt-Bristols, a Le Mans Index of Performance winning renault-DB and the famous Barlow-Simca Special.

The pre-World War II group will include a 1915 Stutz Special owned by the Los Angeles County Museum of Natural History. Driven by the famed Earl Cooper, from 1913 to 1915, the Stutz is part of the museums extensive collection.

Two pre-1930 Lancia's, a Bugatti T-35C from the same period and a Talbot-Lago Grand Prix car, driven by the French Champion Louis Chiron, are also a part of this unusual group.

More than 30 grand touring cars, designed for high-speed travel over the most marginal roads of Europe, will also compete.

The Ferrari's, Alfa-Romeo's, Aston Martin's and other specialized makes weren't orginally designed for the track.

The last vintage event in 1988

Other Events

(A lot of non racing things happened at Riverside)

Some we covered in Volume One, here are a few more)

RALLY 'ROUND THE FLAG, BOYS — Pretty Karen Resnicki, the reigning Miss Redlands, displays the starter's flag used by nearby Les Richter to send contestants on their way Saturday in the Explorer Road Rally. In front (from left) are Jerry Moore and Vernon Fowler of Explorer Ship 4, Redlands, and Phil Pettis and Jerry Hansen of Hemet, where contestants made their half-way stop during the rally. (Photo by James Sloan)

The Explorers Road Rally made a stop at Riverside with Les Richter

Not exactly racing; Ron Pierce said: *"In 1968, I got a invitation from the Javelin Club to sit in the esses with them and got to drive in a parade lap around the track. I had just purchased my brand new 1968 Javelin in Bakersfield After that I attended 2 or 3 races at Riverside a year and I still have the Javelin."*

1970 Memorial Day Air Show

RIVERSIDE—Well, the Red Baron has had it. Sorry, Snoopy, but I've just met Art Scholl. Professor Art Scholl, that is. Old Red wouldn't last two rounds with the Professor.

Forget the Sopwith Camel, check out the Chipmunk.

Funny thing. I came out here to take a look at the ground machines warming up for Sunday's 11th annual Times Grand Prix and wound up with an eye in the sky. Prof. Scholl flies. Like, high. Also low.

On a given day, Art Scholl looks, talks and acts like a professor. A comfortable family man and father of two, he teaches classes and is head of the department of aeronautics at San Bernardino Valley College.

On another given day, Art Scholl is some kind of nut. Wally Schirra, Donn Eisele and Walt Cunningham notwithstanding, Prof. Scholl is generally regarded as the most daring stunt flier in the planetary system these days.

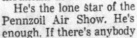

Art Scholl

As a special bonus attraction to this year's Grand Prix, Scholl is going to put on an exhibition prior to the start of Sunday's feature at Riverside Raceway. Denis Hulme, Bruce McLaren, Dan Gurney, Jim Hall, John Surtees and 30 more of racing's finest will roll off the blocks at 1:30 p.m. Scholl will roll over the mountain at 1.

He's the lone star of the Pennzoil Air Show. He's enough. If there's anybody left in the grandstands when he gets done, it's going to be quite a day.

Will Kern, assistant race director of the GP, had a brilliant idea. "I've made arrangements for you to go up with Scholl and take a spin," said Kern. He was looking directly at me. I looked directly at the plane.

It's a DeHavilland Chipmunk, which was used by the Canadian Air Force as a basic trainer during World War II. It's got maybe a few edges on the Sopwith Camel, but it still looks like a toy. A little toy.

Stalling for time, Daredevil Hall settled for watching a movie of Scholl's speciality. He calls his act "Ballet In The Blue" and the fact he's been able to stage it more than once is testimony to the theory man is going to last.

souvenir program $1.00

world air shows, inc. presents

"greatest show above earth"

Commemorating ART SCHOLL

the 1st annual MEMORIAL DAY AIR CIRCUS

riverside international raceway

Tragically, Art Scholl was killed in a plane crash while assisting in the filming of Top Gun in 1985.

417

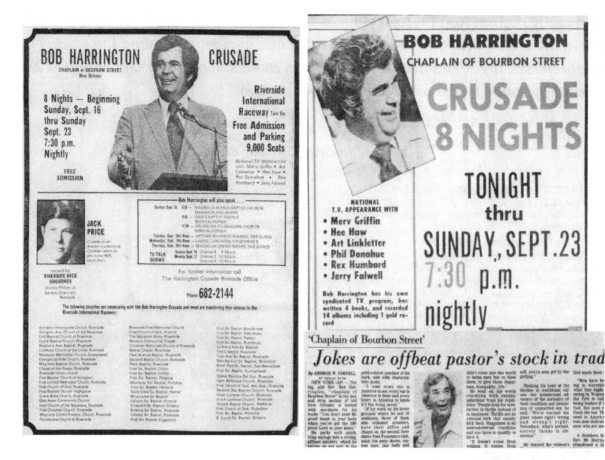

In 1973, Bob Harrington brought big crowds to turn six. Later, Harrington, "The Chaplain of Bourbon Street" divorced and went bankrupt. He died in 2017 at the age of 89.

A disappointing crowd of 5000 attended the 1978 Country Music Festival

'Giant' country festival was good but not a giant

Chapter Seven - Club Racing and Corner Workers

Amateur racing began with the very first race at Riverside in 1957, an SCCA regional in September, followed by a National championship event in November. The SCCA National championship was, at the time, the premier road racing series in the U.S. Racing continued with a few events every year. No prize money and as pro racing evolved, club racing became the last domain for amateur racing. Club racing events were held as supporting events to major races. The last event on the complete course, an SCCA National, took place in July, 1988. A few events were held in 1989 on portions of the course not yet demolished although utilities had been shutoff and plumbing was marginal.

Last, Last Race at Riverside Scheduled

Al Unser and his son, Al Unser, Jr., who staged auto racing's most exciting duel for a national championship two years ago, plan to race each other again in the historic

the Unsers.

Competition will be staged on the traditional 1.5-mile man made off-road track designed to simulate the thrills of racing in Baja in an area

View a video of a 1957 SCCA regional on the attached DVD

Front Deptember 1957 - Bob Drake, Pete Woods and Chuck Daigh

Ron Cummings: *"I took John Albi's Devin Chevrolet to a Cal Club driving school. My instructor was Jim Adams. Albi had built the car in Arcadia in 1960 - 1961, mostly in the evening and on weekends in his family's garage He had owned a MG-TD and a XK-120 Jaguar and ran in some time trials."*

Hansgen, Gregory and Shelby Top Riverside Race Entries

By MAURY POWELL
MOTORACING Staff Correspondent

—MOTORACING Photo

CARROLL SHELBY AND JAN HARRISON
After Spa Victory . . . Riverside This Weekend

WALTER HANSGEN NO. 1 D-JAG DRIVER IN U.S.
He's Entered in Big National Race at Riverside

RIVERSIDE, Nov. 13—SCCA's triple-header West Coast National Championship series comes to a frothing finale here at Riverside International Motor Raceway's 3.2-mile course Nov. 16-17, with everything pointing to this being the "gasser" of them all.

Race Co-ordinator George Cary, Jr., who got the frigid finger from Fate at Palm Springs earlier this month when chill weather set in and cut down the crowd, announces two big names for this one.

He hit the jackpot with Walt Hansgen, Westfield, N.J., who has been giving everybody the "Mark of Zorro" treatment with Briggs Cunningham's white 3-8 D-Jag throughout the East; and Masten Gregory, Kansas City, one of the few Americans to cut the mustard with a European factory team.

I. W. Stephenson, team manager for Temple Buell of Denver, Colo., phoned Cary from Miami today that Gregory's 4.7 Maser would be flown to Los Angeles from Florida. Repairs have been made, Gregory having

flipped the car during the Caracas meet.

HANSGEN BIG ATTRACTION

Hansgen comes here fresh from a string of wins over the East's finest, his latest being recorded at the new Virginia International Raceway, Danville, Va., several weeks ago.

Another Atlantic Seaboard ace is smooth-driving Paul O'Shea, Port Chester, N.Y., a mean man with the new Mercedes-Benz 300SLS. He was third behind Pete Lovely and John von Neumann at Pebble but should go better on this course.

Carroll Shelby, peerless at Palm, cannot be counted out despite a fourth at Pebble. His tire combination on the 3-liter Maser wasn't right, according to Chief Mechanic Joe Landaker, but the Dallas, Tex., ace will be in the thick here with John Edgar's 4.5 Maser.

Johnny von Neumann heads up the Ferrari fire brigade with his silvery 2.5 Testa Rossa. He's augmented

(Continued on Page 9, Col. 3)

NEW COURSE DEBUT NEXT WEEKEND

A group of sports cars barrel through the esses on the first leg of the new 3.3 mile road course at the Riverside International Motor Raceway near March Air Force Base. The plant will open for business next week end with racing Saturday and Sunday by members of the California Sports Car. Club. Track promoters hope ultimately to bring Formula I and II European grand prix racing to the Southland circuit.—(Staff Photo)

Jim Law: *"I was the assistant starter at a regional in 1959. Steve McQueen's Porsche was leaking oil in turn nine and the stewards told me to black flag him. I put out the flag per orders; McQueen gave me the finger and kept going for a few more laps. The stewards stopped scoring him !! After the race, he came up to me and yelled about the black flag. I told him I was just following orders, turned around and left."* Compiler's Note – This was long before LeMans. McQueen was starring in the TV show; "Wanted Dead or Alive."

In April, 1960, the SCCA National Amateur Championship event
attracted a large field. Steve Mqueen in the Porsche

Peter Culkin - 300SL

George Kendall – Abarth Zagato

Three Hour-Long Handicap Races At Riverside

Three unique hour-long handicap races will wrap up a two-day road race program at Riverside International Raceway tomorrow, featuring the Pacific Coast's top sports car drivers.

A field of more than 200, topped by the 1960 driver of the year — Billy Krause, launched the California Sports Car Club event with an eight-race card today.

Competition tomorrow gets under way at 11:30 a.m. with races for formula, ladies, production and modified cars as well as motorcycles.

Favored in the one-hour handicap race for modified sports cars of all sizes will be Krause, winner of the Times-Mirror Grand Prix here last fall. Race chairmen Dave Bracken and Bill Pollock explained entries (a limit of 35) will be started on a time handicap, based strictly on past performances of cars and drivers.

Many of the west's top drivers share billing with Krause. Among them are Ken Miles, Southern California's most frequent main event winner; Eric Hauser, in his new "Lafayette Escadrille"; Lew Spencer, Kontratief Chevy Special; Rick Lewis of Riverside, L-S Special; Jim Chaffee, Pink Elephant Mark II, and George Brindamour, Maserati.

Production headliners includes Dave McDonald, Corvette winner at Pomona and Palm Springs, and Tony Settember. Pasadena's Frank Monise, another two-time winner in 1961 in his new Lotus, and Art Snyder in a new Lola-Climax are two small bore threats in the modified handicap race.

Krause won the Cal Club's first big race of the year (Pomona) as well as the club's last event at Riverside in December, 1959. He finds the 3.275 mile course definitely to his liking.

McAfee tops field of 150 at Riverside

Drivers from four western states, including two-time national champion Jack McAfee of Burbank, throw the 1962 sports car racing season into gear Saturday and Sunday (March 3-4) at Riverside International Raceway.

Racing begins Saturday at noon with seven eight-lap races around the twisting 3.275 mile paved track with its scorching one mile back straight. Sunday's program of 15-lappers starts at 11 a.m.

The Raceway is located six miles east of Riverside at the junction of US Highways 60 and 395.

Dan Gurney, winner of recent Daytona and Nassau races will be honorary marshal and numerous celebrities of racing, movies and television will be in attendance.

The two-day road racing program, first in the Southland since last October, is the inaugural production of the new alliance between the California Sports Car Club and Sports Car Club of America.

McAfee has assumed the featured role in a strong list of modified entries. He will drive a Porsche RS 61 in the over 1500cc main event.

He will draw competition from Northern California, Arizona, Utah and Nevada.

A heavy emphasis from the list of more than 150 entries has been placed on production races. This field will offer such drivers as Ken Miles of North Hollywood and Lew Spencer of Los Angeles (Sunbeam Alpines), Don Wester of Monterey and Jay Hills of Los Angeles (Porsche Carreras), Ronnie Bucknum of La Crescenta (Ferrari GT) and former national champion Paul O'Shea of Hollywood (Corvette).

Additionally, competition is scheduled among Formula Junior cars in unique "claiming" classification, Grand Prix motorcycles and lady drivers.

At stake will be championship points in the first authorized event for SCCA districts 9 and 10 to determine the 1962 champion.

Modified entries have drawn a wide assortment of equipment.

There will be the unveiling in Southern California of the Elva Mark VI, a widely publicized import to be driven by Art Snyder of Gardena.

SCCA and Cal Club split in 1962, with each group putting om their own races and driver licensing. They got back together the next year,

RIVAL SPORTS CAR CLUBS CARRY FEUD TO RACEWAYS

BY BOB THOMAS

Southern California hasn't seen a sports car race since last October — The Times Grand Prix at Riverside.

Yet, this weekend — and next — there will be two road racing events.

Is it coincidence . . . or, is it war?

Rival sponsors call it both.

Drivers, the commodity needed by each for survival, have found themselves in the

tinued. "For one thing, the clubs need everybody to put on a race.

"Yes, I plan to run at Riverside and Pomona. I would reconsider only if I saw something in black and white from the national office of SCCA.

"Honestly, I don't see any difference between the clubs now. They both want to promote safe racing and better the sport. But I don't think there's room for two clubs. There's too much competi-

Dave MacDonald

Driver Gets New Tests

The California Sports Car Club, with headquarters at 1923 N. Hillhurst Ave., in Hollywood, is a pretty thorough organization. They have certain specified rules for their members and demand that they be followed to the letter.

One good example of this concern, both for the sake of safety and fairness to fellow-club members took place Sunday.

Even though Josie von Neumann is the first woman ever to race professionally and a respected participant of the racing clan, she was required to undergo a rigid driving examination before Cal Club officials will give her their permit.

Cal Club Makes Shoulder Harness Mandatory In Races

Recognition of the s h o u l d e r harness as an effective safety device was given recently by the California Sports Car Club region dents, has been a necessary accessory for race cars for many years and was tested thoroughly in competition before it was marketed. not replace a rule calling for seat belts. Both belts and harnesses will be worn by the competing drivers, the club an-

'Cease-Fire' Brightens Picture for Southland Sports Car Fans

BY BOB THOMAS

A "cease fire" seems to exist at long last in the war between the rival Southern California Sports Car Clubs. In fact, it now appears the two armies have called the fied version of the old Cal Club and the rival United States Sports Car Club.

Heading the "new" Cal Club is Otto Zipper of Beverly Hills, one of the area's most popular sports car figures and owner of a 1700cc Shelby has lined up Dave MacDonald, the hot El Monte driver, to handle one of the Cobras. MacDonald is well known for the success he has had in Corvettes, most recently in the Sting Ray aerocoupes.

1963 Cal Club Regional

Pacicfic Coast Championships

california
SPORTS CAR

RIVIRSIDE GP & STOCK

FEBRUARY 1963   **50 CENTS**

PACIFIC COAST DIVISIONAL CHAMPIONSHIP RACES

RIVERSIDE RACEWAY JUNE 22-23, 1963

FIRST RIVERSIDE
NATIONAL CHAMPIONSHIP
SPORTS CAR RACES
NOVEMBER 16-17, 1957

OFFICIAL PROGRAM
50¢

1st 1962 PACIFIC COAST CHAMPIONSHIP SPORTS CAR and motorcycle RACES riverside raceway

official program .50

CALIFORNIA
SPORTS CAR

NOVEMBER 1964

FIFTY CENTS

RIVERSIDE INTERNATIONAL
RACEWAY NOV. 12-15, 1964

AMERICAN
ROAD RACE OF
CHAMPIONS
1964

In 1964, 1966 and again in 1968, Riverside hosted the SCCA American Road Race of Champions, hosting regional champions in a runoff format and replacing the National championship program that had been in place since 1951.

American
Road Race of
Champions
Yearbook 1966

Triumph at Riverside '64

Triumph TR-4 finishes 1, 3 and 4 in CLASS D NATIONAL DIVISIONAL CHAMPIONSHIPS. BEATS MGB, Austin-Healey.

Triumph Spitfire finishes 1, 3, 4 and 5 in CLASS G NATIONAL DIVISIONAL CHAMPIONSHIPS. BEATS Sprite, Midget.

See your Triumph dealer and drive home a winner.
Triumph TR-4: $2849; Triumph SPITFIRE: $2199;

*Suggested retail price POE plus state and/or local taxes, slightly higher in West. Look for dealer in Yellow Pages. Overseas delivery available. Standard-Triumph Motor Co., Inc., 575 Madison Ave., N.Y.C. Canada: Standard-Triumph (Canada) Ltd., 1463 Eglinton Ave. W., Toronto 10, Ont.

Bob Sharp pilots his Champion-sparked Datsun to C/P divisional championship on the '68 SCCA circuit

43 firsts...42 seconds...25 thirds...in national competition across the U.S. qualified 17 Datsun sports cars for the 1968 American Road Race of Champions at Riverside Raceway. An outstanding record and Champion helped spark it! It's more proof Champions deliver outstanding performance. Why settle for less? Always specify <u>Champions</u> for your car!

Champion
spark plugs
...the heart
of a tune-up!

CHAMPION

CHAMPION SPARK PLUG COMPANY • TOLEDO, OHIO 43601

CAR and DRIVER

431

HAPPY HEAD-SHRINKER—Thomas Jervey Kelly (T.J. to his friends) flashes a toothy grin yesterday after completing his practice laps for the ARRC at Riverside Speedway. T. J. is a resident psychiatrist in Miami Beach who races sports cars for a hobby.

Making Final Checkup

Bob Tullius checks the oil level in his Triumph after a practice session yesterday at Riverside International Raceway. Tullius and three co-drivers will try to qualify today for the American Race of Champions and a possible national championship this weekend.

The first American Road Race of Champions was held in November 1964 at Riverside. It was a cold, windy week with temperatures in the 50's. Seventeen classes competed for the title of national champion, pitting the top three from every SCCA division in the country.

Riverside Skeds Race World Series

Entries began mounting for the first American Road Race of Champions, a four-day "world series" of sports car racing which will decide the national driving championship in 17 competition classes at Riverside International Raceway Nov. 12-15.

The long awaited run-off will

Invitations to participate in the Sports Car Graphic Magazine-sponsored event were sent to eligible competitors last week and race officials report an early return. Only the top three points holders from each of the 17 classes in all six SCCA divisions are eligible to compete thus assuring

Ladd Killed At Riverside

RIVERSIDE, Calif. (AP) — Jim Ladd Jr., of Lebanon, Pa., driving what he had said would be his last race, was killed today in the last event of the day at the American Road Race of Champions.

Ladd was third when his Austin-Healy 3000 spun out on a turn and was hit and sent rolling over and over into the infield.

Ladd's death came at the end of two days of sports car racing in which Western drivers scored 11 of 17 victories.

Bart Martin of Hayward, Calif., in a Cooper-Chevvy, scored a one-second victory in the C and D modified event, and Ed Leslie of Carmel, Calif., in a Ford Cobra, won the A and B production model race.

Ladd was just behind the leaders in the D production race —for street-type sports cars— when he lost control approaching the first turn of the fifth lap.

His car was hit by one driven by Charles Gates of Rolling Hills, Calif. The Austin - Healy rolled twice, the roll bar bent and Ladd was crushed against the steering wheel. Gates escaped injury.

Ladd's wife Sue was in the

PIT STOP
East Domination Expected to End

By ED DUNCKELMANN

Eastern sports car drivers are the best in the nation, and if you don't believe it, just ask them. For years they have been pointing with un-humble pride that there never has been an SCCA National Champion from the West Coast.

Out of possibly 1,600 drivers in National races the past four years, no Westerner has even won a class victory. Obviously, the East Coast breeds better drivers and fiercer competitors, so they say.

Well, don't believe it, SCCA's so called "National" Championship title is about as phony as can be.

There have been 49 "National" races since 1961, and every one of them has been in the Eastern States. This year alone, a local driver at his own expense would have had to travel over 60,000 miles to enter this series of races.

This balloon is about to burst and some of the East Coast drivers are crying already and making limp excuses why they are going to get trounced at Riverside in November at the first American Road Race of Champions.

Each one of SCCA's six divisions from throughout the country is sending their top three drivers in each of SCCA's many production, modified and formula classes for the huge title runoff.

While it was all right for them to claim all the "National" titles for a series of 13 local races back East even though our drivers would have had to pay their own way, these great sportsmen are complaining about the expense of one trip to the West Coast ... even though their entry fees, rooms and transportation are being paid for them.

Adding insult to injury, though West Coast drivers have contributed through their entry fees just as much money as the East Coast boys and girls, transportation expenses are not going to be paid for Pacific Coast Division drivers.

Maybe we just have a suspicious mind, but we think SCCA's so called "National Champions" are afraid that no one is going to believe their excuses why they got beat by a bunch of West Coast non-champions.

With six divisions, the odds appear to be that the Pacific Coast drivers should take home one sixth of the marbles. We'll go out on a limb and say that when its all over, half the awards will have stayed right here.

★   ★   ★

Norm Evans, Bib Tullius, Jim Ladd, Jim Adams and Bruce Kellner. Bob Tullius won in the TR-4

Harry Banta Hopes to Reverse Result In American Road Race of Champior

Harry Banta of Reno hopes to reverse the Pacific Coast championship results when he competes against the nation's leading drivers in the American Road Race of Champions, Nov. 12-15, at Riverside International Raceway.

"My biggest ambition right now is to beat Bill Molle at Riverside and even the score for 1964," Banta says while making preparations for the four-day speed classic to de-

tive sports car racing for 11 years.

Among his competition in addition to Molle will be Charlie Barnes of Dallas, Texas, who proclaims quite an impressive maintenance record with his exotic Merlyn Mk. 6.

"I've run the car 18 times this year and the engine has never been removed from the car for maintenance," the 31-year-old driver, says. In those

Why d
from N
at the
San Fr

The H Modified Field

Rick Muther Surprise Winner at Riverside

BY BOB THOMAS
Times Auto Editor

RIVERSIDE — A promising Southern California driver who has designs on the European racing circuit was among eight national amateur sports car champions crowned Saturday in phase one of the first American Road Race of Champions at Riverside International Raceway.

Phase two, a seven-race program over the same 2.6 mile road course, will be held today, starting at 10 a.m.

Started Last

The surprise star of the who has been racing only four years started last in the featured 45-minute race for Class E and F modified sports cars yet blazed to an impressive victory in his tiny Lotus 23 racer.

He hopes the triumph will provide an important step toward professional racing. He drives heavy grading equipment for a living now.

Wood 3rd

Muther was an unexpected starter in the competition which pits the divisional champions and first two runnersup from the six districts of the Sports Car Club of America. His car was wrecked and burned in a Del out due to injuries received in a late season accident.

Muther finished 21 seconds ahead of Ralph Wood of Orinda who won the Class E division in an Elva Porsche. Muther's car was a Class F entry, a classification determined by engine size.

Ed Barker, 45 - year - old driver from Hermosa Beach, won the Class G production car division with his Triumph Spitfire in a close finish with Emmett Brown of Santa Maria. Dan Parkinson of La Canada won the modified race in a homebuilt Dolphin Abarth and Alan Johnson of Los Angeles captured the Class E produc- turn of the nine-turn course. He was forced off the course, while trying to lap one of his rivals. Subith had built up a comfortable lead when the accident occurred on the 18th lap of the 23-lap race. He escaped injury although the car was demolished.

FORMULA VEE (23 laps)—1. Lew Kerr (Niantic, Conn.); 2. Oser Barr (Galston bury, Conn.); 3. William Duckworth (Orlando, Fla.); 4. Jerry Hansen (Minneapolis); 5. Sheldon Dobkin (Miami). Average speed—88.8 m.p.h.

H PRODUCTION (23 laps)—1. Fred Salo (Detroit), Austin-Healey Sprite; 2. Gilbert Page (Putnam, Conn.), Sprite; 3. Clyde Cabrinha (Millbrae, Cal.), Sprite; 4. Robert Durham (Longview, Tex.), Sprite; 5. Dr. Richard Alley (Wichita, Kan.), Sprite. Average speed—78.25 m.p.h.

G PRODUCTION (23 laps)—1. Ed Barker (Hermosa Beach), TR Spitfire; 2. Emmett Brown (Santa Maria), MG Midget; 3. Dr. Dave Kiser (Overland Park, Kan.); 4. Bob Clemens (Utica, Mich.), TR Spitfire; 5. Erwin Lorinez (Newtown, Pa.).

Ralph Wood (Orinda), Elva Porsche; 2. Dave Jordan (Hawthorne), Dolphin Porsche; 4. Alan Friedland (Marion, Pa.), Elva Ford; 5. Mike Hall (Chicago), Elva Ford. Average speed—84.324 m.p.h.

E PRODUCTION (25 laps)—1. Alan Johnson (Los Angeles), Porsche; 2. Ron Grable (Linthicum, Md.), Porsche; 3. Denny Harrison (Los Angeles), Porsche; 4. Herb Everett (Doylestown, Pa.), Porsche; 5. Howard Fowler (Miami Springs, Fla.), Porsche. Average speed—85.047 m.p.h.

F PRODUCTION (25 laps)—1. Richard Hull (Lansing, Mich.), Volvo; 2. Robert Patrick (Flint, Mich.), MGA; 3. Sheldon Shoff (Wilton, Conn.), Lotus 7A; 4. Tim Burr (Little Rock), TR3; 5. Jerry Demele (Stockton), Lotus 7A. Ave. speed—80.6 m.p.h.

435

Steve Dooley - B Production Jaguar XKE

In 1966, a record number of entries (333) showed up to the runoffs

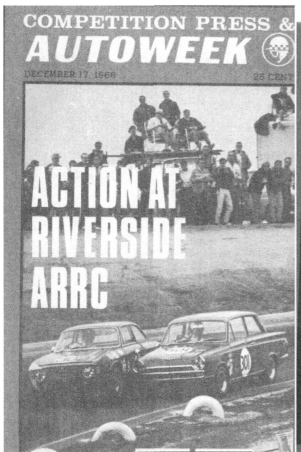

Amateurs Will Burn Rubber, Oil and Gas

RIVERSIDE, Calif. — The largest field of cars and drivers ever assembled for a closed circuit road race will get into action tomorrow in preparation for the weekend's American Road Race of Champions at Riverside International Raceway.

More than 300 participants, representing class champions and top ranked drivers from the seven geographical racing divisions around the country governed by the Sports Car Club of America will take part in this giant "raceoff" which will determine national class champions in each of SCCA'S 22 competition classes.

Beginning with tomorrow's practice session over the challenging 2.6-mile Riverside course, and continuing through Friday's qualifying and the 12 races on tap for Saturday and Sunday, the gigantic field will rack up more than 30,000 miles of racing. They will burn up the equivalent of four tankloads of premium gasoline, wear out more than a thousand tires and carry—or use—something like 2,000 quarts of motor oil.

While no prize money is involved, since the event is for the nation's amateur championships, sports car fans are assured of top quality competition, with the coveted titles at stake. Participation in the ARRC is by invitation only, to drivers compiling the best records in their class during the regular season within their respective regions. The record entry of 333 is assurance that the ARRC is one of the most important sports car events in the world.

Tomorrow's activity will be held from 9 a.m. to 5 p.m. and Friday's qualifying will follow the same schedule.

The Desert Sun
Wednesday, November 23, 1966
Palm Springs, California

3 Riverside Drivers Hurt

RIVERSIDE (Special) — Resting e a s i l y at Riverside Community Hospital today were the victims of the three accidents which slowed down yesterday's American Road Race of Champions, won by Ralph Salyer of Hammond, Ind.

Jack Beall Jr. of Houston, Tex., whose Austin Healey hit a retaining wall in the first race, suffered head injuries. Ron McConkey of Cedar Falls, Iowa, is in satisfactory condition with back and rib injuries incurred when his Jaguar flipped in the second race. Dan Gerber of Fremont, Mich., had only facial cuts to show after his A-B production car was tailgated by one car and then hit broadside by another.

Salyer averaged 97.922 mph as he won the championship for C and F modi-fied sports cars. Second was Bob Aylward of Whichita, Kans.; third, Don Wester of Monterey.

Top placing drivers and their cars:
E Production—1, C a r l Swanton, Woodland Hills, Calif., Morgan; 2, Alan Johnson, Los Angeles, Porsche; 3, Bert Everett, Doylestan, Pa., Porsche. Average winning speed: 85.948.

A, B, C Production—1, Don Morin, Attleboro, Mass., Brabham; 2, Karl Knapp, Pasadena, Calif., Le Grand; 3, Stu McMillen, Libertyville, Ill., Brabham. Average speed: 96.840.

A and B Sedans—1, Ron Grable,

Mt. View, Va., Dart; 2, Bill Pendleton, Eugene, Ore., Mustang; 3, Scott Harvey, Dearborn Heights, Mich., Barracuda. Average speed: 90.173.

A and B Productions—1, Ed Lowther, McMurray, Pa., Cobra; 2, Don Peckham, Torrance, Calif., Cobra; 3, Fred Sutherland, Los Angeles, Cobra. Average speed: 77.552.

C and F Modified—1, Ralph Salyer, Hammond, Ind., McKee Olds; 2, Bob Aylward, Wichita, Kan., McLaren; 3, Don Wester, Monterey, Calif. Porsche. Average speed: 97.922.

C and D Production—1, Jerry Titus, Sherman Oaks, Calif., Porsche; 2, Dick Smith, Fresno, Calif., Porsche; 3, Jim Dittemore, Redondo Beach, Calif., Triumph. Average speed: 85.988.

Walt Hane leading the B Production field

B Production Grid

Road Race Champs Hit Riverside

RIVERSDE, Calif. (UPI)—Six races were scheduled for today to determine titlists in several classes as the third annual American Road Race of Champions got underway at Riverside Raceway.

More than 330 drivers are entered in the Sports Car Club of America sponsored two-day national event. Six more races will be run Sunday.

Small engine class races were on the agenda today. Competition was scheduled for Formula Vee, H. Production, G. Production, C. D. Sedan, G-H Sports Racing and F Production cars today.

In qualifying runs Friday, Bud Morley of Denver, Colo., and Ralph Salyer of Hammond, Ind., tied for the top speed of 103.539 miles an hour.

Salyer drove a McKee Oldsmobile and Morley a McLaren Ford around the nine-turn, 2.6 mile course, both in the big bore Class C sports racing category.

The ARRC came back to Riverside again in 1968.
This would be the last time there.

ARRC At Riverside

THREE HUNDRED-TWENTY-Six drivers from all over the country are competing in the American Road Race of Champions (ARRC), the Olympics of road racing, being held this weekend at Riverside Raceway. The national champions in 20 classes are being determined by 14 race events.

Qualifying for ARRC invitations to compete is based on drivers emerging at the top of their class competition this past season in the Sports Car Club of America's seven geographic divisions.

Each division has held a year's competition of six to eleven national events to determine these champion candidates. Of the top six in each class, the best three who accept ARRC invitations go to Riverside for the runoff.

This is the fifth annual ARRC, an event that alternates between Riverside and Daytona Beach, Florida. Races will be 30 minutes in length using Riverside's 2.6 mile course, with seven races taking place Saturday and seven on Sunday.

Some Scenes from the 1968 ARRC

1968 ARRC - Don Pike, Porsche 911, leading Gary Wright, Alfa, in the B Sedan Race. Pike and Wright were later disqualified, giving the win to pole sitter Alan Johnson, also in a 911

442

Dan Gerber was seriously inured in the B Production race

DICING IN A CORNER — Five Formula Vees enter a turn at Riverside International Raceway in the last American Road Race of Champions in tight formation. The same close action is expected this weekend when the ARRC again returns to Riverside. The Formula Vee race will be held Saturday at 3 p.m. Seven races will be held Saturday and Sunday.

"124 MPH UNDER RIVERSIDE'S CHAMPION BRIDGE!"

It was the chance of a lifetime for me, and a couple of hours at Riverside in the Datsun 2000 proved two things: it's an exciting, exacting track—and Datsun does things with it.

First off, the car feels right, the deep padded buckets supply easy support. The tach and engine instruments are all where they should be. The wheel position is nice: not Italian, but not too close either. The five speed gearbox is a joy, light with short, precise throws.

A flip of the column-locking key and twin carbs take charge right now. The engine warms to running speed in a hurry. 135 horses chuckle in their overhead cam corral.

I'm not a race driver and my car is a perfectly stock 2000. But I must admit to a little excitement as I wheel onto the track and take aim at Turn One. We zip through it. Then up through Turns 2, 3 and 4... The "Esses"... with the power coming on strong, and the sway bars and double acting shocks giving the tires plenty of bite. (I say "We," because driving this car is that kind of personal experience between you and the machine.)

Into tough Turn Six, I slip down into second gear. The synchros and linkage are so slick. The revs soar, the horses kick up their heels.

A second later, I'm halfway down the short chute to Turn 7, toeing the front discs, hanging it all out through the sharp reverse camber.

Accelerating through Turn 8, the long back straight suddenly stretches before me. Now we'll see what flatout means to Datsun! 100 in third gear. I check the dials. Everything normal, 110 in fourth.

Still all systems "Go!" with the engine and tires singing a sweet duet. Now, fifth, with the revs and speed rising again. A long pull. There goes the Champion Bridge over my head. In this cruising gear the tach would never get to 7000. But the speedometer says 124 and we must be hitting at least 120. Plenty fast for me!

Turn 9 comes too quickly. It's a snap going slow. It's a bear at speed. As tricky a sweeper as I'd care to meet. Done right, you come out flying.

I snick the box into third. "G" forces press me into the resilient bucket seat. We catapult onto the short straight and shoot past Start-Finish at over 100.

Sure... I took another lap. Several of them, collecting thrills and a few tidbits you'll never read in *Competition Press*. But the radio plays at over 100, and you can hear it, too. The engine is turning about 4 grand at that speed in fifth, and with the thermostatic fan running free, the quiet up front is uncanny.

The car didn't heat. The oil pressure was fine and steady. And the gas gauge barely moved. I enjoyed myself thoroughly. You'll enjoy the Datsun 2000, too! It still delivers more than any other sports car and does it for an amazing low price— $3096.*

And if you want the same great lines and $300 of no-cost extras for even less money and a little less power...try the 2000's high-stepping stablemate...the Datsun 1600. You'll get a 96 HP OHV engine for the same kind of performance that's made the 1600 an "F Production" class winner at tracks over the country. Parts and service at over 600 Datsun dealers across the country. The Sound Move is to...

DATSUN THE TRACK STAR!

445

ARRC Action Begins Today

By RYAN REES
Sun-Telegram Auto Racing Editor

RIVERSIDE — Zero! Countdown for the "Fastest Week in the West" at Riverside International Raceway has reached the zero mark.

More than 100 entrants have already arrived at the track with a steady stream of cars pouring into the infield area hourly.

More than 425 entries from all parts of the country are expected for the two days of racing Saturday and Sunday to determine 20 national champions in 14 divisions of sports car racing.

Only the top three drivers in each racing class from seven geographic areas in the country have been invited to the Olympics of Racing. However, in some cases the top three haven't been able to come so the next in line have come to try and qualify for a spot on the starting grid either Saturday or Sunday.

And in still other cases, the top three have traveled to Riverside but the next in line have come anyway hoping that one of the top three won't be able to qualify and they will get an opportunity to start.

Some of the entrants have traveled more than 3,000 miles.

They have not traveled the great distance for the hopes of taking home a bundle of loot. Instead, they are racing for the prestige of a national championship and a trophy offered by Nine Flags. Nine Flags, Newspaper Enterprise Assn. (NEA), Riverside International Raceway and California Sports Car Club region of SCCA sponsor the race.

The Sports Car Club of America sanctions the race.

The American Road Race of Champions is held on a semi-yearly basis at Riverside Raceway. On alternate years, the ARRC is held at Sebring in Florida to help even out the traveling distance for the drivers.

The ARRC will be run on the 2.6-mile, eight-turn "short" course at Riverside.

Several former national champions and defending ARRC winners are entered.

Alan Johnson of Los Angeles is the defending champion in the C Production event with his Porsche. Bill Campbell of Cantonment, Fla., will be trying for his third straight title in the Formula Vee race. He drives a Zink.

Also going for a third national title in a row will be Paul Jett of San Antonio, Tex., in his Lotus in the F Sports Racing class.

Richard McDaniel of Hurst, Tex., is seeking a third straight C Sedan crown with his BMC Cooper and Dan Parkinson of LaCanada, Calif., is after his third D Sedan trophy in an Abarth.

The Fastest Week will conclude next Sunday when the Rex Mays 300 is held for Indianapolis-type racers. Forty-nine entries have been received including Bobby Unser, the 1968 Indianapolis 500 winner, his brother Al, Mario Andretti, A. J. Foyt, Jack Brabham and defending champion Dan Gurney.

Ticket prices for the ARRC are $1 for today and tomorrow, $2 for Friday, $3 for Saturday and $4 for Sunday.

Tickets are available at all Mutual Ticket Agencies and at the raceway.

Rialto Road Runners Win

The Rialto Road Runners 10-11 year team easily captured the first place team trophy for their age group at the California State and U.S. Western States Cross Country Meet at Sacramento Sunday. The meet was run under the auspices of the Amateur Athletic Union.

Rialto's winning score of 21

Rosie Saavedra, 18th; Sue Shite, 17th; Juanita Cobbs, 19th and Kathy Leon, 21st for Rialto.

Rialto's women's team brought home a second place trophy. Will's Spikettes placed first with 26 points, Rialto second with 47 points and Long Beach third, 72 points. Running

ARRC Looms as Race of Year

RIVERSIDE, Calif. (NEA) — Another Olympics, this one home-grown, is taking shape in the desert of Southern California. It's called the American Road Race of Champions and, for anybody interested in cars, it's where the action is.

This major competitive encounter for sports cars in the United States — sponsored by Newspaper Enterprise Assn., this newspaper and Nine Flags —is set for Nov. 29-34 at Riverside International Raceway.

Some 400 drivers, drawn from the top sports car competitors in the country, have been invited to race in the 20 classes set up by the Sports Car Club of America.

MILLIONS of dollars of machinery, ranging from the more conventional Mustangs, Corvettes, Porsches and Alfa-Romeos to the exotic Bobsys, Zinks, Hebras, Quantums and Merlyns, will be hauled to California from every state in the Union.

Unlike other big races, the drivers are amateurs in that they race generally for one reason; for the fun of it. No prize money is offered; instead, each of the 20 national champions will receive the unique Nine Flags trophy, a sculptured figure of a race starter flashing the checkered flag. The trophies were created by Bill Crawford, editorial cartoonist for NEA and this newspaper.

INVITATIONS to the ARRC go to the six point leaders in 20 racing classes in SCCA's seven racing divisions. Each division has held a year's competition of six to 11 events to determine those champion candidates. Of the top six of each class, the top three who accept ARRC invitations go to Riverside for the runoff.

"You can see," explains John Bishop, executive director of the SCCA, "that the ARRC is about as grassroots as you can get. There are literally thousands of drivers all over the country who race hourly with one thing in mind: 'get enough points to qualify for the ARRC.' Obviously, the competition at the big race will be something fierce."

And there is no typical race driver. Occupations are, to put it mildly, unusual. There are doctors, engineers, real-estate dealers, funeral directors and stock brokers. At last year's race, a retired professor, a retired member of the Kingston Trio, a demolition expert and a nuclear-physicist were among the competitors.

Since each race lasts but 20 minutes, the driver who makes one slight miscalculation, the car that's a shade under first-class mechanical condition — well, both have traveled a long way to be placed in the also-ran category.

BUT that's what makes the ARRC the nearest thing to the Olympics. The 400-meter runner a shade off in form doesn't have the time to correct.

In the case of auto racing, both man and machine must be in perfect harmony. The too-fast driver in the too-slow car simply doesn't win races.

Sports car racing is very much the family sport. While wife, girlfriend or kiddies can't do much while the guy is wrestling his car around the course, they do plenty before the green flag is dropped.

Unlike professionals, the average sports car driver doesn't hire a pit crew but relies on family and friends. They, too, have got to love taking an engine apart, refiguring the suspensions and walloping in crankcase goo. And, during the season, the average driver probably spends some 40 extra hours a week on his car.

But the back-breaking, costly preparation is forgotten when the green flag drops. It's the race that really counts.

**1966 six hour enduro was won by Don Pike, Dick Smith
and Chuck Cantwell in a Mustang**

6-Hour Race at Riverside

**Lew Spencer signalling
winner Don Pike**

ROAD RACING—A 55-car field will tackle a marathon challenge at Riverside International Raceway Sunday at 1:30 p.m. when the California Sports Car Club stages a six-hour Enduro to complete a two-day regional program over the 2.6-mile circuit. Entries include Alfa Romeos, Ford Cortinas, SAABs, Cobras, Mustangs, Porsche 904s, Lotus Elans and Stingray Corvettes. Favored is the Cobra driving team of Don Peckham of Torrance and Jim Dittemore of Redondo Beach. Qualifying and sprint races will be held Saturday, followed by a "Hootnanny" at the race track. The enduro is open to production cars and sedans . . . Dan

The California Sports Car Club Region of the Sports Car Club of America stages the 6-hour enduro at River-

side International Raceway, featuring a Le Mans start for more than 50 production sports cars and sedans.
The all-day Sunday affair

Also in 1966, supporting events to the USRRC included a thirty minute race production sports car race, and a precursor to the Trans Am; a 100 mile sedan sedan race called the Mission Bell trophy. Don Pike won overall in a Ford Falcon and a class win for Pete Brock in a Hino

Jim Law: *"I was right there with the Hino with my Saab. These were supposed to be production cars but Parkinson's Fiat Abarth (You can''t tell me there were 5000 made) was just a lot faster !! Meanwhile the other team Hino rolled up into a ball. Brock couldn't fit in his enclosed trailer so we swapped; I was the embarassed guy with the wreck on my trailer; Brock had a Saab hidden in his!!"*

Frank Sheffield's film from 1967
Watch the entire video on the attached DVD

Davey Jordan

Davey had a long and varied caree, not only in club racing but also in the USSRC, Can Am and Formula 5000 with successes at both Sebring 12 hour and Daytona as well.

"I started racing in 1959, driving my own Porsche Speedster. Race it for 4 years, winning the Pacific Coast Championships in 1961 and 1962 in the "F" production class. In 1961 I was Cal Club "Driver Of The Year". I drove Otto Zipper's Dolphin Porsche to a second in E Modified at the ARRC at Riverside. In 1967 I drove Vasek Polak's 911s in Nationals with 12 firsts and 3 seconds in D Production

Davey and his wife Norma, winning in 1961

Davey Jordan and Vasek Polak

"Shelby hired Scooter Patrick and I to run the Toyota 2000GT's in C production in 1968. it was a big deal, I had been a pretty successful club racer and racing for Shelby was a really big deal, a step up for me. Ronnie Bucknum did the initial testing, pronounced the cars front runners. Goodyear made us trick tires, then SCCA disallowed the Webers we were running and forced us back to Solexes. We just didn't have enough horsepower after that, even with Lew Spencer and Phil Remington spearheading the team. We just got beat by Porsches everywhere. But it was a great year - I had never done a season with a big team like that before. Unquestionably it was the biggest highlight of my career. I have had more memorable positive moments, but racing for Shelby was a big deal.

Compiler's Note: Most people suspected that Shelby, who was the Toyota distributor for texas and the Goodyear race tire distributor convinced Toyota to give him money, knowing the cars wouldn't win"

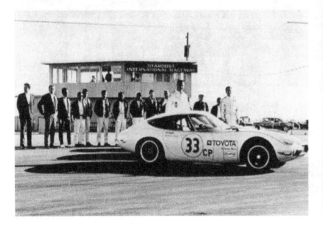

Assorted Club Racing Photos

HISTORIC BUILDING BOOM——
——EXPERIENCED BY MORENO VALLEY IN 1971

The view eastward over the Moreno Valley is spectacular. In the left foreground is the junction of Highways 60 and 395. Directly above (center) is Riverside International Raceway; to the south (right center) is March Air Force Base. East of March, between the Russell Mountains and Bernasconi Hills lies the site of Perris Lake (see map on next page). The snow capped mountain is Mt. San Jacinto, beyond which lies Palm Springs.

The land on which you—and Riverside International Raceway—are sitting is located in the northwestern part of Moreno Valley. Rich in history, beginning with pre-historic times, the valley is today one of the most prolific areas in Riverside County in terms of agriculture and population growth.

Population today is more than 20,000, twice as many as five years ago and a far cry from the 228 recorded souls in 1892. March Air Force Base was re-activated in 1927, after being closed at the end of World War I, as a primary flying school. With the advent of World War II, the base was enlarged, and since then has continued growing.

Agriculture products of the valley include walnuts, avocados, rye, beets and flowers. Livestock raised includes rabbits, chicken and turkeys. To the east and south are many beautiful, working horse ranches, some of which may be seen along U.S. 60 east of the raceway.

Also east of the track is the site of the Perris Dam, southern terminus of the California Aqueduct. When Perris Lake is filled to its 120,000 acre ft. capacity, it will have a total area of 2450 acres contained by 9.7 miles of shoreline. 100,000 tons of sand will be hauled in to create miles of swimming and sunning beaches, providing Southern Californians with a vast new recreational area. The project is now one-third complete with water reaching the lake during the summer of 1973.

Accompanying the lake and dam construction is a record-shattering building boom. Nearly $14 million in new building permits were issued during 1971, including 73 single family units, several luxury apartments, and a new motel.

"The building progress that Moreno Valley experienced in 1971 is only an indication of what is going to happen here," says Burton E. Smith, senior vice-president of Southern California Financial Corporation, owners of the huge Hendrick Ranches development in the Moreno Valley area.

"With the influx of population coming from Los Angeles and Orange Counties, coupled with the mid-1973 completion of Perris Dam and recreational facility, there is no doubt in our minds that Moreno Valley will experience a dramatic population increase and building boom in the next few years," Smith said.

Riverside Raceway Faster, Safer and Better for Fans

BY SHAV GLICK
Times Staff Writer

Faster, safer and much improved for the spectator.

Those are the apparent results of Riverside International Raceway's massive improvement program which has changed the face of the world famous road racing plant.

The most notable change is in the configuration of Turn 9, the high speed U-turn at the end of Riverside's long backstretch. The turn, once considered one of the most dangerous in auto racing, now swings to the left about 1,000 feet below the Champion Bridge and begins a more gradual turn exactly twice the old radius.

The new Turn 9 is also banked eight degrees, enabling cars to go through it at higher speeds—but with greater safety. The secret of speed at Riverside is how fast you can come out of Turn 9 and head up past the start-finish line and through the Esses.

Greater Speeds

Most of the drivers who have road tested the newly paved course this week agree that speeds should be greater with the new turn. None of the other familiar turns was altered although the entire surface of the track has been given a double layer of asphalt.

Despite long delays brought on by the heavy...

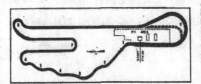

THE NEW LOOK—This is how Riverside Raceway's Turn 9 will look when the Times Grand Prix is held Oct. 25-26. Dotted line shows tight turn of old course.

...with press and television personnel.

Sunday's nine national championship races will be the last Cal Club regional event of the year held in Southern California. More than 250 sports cars, including the Can-Am type Lolas and McLarens, big-bore American sedans, Formula machines and production cars will be entered in a final bid to qualify for the American Road Race of Champions which designates national champions.

The feature race will match the Porsche 910 driven by four-time national champion Alan Johnson of Corona del Mar against the Alfa Romeo T-33 driven by Scooter Patrick of Manhattan Beach in the D sports racing division.

BIG CARS — Indianapolis 500 winner Mario Andretti, who clinched the national driving championship last week, heads the field in Sunday's Golden State 100 in...

Raceway ... Gary Kleckner and his "Chevota" will be back at San Fernando Raceway Sunday for a shot at his wheel-standing record ... Something different is planned for Oct. 19 at Orange County Raceway when a drag program for cars of pre-1954 vintage is scheduled ... The SoCal American Motors Dealers Assn. is hosting a clinic for car owners Friday night at Orange County Raceway with Clyde Morgan demonstrating starting techniques ... When Danny Ongais drove Mickey Thompson's Mach I Mustang to a national funny car record of 7.32 seconds (199.67 m.p.h.) it earned the team a spot in the World Finals next month in Dallas.

MOTORCYCLES—Class A speedway riders will qualify Friday night at Orange County Fairgrounds in Costa Mesa for the national championship...

ships Oct. 3 at the same track. A similar program scheduled last week at Whiteman Stadium was canceled ... Mel Lacher will be after his fifth straight main event win in Friday night's flat track program at Ascot Park ... Gary Scott, Jimmy Raymond and Paul Wilde will duel tonight in Trojan Speedway's combined TT steeplechase and flat track ... Bart Markel in an early entry in the U.S. 8-mile championship race Oct. 4 at Ascot Park.

STOCK CARS—Jim Insolo with three wins in a row, is...

the driver to beat night at San Gabriel Speedway's NASCAR program for sportsman cars ... Bay and young Chuck resume their duel way in another ... Jalopie Bakersfield Speedway night ... Sunway holds a 60-lap championship race Saturday for Tornado division...

MIDGETS—Friday three-quarter midget Trojan Speedway rookie-of-the-year Mike Olivero of Downey last week won...

OFF-ROAD—...competition for racing cars, buggies, wagon sedans is Sunday at Saddleback located on Santiago east of Orange, who won the 1968 race for limited will compete.

NEWSWORTHY—Gibbs of West were added to N Reel Assn. staff ... Indianapolis 500 Hooks is touring aboard the Cors...

Riverside Raceway Use Set for Public Hearing

RIVERSIDE (RCN) — Proposed motorcycle trails and scramble events and music festivals at the Riverside International Raceway are running into opposition from nearby property owners.

Appearing at the Central Area Planning Council session, the opponents of the additions to the racetrack near Sunnymead forced a public hearing to be opened instead of routinely continued at the applicant's request. Neither the applicant nor the Planning Department was ready to present the case but county counsel ruled anyone in the audience wishing to speak at the advertised hearing could do so.

Then in order to protest, the opponents demanded that Les Richter, president of Riverside International Raceway, reveal the plans for expanded use of the facility. He declared there is nothing being planned in the line of rock music festivals, which he pointed out are virtually outlawed in the county by ordinance of a couple years ago.

The music events would be along the lines of those that have been staged in other sports facilities such as Dodger and Anaheim stadiums, and at Swing auditorium in San Bernardino.

"We are not talking about any three-day hard rock session," Richter declared.

The conditional use permit case has resulted from county counsel advice that the uses permitted at the speedway should be clarified, in particular a rocket-firing type event on the racetrack. Arthur West of Laguna Beach, who owns property across the street from the raceway, led the opposition after he forced the hearing to be opened over the declines of the six-member council.

...destructive to the neighborhood," he stated.

Residents of the area complained of cans and bottles and rubbish polluting the streets following race events at the track. They also said the traffic created is a problem already and they complained of music from the loudspeaker system on Sunday mornings. Carl C. Watson of Edgemont commented: "All music is not music."

Spokesmen for the Riverside Chamber of Commerce and the Junior Livestock Show (which is slated to move in the speedway for its events) supported Richter's application.

The planning department recommended approval, stating the uses would be compatible with the existing raceway, which is located on a total of 540 acres. The report, however, points out "the property is in the heart of the Edgemont-Sunnymead area, surrounded by a great deal of multiple family zoning."

After listening to an hour of testimony, the council voted to continue the hearing to June 20 to 9:45 a.m.

Merchants-City Child Care Service for Shoppers Nixed

SAN BERNARDINO — Mayor W. R. Holcomb yesterday vetoed a City Council request to have the city administrator study a joint venture with merchants to provide child care services for downtown shoppers.

The veto came promptly after the council approved the request on a 4-3 vote. "We should let private industry do the study," Holcomb explained.

Councilman Robert L. Hammock, who proposed the study, said, "It is important to attract the maximum number of shoppers into the city. I understand that some merchants are interested in helping with this venture."

He said he expected the services to be privately run, but he suggested "we just have the city help set it up."

Hammock envisioned having the service available to customers of Inland Center, Central City Mall and other downtown shopping areas.

Councilmen William Katona, Lionel Hudson and Drusilla Secombe joined Hammock in voting for the study. However, Katona said he approved of the idea only if city funds were not to be used.

County Counsel Gets Task Of Contesting Range Suit

Deke Houlgate and Dusty Brandel promoted everything from Club racing to USAC

Rod Bean: *"I went SCCA racing in late 1972, couldn't afford to race an Elan, the winning car in the class so I bought, as my first race car, a sanitary, but under prepared, D Production Yenko Stinger. My third regional race, on the Riverside short course, I started) a couple of rows below the fast guys, which was about par for my car, based on my first two races. Most non Californians thought of Riverside as sunshine and palm trees year round but I knew better*

On the first lap, it started to snow - Big flakes that looked serious, but it didn't stick, only making the track good and wet. I hadn't yet raced in the wet but I liked it. The Stinger, with the engine over the drive wheels, liked it too.

I found it quite easy to pass all the fast guys, one actually giving me "slow down" signals. Being a new guy, my first reaction to that was to wonder if we were under a full course yellow. But there were green flags, so I just kept going. Pretty soon, I couldn't see anybody else back there.

Then it stopped snowing and a dry line appeared, not that I was smart enough to use it. But the two orange B Sedan BMW 2002s from Hyde Park Motors did' driven by Carl Fredericks and Jeff Kline. Carl gradually reeled me in, eventually passing me. Then a light bulb came on in my head and, seeing what was happening in front of me, I did the same thing, pressing Carl. And we drove our hearts out for the rest of the race, never seeing another car.

Losing the overall win by a couple of hundredths to a car in another class didn't bother me because I had had so much fun. Carl had fun too. We drove the cool off lap laughing. And I learned something about racing in the rain. I never saw snow at Riverside again. Too bad

CSCC REGION SCCA REGIONAL CHAMPIONSHIP RACES
SEPT. 14-15, 1974

RIVERSIDE RACEWAY
2.55 MILE 'SHORT COURSE'

Frank Sheffield: *"I had a 1967 MG B roadster, well set-up handling-wise, bone stock engine with hi-rev valve springs, and headers. Reliable, fast enough to learn some car control. Then I flattened tail light and the crumpled the panel behind the front wheel, a consequence of spinning in historic turn nine and meeting the boiler-plate wall. The car was Bourgeois Blue, the wall was white, with blue markings. Bill Swan and I drove this same car to seventh overall and a class second in a three hour enduro race in July, 1969. We used the upper radiator hose from Sid Cole's MG A as a filler spout on the refueling rig that safety steward and orchestra leader and land speed record 300SL owner Don Ricardo was hesitant to approve. Great Fun."*

Joe Scalzo: *"In 1962 came the arrival of the rear engine Elva and the obsolescence of the front engine Lotus XI. Frank Monise took part in the vehicle's swan song battle, a thriller fought on the long course at Riverside. Opposing him was a fast driver named John Timanus who had acquired the model XI that future Lotus martyr Pat Pigott had guillotined at Vacaville by wrapping around a telephone pole. The battle fought by Monise and Timanus went into the Valhalla where all great racing battles go. Monise, fittingly, won."*

Doug Stokes: *"I forgot to mention that writer/racer Jerry Titus signed off my SCCA competition license at Riverside after I bribed him with a joke booze flask (empty of course) that was made out of foam rubber in the shape of a baloney sandwich."*

FORMULA

BOB EARL INTERVIEW   PRO FB   SMR   SUPER VEE '73

Bob Kirby Wins Rough TransAm Regional; Bash Halts Main

A three-car accident on the first lap of the big-bore regional feature accompanying the Mission Bell 250 Trans-Am event brought out the red flag when the course was blocked. The turn one incident involved Neben Evol's Sting Ray, the A S/R Capella of Andre Gessner and Roger Hilton's Camaro. Although the cars were badly damaged, there were no injuries to the drivers.
(Peter Borsari & Autoweek photos)

By Joyce Uphoff

RIVERSIDE, Calif., Sept. 8 — Bob Kirby drove his trusty black Porsche to a wire-to-wire win over the 38-car field of the E, F, G and H production race during the SCCA regional program accompanying today's Mission Bell 250 Trans Am event.

Kriby nosed ahead of Alan Ward's second-place finishing Gp Alfa at the start and was four seconds ahead at the finish. Kirby took the flag and drove as far as turn four when his engine blew.

Fritz Taggart drove a steady race in his Fp Alfa and captured his class and third overall. First in Hp was the Sprite of Roy Miller, who finished ninth overall.

The excitement of the A sports/racing, A-B sedan and A-C prod race was in the first lap at turn one, when four cars attempted to negotiate the turn four abreast. Three cars ended up on the hay bales, and although there were no injuries, the race was red flagged to clear the course.

At the re-start, Ed Marsh, Lotus held the lead until turn six of the last lap when Harvey Lassiter, McLaren-Chevy, passed him to win the race. The Ap class went to Dale Harris, Sting Ray, who was third overall.

A hard-fought battle between Steve McMillen, Eisert-Chevy, and Jerry Entin, LeGrand-Chevy, was won by Entin in the F/SCCA event. McMillen posted the fastest lap at 1:32.0 for an average speed of 100.00mph. Entin pressed and finally passed McMillen four laps from the finish. McMillen was forced to retire on the last lap with an overheating engine. Max Collicott, Lotus, took F/B and was 55 seconds behind the leader. F/C went to another Lotus, driven by Brian Knowles.

Ed Wakely drove a smooth, steady race in his B S/R Porsche to win the race for B-D sports/racing, C-D sedans. He averaged 90.8mph to finish 17 seconds ahead of the C S/R Platypus of Stan Sorenson, who won the class. C sedan winner was Dennis Lyman in his rapid Mini. One lap back was the D sedan winner, the NSU of Walt Schomburg.

Jim Kennedy won the Formula Vee and Formula 4 race in his LeGrand F/4. He was followed by F/V winner, Herb Brownell, Zink, 11 seconds behind at the finish. The best duel of the race came from Dennis Sherman, McKnight, and Dick Hayes, Beach. They stayed in close contention for third and fourth place, with Sherman barely pulling ahead to capture third.

CLASS WINNERS: Ap - Dale Harris, Sting Ray; Bp - Richard Hearn, Sting Ray; Cp - Fred Johannson, Lotus Elan; Dp - Fritz Warren, TR4; Ep - Bob Kirby, Porsche; Fp - Fritz Taggart, Alfa; Gp - Alan Ward, Alfa; Hp - Roy Miller, Sprite; A S/R - Harvey Lassiter, McLaren-Chevy; B S/R - Ed Wakely, Porsche; C S/R - Stan Sorenson, Platypus; D S/R - Jim Bailie, Fiat; A Sedan - Jerry Cook, Covair; B Sedan - Keith Bleecker, Porsche; C Sedan - Dennis Lyman, Mini; D Sedan - Walt Schomburg, NSU; F/A - Jerry Entin, LeGrand-Chevy; F/B - Max Collicott, Lotus; F/C - Brian Knowles, Lotus; F/V - Herb Brownell, Zink; F/4 - Jim Kennedy, LeGrand.

1974 Formula Ford Action

Tom Weichmann, Dave Parke, Dennis Firestone and Alan Holly

Allen Holly leading Dick Cooney

Firestone followed by Kastner

Dick Shirey

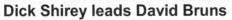

Dick Shirey leads David Bruns

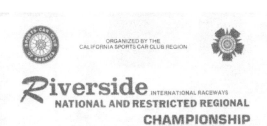

**Formula Vee at an SCCA National - Dick Murray leads
Tim Kuykendall, both in Zinks**

SPORTS CARS—The stock cars held their last go-around at Riverside International Raceway last weekend. Now it's the sports car set's turn. The California Sports Car Club, along with Sports Car Club of America affiliates from Las Vegas, San Diego and Arizona will hold a three-day program July 2-4 with national and regional championship races on the twisting road course. Chairman **Jim Snelling** is inviting any driver who ever competed at Riverside to contact the SCCA office at (818) 508-7811.

Pittinger leading, Shirey, Marvin and Ferguson in turn six

Charley Budenz - *"I grew up in Riverside, became a volunteer ticket taker at the track. Then had a career in the Navy including three combat tours in Viet Nam.. I competed in autocrosses while stationed in various locations, then after attending a drivers school at Riverside, bought an insurance salvage Fiat 124 and built it into a racecar. Competing in regionals and nationals through the 70's and 80's, I did pretty well, never finishing lower than third !! Driving it at Riverside, flat out through one and two, braking and downshifting at six, sometimes using seven and eight, sometimes the club course that cut across from seven to the back straight. That long straight, braking at the last minute for the dogleg and a slingshot around nine onto the front straight – what a blast. Incidentally, the reason for the tall roll bar is that my partner and codriver was 6'5".*

OFF AND RUNNING

Father, son combine talents in racing cars

By BILL ROLLINS, *Special Sections Writer*

Ideally, a race car driver ought to be three things—an orphan, rich and impotent.

At least, that's the opinion of the venerable Enzo Ferrari, 90, whose red cars have the winning record to prove that he knows what he's talking about.

Such a driver, Ferrari said, would not have to deal with the pain of losing loved ones, the misery of poverty, the distraction of women.

Bill Auberlen, 19, of Rolling Hills Estates, meets none of Ferrari's criteria. He just wins races.

Dueling wheel-to-wheel against more experienced drivers in physically faster cars, some of them backed by $3 million budgets, Auberlen is roaring to national recognition among sports car drivers.

Bill's father, Gary, is his inspiration and sometimes co-driver. They work together for their wins, personally building and rebuilding engines and cars.

Last year, Bill competed in only half of the International Motor Sports Assn. (IMSA) circuit (usually 14-16 races), and finished 12th in point standings.

After a second-place finish in the GTU class at Daytona this year, the Auberlens came in sixth at Sebring, with Bill driving 7½ of the 12 hours. The car is now in second place and Bill is No. 4 in driver point standings with nine more races to go.

"Without my Dad, none of this would have been possible," said Bill. "He has spurred me on and

"I think motorcycle racing is one of the best training grounds for car racing," Bill said. "The starts are very close, with the handlebars overlapping sometimes. You learn control when you're close and get a good sense of judgment.

"It also taught me maintenance, and how to treat a transmission so that it will last."

When Gary began racing cars about six years ago, Bill was part of the pit crew.

Bill tried driving his Dad's Porsche 911 when the Porsche Owners' Club rented the Riverside track for time trials.

"He took to it like a fish to water," his father said.

When Bill was 17, he became the youngest ever to attend the Sports Car Club of America (SCCA) driving school at Riverside.

Two sprint races are held at the end of the school. Bill won them both against physically faster cars.

He attended a second driving school at Carlsbad in a borrowed 510 Datsun. Again, he won both races at the conclusion of the school, proving that it was more than the car.

With this preparation, father and son entered their first race together, a three-hour enduro at Riverside, finishing first in class and second and third overall.

Gary's ultimate objective was the 24-hour Daytona race sponsored by IMSA.

Bill applied for the license necessary to enter Daytona, but with

Photo courtesy of GARY AUBERLEN

Photos by DAVID NEWLAND

Bill Auberlen finished second in the GTU class at Daytona this year, at top. Bill, shown above at left, works in his father Gary's speedometer shop in Redondo Beach, above at right.

462

1972 - Bobbie Cooper, #23, says this was her first race.

Rod Davis leading in #24, Dwayne Anderson in #42

Racer Cramer mixes business with pleasure

Peter Cramer, vice president of Peyton Cramer Ford, has quite a list of racing accomplishments.

His first race was in 1979 at a regional SCCA formula Ford race, where he placed third. In 1980, Cramer competed in Jim Russell School's world scholarship championship series, winning four of more than 30 races. He placed sixth in British championships, third in Willow championships, and 10th in F&O Focus series as part of the Von Berman factory team. He did a formula 1 test for Murray Taylor, but no sponsor materialized.

In 1981, he set a new lap record for formula Ford in the first race at Riverside, but was shunted off the track in the race by another car. His father asked him to quit racing and go to work in the family business.

Cramer's father, Peyton Cramer, was a business associate of Carroll Shelby in early Shelby American days, later a business partner of Peter Brown, and currently a multi-auto dealership operator based at Redondo Beach.

So, in 1981, Cramer started as a new

car salesman and progressed to finance manager and sales manager.

Then in 1988, in the first eight races of the season in Showroom Stock B, he won SCCA regionals at Willow Springs and Holtville; nationals at Phoenix twice and at Riverside; and led in Holtville national until his engine quit.

Cramer is currently first in SCCA national points. He is also holder of the track record at Riverside and Willow Spring and Firebird International Racing in Phoenix. He is scheduled to drive in the IMSA GTO Series for Francois Coughin Racing Team from France in a Peugeot 205 T-16.

On the business side, Cramer serves as vice president and general manager of Peyton Cramer Ford-Peugeot in Redondo Beach. He is president of Peugeot Dealer Advertising Association of Southern California and Bay District Motor Car Association of Los Angeles, sponsors the Galaxia Task Force and K-9 Patrol Team of the Redondo Beach Police Department and is active in the Child Passenger Safety Committee of Los Angeles County.

Peter Cramer (above), and at left racing a Peugeot Sport.

Women get credit they deserve

To honor some of the commuters and the increasing number of women automobile buyers, Peninsula Pontiac in Torrance is offering over the summer free seminars "For Women Only." The free summer seminars will cover many topics of concern to the woman buyer such as service, maintenance, financing and the selection of a new or used

car, as well be any great mystery. Therefore they are striving to make the whole process of selecting, purchasing, maintaining and financing of a new or used car as easy to understand and as rewarding as possible.

In latter answer the questions expressed by women in regards to the finances of a new Pontiac, the motor

463

The John Mueller / Mark Yanez / Joe Jordan RX-3 at the 1985 Enduro

Richard Wakefield leads a gaggle of Formula Fords

Fred Whitehead - Formula Atlantic in 1980

Mike Hull leading the Formula Ford race – 1976

Rod Bean: *"I think it happened to everyone once - One time, when I was racing the Yenko Stinger, I was planning on a race weekend at Riverside, needed the points, but my tow car was down. I had several Corvairs so I grabbed a '67 140hp automatic from my collection, put a rented bumper hitch on it (visualize the minimalist Corvair bumpers - car + trailer = 3200 lb.) and towed from Hermosa Beach on the old, winding, Highway 60 through the mountains. I used to put the race car on the trailer backwards, so the tongue weight was fine. And also, the tow car Corvair did an unexpectedly fine job hauling. But when I pulled into that Riverside Raceway registration area (parking for registration was on a very bumpy dirt surface), the hitch detached itself and went straight into someone's nice motorhome, fortunately, at low speed. I looked in the mirror and wondered where the car had gone. This was the nature of my racing at the time; a rusty trailer and a girlfriend as my only pit crew - secretary and girl Friday."*

Mark Mitchell: *"The fall Cal Club enduro; 1987, Over a 120 cars on the grid. We used to line up on the inside apron of turn nine with the co driver on the banking waiting for the starter's gun to go off. He would run the key to the starting driver who was already buckled in the car. I was driving an '82 Mustang GT in SSA at that time and was the starting driver. Gun goes off, Co driver runs the key down to me, I dump the clutch, got a good start and took off. Passed 14 cars on the first lap and passed the overall leader going into the dog leg. One of my most cherished moments of racing, looked in the rear view mirror seeing dozens of cars. My co-drivers and pit crew were going nuts; they couldn't believe I made up do many spots on the opening lap I led for about a dozen laps until the first yellow; then Lance Stewart in a Corvette and the Jon Milledge/ Walt Mass 944 finally caught me. Wow, these were the best of times"*

Worker Stories

The Flag Team in 1979 - Thanks for all your hard work

Dante Puccetti: *"It was qualifying at the June, 1981 Warner Hodgdon 400 - They yelled watch out as I heard the engine roar. Jimmy Means; throttle jammed wide open at 140 MPH is bounding straight at us. I'm looking at the chrome grill of an out of control 4300 pound Plymouth heading straight up the hill. Fifty feet away and closing. Adrenaline pumping, I dive to the right behind the wall. The car is coming straight at me. The wheels are in the air so the brakes and the twisting steering wheel aren't factors in stopping it. My only protection is a three tiered tire wall. The car hits the inside of the pavement on the far side of the track; I heard rubber screeching and the car breaking up as I saw the last bounce out of the corner of my eye. I already knew; You can't run away from a racecar, as they will always catch you so run perpendicular to the car. I reached my safety zone on the inside, at the same time Means slammed into the tire wall where I had been. The car created three parallel thirty foot by one inch-wide fissures on the ground. After the dirt settled, and my hearing returned, not one side of Means white and red number 52 was undamaged. The crinkled hood was hanging off the front, while the trunk dangled on the pavement dancing with the still violent vibrations; the driver's side was three feet shorter than it was before. Means was qualifying for the NASCAR race; like may NASCAR drivers not yet up to road course driving, he took a different approach to the esses, offline through turn five, approaching us entering the inside of turn six off the track on driver's right. We on the SCCA flag team were a bit rattled, but Turn Marshal Donny Anderson assisted Jimmy out of the wreck. He was not injured but didn't qualify"*

Here's Dave Marcis being attended to by the emergency crew

July 1982 $1.50

SportsCar

The Official Publication of the Sports Car Club of America

Psyching Out The Competition
Audi Unleashes Its PRO Rally Steamroller

SPORTS CAR®
Salutes
The Workers

Victor Van Tress: *"In 1981 and '82 I raced a Mustang V8 in Showroom Stock A. It had a top end edge on everybody - 10 mph faster than any car in its class plus Ford paid contingency money. But it's handling left something to desired - you still had to get through corners and I wound up closing on the people in front of me on the straight and lost them in the corners. Still finished third somehow. At one national race at Riverside, I was saw the voltage dropping and the temperature going up. Clearly had a problem and so I pulled off in Turn Seven, opened the hood, looked in there and saw that the serpentine belt tensioner had broken and it wasn't going to go anywhere. So I walked over to the flag station, having already been a corner worker before I started racing and as I approached my friend and fellow corner worker, Donny Albright, he handed me a blue flag. So I started flagging the cars as they were coming out of seven. I would give them the flag if they were being passed or holding anybody up. I think it was John Norris that actually recognized that it was me flagging in the helmet and driver suit and all. Finish the session, got the car back into the pits. I rerouted the belt and managed to get it to drive home."* Compiler's Note: Victor later raced in the Renault Cup and was SSB National Champ in 1987 in a Peugeot".

Ray Crampton: *"My first day flagging - 1971. My flag partner tells me, "Don't run away without telling him !!" Minutes later a car misses Turn 7A. He runs - "What about me, Thanks for telling me trouble was coming." Never saw the guy again after that day"*

Tim Johnson; *"Observing at turn four during a Formula Vee / 440 National Vee driver misses the apex at turn two, spins, hooks a few tires on the edge of the pavement and winds up immobile, right at the edge of the racing line at turn four. Standing Yellow at turn two and waving like crazy yellow at four. I called for a tow, which was stationed there (for once). They sneak out and Schultz and company are hooking it up for a drag and go. Just then the formula vee in his racing line, raises his hand and lifts. The following driver has no time to respond and drop kicks the lead 440 into and over the broken Vee. Schultz and company go full subterranean as the 440 goes over their heads and lands right side up on the back of the tow truck. I got a chewing out for calling for a tow ("Could you have left it there?") and the tow crew had another scary story for the beer bust."*

Pat Mumbower: *"I was working blackboard on the back straight, facing up track with my right foot barely touching the white line. Bobby Allison goes by on a qualifying lap. Gives me a move over sign; I comply. Next lap, his right side tires on the white line where my foot was. Big grin and thumbs up from Bobby."*

At the "Last lap" in 1989

Bill Morgan: *"Phil Deushane and I were flagging driver's left at the exit of turn six.*

One of the formula 440 cars had retired and parked on the inside of the turn. When the checker fell the tow crew hooked up a strap and began to pull the car back to the pits. About halfway to turn seven, it got squirrely, whipped back and forth across the road and turned sideways. The driver didn't let go of the tow strap and the car flipped over. Meanwhile, the entire field is entering turn six on the cool down lap, still carrying a lot of speed. Phil and I grabbed every flag we could carry, signaled frantically to the team on the wall at six for waving yellows, and ran onto the middle of the track waving yellows, whites, surface, and pointing to the outside of the road. Thank goodness this was before the idiotic practice of corner workers twirling flags during the cool down lap."

Tim Johnson: *"A really hot day in July - small bore D / E / F / G production cars at a national, running the long course. All running together, racing hard the whole race. I'm observing at turn seven, enjoying the show. Checker happens, yay - thumbs up, waving at drivers, great race. Suddenly, a black MGB coming off seven7 and heading up the road to turn eight comes to a stop in the middle of the track, driver slumped over hanging from his belts. Mary Anne_takes off from the turn seven7 bowl at a dead run, arms raised for the may day. Emergency shows up, extracts the driver, hooks up an IV and hauls him off to the track medical unit. The driver had passed out from heat exhaustion. He was so focused on the race and staying conscious that he didn't see the checker and thought he was still racing the other cars on the cool off lap. He knew he wasn't going to make it any further so he just switched off the power right before he collapsed."*

Steve McCarthy: *"1988 – Waltrip got nudged by Allison at the entrance to two. Waltrip, in the Tide car tried to kill the Turn 2 flag crew! Went straight at 'em and flattened the guardrail. I was Turn Marshall at turn six. Saw an ice chest shoot up in the air through the dust. We thought he'd killed people. Thankfully, no one was seriously hurt. Just a bruised knee for one. A very scary moment. John Dillon was at that flag station and wrote a song about it called "Darryl Waltrip took out my flag station but I'm still flaggin' blues.* **Compiler's Note – Listen to John Dillon's songs;"** "'ve got the Darrell Waltrip tried to kill me blues" and "Riverside is Closing" on the attached dvd

John P. M. Dillon

Songwriter (ASCAP)

I'VE GOT THE
DARRELL—WALTRIP—TOOK—OUT—MY—FLAGGING—STATION—BUT—I'M—STILL—FLAGGING BLUES

Lyrics copyright c 1988 John Dillon
Music copyright c 1988 John Dillon and Jeff Porter
February 3, 1989 version

I was working in the esses, clutching a yellow flag
I was working in the esses, holding that yellow flag
When Darrell Waltrip came to visit
(Without an invite, I might add)

He snuck in on us backwards, waiting for his ride to stop
He came sliding at us backwards and he wasn't gonna stop
And when he smashed into our barricades
He gave us flaggers quite a shock

    I've got the Darrell-Waltrip-took-out-my-flagging-station-but-I'm-still-flagging blues
    I've got the Darrell-Waltrip-took-out-my-flagging-station-but-I'm-still-flagging blues
    Although his ride is orange and white
    He left us with a pile of blues

His car is white and orange, just like a giant box of Tide
He left us some sheet metal, so he'd be lighter on one side
But why'd he have to leave us
A pile of blues on the side

    I've got the Darrell-Waltrip-took-out-my-flagging-station-but-I'm-still-flagging blues
    I've got the Darrell-Waltrip-took-out-my-flagging-station-but-I'm-still-flagging blues
    Although his ride is orange and white
    He left us with a pile of blues

Although Darrell did the driving, they say that Allison's to blame
Although Darrell did the sliding, Bobby Allison's to blame
You know it really doesn't matter
Our station's missing just the same

    I've got the Darrell-Waltrip-took-out-my-flagging-station-but-I'm-still-flagging blues
    I've got the Darrell-Waltrip-took-out-my-flagging-station-but-I'm-still-flagging blues
    Although his ride is orange and white
    He left us with a pile of blues

    I've got the Darrell-Waltrip-took-out-my-flagging-station-but-I'm-still-flagging blues
    I've got the Darrell-Waltrip-took-out-my-flagging-station-but-I'm-still-flagging blues
    Not even a ton of his sponsor's stuff
    Will clean out all these blues

Dante Puccetti: *"One IMSA practice, two flaggers and I are sitting on the Armco barrier inside turn eight during the break, before the GTO practice session. A BMW sedan approached. Driving was Elliott Forbes Robinson, the passenger was P.L. Newman, P.L. was an excellent racer and wanted appreciation for his racing skills. EFR was a highly respected racer showing Newman the line through the complicated double apex turn eight as this was Newman's first look at the course. They walked over near me and EFR said, "enter the turn on the outside, turn tight in here, jump on the binders and steer at the marshals. Momentum will carry you out to the proper line. "Wait," I said, "don't aim at me. I have enough trouble dodging cars that aren't trying to run me down."They laughed, and Newman said with a little smile as he looked around, assessing my precarious position, "You look perfectly safe here."I said, "Thanks, P.L, don't jump on the binders too late. Stop back after practice, and I'll show you how you are working through this corner.""OK, you stay safe now," Newman said. He was a shy man in his personal life and parsed his words. I knew PL was a championship racer, and I accorded him that stature. EFR and P.L. drove to the exit of eight to examine the entrance to the back straight. The next time I saw P.L. Newman, he aimed at me with his #33 Datsun 280ZX, dicing in a pack of race cars, and his concentration was phenomenal. P.L. slid through my turn lap after lap, and he never dropped a wheel off once. He and EFR finished first in class.*

Ray Crampton: *"A NASCAR race; working Turn Six - Two or three cars come together and hit the wall. We all go out to sweep up the gravel. The crowd cheers the cleanup and as we're headed back, I doff my cap and bow. The crowd erupts in cheers and laughter"*

The Sam Posey – Ron Courtney crash 1969

Tim Johnson: *"An SCCA Driver's School in the 80's - This guy had a very nice bright red Porsche 944. He was a typical first timer but eventually found his way around the track with reasonable success and all corners still on the car. Then Sunday morning racecar driver syndrome hits after a night of whatever and bench racing. The 944 guy is the first car on track in the first session and he is now a race car driver. Hard out of pre grid, hard through turn one and even harder through turn two and well beyond, missing the apex by about half a mile. Off he goes, driver's left sliding sideways through the dirt as the earth falls away from the track. Then he encounters the soft sand at the bottom of the drop and rolls at least five times. No longer a very nice car and the end of school for him. The rest of the story going was it was his girlfriend's car, she was out of town and, she didn't know he had the car!!"*

Victor Van Tress: *"One time I was working with Dick Robinson at the outside of turn six during a Formula Ford race. In those days the Formula Ford field was it was huge. There was one driver who really didn't pay much attention to whatever traffic was doing around him. No matter how many flags you showed him, he didn't acknowledge or change his pattern. After a while Dick Robinson turns to us and says hold on to me. At turn six corner workers are standing on top of the wall, elevated from the track. We didn't think much about it until all of a sudden he started to lean forward towards the track. We grabbed him and he was hanging off the side of the wall. He pulled a blue flag out and hit the driver of the Formula Ford in the head with his fist on the driver's helmet. We pulled him back up and the next time that driver came around he was way over on driver's right with his head turned way over to the left with some great big eyes wondering what the hell hit him."*

Ray Crampton: *"At a NASCAR race, the emergency vehicles stop on the parade lap and pick up the flaggers. We do a lap with them and get back to our stations – someone stole my racejacket !! Note – flaggers always carry a hunting knife to cut seat belts or harnesses if a driver is trapped. Always wondered what a driver would think, seeing someone running toward them waving a big knife.*

Chuck Weinstein flagging for the huge Lyn St. Jjames / Doc Bundy wreck in 1986

Chapter Eight - Motorcycle Racing

Motorcycle racing began at Riverside in February 1958. Joe Leonard, later to be an Indy car driver, won the 100 mile AMA Pacific Coast Championship race in front of 6500 fans on a windy day. Leonard picked up $500 for the win with Bob Sirkegian in second and Brad Andres in third

J. C. Agajanian Presents

100-MILE GOLD CUP

MOTORCYCLE ROAD RACES

Sanctioned by American

Motorcycle Association

Riverside International Motor Raceway

OFFICIAL PROGRAM

50c

Managing Director J. C. Agajanian, Eddy Kretz Jr. talk over today's racing program with lovely actress Sandra Giles, starring in picture "Daddy O'" and television series "Cab Girl" to be released soon.

Andres in Easy Motorcycle Win

RIVERSIDE (UPI)—Brad Andres of San Diego easily won the 100-mile Gold Cup Motorcycle race Sunday although the event was marred by accidents that sent four cyclists to Riverside Community Hospital.

Johnny Rich of Venice suffered a broken leg; Ross Baccarella, Lynwood, fractured spine; Greg Carroll, Los Angeles, fractured hip; and Calvin Rayborn, Imperial Beach, internal injuries. Second to Andres in the main event at Riverside Raceway was Harold Ball. Dave Lorenz was third.

Leonard Drives Motorcycle to Riverside Win

BY JACK CURNOW
Times Staff Representative
RIVERSIDE, Feb. 2—Joe

MOTORCYCLES IN RIVERSIDE RACE

RIVERSIDE, Sept. 13 — Joe Leonard, three-time United States motorcycle racing champion, heads a brilliant field of 100 riders who will compete in J. C. Agajanian's 100-mile Riverside Gold Cup motorcycle road race at Riverside Raceway tomorrow.

The big professional show, offering guaranteed minimum prize money of $2500, starts at 2:30 p.m. with qualifying at 12 noon. There will be a 50-mile race for amateur lightweight riders in the morning at 9:30 and this event has also drawn

Leonard faces a great field that includes Dick Dorrestyn, Dick Mann, George Everett, Brad Andres, Johnny Gibson, Pat McHenry, Don Hawley, Ed Kretz Jr., Bob SirKegain, Jack O'Brien, Duane Francisco, Ron Emmich, "Tiger" Johnny Rich, Tex Luce and Al Gunter.

Leonard Wins Motorcycle Race At 81 MPH

RIVERSIDE (UP)—Joe Leonard, of San Jose, averaged 81 miles an hour Sunday to capture the 100-mile Pacific Coast championship motorcycle race at Riverside Raceway.

Leonard, the nation's motorcycle racing champ for three of the last four years, led for all but

Mary McGee: I ran at Riverside three times, on a Honda CB92 in the 125cc class. That

long straight, exciting turn nine, the esses and turn six, what a thrill. Then Steve McQueen told me to get off that pansy road racing bike and come out to the desert, I went desert racing and never got back to Riverside

Compiler's Note –

Mary was the first woman to compete in motorcycle road racing and motocross in the United States. She is a member of the Trailblazers Hall of Fame and the AMA Motorcycle Hall of Fame

Mary McGee
One of the first female motocross and road racers
Inducted: 2018

Mary McGee learned to ride motorcycles in 1957 on a 200cc Triumph Tiger Cub, and later took up motorcycle road racing to try to improve her car-racing skills.

In 1963, she switched to dirt riding and rode her 1962 250cc Honda Scrambler in an AMA District 37 enduro. She started riding Baja events in 1967 and, in 1975, McGee rode the Baja 500 solo, which was one of her most memorable accomplishments as she finished ahead of several two-man teams.

Also in the 1970s, McGee worked for *Motorcyclist* magazine and joined a 24-hour endurance road race in Las Vegas, in which the magazine's team changed riders every hour on a 650cc Suzuki.

Throughout her adult life, McGee has served as an ambassador for motorcycling, whether as a pioneering female competitor or through her speaking engagements that encourage women to try motorcycling and racing.

"I would like to see more women — and more younger women — get involved. It's not whether you finish first, second or last. It's the struggle to finish. It is the journey of your life," McGee is quoted as saying.

HEAD FIRST—Preston Petty skims along track on his head after being thrown from motorcycle in Times-Mirror Grand Prix event at Riverside. Petty regained his feet, escaped with minor injuries.

Times photo by Art Rogers

Absent from Riverside in 1964 and 1965, motorcycle racing came back in a big way when Les Richter announce plans for a U.S. Grand Prix for Motorcycles

Riverside bike races set

RIVERSIDE, Calif. — Motorcycle racing, absent from Riverside International Raceway's schedule of events for the past two years, will return to the 2.6-mile road course on Sunday, May 22 for a National Open meet sanctioned by the American Cycling Association (ACA).

According to Raceway President Les Richter, the seven-race card will serve as a verification event to certify Riverside's circuit for a U.S. Grand Prix for motorcycles later this year.

"We've already applied to the FIM in Geneva, Switzerland, for the sanction," Richter explained. "According to procedure, any course requesting a Grand Prix race for motorcyles must first hold a national race under supervision of an FIM representative, in order to obtain the necessary certification."

Richter added that the outlook for obtaining FIM blessing is very good and if the sanction is granted, will mark the first time a U.S. Grand Prix for motorcycles has been held on the West Coast.

Motorcycles Back at Riverside Track

Motorcycle racing, absent from Riverside International Raceway's schedule of events for the past two years, will return to the 2.6-mile road course today for a national open meet sanctioned by the American Cycling Associ-

American Federation of Motorcyclists Inc. 1954-1975

Los Angeles Chapter

AFM

OFFICIAL 1975 ROAD RACING PROGRAM

JAWS

MULHOLLAND SHOCK ABSORBER CHALLENGE CUP

Riverside Raceway, California
October 2nd/3rd, 1976

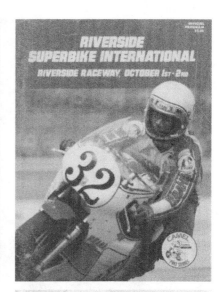

RIVERSIDE SUPERBIKE INTERNATIONAL

RIVERSIDE RACEWAY, OCTOBER 1st - 2nd

AMERICAN FEDERATION OF MOTORCYCLISTS, INC.

AFM

LOS ANGELES CHAPTER

ROAD RACES

RIVERSIDE
INTERNATIONAL RACEWAY
NOVEMBER 12, 1978

A.R.R.A. Presents
RIVERSIDE
INT'L RACEWAY
Program

THE FINAL ROAD RACE OF THE 70's DEC·2·1979

Budweiser Six-Hour

AMERICA'S PREMIER MOTORCYCLE ENDURANCE RACE

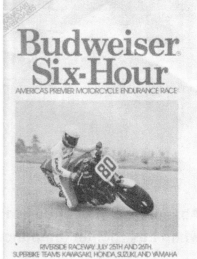

RIVERSIDE RACEWAY JULY 25TH AND 26TH.
SUPERBIKE TEAMS KAWASAKI, HONDA, SUZUKI AND YAMAHA

Budweiser Grand Prix
AMERICA'S PREMIER MOTORCYCLE ENDURANCE RACE

BUDWEISER SUPERBIKE

RIVERSIDE · APRIL 14-15
PORTLAND · AUGUST 11-22
WILLOW SPRINGS · SEPT 15-16

KERKER   BELL   LOCKHART   AMA
ND SPARK PLUGS   Kawasaki

Practice for the 1977 AFM race

Lawson loses locals at AFM Riverside RR

By Lori Tyson

RIVERSIDE, CA, FEB. 21
1981 AMA Superbike Champion Eddie Lawson took one of a pair of KR500 GP bikes, brought to the track by Kawasaki to the Formula One victory at the American Federation of Motorcyclists' race at Riverside International Raceway. But, as Lawson was not running for points, John Glover on the Warland Engineering Superbike took home the trophy, after keeping up with Lawson pretty well, considering the difference in the Open Stock Production clash with Statum finally taking the win. Both men were riding Suzukis and rode a good hard race, with Statum grabbing the lead for good on lap seven of the eight lap race.

Champion Motorcycles' Lee Fleming, back on a big bike again, captured the number three spot.

In the 450cc Modified Production money race, Ron Hlavka took the holeshot and held on to take the trophy and the cash. Dale Alexander and Clinton Whitehouse had quite a battle for second, with Alexander the winner.

All of the GP races had an interesting change this time — a European bump start — and the 250cc GP was one that had everyone practicing in the pits for the start. Everyone, that

THE GRADUATES — Richard Lovell and Keith Code (right) pose with students who graduated from their motorcycle racing school in Riverside. Duo teach riders how to road race on tracks.

MOTORCYCLE RACING SCHOOL

For $110, They Put You in Driver's Seat

By TOM HAMILTON
Times Staff Writer

RIVERSIDE — Ever wonder what it would be like racing a motorcycle on Riverside Raceway's 2.5-mile course? Perhaps envisioned yourself as a road racing champion but didn't have the money to try?

For all the frustrated Kenny Roberts in the world, former pro racer Keith Code and his partner, Richard Lovell, have just what a hopeful road racer is looking for — the California Superbike School.

For $110, an aspiring rider can race a new Kawasaki KZ550 for 40 miles at Riverside. Even the leathers and helmets are supplied.

Code and Lovell, who started the school last May, have taught 100 students. The duo own 10 identically prepared superbikes and have invested $12,000 for the school's equipment.

Code, who campaigned on the American Motorcycle Assn. superbike series from 1977-79, came up with the idea four years ago and finally convinced Kawasaki it would work.

Lovell, who raced 250 Grand Prix bikes, was an instructor at a similar school in England — the British Motorcycle Racing School. He estimates in 13 years about 2,000 students have gone through the course in England.

"We haven't heard a bad word about the school from any of the students who have ridden here," said Lovell, 27, of Manhattan Beach. "In fact, we've had five stu-

will I be able to announce these races, I'll be able to ride in them."

Robert Kutz is a Laguna Beach lawyer who says, "I always wanted to try something like this. When you stop to think about it, this is a remarkable program. I think they give you too much for your money."

One by one Code goes over the time charts. Many of the students broke the two-minute barrier on the 2.5-mile course. Kenny Roberts owns the track record at 1:27.

Keith Code's Super Bike School was created in 1976. Here's Keith with Superbike Champ Eddie Lawson in 1982

Here's the staff in 1981 - Wayne Rainey, Eddie Lawson, Jimmy Felice, Bubba Shobert, Ronnie Jones, Steve Storz, Don Shoemaker and school crew on the front straight.

The Orange County Motorcycle Club put on the Great Bear Grand Prix at Riverside from 1973 to 1979 as a successor to the Elsinore Grand Prix. Viewfinders Motorcycle Club then took over until xxx. Conditions over the twelve mile combined pavement and dirt course sometimes included rain, hail, cold or heat, depending the April weather.

Paul Dube; *"The first time I saw Riverside Raceway was also my first motorcycle experience at the Riverside Grand Prix. I had seen pictures but actually being there was an entirely different experience and racing in front of thousands of race fans instead of maybe a hundred or so was overwhelming but also exciting. I rode my Suzuki 125 motocross bike. To prepare the bike I first balanced the tires using fishing weights. Next I put in a fatter main jet and changed the gearing to the tallest gear the bike would pull. The course was run backwards. You entered onto the asphalt somewhere around turn six and ran wide open down through the esses and halfway through turn nine before turning back down into the dirt sections. I had never ridden that fast on that little bike before; I just tucked in like the flat track riders do down the straight a ways. I remember sitting up just before turning down in turn nine on the first lap and the wind almost pulled me off the handlebars, I held on tighter from then on."*

Ron Williams:*"At the 1974 Great Bear - I remember making the mistake of taking my foot of the pegs to stretch my leg a bit on the paved straight. My leg slammed back and I had to wait until I slowed down going back onto the dirt to get my foot back on the peg. Huge amount of wind at over 100 mph".*

Rick Guinn

SCHEDULE OF EVENTS

FRIDAY, MARCH 22, 1974

6 pm to 11 impound open for Saturday races

SATURDAY, MARCH 23

7:30 am	Pits open
8:00 am	Riders' Meeting
8:15	Impound opens for morning race
8:30	Bikes leave impound for starting line
9:00 am	National Anthem
9:05	Morning race begins
	250 Novice
	175 Novice
	125 Novice
	100 Novice
	All Powder Puff
12:15 pm	Impound opens for afternoon race
12:30 pm	Bikes leave impound for starting line
1:00 pm	Afternoon race begins
	250 Amateur
	175 Expert
	175 Amateur
	125 Expert
	125 Amateur
	100 Expert
	100 Amateur
	175 Unclassified
	125 Unclassified
	100 Unclassified
6 pm to 11 pm	Impound open for Sunday races
7 pm to 10 pm	Street Dance

SUNDAY, MARCH 24

7:30 am	Pits open
8:00 am	Riders' Meeting
8:15 am	Impound open for morning race
8:30 am	Bikes leave impound for starting line
9:00 am	National Anthem
9:05 am	Morning race begins
	Open Old Timer
	500 Old Timer
	250 Old Timer
	175 Old Timer
	125 Old Timer
	100 Old Timer
	Old Timers' Association
	Heavyweight Hacks
	Lightweight Hacks
12:15 pm	Impound open for afternoon race
12:30 pm	Bikes leave impound for starting line
1:00 pm	Afternoon race begins
	Open Expert
	Open Amateur
	Open Novice
	500 Expert
	500 Amateur
	500 Novice
	Open Unclassified
	500 Unclassified
	250 Unclassified

POPULAR CYCLING PHOTO

Steve Webb: *"Right off the start, wide open through turn nine, and I look back over my shoulder and lose all my tear offs before we even hit the dirt – lesson; better goggles !!"*

Chris Real: *"I signed up late and was in the second to last row. I raced hard and passed everyone in my 175cc class. I had a guy chasing me the entire race, who I thought was on a 250. On the last half of a lap we were side by side. He passed me 100 feet from the finish as I backed off as I had smashed my hand on a course marker barrel. When we shook hands I saw that he was on a 175 and had started in the row behind me! Lost first by 15 seconds. The lesson was clear, race to the end of the race."*

Paul Dube: *"In 1974, at the OCMC Great Bear Gran Prix, I rode a 250 square barrel Maico for the Outpost Café owned by a gentleman by the name George Newton. There was a lot less asphalt this time and more of a stadium type layout with jumps at the start/finish line."*

Don Chalmers

Herbert Brownell; *"I had the flu for several days before the race but rode anyway. Around the halfway mark, the bike fouled a plug. When I got off the bike, the heat overwhelmed me and I collapsed and passed out for a few moments. Changed the plug, rode back to the pits and retired; exhausted and totally worn out. But, still great fun, an exciting event that combined the dirt and asphalt !!"*

Cathy Riddle: *"I started riding enduro's at 11, then found myself wanting to just go*

faster started to hare and hounds. At 14 I discovered my high school had a motocross team so I had to learn how to corner, which served me well in the grand prix's. Two years later I won my class riding against a a girl on a 500cc bike. She passed me on the straights, but I outcornered her and pulled out the win. I think we both lapped all other racers.

Trophied a few times at Riverside. At my first Grat Bear, I endo'd near the finish and was taken to the pits by ambulance to my waiting parents with the bike in about twenty pieces. When I won my class , I got my trophy and the girl who won the wet t-shirt contest got a trip to Hawaii. I was bummed. I was only 16 so I didn't yet know much about the real world !!

As a teenaged racer, I didn't recognize any "women's" issues, just thought it was fun to beat the guys in the 250 open class). Being a girl racer had some benefits; a

mutual friend fixed me up with Larry Roessler before he was a star. I chased him around the track all afternoon; he was too fast and and we never really hit it off. A middle school classmate teased me, saying he was faster then I beat him in a high school motocross.. There was also an incident of "boy hates being beaten by a girl" when a dude intentionally crashed into me a few yards off the start line. I wrapped my gear shift around the foot peg when I and the bike slid uphill for some distance, lost most of the skin off my right side and upper back. It was on my sixteenth birthday and I was starting my new job that same night as a hostess at the restaurant whose jersey I wore. It was painful, but I made it to the job. That was also the day two local Yamaha shops offered to partially sponsor me; offering free mechanical and local restaurant also provided some monetary support in return for wearing a jersey they made for me with the restaurant's logo. I had to alternate wearing the restaurant's jersey and Yamaha jerseys at all local races.

I was an amateur and somewhat competitive for only about four years. Those years taught me so much - I learned to dig deep in order to accomplish a goal. I always rode both loops which could be exhausting, especially after a crash – or if it took many attempts to take a tough hill. Sometimes I wanted to cry or quit because it was hot and I was hurting. But waiting for the sweep crew wasn't an option for my ego. That resilience has helped me get through some challenging times in my life."

Chris Real: *"Riverside International Raceway has very special memories for me as I have raced and crewed on many vehicles there. In 1978 I ran the off-road motorcycle Grand Prix at Riverside. The race was part of the AMA District 37 desert schedule, and was put on by the Viewfinders Motorcycle Club, one of the best clubs in Southern California off-road racing.*

In off-road Grand Prix races the starting procedure is to usually have about 10 riders on a row, and the riders are started at intervals, usually about 10 - 30 seconds apart.

Often several classes race at the same time, so the "wave" starts allows everyone to have the chance to race each other in their class. In the event you are a late sign up, your starting row is in the back, but the scoring is on time.

The paved and dirt course had numerous obstacles, water in places, big jumps, high speed roads and we raced close to fences, hay bales, pickets and barrels. I signed up late and started in the next to last row. Since racing on pavement was not new to me the paved sections of the road racing course were extremely fun and I had a new, fast motorcycle, my 1978 Yamaha 175cc IT that had some serious modifications done.

I raced hard and had good fortune in not getting stuck anyplace and I passed everyone in my class. I had a good race with another rider who I thought was on a 250cc bike and not in my class for several laps and he chased me the entire race. I could always hear him behind me and occasionally he would make a pass. It was really good fun racing that close for an hour plus. On the last lap I hit a course marking barrel and wacked my hand hard and had to back off. I kept going but my competitor gained on me and passed me about 100 feet from the finish line.

When we stopped in the finish area, we got our finisher pins and shook hands while laughing. That's when I noticed that his bike was not a 250cc and he was riding a 175cc bike in my class and he had started in the row behind me! I had lost P1 because I backed off and he had just a slightly better day than I did. I have kept the trophy in my garage as a reminder that good fair competition is the best, even if sometimes you don't win. The lesson learned that day was clear, race to the end of the race and be proud of playing fair and hard."

1979 AFM Race

Kevin Bracken: *"That's me (ugly brown leathers) almost center of the pic. A very early '79 race because of the white front fairing and SS front fender on my Ducati Darmah. My memory says it was '79 AFM 3rd race of season. I'd crashed out at Sears three weeks prior in practice at turn two and broke my right collarbone. I crashed out at this race by dragging my right header exiting seven. No injury that time. Didn't crash for a long time after that!"*

David Gibbons: *"Months after this we got to go straight from this first right to the far north east corner and, man that was a long straight leading to the left that had no name or number. As I recalled I then stayed to the left to set up for the chunky banked right 180 to the front straight. I got to ride that long straight on an open bike one weekend and man, that little left at the end just before the banked right. That 180 was for sure exciting and at what, a buck 65? It deserved a number."*

Murray Kapko and dad – 1980

Dennis Tipton: *"Riding my Husky 500XC, I was near the end of my ninth ten mile lap, worn out and not real excited about going another lap when I saw behind me, in the switchbacks, the leaders on their last lap. I slowed down just enough to be the first guy to do nine laps instead of the last guy to do ten. Only time I was happy about wimping out !!"*

Roeseler captures Great Bear GP

Sun news services

RIVERSIDE — Larry Roeseler of Fontana stopped in the pits to throw his dislocated knee back in place and went on to win the main event of the Great Bear Grand Prix Sunday at Riverside International Raceway.

The veteran desert racer gave up the lead to race favorite Bob Balentine of Mojave when Roeseler crashed and aggravated an old injury on the third lap.

The pit stop dropped Roeseler back to fourth in the 96-mile motorcycle race but he regained the lead as Balentine dropped out on the fourth lap of the eight-lap race around a 12-mile, 70-turn obstacle course.

Roeseler, riding a 500cc Husqvarna, averaged 36.5 miles an hour.

Max Eddy of Barstow finished fourth overall in the main event and also captured the 250cc expert title on his Husqvarna. Two other Barstow riders made the top ten in the main — Rodney Brand placing fifth overall on a 250 Kawasaki and Troy Hallis seventh on a 500 Suzuki.

Steve Harper of Crestline, averaging 32.542 mph, beat out Ron Monreal of San Bernardino for the novice title. Both were on 500 Yamahas. Alson in the novice event, Edward Shinault (500 Husky) placed sixth and Chino's Greg Zitterkopf (250 Maico) took eighth.

Terry Tingle, 35, of Torrance was listed in good condition at Riverside Community Hospital, where he was treated for broken ribs and possible internal injuries. Tingle was struck by a motorcycle when he fell during the novice race.

Officials of the sponsoring Orange County Motorcycle Club said that the world's largest motor racing entry list was down more than 20 per cent this year, with a total of 1,620 riders competing in the two-day event.

Some Action at the 1979 Great Bear Grand Prix

Scott Dinger: *"In 1975 a buddy from work named Power Johnson told me that once you race Great Bear you will race it every year. I had a brand new Yamaha MX250 Mono, put a desert tank on it. I'm a novice at the time and unsure about the jump so I take the mud hole route. As soon as my plug wire got wet the bike stalled and I dropped it in the deepest part of the water hole. I had to wring the foam filters out then put the bike upside down on it's seat and handlebars, pull the plug and pump muddy water out of my cylinder. I finished the race running a few laps down but always went back. Those were good times."*

Dan Clark: *"Crashed near the start, injured. But Rick Sieman passed me on his Maico, and I got off my ass and went and chased him down. Couldn't lose to Super Hunky. Never would have heard the end to it."*

(Above) Shown on his 175cc bike, Larry Roeseler won two classes. (Inset) Balentine goes around the ailing Roeseler.

Great Bear GP: Roeseler 2, Balentine 1, Harper 1

Robbie Zela: *"What a great event - it was an early morning hot engine start in rows of fifteen. And, if you were past row five you probably got to race buzzed off the exhaust fumes that seemed to be mostly nitromethane. - First lap, I was all alone, not* *knowing if I was going fast enough. The guys started passing me and I turned it up a bit"*

Steve Davies

In 1980 The Viewfinders Motorcycle Club took over the running of the Great Bear Brand Prix, renaming it the Viewfinders Grand Prix,

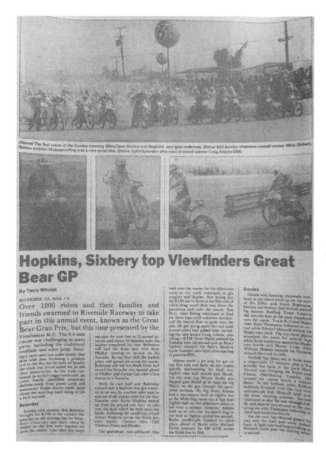 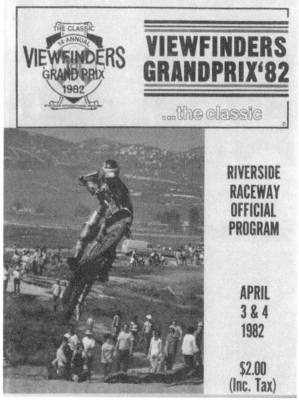

1983 Super Bike 100 - Mike Baldwin won on a Honda Interceptor 750 in front of a crowd of 4800 on a windy dusty day. Wayne Rainey was second on a Kawasaki, Fred Merkel third also on a Honda with Wes Cooley in fourth on a Kawasaki.

Wayne Rainey

Wes Cooley

Don Emde: *"Riverside was my favorite track and the track was good to me, from 1966 thru 1973, I never crashed there once. My first roadrace was at Riverside in 1966. I had been racing some amateur scrambles races in the San Diego area where my parents had a motorcycle shop. A mechanic who worked there had been racing in So Cal club races and as a race at Riverside was approaching, he told my dad that if it was okay, we had a 250cc Harley-Davidson Sprint roadracer that my older brother had raced parked in the back room. He told my dad that he could get it running and take me to the race. So it was all set up. We got the bike running and I went to Riverside. I didn't know anything about roadracing except for what I had read in Cycle World and other magazines, so I took it easy and got thru a couple of practice sessions trouble free. I guess since I was new, I was lined up on the back row for the 250cc race and off I went when the race started. Unfortunately, the Harley Sprint only lasted a couple of laps until the connecting rod broke. I had to get towed*

in on a trailer and my day was done. I didn't really get going fast enough to have any real impressions about the Riverside track, other than when I got home, I knew I wanted to go again. But we didn't have another roadrace bike, so the rest of the year I just did scrambles racing.

I got a big break for in 1969 when Mel Dinesen, a Yamaha dealer from Bakersfield, offered to sponsor me in roadracing. So now as I began my fourth year in roadracing, I was racing all those ACA and AFM races entered in four classes at each race. Mel brought a 100cc Hodaka converted for roadracing, a 250cc and 350cc Yamaha GP style racer and a 350cc street bike for the Production class races. We won a lot of races everywhere, including Riverside. One of my best memories was pushing myself to go faster and faster through the left hander and into and through the esses at Riverside. As I approached the start/finish line to get over to the right side of the track, I'd stay full throttle thru that turn and into the esses I would just let off long enough for a quick downshift, then full throttle while leaning back and forth thru the lefts and rights. No section of any racetrack I ever raced was ever more fun than that for me."

Compiler's Note - Born into a motorcycle family (His father won at Daytona in 1948 and owned a motorcycle dealership), Don had a great racing career including an AFM championship and a win at Daytona in 1972. A member of the AMA Motorcycle Hall of Fame, he went on to publish a book on the history of the Daytona 200, as well as a couple of others and became the publisher of Motorcycle Dealer News. Find more information at www.emdebooks.com

Chapter Nine - The Movies, TV and Ads

Due to its proximity to the Southern California entertainment industry, Riverside was a frequent filming location for Hollywood movies, television shows and commercials. Every ad agency had Riverside on their speed dial for photo shoots

We didn't include every film or TV show as there are just too many but selected the ones you might find most interesting. In case you missed it, there are two great films on the Volume One DVD; "The Racing Scene" and Bruce Kessler's "Sound of Speed"

Steve McQueen posed for photos and drove this Chuck Jones owned Lola T-70 in a practice session but never raced it. It was driven by Skip Hudson in the USRRC series.

1959 - On the Beach

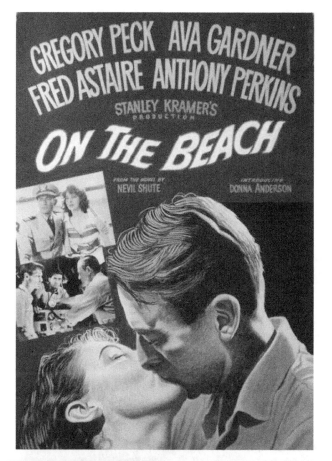

Gregory Peck, Ava Gardner, Fred Astaire and Anthony Perkins star in this apocalyptic vision of the aftermath of nuclear war

Watch the trailer on the attached DVD

1959 - Road Racers

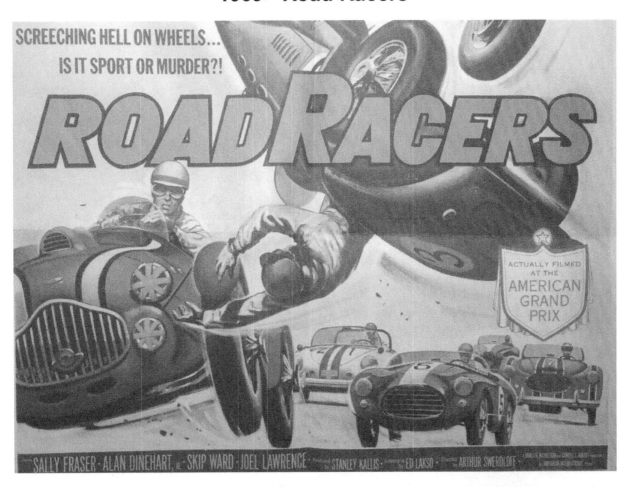

The father of a racecar driver blames him for a death on the track, disowns him, and sponsors a rival racer. Stars include Joel Lawrence and Sally Fraser. Cars seen in the film include Max Balchowski's Ol' Yeller, a Kurtis 500X, a Ferrari 412 and many more.

Watch the trailer on the attached DVD

1964 - The Killers

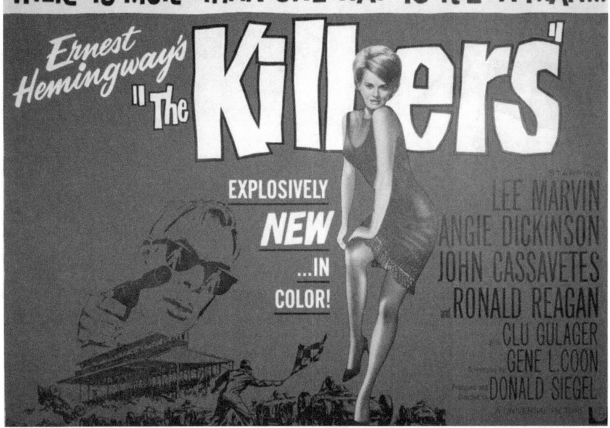

Lee Marvin as hitman Charlie Strom and Angie Dickinson as his sometime girlfriend kIll a former racecar driver who was once involved in a mail truck robbery. Ronald Reagan plays the role of former gangster, now businessman Jack Browning

Watch the trailer on the attached DVD

1964 - Viva Las Vegas

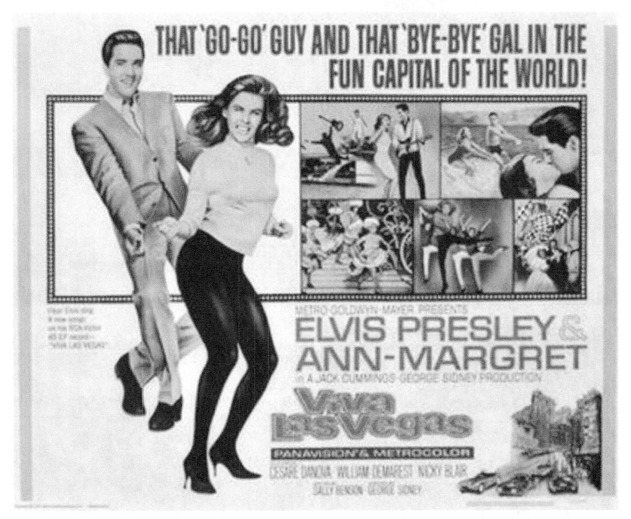

Elvis Presley stars as a racecar driver in Las Vegas, working as waiter to pay for his new engine. He competes with Ferrari racer Count Elmo for the attention of Ann Margret. This is considered to be one of Elvis' best films. Most of it was filmed in Vegas, but there was some time spent at Riverside and also in Dan Blocker's garage.

Watch the trailer on the attached DVD

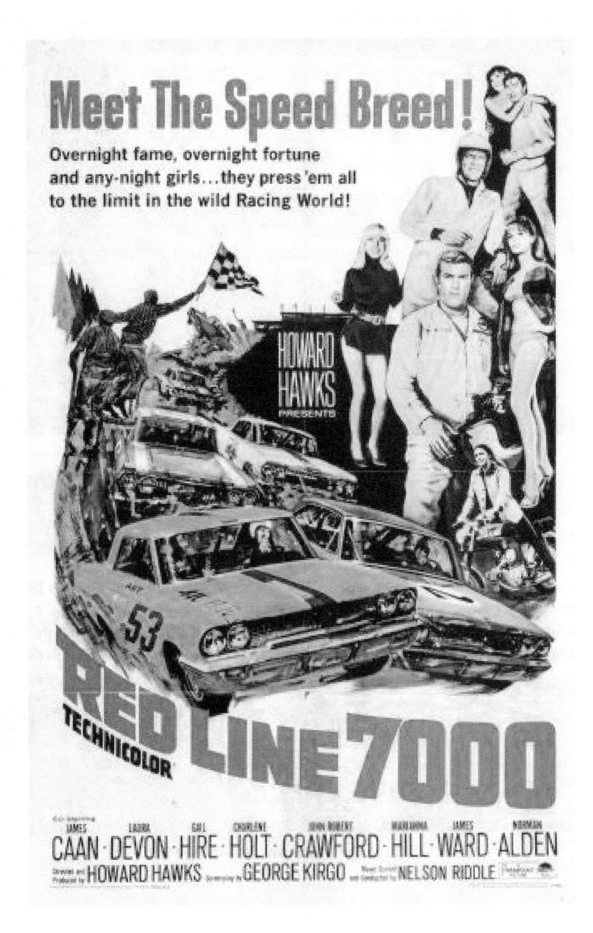

James Caan and Laura Devon star in this story of three racing drivers and three women, who constantly have to worry for the lives of their boyfriends. Not much Riverside is shown here but we can ask the assistant director, Bruce Kessler, who raced a lot at Riverside

Watch the trailer on the attached DVD

1966 - Spinout

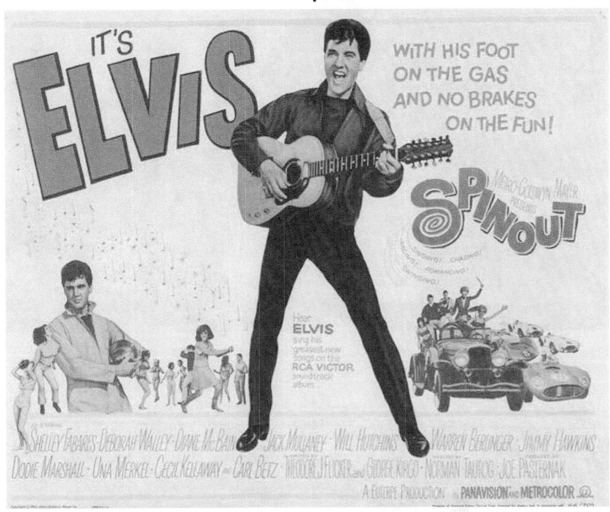

Elvis, as band singer / racecar driver Mike McCoy, must choose between marrying a beautiful rich girl, Shelley Fabares, and driving her father's car in a prestigious race.

Watch the trailer on the attached DVD

1966 - Grand Prix

James Garner stars as driver Pete Aron, world class racer who is dropped from the team, finds another team and is having an affair with his ex teammates wife. Directed by John Frankenheimer, it ranks near the top, although dated, in racing films

Watch the trailer on the attached DVD

Fabian and Track Announcer Sandy Reed

Fabian, as stock car racer Tommy Callahan, is forced to join Pete Madsen's thrill circus after his blackouts cause a fatal accident that gets him thrown off the circuit. He shows Pete's daughter Francie, Annette Funichello and her boyfriend, Eddie Sands, everything he knows about driving. They become fierce rivals after Eddie wins the first time out.

1968 - The Love Bug

Dean Jones, as racecar driver Jim Douglas, is reduced to driving in demolition derbies. After seeing a used car lot abusing a 1963 Volkswagen. Jim defends the VW and it leaves the used car lot and parks itself in front of Jim's house. After a number of actually funny happenings, they go on to win a race. There are a lot of interesting cars in the film, a Ferrari 250GT Berlinetta, a Lamborghini 400 GT and a 1963 Apollo GT, among many others. This was the second highest grossing film of 1969, earning 51.2 million dollars. Later productions; "Herbie Rides Again", "Herbie Goes to Monte Carlo" and "Herbie Goes Bananas" were not filmed at Riverside.

View the trailer on the attached DVD

1969 - Winning

HEAD OVER WHEELS—Without benefit of a stunt man, actor Paul Newman flips twice in a stock car during filming at Riverside Raceway. And just like the script called for, Newman crawled away unhurt.

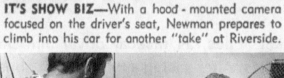

Paul Newman is Frank Capua, a rising star on the race circuit who dreams of winning the big one, the Indianapolis 500. He meets Elora, played by Joanne Woodward, but neglects her to focus on racing She has an affair with his rival, Luther Erding, played by Robert Wagner. Frank wins the Indy 500. A number of <u>racecar</u> drivers and people associated with racing appear in the film, including <u>Bobby Unser</u>, Charlie Hayes, <u>Tony Hulman</u>, <u>Bobby Grim</u>, <u>Dan Gurney</u>, <u>Roger McCluskey</u>, and <u>Bruce Walkup</u>. Compilers Note: I drove in a filming session the day after the Road America 500 USRRC race and was paid $300.

Watch the trailer on the attached DVD

1978 - Good Guys Wear Black

Chuck Norris, Anne Francis and James Franciscus star in this Viet Nam veteran conspiracy film. An ex-US Army commando must find the reason why his comrades from his unit are being systematically murdered before he is next.

Watch the trailer on the attached DVD

1973 - Stacey

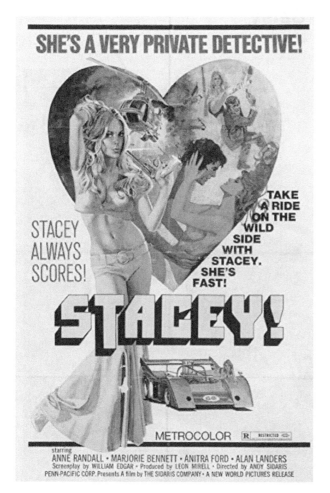

Former Playmate Anne Randall stars as Stacey, the center fold private eye and race car driver, is hired by an ageing millionaress to spy on her heirs. She is, among other things, cornered in a race track gun battle and chased by a helicopter. Can Am driver Lothar Motschenbacher supplied his McLaren for this film, produced by Andy Sidaris, who also produced James Garner's "The Racing Scene" found on the DVD that accompanies Volume One.

1978 - The Betsy

An auto tycoon, played by Laurence Olivier, to spite his son, Robert Duvall, hires outsider, racecar driver Tommy Lee Jones, to develop a ground breaking new car for the family owned manufacturer. Jones, as Angelo Perino, has just recovered from a serious crash and realizes his racing career is finished. Described by reviewers as a trashy soap opera filled with lots of sex, cars and greed.

View the trailer on the attached DVD

1981 - Circuit

A behind the scenes semi - documentary covering the 1981 Can Am season. Stars a number of team owners including Paul Newman and Carl Haas and drivers Teo Fabi, Danny Sullivan, Al Holbert and Geoff Brabham.

No trailer was available buy you can view the film on youtube - https://youtu.be/kidFHfSJhd4

TV Shows

1961 - Route 66 "The Quick and the Dead" episode

Tod and Buz are in California for the Riverside Grand Prix auto races. Tod decides to enter in the Stock Class. Doing well in practice, he is asked to drive in the main event. Tod drawn into the conflict between a veteran driver, his daughter and second wife,

1979 - Chips "Drive Lady Drive" episode

Ponch, Jon, Bear, and Lenny go to Palma Vista. While there, they help an orphaned 10 year old girl find a new home, arrest a councilman's two sons and city manager's daughter on some serious traffic charges, and break up a hijacking ring. Ponch falls for a lady race car driver, but loses out in the end.

1985 - Knight Rider "Knight Racer" episode

Michael Knight helps friend who is involved in racing and thinks his team is being sabotaged. Knight goes undercover as a driver and finds himself in the sights of a hitman.

1979 - Rockford Files "Never Send a Boy To Do a Man's Job" episode

James Garner, as Jim Rockford, assembles a cast of con artists to recover a printing plant that a swindler has stolen from new detective, Richie Brockelman.

1984 - Simon and Simon "What Goes Around" episode

The brothers are employed by racecar driver Dwayne Bellwood after three of his Indy cars are sabotaged.

1976 - Gemini Man "Buffalo Bill Rides Again"

A renegade physicist, played by Ed Nelson) plans to test his device to explode a rare metal on a race car driven by Sam's friend, played by Jim Stafford. Ray Elder's car is used in the film. -

1976 - Mystery Science Theater "Riding with Death" episode

A government agent with the ability to become invisible tracks down enemies with the help of a truck driver / racer. This utilizes part of the "Buffalo Bill" footage

Chapter Ten - The End

The last NASCAR race was the June 1988 Budweiser 400, won by Rusty Wallace, followed by the August SCORE Off Road event. And then throughout 1989, Cal Club Region SCCA held a half dozen "last race at riverside" races on shortened versions of the course and the Skip Barber School did the same. Attendees at the school reported that they drove down the pit lane, made a tight turn on a new patch of road that led to turn nine. The rest of the course hasd already been bulldozed

Fritz Duda, who was part of a group that bought into the track in 1973, announced in 1984 that the track would close in 1986, being squeezed out by urban growth. Relocation plans included a site in Valencia, another in Corona or Valencia as well as one near Glen Helen, None of these seemed realistic at the time. Final closing for the construction of the Towngate Mall on the racetrack site took place in early 1990.

Duda announced this in 1983

Inland Empire is starter in new raceway-site race

By RICK BURNHAM
Sun Business Editor

LOS ANGELES — It appears the Inland Empire stands a good chance of keeping professional racing — and the millions in revenue generated — within its boundaries, even though officials said Wednesday they will close Riverside International Raceway and may relocate elsewhere in Southern California within three to five years.

Speedway officials say continued urban growth (residential and commercial development) near the existing track and the lack of quality hotels, motels and restaurants are major reasons for the move.

It's no secret that the raceway's existing

analysis

500-acre site is surrounded by a growing number of residential and commercial projects, including four planned shopping centers.

And it's been rumored for months that the raceway property may be more profitable if sold for those types of development than if continued as a speedway.

A year-long study done for the speedway by Christensen & Wallace Inc., of Oceanside, claims the raceway has a total economic impact of between $82 million

and $137 million in the San Bernardino-Riverside-Pomona area — about $34 million of that directly and including between $2 million and $3 million in various local taxes.

Raceway officials will take the next 12 to 18 months to look at sites from Santa Barbara to San Diego, including San Bernardino and Riverside counties, chairman Fritz Duda said Wednesday.

But based on the economic facts of life — especially the projected costs for property acquisition — San Bernardino and Riverside counties stand a good chance for the new site.

Duda says the estimated cost for building the proposed motorsports and auto-

motive technical center facility — including a 1½- to 2-mile super speedway oval, international road course, dragstrip, and an industrial and auto testing complex — is between $12 million and $15 million, depending on the actual site chosen.

Duda said after a press conference Wednesday that $4 million to $5 million of the total represents the estimated cost to buy the 300 to 400 acres necessary for such a development, assuming no public assistance in the form of financing, tax breaks, or an outright gift.

That means spending roughly between

(Please see Raceway, B-5)

1984

Raceway will move to Corona site

By MARK LUNDAHL
Sun Staff Writer

RIVERSIDE — Riverside International Raceway's majority owner made it official Friday, announcing plans to relocate the racing complex to the Prado Dam recreational area near Corona with an opening tentatively scheduled for April 1987.

The announcement was a blow for San Bernardino County officials who had hoped to lure the raceway to the Sycamore Flats area near Glen Helen Regional Park

rector Gary Patton said Friday that San Bernardino County will continue to push hard for a racing facility there.

Riverside International Raceway majority owner Fritz Duda shared a podium with Riverside County supervisors and Corona city officials in announcing the plans for a 700-acre, multi-purpose regional park and its centerpiece — an oval auto speedway and road course.

Riverside County officials said they plan to also include camp-

courts and equestrian riding areas within the park, just east of the Prado Dam spillway, north of Highway 91.

The project is subject to approval by the Army Corps of Engineers, which owns 600 acres of the proposed park land and currently leases it to the city of Corona. Officials said they must also acquire another 100 acres of private land.

Officials said they hope to clear all legal and environmental hurdles by 1985, begin construction by 1986 and hold the first

Glen Helen site remains in the running for RIR relocation

The world soon may hear Riverside International Raceway's September song.

Early this summer, Dan Greenwood, president of Riverside Raceway, said a decision on a relocation site for the Edgemont plant, which closes the end of the 1986 season, would probably be made by the end of this month.

As the days dwindle down to a precious few, Greenwood is still looking at three possible locations. Sycamore Flats in Glen Helen Regional Park is still on the list, as is the Alber Hill site near Lake Elsi-

Motor racing

Katie Castator

closure of RIR without relocation. This interview was the latest.

To us doubters, he replied: "If we aren't still interested, then I'm wasting 80 percent of my time. I talked to Mr. (Fritz) Duda (RIR owner) at 7 our time last night. As of that discussion, he seriously wants to be in the business. I just sometimes wish we were a baseball franchise where some town builds the facility and gives it to you."

Obviously, theirs is to make the decision. Ours is to wait on pins and needles.

that's what everybody tells me. So I'll probably crash in turn one."

He'd scraped the concrete retaining wall in turn one that day.

Explained Foyt: "The car kept wanting the rear end to come around all day. We couldn't get enough sidebite no matter what we did, so I figured I'd leave my foot in it and see what it'd do."

Foyt obviously did not heed Cale Yarborough's warning that if you make a mistake at Darlington, you're gonna hit something.

"But I'm a rookie, I'm allowed

for the season championship. The season concludes Sept. 28 with the decisive races for limited, streets and Figure 8.

Randy Becker of Highland leads Dan Clark of Lake Matthews by 70 points in the super modified division. In streets, John Hillbish of Ontario has a 20-point edge over Jon Hauser of Hesperia. Dennis Artoff of Highland leads Tom Nunn of San Bernardino by 90 points in ponies. The limited leader is John Menschner of Rialto, who is 110 points ahead of Kevin

Croswell of Apple Valle ure 8, John Lathrop of has 20 points on David F erside. The lead in that has changed the last f they've run.

Special post-season planned for October, wit Lite 100 coming up Oct. State championships wee 12-13. All championships go to the Anderson Scho retarded but trainable

Riverside Raceway Considers Move to Valencia

Negotiations between Newhall Land and Farming Co. and Riverside International Raceway officials may bring a combined oval-road track and drag strip to the Valencia area by the end of the year.

The now-defunct Indian Dunes off-road facility is one of two sites near Valencia that Riverside officials are considering leasing. Both sites are owned by Newhall Land and Farming.

"We've talked in generalities," said Daniel Greenwood, president of Riverside International Raceway. "The negotiations have been very preliminary. By next week we'll have a clearer idea as to whether it will go forward."

Michelle Pappalardo from Burroughs.

The City lineup: Karen Walker and Teri Rupe, El Camino Vincent, Chatsworth; Stephanie Remington and Diane Kennedy; Michelle Van Kirk and Kim Green, Cleveland Borrego, Monroe; Diane Lopez and Katrina Garcia, Syl Hernandez and Rosi Castro, Bell; Lisa Bautista and Sus Banning, and Lisa Cantor from North Hollywood.

Information: (818) 341-7314 or (818) 843-2150 ext. 170.

■ Robinson Leads Going Into Mesa Marin

TownGate to Become Big Mixed-Use Center

Even if TownGate never gets its 1.25-million-square-foot regional mall, it will still be one of the largest real estate ventures ever undertaken in the Inland Empire.

Phase 1, which begins next spring, calls for the construction of a 460,000-square-foot commercial center. According to the developer, Dallas-based Fritz Duda Co., anchor tenants will include an Ole's home-improvement store, a Mervyn's department store and an Edwards eight-plex theater.

Other tenants are expected to

include a day-care facility, senior citizens' activity area, library and church site.

Adjacent to the town center is a 25-acre school site. The school will serve grade-schoolers and junior high students living in TownGate and nearby areas.

The 12.6-acre neighborhood park will include extensive recreational facilities, including an Olympic-size pool.

Civic Center Buildings

TownGate also includes a 26-

Inside: Complete National And Regional Action From Memorial Day Races

CALIFORNIA
SPORTS CAR
CLUB NEWS   JULY 1988 $1.50

THREE OF A KIND
Hunter Dealt FF Royal Flush

last lap of riverside
official event program

Starts on Page 11: Fourth of July race schedule,
track map, memories from Cal Club drivers and
a look back over 31 years of racing.

THE OFFICIAL PUBLICATION OF THE CALIFORNIA SPORTS CAR CLUB REGION

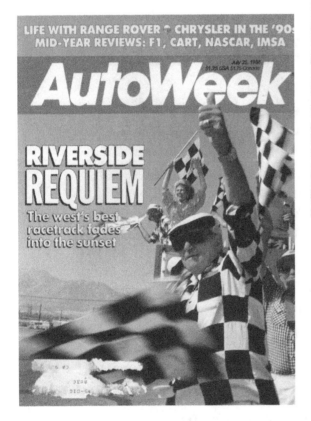

LIFE WITH RANGE ROVER • CHRYSLER IN THE '90s
MID-YEAR REVIEWS: F1, CART, NASCAR, IMSA

AutoWeek
July 25, 1988
$1.25 USA $1.75 Canada

RIVERSIDE REQUIEM
The west's best racetrack fades into the sunset

The last big SCORE at Riverside

By KATIE CASTATOR
Sun Sports Writer

This is it once again.

This weekend's 16th annual Stroh's SCORE Off-Road World Championship is absolutely, positively the last race at Riverside International Raceway before it closes for good.

"For the last three years, we've heard. This is it — the last ever," said Steve Millen, a member of the Toyota team that has dominated the track classes the last five years at Riverside's off-road show. "But now it seems certain there will be no more dirt flying at Riverside."

Dirt, mud, sheetmetal, and tempers — all have flown at the storied plant. Millen, a transplanted New Zealander, has seen almost everything but the checkered flag there, largely because of teammate Ivan Stewart of Lakeside.

Stewart, the 43-year-old, all-time champion of Riverside, won the Mini Metal Challenge in 1983 and '84. Millen took second both years.

"As I recall, Steve Millen and I raced back and forth for the lead both years," Stewart said. "I'm sure he'd like to win this last one.

"But I'd really like to win this one, too. I'd like to go down in history as the last driver to win at Riverside. At least, I think this is the last race. Do they have another race after this?"

It appears not. This really is it.

Stewart is not mourning the loss of Riverside, however. "It really doesn't upset me," he said. "I've had a lot of fun at Riverside but it's progress. It's got to go and we've got to go somewhere else."

The off-road racing veteran of 16 years raced the inaugural off-road championship in 1973 and hasn't missed one since.

He has won six world championship titles there in various classes. In 1983, he started a three-year win streak in the Mini Metal class for mini pick-up trucks. Those three years, Stewart also was the sports truck points champion of Mickey Thompson's off-road stadium series.

He's leading in points in the stadium series again this year.

Thompson, the founder of SCORE who was killed by two gunmen last May, initiated his concept of short-course, off-road racing at Riverside.

"I remember Mickey standing in the back of a pick-up truck at a drivers' meeting before the first World Championship in 1973, pointing to the empty stands and declaring that one day spectators

See RIVERSIDE/C5

Last, Last Race at Riverside Scheduled

Al Unser and his son, Al Unser, Jr., who staged auto racing's most exciting duel for a national championship two the Unsers.

Competition will be staged on the traditional 1.5-mile man made off-road track de-

---

Last Winston race today at Riverside

RIVERSIDE, Calif. (AP) — Ricky Rudd, of Victoria, British Columbia, won the Toyota pole today qualifier for today's Budweiser 400...

Budweiser 400

Last Go-Round Recalls
Legends of Famed Track

And Now, Riverside Roars Into History

By BILLY GLICK
Times Staff Writer

RIVERSIDE — The closing of a race track is nothing new. But the closing of Riverside International Raceway is like no other...

Closing Of Riverside Evokes Memories Of Fabled Track

RIVERSIDE, Calif. — No matter who wins today's Budweiser 400, it'll always be remembered as the date they closed ol' Riverside Raceway down.

After the NASCAR Winston Cup Series stock car race is completed at about 7 p.m., no more major events are scheduled on the 2.62-mile road course that dates to the mid-1950s.

Only an off-road scramble remains to be run in August. Then, the bulldozers that already are plowing up the desert terrain along the track's backstretch will move onto the 700 acres of speedway property.

motorcycles, go-karts and off-road machines.

"The place has been the site of dozens of movies and commercials. Also automotive tests."

Richter's most humorous recollection involved one of the tests.

"Ford was matching its pickups against Chevrolet and Dodge," he said. "They were going to run 67,000 miles consecutively in 1967. Naturally, this was boring to the drivers, especially on the night shifts.

"Topless dancing had just come in then. So we had this idea. We hired two or three of these strippers and stationed them around the track. They'd suddenly appear, naked, making like they were hitchhiking. Then they'd dart into the darkness. The trucks were equipped with radios, and you can imagine the

546

In July, 1988, 729 racers from all over the United States assembled for first of a few "Last Laps of Riverside" complete with a Last Lap Ceremony and worker photo op. As they knew it at the time, that was the last hurrah for SCCA racing at Riverside International Raceway.

Then, another chance - in July, 1989, another regional, remembered as being primitive with utilities shut off in most areas and marginal plumbing. A generator had to be used to power timing and scoring and race control. A track that was already known for hot weather had become even less hospitable and even the track itself left something to be desired. While the original pavement remained from turns nine to seven, a stretch of new pavement had to be laid to connect the exit of seven with the entrance tof nine. The resulting 2.5 mile course played host to nearly 150 drivers who braved the heat and facilities to bid a final farewell.

Motor Racing / Shav Glick

Record Entry for Amateur Finale at Riverside

Members and alumni of the California Sports Car Club and affiliated regions of the Sports Car Club of America—eager to drive the Last Lap of Riverside—have swelled the entry for this week-end's final amateur racing weekend at Riverside International Raceway to a record of more than 700 cars.

Cal Club officials said that the number may go above 800 before the first national championship race is held Saturday. The program calls for six national races Saturday, five regional races Sunday and two Monday.

Tom Marx, fresh from a victory in the Firehawk endurance series at Watkins Glen, N.Y., will drive a Nissan 200 SX in the first race Saturday and then turn the car over to actress Sandra Bartley for Sunday's first race.

After Monday's races, the Cal Club has planned a nostalgic program highlighted by former track champions from the 1950s and '60s taking the Last Lap of Riverside

and the Pennzoil 100 for sports cars in 1967.

Four men who drove in the first race ever run at Riverside, on Sept. 21, 1957, will drive again Monday. They are Andy Porterfield, Frank Monise, Bob Kirby and Bob Snow.

Many modern-era drivers who had hoped to be at the final event, such as Dan Gurney, John Morton, Elliott Forbes-Robinson, Chris Cobb and Dennis Aase, will instead be at Watkins Glen for an International Motor Sports Assn. event this weekend. However, some of them indicated they may make it to the nostalgia party late Monday afternoon.

Still coming at Riverside are an antique car event July 16-17 and the SCORE closed course world off-road championships Aug. 13-14.

SPRINT CARS—Lealand McSpadden, the West Coast's hottest sprint car driver, will go for his fourth straight California Racing Assn. victory Saturday night at Ascot Park in the annual Firecracker 50. McSpadden has won seven main events in the Parnelli Jones Firestone sponsored

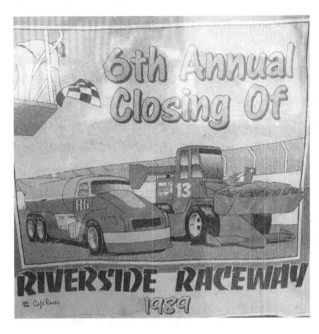

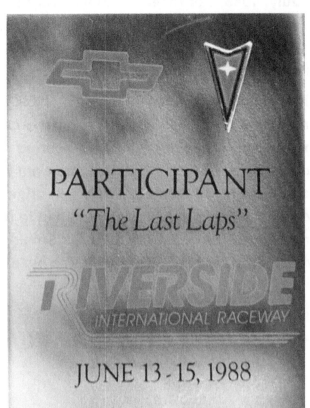

THE CALIFORNIA SPORTS CAR CLUB
AND
OH BOY! **Oberto** PRESENT
A TRIBUTE TO
RIVERSIDE INTERNATIONAL RACEWAY
RIVERSIDE, CALIFORNIA
JULY 2 - 4, 1988
I WORKED
THE LAST LAP AT RIVERSIDE RACEWAY

GENERAL ADMISSION $10.00
NO CASH REFUND OR EXCHANGE

000466

Wheels

FAST
TRACK

When

RIVERSIDE

meant

RACING

BY: TAMMY MINN

PHOTOS COURTESY OF RIVERSIDE
INTERNATIONAL RACEWAY MUSEUM

Racing legend
Dan Gurney at
Riverside Raceway

Read this Inland Empire Magazine article on the attached DVD

Ed Dellis: *"Not a race, but I went as passenger for the very last lap on that track in a '69 Z/28 Camaro with Chevrolet Chief Engineer, Mr. Fred Schaffsma - .pretty sure I mentioned this earlier. The event was called "Last Lap at Riverside" and served as the long-lead for the first ZR-1 Corvette....a C4. I believe I was in July '89, and the model year was a '90. Fred knew I owned two '69Zs in high school and college, so he was very proud to show me his then-new-to-him green/black-striped one that he picked up earlier that day...a rust-free "California car". After a somber closing ceremony and everyone was packing up heading home heads-down with our tails between our legs, Fred said, "Hey Ed! Ya wanna do the Last Lap at Riverside in my Z?" Knowing we'd get only 1 lap in before the remaining security personnel chased us off, he quietly rolled out of the pits, and proceeded to tach redlines in every gear ON A COLD MOTOR! When we came back in under a waiting security guard's...ahem..."encouragement", Fred and I remained quiet and just looked at each other knowing we just closed the chapter on one of racing's greatest legendary race tracks.*

Vintage Motorsports articles on the attached DVD

RIVERSIDE IS CLOSING (3:13)

Lyrics copyright © 1988 John Dillon (ASCAP)
Music copyright © 1982 John Dillon (ASCAP)

(JJ061988)

Riverside is closing
The racetrack soon will be just a city street
Big bucks want it all for condos and a shopping mall
Don't they care about the fans at all?

CHORUS:
But let's all remember the good times
Let's not forget the turn at six or the dogleg into nine
Let's remember all the good times
The pride we showed at Riverside
The times we shared at Riverside

The racetrack brought us progress
Technology from racing cars is now out on the street
But progress goes full circle now, they're tearing this old racetrack down
Don't they know they're killing sacred ground?

REPEAT CHORUS

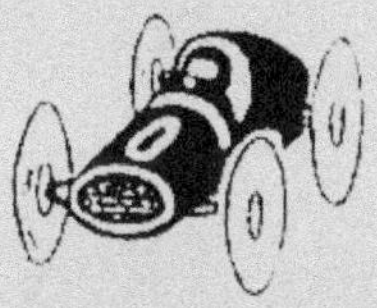

We won't forget the engine screams
Or the smell of racing gasoline
Or the thrill of sliding through the esses clean
We won't forget those checkered flags
Or the super fans we had
The track may go but our memories will race on . . . and on and on

We're gonna miss this old lady
The proving ground for excellence, the greatest in the land
A racetrack with a lot of grace and the finest folks who ever raced
Who'll be left to set the pace when she's gone?

REPEAT CHORUS

Riverside is closing
Farewell Riverside

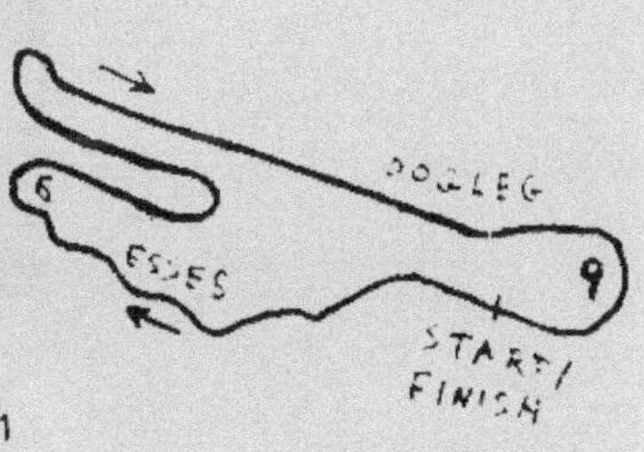

Performed by Jeff Porter
Produced by JPRS Productions, 9252 Picadilly Circle, Anaheim, CA 92801
Published by RaceHead Publishing, P. O. Box 6026, Fullerton, CA 92634
Engineered by Dennis Rose at Golden Goose Studios, Costa Mesa, CA

Listen to the John Dillon recording on the attached DVD

R.I.P

Made in the USA
Las Vegas, NV
01 March 2025